QUEER MUSLIM DIASPORAS IN CONTEMPORARY LITERATURE AND FILM

Series editors: Amina Yaqin, Peter Morey, Rehana Ahmed, Claire Chambers, Anshuman Mondal and Stephen Morton

This series will explore literary and cultural texts emerging from contexts in which majority/minority power dynamics operate, in the light of debates about contemporary multiculturalism. It will analyse texts marked by, or inscribing, a disequilibrium of power and/or cultural capital – such as the relations between majority white and BAME communities in Britain and other countries of the West – addressing the experiences, issues and anxieties arising from the perceived clash of ideas and values. Its aim is to develop a collective body of scholarship offering new insights on literature produced by and about diasporic and minority communities that is situated in a contemporary landscape where notions of multicultural tolerance have been challenged by political and populist discourses at best wary of, and at worst directly hostile to, multiculturalism.

Queer Muslim diasporas in contemporary literature and film

Alberto Fernández Carbajal

Manchester University Press

Copyright © Alberto Fernández Carbajal 2019

The right of Alberto Fernández Carbajal to be identified as the author of this work has been asserted by him in accordance with the Copyright, Designs and Patents Act 1988.

Published by Manchester University Press
Altrincham Street, Manchester M1 7JA
www.manchesteruniversitypress.co.uk

British Library Cataloguing-in-Publication Data
A catalogue record for this book is available from the British Library

ISBN 978 1 5261 2810 2 hardback
ISBN 978 1 5261 180 3 paperback

First published 2019

The publisher has no responsibility for the persistence or accuracy of URLs for any external or third-party internet websites referred to in this book, and does not guarantee that any content on such websites is, or will remain, accurate or appropriate.

Typeset by Newgen Publishing UK

*For Clare Barker and
dedicated to the memory of
Anthony Carrigan
(1980–2016)*

Contents

List of figures	ix
Preface and acknowledgements	x
Introduction: Queering Islam and micropolitical disorientation	1

Part I Queer interethnic desire — 31

1. Of interethnic (dis)connection: queer phenomenology, and cultural and religious commodification in Hanif Kureishi's *My Beautiful Laundrette* (1985) and *The Buddha of Suburbia* (1990) — 33

2. 'Are we on the same wavelength?' Interstitial queerness and the Ismaili diaspora in Ian Iqbal Rashid's poetry and films — 62

3. Queering Orientalism, Ottoman homoeroticism, and Turkishness in Ferzan Özpetek's *Hamam: The Turkish Bath* (1997) — 87

Part II Negotiating Islamic gender — 107

4. Countermemories of desire: exploring gender, anti-racism, and homonormativity in Shamim Sarif's *The World Unseen* (2001) and *I Can't Think Straight* (2008) — 109

5. Between gang and family: queering ethnicity and British Muslim masculinities in Sally El Hosaini's *My Brother the Devil* (2012) — 131

6. The good, the bad, and the ugly? Unveiling American Muslim women in Rolla Selbak's *Three Veils* (2011) — 155

Part III Narrating the self in queer time and place	179
7 A postcolonial queer melancholia: matrilinearity, Sufism, and *l'errance* in the autofictional works of Abdellah Taïa	181
8 The druzification of history: queering time, place, and faith in the diasporic novels of Rabih Alameddine	204
9 Written on the body: a queer and cartographic exploration of the Palestinian diaspora in Randa Jarrar's *A Map of Home* (2008) and *Him, Me, Muhammad Ali* (2016)	228
Conclusion: Thinking across	250
Index	272

Figures

1	*My Beautiful Laundrette* (1985), directed by Stephen Frears	43
2	*Touch of Pink* (2004), directed by Ian Iqbal Rashid	77
3	*Hamam: The Turkish Bath* (1997), directed by Ferzan Özpetek	92
4	*The World Unseen* (2008), directed by Shamim Sarif	122
5	*I Can't Think Straight* (2008), directed by Shamim Sarif	123
6	*My Brother the Devil* (2012), directed by Sally El Hosaini	140
7	*Three Veils* (2011), directed by Rolla Selbak	159

Preface and acknowledgements

On 12 June 2016, a man called Omar Mateen, an American Muslim of Afghan heritage, committed the deadliest crime against LGBT citizens in the whole of American history: he walked with his gun into Pulse, a gay nightclub in Orlando, Florida, popular with queer citizens of many different ethnicities, and killed 49 people, leaving another 53 injured, before being shot dead by the police. The Orlando massacre took place while I was in the midst of writing this book, and, on reflection, it tragically encapsulates the complications assailing queer Muslims in the diaspora. The initial responses to Mateen's murderous rampage illustrate the acts of disavowal that ensue when no single community is ready to claim ideological influence over an individual's actions. On the one hand, Mateen was quickly identified as a Muslim extremist – the classical terrorist scenario following 9/11 – in the light of his call to the American police to disclaim his allegiance to Islamic State (Kirby, 2016). As it was later discovered, Mateen's radicalisation was politically inconsistent, intermittently showing support for antithetical groups such as the Islamic State of Iraq and the Levant (ISIL) and Hezbollah (Perez et al., 2016). So, while clearly harbouring resentment against the West and being sympathetic to Islamist groups in the Middle East, Mateen was not a 'straightforward' Islamic terrorist with clear links to any organisation. It is possible that his subscription to the Islamic State may have constituted an attempt at justifying, in his own eyes, the crime he was perpetrating against Florida's LGBT community.

On the other hand, while the Islamic State was more than willing to enlist Mateen as one of its own, Muslim commentators were quick to disqualify Mateen as a Muslim, since his behaviour was clearly inadmissible, especially during the sacred month of Ramadan. As it percolated, it would seem Mateen was himself an occasional customer at the Pulse nightclub, marking him as a closeted homosexual. By that point, however, he had already been disowned by queers and

Muslims alike. These processes of disidentification crystallise the exclusion faced by queer Muslims in the West. Because Mateen was a Muslim and committed a crime against the queer community in Orlando, he was automatically constructed as an outsider, either as a typical Muslim homophobic extremist or as a closeted Muslim unable to deal with his homosexuality, which pointed, in their view, to Islam's clear problem with homosexuals. While our initial thoughts should always be with the innocent victims at Pulse, the troubling case of Omar Mateen should draw our attention, in a preliminary manner, to the identity conflicts involved in Muslim queerness. As Aamina Khan writes:

> LGBTQ Muslims have always been stuck in a dichotomy, pressured to choose between their queerness and their Muslimness. And the Pulse shooting made that dichotomy even starker as we witnessed a tragedy, and all the victims of it, being used by politicians and lawmakers to target the Muslim community. (Khan, 2017)

It is this deeply entrenched dichotomy that might have drawn Mateen himself to his murderous behaviour, with the media being filled in its aftermath with disclaimers about Mateen's mental instability, his sexual ambiguity, his extremist views, and his un-Islamic behaviour, in a partisan way that did not attempt to make sense of the complex logic behind his terrible actions.

It is feasible that Mateen's unjustifiable crime may have started from a place of self-loathing: Mateen must have found it arduous to come to terms with his identity as a Muslim critical of the West's military and moral preponderance, and with his own troubled sexuality, which he attempted to cover up publicly, most explicitly through his marriages to two women. Asked about his son's apparent homosexuality, Mateen's father, Seddique Mateen, responded: 'It's not true. Why, if he was gay, would he do this?' (Pilkington and Elgot, 2016). One answer might be that he found it impossible to reconcile his same-sex desire with his internalised homophobia, which must have been encouraged by his father's own homophobia (Hennessy-Fiske *et al.*, 2016). He responded to his bitter perception of the West's aggressive foreign policy by attacking the multiethnic queer citizens at home in the Pulse nightclub who routinely drew attention to his inexorable internal dilemma, singling him out as a 'sinner' within his own ethno-religious community. It is important to remind ourselves that not every queer Muslim is Omar Mateen, the way not every Muslim is a terrorist, or every queer person an apostate, but the tragic case of the Orlando massacre helps us begin questioning the processes of social and discursive exclusion at work in the

West regarding issues of Muslim identity and queerness. While these two identity categories may appear to many people to be mutually exclusive, anti-normative sexual orientations remain a matter of everyday life for many people of Muslim heritage, despite secularising Western LGBTIQ discourses and mainstream heteronormative Islamicate values.

In this study, I will be exploring contemporary literature and film's depiction of queer diasporic Muslims' mundane struggles with these intersecting identities, in an attempt at complicating restricting assumptions about Muslim identities and sexualities. In taking a diachronic critical view of chiefly fiction – and some poetry – and films dealing with Muslims, migration, and same-sex desire from the 1980s to the present day, I am undertaking the first scholarly study of this kind, bringing together the work of artists of various national, cultural, class, and Muslim backgrounds, and with very different experiences, and patterns of, migration. As a postcolonial scholar, I have always been on the lookout for those human subjects with a history of colonialism who are oppressed or misunderstood, and the distinct plight of queer Muslims in the diaspora, torn as they are between expected allegiances to the allegedly opposed camps of Western liberalism and Islam, makes their case an urgent one to argue in our highly polarised Western societies. As I argue in Chapter 1, via Momin Rahman (2014), the most productive way of approaching queer Muslims is intersectionally, attending to the particular triangulation of homophobia and Islamophobia. I therefore offer this study as a double critique of both Western prejudice against Muslims and of the particular problems assailing queer Muslims as sexually dissident.

Reading the work of Moroccan writer Abdellah Taïa while preparing my first book for publication, in the summer of 2013, became the initial spark of this project, especially upon discovering there was a scarcity of scholarship attending to the fictional depiction of queer Muslims. It is with a view to reclaim them from academic obscurity that I conceived this project, which was eventually funded by the Leverhulme Trust. While my original research plans juxtaposed diasporic and nationalist perspectives, a growing archive of literature and film, added to temporal constraints, meant I ended up concentrating chiefly on the experiences of queer Muslims in the diaspora. I found their unique situation, divided between the need to represent Islam in the West while reclaiming their queerness against both residual Western homophobia and Islamicate homophobia, as perfectly poised to begin disorientating the ontological certainties of many Western subjects, Muslim and non-Muslim. This ability to speak critically to two camps attracted me the most to the study of queer diasporic Muslims, and the necessity to explore with nuance the ideological complexities of their creative narratives,

Preface and acknowledgements

which paint a far more granulated picture than that of the fiercely partisan and ethnocentric Western media.

One of the questions I am routinely asked when I mention I research queer Muslim diasporas is whether I am a Muslim. It should be prudent to disclaim that I am not, although not subscribing to Islam does not presuppose a lack of empathy with Muslims' political plights, or an inability to study their aesthetic representation academically. I was brought up a Catholic in Spain, a faith that subsequently lapsed. I moved to Britain in my early youth, partly, as I found out in hindsight, in an attempt at finding a place of safety where I could be freely gay, without societal or familial pressures surrounding my sexual orientation. My interest in faith, sexuality, and migration is thus rather personal, yet, as a postcolonial scholar, I am also sensitive to issues of social justice and to reclaiming the perspectives of those people who suffer from systemic discrimination. I am aware that the positionality of queer Muslims is vastly different from my own, and subject to structural issues of racism and Islamophobia. While I know our situations are nowhere analogous, this study is incepted from a position of solidarity. By paying scrupulous attention to textual and cultural detail, I vindicate queer Muslims without castigating their ethno-religious filiations, hence contributing to the collective project of curbing Western Islamophobia. I am an advocate of work that challenges ethnocentric identity politics and the idea that scholars can only ever work on people and subjects just like themselves. This instinctive ontological wedge driven between communities only serves to perpetuate societal fragmentation and communitarian insularity. If there is to be a collective dismantling of Western networks of desire – such as white supremacy and systemic Islamophobia – then such a struggle must be collaborative, and it must be carried out by Muslims and non-Muslims alike.

Nonetheless, any white, Western, gay, and male scholar approaching the topic of Islam, Muslims, and homosexuality must be ready to pre-empt accusations of Orientalism, even when not writing, with a few punctual exceptions, about the so-called Orient, but mostly about Muslims in the West. In his book *Orientalism*, Edward Said famously argues that the Orient is constructed discursively by the agents of the West, determining it in the Western imagination as a place of Otherness. However, as I suggest elsewhere, 'critics of Said's work, like Robert Young and Aijaz Ahmad, have observed that his notion of discourse is "too determining and univocal" (Young, 2007, p. 386) and that the study as a whole allows for "no site of resistance" (Ahmad, 1992, p. 195)' (Fernández Carbajal, 2014, p. 6). In other words, according to Said's critics, his notion is too totalising: anyone writing about the Orient in the West is, by default, an

Orientalist; and, in Ahmad's thinking, Said allows for no possibility of resistance to Orientalism from within the West itself, a feat that constructs every Westerner as inexorably complicit with cultural imperialism, without any regard for their political leanings, the specifics of their work, or their intentions. Orientalism becomes, in practice, an ontological prison, one that this study attempts to break out of, examining, with dissident impetus, the ways in which fictional depictions of queer Muslims challenge the conscious or unconscious bias of their implied Western audiences.

In approaching Islam and Muslims from a perspective of solidarity, one must remain wary still of the pitfalls of not just Islamophobia but also Islamophilia. As Andrew Shryock soberly asks regarding the pervading anti-Muslim prejudices of the West:

> Without a careful assessment of contemporary geopolitics and deep historical relations between Muslim and non-Muslim societies, it is hard to understand what people are afraid of when they fear Islam. Given the scant knowledge of Islam most Americans and Europeans bring to the creation of their anti-Muslim stereotypes, can we be sure that Islamophobia is ultimately about Islam at all? (Shryock, 2010, p. 3)

Shryock's pressing question entreats us to consider the wider historical frameworks that turn Muslims into 'Other' figures in Western societies. Since, according to him, Europeans and Americans have very little knowledge of Islam, it may be that their Islamophobia has no root in Islam itself; rather, this is a problem of racist and xenophobic bias deeply imbricated in ongoing processes of Western imperialism. Nonetheless, in attempting to curb Islamophobia, one must be careful not to fall into the tempting trap of Islamophilia. According to Shryock, Islamophilia is borne out of the need to curb Islamophobia, but it creates the binary of the 'good' and 'bad' Muslim, with the acceptable Muslim becoming a stereotype uniting all the seemingly beneficent features Westerners ascribe to peaceful, liberal Muslims, thus ultimately prescribing what a 'good Muslim' looks like. This study does not set out to challenge Islamophobia by creating an idealised and equally problematic Islamophilic construction of Muslims in the West; it does not set out to offer a blueprint of perfect Muslim citizenship but will be critical of both Western networks of desire and of the Islamicate heteropatriarchal tendencies articulated in depictions of Western Muslim communities.

As regards the book's overall structure, the study is divided into three sections, with three chapters each. Although there are, unavoidably, some thematic overlaps across these sections, they allow me to map out queer Muslim diasporas according to different angles of representation. First, I offer a free-standing opening introductory chapter, 'Queering Islam and micropolitical disorientation', where I set out my main conceptual framework, in dialogue with Gilles Deleuze and Félix Guattari, Jasbir K. Puar, Gayatri Gopinath, and Sara Ahmed, among others. Here, after offering a preliminary interrogation of the history of homosexualities in Islamic history, I suggest that queer Muslims in the diaspora engage in a micropolitical dynamic which disorientates the macropolitical identity categories of Western societies, thus offering alternative ways of becoming. However, in defining queer micropolitical disorientation, I do not offer a methodology that I then impose onto all the films and texts studied. Applying one single theory to such a variety of cultural texts would be tantamount to epistemic violence. Conversely, each chapter in this book is attentive to the material and cultural contexts relevant to each individual artist, and so, as we will find, each film, book, and relevant scholarship suggest a specific vocabulary to deal with their disquisitions of Muslim queerness. In addition, in formulating my main concepts and methodology, and following the recent example of Sara Ahmed (2017), I have attempted not to crowd the book's conceptual dimensions with references to dead white men, although at least two of them have found their way in. I give prominence in my thinking to the work of queer women of colour, most prominently Ahmed and Gopinath, in an attempt to infuse the study of queer Muslim diasporas with terminologies forged by thinkers who are themselves queer, diasporic, non-white, and feminist.

In Part I, I begin the study of the queer Muslim diasporic archive by focusing on 'Queer interethnic desire', as a means of ascertaining how artists of Muslim heritage negotiate sexual orientations and ethno-religious identities across ethnic lines. Chapter 1 opens this section with a canonical film and text: chiefly Hanif Kureishi and Stephen Frears' *My Beautiful Laundrette* and Kureishi's *The Buddha of Suburbia*, with reference also to shorter texts by Kureishi. Here, I explore the countercultural impetus of Kureishi's work in predicating queer diasporic Muslim transgression across ethnic divides, drawing attention to the colonial inception of racial hierarchies and to the need to challenge Thatcherite neoliberalism in order to incept productive queer interethnic relationships. While Kureishi's characters' initial queerness in both *My Beautiful Laundrette* and *The Buddha of Suburbia* is a sign of micropolitical disorientation, their aspirations to join the culturally dominant group and their heterosexual normativity reveal the risk of complicity in joining the mainstream, and so it is queer characters who refuse to kowtow to societal and familial expectations that remain ultimately transgressive. Chapter 2 goes on to examine the work of Canadian Ismaili poet and filmmaker Ian Iqbal Rashid, with a particular focus on his short films and his debut feature, *A Touch of Pink*. In this chapter, I analyse how his characters are positioned at the interstices between Islamic Ismaili traditionalism, colonial modernity, and diasporic post-modernity, arduously trying to reconcile inherited ideas of Muslim identity with their anti-normative sexualities, also in defiance of inherited colonial social structures. Chapter 3 explores diaspora in reverse in *Hamam: The Turkish Bath*, the debut film of Turkish-Italian filmmaker Ferzan Özpetek. In my reading of the film, I propose Özpetek's cinematic narrative excavates and transforms Ottoman homoeroticism from an interethnic perspective and against the contemporary sway of Kemalist and Islamist homophobia, in spite of academic charges against his alleged Orientalism in his depiction of his native Istanbul.

Part II is invested in 'Negotiating Islamic gender', and although the section is focused on the work of three female Muslim filmmakers and a novelist-cum-filmmaker, the section explores their different constructions of both Islamic femininities and masculinities. Chapter 4 examines the work of British writer and director Shamim Sarif, focusing on her novels and films of the same name: *The World Unseen* and *I Can't Think Straight*, novelistic and cinematic narratives depicting same-sex desire between diasporic Muslim women and between British Muslims and cosmopolitan Christian Arab women, respectively. My analysis suggests that, while Sarif, brought up in Britain, lacks an Islamicate homoerotic archive and relies chiefly on the tropes of Euro-American lesbian cultures, occasionally subscribing to a homonormative envisioning of sexuality, her work, via Joseph Roach (Gopinath, 2005), offers countermemories carving a niche for diasporic same-sex desire against the blindsiding of the dissident sexualities of women of Muslim heritage in Britain. Chapter 5 then analyses the work of British-Egyptian filmmaker Sally El Hosaini, concentrating most amply on her debut film, *My Brother the Devil*, which critiques the limited models of masculinity offered to young British youth of North African Arab descent by their first-generation diasporic parents and by their multiethnic British gangs. I argue the film posits Islam as the trigger of a new model of masculinity that is relational and empathetic, while forfeiting the hypermasculinity of gang culture and the heteronormativity of the diasporic Muslim family. Lastly, Chapter 6 explores the films of American-Palestinian Rolla Selbak, in particular her first professionally produced film, *Three Veils*, a narrative dealing with the individual yet entangled stories of three American Muslim girls, whose Islamic femininities are at stake. I suggest that while the film tackles controversial topics such as arranged marriage, rape, gender violence, homosexuality, and queerness, it does so in a way that highlights the common humanity of American Muslim women and men, in an attempt at critiquing the ongoing problems of Western Muslim communities while also qualifying Western stereotypes about Islam and Muslims.

I finally devote Part III to the topic of 'Narrating the self in queer time and place', exploring the ways in which queer Muslims write the diasporic subject, in an explicitly autobiographical manner or with semi-autobiographical inspiration, into historical narratives of Islamicate eroticism, nation, and migration. Chapter 7 examines the autofictional work of Abdellah Taïa, most extensively his novels *An Arab Melancholia* and *Salvation Army*, and his articulation of postcolonial queer melancholia, which is connected to the ongoing social injustices of the postcolonial Arab world and to his early and traumatic experiences of homophobia in his native Morocco, which are complicated by unequal relationships with Europeans and the lack of real freedom in the often ethnically inhospitable spaces of contemporary Europe. Nonetheless, I suggest Taïa posits a model of queer fraternity in the diaspora which, however ephemeral, temporarily dissolves the barriers created by European colonial hierarchies, while inscribing his work within the historical continuum of pre- and Islamic Arab poetry. Sufism and women's religiosity are also offered as antidotes against the strictures of literalist Islam. In turn, Chapter 8 visits the work of American-Lebanese Rabih Alameddine, a painter and writer of Druze heritage. My readings of his work suggest that Alameddine's diasporic novels – *The Hakawati*, *I, the Divine*, and *KOOLAIDS: The Art of War* – 'druzify' religious perspectives, suturing texts such as the Bible and the Qur'an in an attempt at syncretising religious traditions and at going against the current of mainstream heteropatriarchal religious interpretation. I suggest time and place are also queered in Alameddine's debut novel *KOOLAIDS*, blending the spaces and temporalities of the Lebanese Civil War and the American AIDS crisis. Queerness, AIDS-induced visionary reveries, and queer models of family, I argue, are offered as strategies of resistance against the clout of Islamicate heteropatriarchal values and ethno-religious exclusivism. In Chapter 9, I examine the literary work of American-Palestinian Randa Jarrar, in particular her first novel, *A Map of Home*, with reference also to her recent collection of stories, *Him, Me, Muhammad Ali*. My critical analysis explores the burdens on the second-generation diasporic citizen of the lost Palestinian homeland and the construction of the queer body as the repository of both personal liberation from Palestinian nationalism and Islamicate heteropatriarchy. While Jarrar's work is painfully – if also playfully – conscious of the ongoing abuse of women at the hands of Arab and Muslim patriarchy, there is also a certain degree of empathy in her depiction of the societal expectations placed on Muslim men. In the light of internalised Islamicate homophobia, Jarrar's texts offer, I argue, irreverent queer exegesis and the emancipatory reclamation of the queer female body.

Acknowledgements

I have incurred many debts in researching and writing this volume. First, I must thank the Leverhulme Trust for granting me the Early Career Fellowship (ECF-2014–067) that made this project possible, and the University of Leicester for hosting me during the writing of this book. Thanks are also due to my referees for this Fellowship: John McLeod, Ananya Jahanara Kabir, and Lindsey Moore; they remain stellar role models as well as cherished friends. My mentor at Leicester, Corinne Fowler, was an advocate of this project from the very moment I mentioned it to her. I must thank her for her support and for her guidance with my written work. At Leicester, I must also thank Emma Parker, who alerted me to the work of Shamim Sarif and Randa Jarrar; and, for their general support: Michela Baldo, Anne Marie D'Arcy, Lucy Evans, Zalfa Feghali, Sarah Graham, Marion Krauthaker and Matt Coombes, Rachel Mason, Gail Marshall, Leighan Renaud, Marc Scully, Tracy Simmons, and my first doctoral student, Nisreen Yousef, who makes me proud. My 'roomies' Barbara Cooke and Geoff Belknap also deserve my gratitude for providing welcome distractions when I chanced to be in our office. Warmest thanks also to Richard Vytniorgu, the last Leicester-related friend. At the University of Roehampton, I must thank my head of department, Laura Peters, for providing me with the time necessary to prepare this book for publication and for her kindness, and to all my colleagues, too many to mention, from whom I must single out Rachele Dini, Ian Kinane, and Mary Shannon for their caring collegiality.

At the University of Leicester, I organised a public-facing event series called 'Queering Islam' and a one-day symposium on 'Islamophobia and homophobia', all of whose speakers have shaped my thinking. Thanks are due to Samar Habib, who has become a loyal friend, to our symposium keynote, Amanullah De Sondy, and to Peter Cherry (who first alerted me to Sally El Hosaini), Tareq Sayyid Rajab de Montfort, Rusi Jaspal, Tehmina Kazi, Asifa Lahore, Shamim Sarif, Rolla Selbak, Asifa Siraj, and, last but not least, to Aleardo Zanghellini, who invited me to present at the University of Reading. Other colleagues and friends who expressly asked me to share my expertise must also be thanked: Pilar Cuder Domínguez, David Firth and Sarah Newport, Alice Guthrie and Daniel Löwe, Martin Halliwell, Gina Heathcoate, Laura Hegarty, Madhu Krishnan, Ebtihal Mahadeen, Amber Pouliot, Maria Rovisco, Esra Mirze Santesso, Lindsey Moore and Nadia Atia, Nicole Thiara, Lucinda Newns, and Janet Wilson. My gratitude to Alexandra Chreiteh, Saleem Haddad, and Amahl Khouri for teaching me about the current state of queer Arab writing. I must offer my sincere thanks to Abdellah Taïa, who welcomed me to his home in Paris for a very long interview, and who selflessly offered me his friendship along with it. His fineness of spirit remains a source of inspiration and courage not just to me but to many people in the Arab and Islamicate world.

I must thank those people who have had a hand in publishing my work: Caroline Osella, Amina Yaqin, Rehana Ahmed and Rachel Carroll, John McLeod, and the research team at Interpreting Communities, led by Godela Weiss-Sussex and Malachi McIntosh, with whom I collaborated for a while, and most particularly Margaret Littler, who introduced me to Ferzan Özpetek's films. Shorter and different versions of Chapters 1, 4, and 8 have appeared as follows: 'Powders Revisited: Queer Micropolitical Disorientation, Phenomenology, and Multicultural Trust in Hanif Kureishi and Stephen Frears' *My Beautiful Laundrette*', in *Muslims, Trust and Multiculturalism: New Directions*, edited by Amina Yaqin, Peter Morey, and Asmaa Soliman, Palgrave Macmillan, 2018, pp. 217–40; 'Countermemories of Desire: Female Homosexuality, "Coming Out" Narratives, and British Multiculturalism in Shamim Sarif's *I Can't Think Straight*', *The Journal of Commonwealth Literature* 53.2 (2018): 255–69; 'The Druzification of History: Queering Time, Place and Faith in Diasporic Fiction by Rabih Alameddine', *Études Anglaises: New Diasporas, New Directions* 70.1 (2017): 78–94. I thank the various journal editors and publishers. I also thank Ian Iqbal Rashid for his permission to quote from his poems 'An/Other Country', *Song of Sabu*, and 'Bastards of the Diaspora', and for his kind friendship and encouragement more generally, which I truly appreciate. I should also thank my two editors at Manchester University Press: Rob Byron, an amenable soul who showed interest in this book from our first conversation at the Aga Khan University in London, and Paul Clarke, who cheerfully took it on in order to turn it into the first volume of the Multicultural Textualities series.

My colonial and postcolonial comrades, particularly the executive and regular members of the Postcolonial Studies Association and ACLALS, must be thanked, especially Claire Chambers, Anshuman Mondal, Nicola Abram, Sarah Arens, Rabaha Arshad, Clare Barker, Veronica Barnsley, Catherine Bates, Anna Bernard, Elleke Boehmer, Howard J. Booth, Lorna Burns, Isabel Carrera Suárez, Anthony Carrigan, Helen Cousins, Dom Davies, Sharae Deckard, Om Dwivedi, Luz Mar González Arias, David Farrier, Rachel Fox, Syed Haider, Caroline Herbert, Lola Herrero, Christinna Hobbs, Kate Houlden, Graham

Huggan, Sarah Ilott, Rena Jackson, Sam Knowles, Ole Birk Laursen, Sarah Lawson Welsh, Jenny Leetsch, Milena Marinkova, Belén Martín Lucas, Kasia Mika, Sorcha Ní GiollaDhuinn, Brendon Nicholls, Stuart Murray, Jade Munslow Ong, Daniel O'Gorman, Emma Parker, Maya Parmar, Beatriz Pérez Zapata, Ed Powell, Shital Pravinchandra, Don Randall, Sue Reid, Samantha Reive Holland, Gillian Roberts, Amy Rushton, Cristina Sandru, Esha Sil, Veronika Schuchter, Rob Spence, Robert Spencer, Florian Stadtler, Caitlin and Cheryl Stobie, Anastasia Valassopoulos, Abigail Ward, Matthew Whittle, and Chantal Zabus. The 2018 edition of the Critical Muslim Studies summer school at the School of Arabic Studies in Granada provided a fertile, if at times treacherous, ground for thinking about Muslim issues as I was finishing this book. I must thank the students who granted me their hospitality, most especially Fatima Akhtar, Zareef Tajwar Karim, Zarah Mayeesha, Leonie Blacknell-Taylor, Chantal de Rudder, Catherine Sameh, and Jenny Yanez; and among the lecturers, Shahid Mathee, Santiago Slabodsky, and Amina Teslima.

The most personal debts are always the most numerous, yet there is never enough space to convey them all. My family, both of birth and acquired, sustain me in my toils with their love and support. My heartfelt thanks must first go to my parents, Gabriel and Ana María, my sister Lucía, my nephews Elías and Darío and their father Carlos, my aunts Ángeles Carbajal and Tarsila Fernández, my cousins, particularly Ana Prado; and my family in law: Teresa, Richard, Rebecca, Christopher, Anthony, Christine, and the late Bill Strange, Steph and Dani O'Brien, and James William Strange. My friends in Britain, Spain, and across continents ought to be thanked for their ongoing support, even when it means seeing little of me; they are far too numerous to be individually mentioned, so I trust they know who they are and how much I adore them. Last but never least, I must thank my most immediate family: the love of my life, William Strange, who must often put up with my swift disappearance into the attic and various other places, such as London, Córdoba, or la Casa del Chapiz; our cats Gigi, Karim, and Percy; and, finally, our son, Billy, whose smile gives me, each single morning, a reason to live.

Introduction: Queering Islam and micropolitical disorientation

> To say that male homosexuality flourished in Islamic societies would be an overstatement typical of orientalist discourse, but it would be no exaggeration to say that, before the twentieth century, the region of the world with the most visible and diverse homosexualities was not northwestern Europe but northern Africa and southwestern Asia. Indeed, the contrast between 'Western' and 'Islamic' homosexualities is not so much one of visibility versus invisibility or modern freedom versus traditional repression, but of containment versus elaboration, of a single pattern of homosexuality defined and delimited by institutions and discourses closely linked to the modern nation-state versus the variety, distribution, and longevity of same-sex patterns in Islamic societies. (Murray and Roscoe, 1997, p. 6)

HOMOSEXUALITY IS, arguably, one of the thorniest contemporary topics surrounding Islam and its relationship with civil rights. To this day, same-sex acts are still a significant taboo even among Muslim communities in the West, and they remain a contentious issue in many Muslim-majority countries, where levels of tolerance can vary between clandestine social acceptance and exemplary state punishment. Whereas homosexuality has been decriminalised in places such as Turkey and Indonesia – while in India it has been decriminalised, recriminalised, and decriminalised once again – stepping out of line with normative sexualities can lead many Muslims to face imprisonment or even the death penalty, in countries such as Malaysia, Nigeria, Iran, and Saudi Arabia (Habib, 2010). Whether these Muslims are the victims of systemic homophobia or of state retribution, such harsh living conditions, often intersecting with issues of war or financial scarcity, sometimes entail migration to countries where homosexual acts are not punished by the state: notably in Europe and North America, where, in turn, perceptions of their incompatible sexual orientations and religious identities can result in internal conflict. This study argues that the fight against homophobia and Islamophobia ought to be a joint one: it is only through a double critique that we can start challenging mutual suspicion and begin to forge some form of transnational understanding of overlapping identitarian and cultural identifications.

One of my aims in this initial chapter is briefly to chart the history of homosexuality in Islam, a living reality often elided in contemporary Islamist discourses that vilify or simply negate sexual non-normativity, against the richness and longevity cited by Stephen O. Murray and Will Roscoe in this chapter's epigraph, taken from their seminal book *Islamic Homosexualities: Culture, History, and Literature*. As we will see shortly, Islamic homophobia is imbricated in a complex and long history of European colonialism, anti-colonial insurgency, and postcolonial Islamic revivalism, which links it, in varying and often overlapping degrees, to Western homophobic discourses. I also interrogate current debates surrounding Western approaches to Muslim homosexuality and suggest an assembled essentialist and constructionist queer approach as the most appropriate critical method to avoid identitarian prescription and the aggressive homonationalist discourse of what Joseph Massad (2007) calls the 'Gay International'.

This chapter also explores the relatively recent concept of 'queer diaspora', and the promises and pitfalls of comparative queer criticism, in interaction with prominent critics such as Gayatri Gopinath and William Spurlin, while also examining current debates on queer Muslim intersectionality by the likes of Momin Rahman. While admitting to the intersectional positioning of queer diasporic Muslims, I also argue that they should not be constructed merely as paradigmatic of intersectionality, but rather as agents of micropolitical disorientation in societies where different forms of macropolitical segmentalisation constantly intersect. As will become apparent in dialogue with Sara Ahmed, it is often too easy to romanticise queer diasporic subjects as inhabiting alternative semiotic spaces, when in fact their routine lines of flight from normativity, which I formulate via Gilles Deleuze and Félix Guattari, reveal their mundane micropolitical disorientation of normative social categories. As such, I present queer diasporic Muslims neither as exceptional figures nor as inhabitants of a different semiotic dimension; instead, like most of their other coreligionist and diasporic comrades, queer or otherwise, they should be seen as contributing to the disorganisation of solidified ethnic and sexual categories in our allegedly liberal West. I also discuss the work of Timothy Fitzgerald in order to reveal how, despite their constant pitting in Western discourses, 'secularism' and 'religion' are interdependent concepts only conceptually separated during the European Enlightenment, demonstrating that the supposedly secular West is still highly steeped in Christian aesthetics. Lastly, I briefly propose an antithetical interpretive methodology in dialogue with Bruce Lawrence and Edward Said, whose interrogation of tendentious discourses on Islam and Muslims propagated by Western media helps me complicate the often simplified relationship between 'Islam' and 'the West'. By explicitly pitting my analysis against such ongoing polarisation, I am answering back to power and its networks of desire, challenging the persistent stereotyping of Muslims. In so doing, I offer queer Muslims as negotiatory figures whose disorganisation of normative ideologies can challenge, on the one hand, Muslim and non-Muslim homophobia and, on the other, monolithic Western views on Islam and Muslims.

Islam and homosexuality

Islamicate[1] cultures – that is, cultures whose evolution have been significantly influenced by their contact with Islam – have a long and complex history of same-sex acts and desire, if not always of *homosexuality* as we have come to understand it in the West since the nineteenth century. Oliver Leaman observes that homosexuality is often constructed by Islamist commentators as a 'feature of Western decadence and something that does not and should not exist in Muslim communities, and if it does, then it is merely as a reflection of the unwelcome spread of corrupt ideas from without' (2014, p. 86). This statement summarises the thrust of contemporary Islamic homophobic discourses, whereby *homosexuality*, understood as a deviant lifestyle, is regarded as an extraneous influence with no real place in 'proper' Islamic societies. Leaman recounts the visit of the former President of Iran, Mahmoud Ahmadinejad, to Columbia University in 2007, when Ahmadinejad confidently asserted that there were no homosexuals in Iran. Leaman recalls that this statement met with raucous laughter from the audience. Although Ahmadinejad himself must have known that his tendentious statement was, even from the most technical point of view, a fallacy, it constitutes, nonetheless, a clear message of defiance: the state of Iran will not tolerate a Westernised envisioning of sexuality, and *homosexuality* has therefore been wiped out from the national plain – if not fully physically just yet, at least discursively. What can be gleaned from Iran's unrelenting official position regarding homosexuality is that sexual non-normativity has become for many Muslim countries and communities an issue of political strategy: it helps them situate themselves in complete opposition to the alleged moral laxity of the aggressively modern but also highly simplified West.

To the chagrin of contemporary Islamists keen to deny the existence of homosexuality in Muslim-majority contexts, it is undeniable that Muslim societies have a tradition of homoeroticism, and that such tradition has not been part of a hushed-up clandestine subculture, but has belonged in the cultural mainstream. The work of Khaled El-Rouayheb, particularly his book *Before Homosexuality in the Arab-Islamic World, 1500–1800*, has been of utmost importance to the reclamation of the history of Islamicate same-sex desire. El-Rouayheb (2005) observes that Islamicate literature from the early Ottoman period was brimming with homoeroticism, bluntly articulated in such disparate genres as dictionaries of biography, poetry anthologies, and collections of erotic essays. According to him, '[t]he biographical entries on Sufis of the period confirm that the practice of contemplating handsome beardless boys was still thought a living tradition' in the mid-eighteenth-century Islamicate world. Although now regarded by some Islamic commentators as the 'decadent' poetry of the Ottoman Empire, the *ghazal*, one of the main poetic genres in the Islamic world between the thirteenth century and nineteenth century, featured constant pledges of love from the male poetic persona to an adolescent male. Jocelyn Sharlet explores the case of Abu Nuwas, the famous Baghdadi poet who knew he would never be able to enter into socially accepted partnerships with his younger lovers, yet devoted much of his poetry to the expression of this particular homoerotics. Sharlet argues that '[c]oncealment of homoerotic desire gives way to occasions to put love on display in the sociable circulation of poetry and anecdotes, both orally and in writing' (2010, p. 44). This dynamic of self-effacement and public dissemination creates a primal paradox in Islamicate cultures: they may not allow socially sanctified homosexual unions, but such lack of social ratification found a projection onto public culture through the expression of the poet's frustrated homoerotic affections. Hence, while exclusive homosexuality might not have been deemed societally tenable, the tragic expression of unfulfilled homoeroticism was certainly to the taste of Islamicate readerships and audiences, and thus a platonic and ill-fated form of homoeroticism found a niche in mainstream Islamicate cultures.

Homoeroticism did not belong exclusively to the allegedly decadent Ottoman period, however, and it certainly did not involve only platonic relationships. Nonetheless, the terms *homosexuality* and *homosexual* do not automatically equate with what takes place in Muslim-majority countries. As El-Rouayheb also reminds us, the terms *homosexualität* was coined in the late 1860s by Austro-Hungarian writer Karl Maria Kertbeny, but it is not necessarily synonymous with the much older concept of *sodomy*. He cites Michel Foucault's idea that the term *sodomite* could only apply 'to the perpetrator of an act' (El-Rouayheb, 2005, p. 5).

Thus configured, someone who has an inclination towards the same sex but does not engage in same-sex acts cannot be considered a sodomite. As El-Rouayheb states: 'On this account, homosexuality is no more synonym for sodomy that heterosexuality is equivalent to fornication' (2005, p. 5). We can glean from this discussion that 'homosexuality' is more in keeping with an essentialist conception of sexual identity, with a focus on feelings and immanence, as opposed to a constructionist approach to sexuality, which regards sexual acts as a form of performativity. This difference between essential identity and constructionist social performance is important when dealing with the configuration of same-sex acts in the so-called 'Muslim world', which seems attuned to inherited Hellenistic and Roman models focused on sexual roles. This homoerotic genealogy is an episteme that retains currency to this day: Max Kramer's (2010) study of contemporary internet chatrooms reveal many Muslims still categorise people according to whether they are sexually 'active' or 'passive' penetrators, not according to the gender of their chosen sexual partners, and certainly not in terms of exclusive desire towards any particular gender. Kramer observes that a man who penetrates another man is perceived as 'masculine', and thus would never be labelled as 'homosexual', a tag reserved for the penetrated party, especially if that person is an adult male. Indeed, as a Turkish correspondent emphatically put to Kramer: 'no no – am not homosexsüel – aktif aktif' (2010, p. 139).

Kramer also explores cases of middle-aged men from the Middle East and the Maghreb, of different social classes and occupations, who are married and have children, but who also find an outlet in homosexual relations with other men. These married men perform their societal and moral duty according to Islamic principles: they court women, they marry women, they have children. Having fulfilled their God-given and societally constructed roles, they can then comfortably lead a double life as husbands and fathers while giving vent to their homoerotic desires privately, sometimes in full knowledge of their immediate family, whose social and financial dependence on heteropatriarchy may encourage them to remain silent about these matters. In Kramer's account, as long as men marry, have children, and carry out their sexual dealings discreetly, they can feasibly enjoy relations with other men *'without being socially discredited'* (2010, p. 144, emphasis in original). Male same-sex acts are alive and well in Islamicate societies, albeit to the detriment of women and their elided desires and emotional needs. Moreover, what is repressed or punished in Muslim communities is not attraction between men per se, but, as Jayesh Needham (2013) suggests, the men's public definition as homosexual, i.e., having a sexual identity of exclusive sexual involvement with men. This social discouragement of same-sex relationships leads many men to marry women, while reserving their same-sex desire for clandestine extramarital affairs. Are these men primarily attracted to men but societally forced into marriage, or is this an endemic case of what the West would call rampant Arab bisexuality? Both cases seem feasible, yet the work of Joseph Massad (2007) leans towards the latter option, by arguing that a Western-style conception of sexuality as essential and gender-exclusive is not vernacular to Muslim cultures.

A self-confessed disciple of Edward Said, Massad argues in his book *Desiring Arabs* that the construction of essential sexual identities, such as *homosexuality*, is a Western invention, and that Muslim men engaging in same-sex acts or infatuated with younger men would not necessarily consider themselves to be exclusively *homosexual* in the way we have come to understand in the West. In his view, applying a Western conception of sexual identity to Islamicate countries is an extension of imperialist taxonomies attempting to define the 'Other' according to prescriptive Western notions. Massad argues in an impassioned syllogism that '[t]here is nothing liberatory about Western human subjectivity including gays and lesbians when it does so by forcibly including those non-European who are not gays or lesbians while excluding them as unfit to defend themselves' (2007, p. 42). At heart, it would seem this is a problem of self-definition: there are many people in Muslim-majority countries that would not describe themselves as *gay* or *lesbian*, let alone *homosexual*, not just because such terminologies do not translate easily to their vernacular Islamicate cultures, but also because the Western exploitation of binaries – i.e., masculine/feminine, homosexual/heterosexual – forecloses behavioural complexities in Islamicate societies. In trying to reclaim homosexual Muslims, Massad argues some Western LGBTIQ activists, which he calls the 'Gay International', project onto a different cultural landscape their own Western ideologies, just like the Orientalists of yore. Kramer also points to the irony in the situation: the Muslim world, so often constructed as an 'Eden for same-sex practices' (2010, p. 134) – as evidenced in the manifold works of Gustave Flaubert, André Gide, Paul Bowles, William Burroughs, Jean Genet, and Joe Orton – is now portrayed as acerbically homophobic and in need of sexual liberation, which the West will gladly procure. To Kramer, forcing down on Muslims a Western formulation of 'sexual Orientation' amounts to almost a 'second colonization' (2010, p. 153). He also observes that a model of exclusive orientation creates undue polarisation even in the West, where people are pressurised into belonging to one particular sexual group, potentially forcing heterosexuality – and homosexuality – onto subjects who might express and define their sexualities more fluidly.

Introduction

There are some downsides to the form of cultural protectionism that Massad propounds. While it is important to remain sensitive to cultural nuances and to be wary of epistemic violence, the influence of global flows of communication, embodied in the widespread availability of Western models of homosexuality through the media and the internet, means that conceptions of sexuality in Islamicate societies, including diasporic Muslim communities in direct contact with Western ideologies, are gradually changing, whether this change is welcome or not, or whether it is seen as a form of cultural contamination or as the inexorable symptom of globalisation. As such, the way social and cultural critics account for the existence of these transnational forms of homosexuality ought to be commensurate with their burgeoning expression. Scholars such as Samar Habib (2010) see Massad's position as too reductive, for it consigns Muslim men and women who have a near-exclusive sexual preference to non-existence, or to a state of mere complicity with Western imperialism. If we are really to account for the complexities of the globalised contemporary world, we should be ready to acknowledge epistemic overlaps in the formulation of sexual identification. Rather than selectively embracing one model of sexuality according to a single school of thought, as either essentialist or constructionist, we need to remain attuned to nuances in the cultural articulation of such matters, and willing to concede to inconsistency, which, in the case of diasporic subjects, is a matter of everyday existence. Moreover, critiquing the colonial and neocolonial networks of desire that have given way to such cultural overlaps in the wake of rampant globalisation is one thing; attempting to downplay or erase the effects of such exchanges on actual human experience is another. As we will see through the course of this book, representations of queer diasporic Muslims are capable of making reference to a plethora of cultural and ideological influences, both local and global. In many cases, the latter are not perceived as an imperialist imposition or as destroying cultural authenticity, but, instead, they are accepted as the inevitable result of living in the diaspora. Like any other human phenomenon, sexuality is not exempt of cultural confluences and ideological intersections. Admitting to such interconnection and analysing its effects on the expression of non-normative desires should be key to understanding queer diasporic positions, while also contributing to blurring the boundaries between 'East' and 'West' stubbornly drawn by both Euro-American ethnocentrism and Islamism.

Even the continued aversion of Islamist commentators to homosexuality cannot be considered in isolation and should be framed more explicitly within the historical context of European colonialism and postcolonial Islamic revivalism, which, despite their power contestations, share some of their homophobic ideologies and discourses. If, as we have seen, homoeroticism was a part of mainstream Islamicate cultures well into the eighteenth century, the global onset of homophobia in the nineteenth and twentieth centuries can be traced back to the West's accession to global power, a time when homosexuality, formulated as an innate moral deviation, became the object of intense scrutiny both 'at home' and in the colonies. El-Rouayheb (2005) sees the expurgation of homoeroticism in literature as part of this colonial legacy. He cites the case of Richard Burton and his translation of the *Thousand Nights and a Night*, first published in 1885. Burton's highly eroticised version of the *Arabian Nights* is testament to his exaggerated fascination with Oriental homoeroticism[2] and is far from being the collection of children's stories later published by Andrew Lang in 1898. El-Rouayheb observes that the edition of Burton's *Arabian Nights* published in Cairo in 1930 elided all the homoerotic stories, including those concerning the real poet Abu Nuwas already mentioned. This sanitised edition was followed two years later in Cairo by an equally expurgated publication of Abu Nuwas' poems, which, unlike previous editions, did not include the homoerotic poems for which Nuwas is famous. The postcolonial expurgation of any references to homoeroticism, whether exaggerated by Orientalists such as Burton or vernacularly articulated by Islamicate poets like Abu Nuwas, reveals that colonial and postcolonial Muslims have inherited the distaste towards homosexuality of the European colonial elites.

Whereas at first this homophobia was symptomatic of colonial mimicry, the postcolonial aversion towards homosexuality would become a feature of Islamic revivalist ideologies trying to define themselves in direct opposition to the West. Roy (2004) convincingly argues that the onset of Islamic neo-orthodoxy in the second half of the twentieth century was due to a postcolonial impetus to define Muslim-majority societies in direct contrast to Western ideologies. He also suggests that the contemporary construction of homosexuality by controversial Muslim *mullahs* replicates the medical rhetoric of right-wing Christian conservatives. He chooses the prominent example of Muzammil Siddiqi, the former president of the Islamic Society of North America, who describes homosexuality as 'a moral disorder, a sin and corruption. [...] Homosexuality is dangerous for the health of the individuals and for society. It is a main cause of one of the most harmful and fatal diseases' (Roy, 004, p. 215). According to Roy, this contemporary rejection of homosexuality on medical grounds is not formulated in relation to Islamicate traditions, but follows, instead, the allegedly scientific model prevalent in the West. Although there is historical evidence that classical Muslims already discussed homosexuality in medical terms (Habib, 2009), it is reasonable to infer that contemporary Islamists seem to be taking their cue from Christian homophobia. In addition, Siddiqi's leaning towards medical terminologies and away from religious and moral imperatives seems to betray a desire to be perceived as 'up to date' with modernity. It would appear, then, that it is not homosexual acts but rather the homophobic discourses medicalising it that constitute a foreign imposition on Islamicate cultures, articulated via colonial Western ideologies and dressed up as Islamist self-affirmation.

As we have just seen, Western imperialism and postcolonial Islamic revivalism are complicit in the condemnation of homosexuality. However, the tendentious Western view that Islam is intrinsically homophobic should also take into consideration not only the influence of European colonial history, but also the complex trajectory of Islamic debates on same-sex acts, which have not been as unanimous as contemporary Islamic commentators would have us believe. Barbara Zollner suggests that neo-orthodox Islamic scholars are too quick to condemn homosexuality 'with stern conviction and without a grain of doubt. Nevertheless, those familiar with the intricacies of Islamic law should immediately be suspicious of this affirmation' (2010, p. 197). Such suspicion is warranted by the lack of consensus in Islamic juridical debates – the *fiqh* – about the nature of same-sex transgression and its suitable punishment. Zollner takes on those liberal commentators who seek to reclaim the perspectives of queer Muslims by essentialising Islamic law, which she does not deem universally homophobic. This is something that can be extended to some feminist debates[3] on Islamic doctrine, which also refute the view that *tafasir* – the various scholarly commentaries on the Qur'an – and the ensuing *fiqh* are unanimously patriarchal. Although, as Zollner observes, Muslim jurists regard divine will as the gauge for their laws, Islam's sacred scriptures need interpretation in order to derive such rulings, and as such the primary instinct behind jurists' decisions is *ijtihad* – independent reasoning.

If the rulings on homosexuality have not been consensual in the first instance, it is because the primary source of Islamic belief, the Qur'an, is not unambiguous about same-sex relations, and thus subsequent commentaries and rulings have had to grapple with this nebulousness. The matter of most contention when debating Islam's condemnation of same-sex acts involves recurring references in the Qur'an to Lot's people, the inhabitants of Sodom and Gomorrah, as described also in the Bible, and some alleged references to female-on-female sexuality. The work of Scott Siraj al-Haqq Kugle (2010) has been instrumental in 'queering' the Qur'an, the *ahadith* – sayings by and about Prophet Muhammad – and the various interpretations of these texts, as well as the *fiqh*. He makes particular reference to the contending schools of thought debating the issue. It is clear from

Kugle's commentary that Lot's people rejected his prophethood, and that they were grossly inhospitable to his guests by using rape and theft as methods of dissuasion. According to Kugle, although anal intercourse is at stake in the episode, which makes references to lust, it cannot be divorced from the context of sexual coercion, including adultery, since Lot's people were married men; in addition, it is important to remember that the transgressions of these men also included theft and the negation of God and his prophet, which played a major role in their being annihilated by a divine storm, together with Lot's wife, who also rejected his message but was not a man who performed anal penetration. Persistent textual references to the men's 'abomination' in waylaying other men and abandoning their wives made it necessary for some Muslim jurists to coin terms that could describe them and their actions: *liwat* and *luti*, which can be roughly equated to the biblical terms *sodomy* and *sodomites*, respectively.

Whereas these jurists interpreted this episode as being, on the most part, a condemnation of anal penetration, Kugle cites the example of classical Andalusian scholar Ibn Hazm, who placed emphasis on the men's rejection of Lot's prophethood and their adultery. According to Ibn Hazm's commentary quoted by Kugle:

> The [divine] stoning which punished them was not for one type of immorality [*fahisha*] in specific, but was rather for their infidelity and rejection [*kufr*]. Those who claim that stoning is the punishment for this immorality [anal sex between men] are not following the command of God unless the one guilty of it is a rejecter of God's Prophet [*kafir*]. (Kugle, 2010, p. 51)

Whereas neo-orthodox Islamic scholars such as Siddiqi would argue that the case of Lot's people involves a categorical, God-ordained rejection of homosexuality, this instance of *tafsir* proves there is complexity to the matter. Kugle argues, via Ibn Hazm, that '[t]he role of male-to-male sex acts is marginal to the essence of the story and its moral lesson' (2010, p. 53). I would add that the contextual details involving Lot's tribe do not correspond strictly with either our contemporary conception of homosexuality as a consensual act between same-sex adults or with any other cultural configuration of human relationships as based on egalitarian intimacy. It should not be obviated that Lot's people were married men and that they were being unfaithful to their wives when forcing their lust on Lot's guests. They were also using sex coercively, as a weapon, not as a form of sensual connection with another human being, which is, together with reproduction, one of its main purposes in Islamic doctrine. Kugle argues that sexual desire (*shahwa*) is one of several human desires, including the enjoyment of 'food, wealth, and power', and that these desires 'might be good or bad depending on the intent, intensity, and ethical comportment of the desiring than on the specific object or experience desired' (2010, p. 50). In light of this, sexual desire is not considered bad per se, but rather its good or evil is incumbent on its motivations. It is arguable, then, that Lot's people were therefore illicitly using their sexual desire with the wrong intent.[4]

The Qur'an mentions another form of immorality – or *fahisha* – that can take place between several women, although it is not given a concrete name. Subsequent *tafasir* have argued this transgression entails *sihaq* – the act of rubbing – a neologism associated with female-to-female sex acts.[5] Kugle (2010) cites a tenth-century interpreter, al-Isfahani, as the first to suggest this *sura* is concerned with female same-sex acts, an interpretive position embraced centuries later by al-Zamakhshari and al-Baydawi, and more recently by Rashid Rida. Kugle concludes that patriarchal interpretation has found it easy to scapegoat sexual morality in order to avoid the more urgent topics of economic and social justice, especially surrounding women. I would suggest that, if Kugle fails to provide an example of *tafsir*, apart from his own, challenging this bias against sex between women, it is because the Islamic focus on sexual transgression has been far more generally directed towards penetration than towards any other forms of sexual contact (Habib, 2007). Some jurists grappling with rulings on female sexuality did not equate *sihaq* with *liwat*, and saw the former as a minor transgression not requiring equal punishment. In fact, Junaid bin Jahangir cites Salafi scholar Yusuf Qaradawi's statement that '[l]esbianism is not as bad as homosexuality, in practical terms' (2010, p. 299). This is not so much a case of benevolence towards women as proof of the general Muslim obsession with masculine sexuality, and with anal intercourse as being metonymic of homosexuality.[6] Female homosexuality, which Qaradawi's statement does not even count as homosexuality, is putatively erased from the map.

The *ahadith* add further complications to the *fiqh*, or the tradition of Islamic juridical rulings. In essence, the *ahadith* are sayings or anecdotes attributed to the Prophet Muhammad or his followers which were observed by his disciples and passed down orally, until they were textually transcribed. A plethora of *ahadith* have been compiled in disparate collections, and a whole Islamic scholarly tradition was once devoted to their study and to the verification of their authenticity.[7] Because of their reliance on the words of a series of followers, who may have wanted to advance their own sociopolitical standpoints, the *ahadith* can be instruments of elucidation, but also, as Kugle warns, of coercion. Zollner (2010) cites the case of twentieth-century Iraqi scholar Taha Jaber al-'Alwani,

Introduction

who, typically, mentions the story of Lot's people as proof of God's condemnation of homosexuality in the Qur'an, and who then justifies the use of the capital punishment by strategically referring to a *hadith* stipulating that, if caught, both active and passive partners ought to be killed by burning or stoning. On closer inspection, Zollner (2010) observes, in concurrence with previous work by Kugle and Habib, the *hadith* singled out by al-'Alwani and anthologised by Abu Da'ud, is not found in the al-Bukhari and the al-Muslim collections, two of the most respected compilations of *sahih* – truthful – *ahadith*, which suggests classical Islamic scholars doubted its authenticity. This is a useful example of how any individual *hadith* may be strategically used to condition the punishment of homosexuality, even when such *hadith* goes against interpretive consensus. Moreover, Kugle (2010) goes as far as suggesting that no single *hadith* reporting on homosexual or transgender behaviour is *mutawatir* – i.e., containing multiple credible links back to the Prophet – a qualification classical Islamic scholars decided was vital in asserting the decisiveness of the narrative when attempting to dispense justice.

The fact that disputed *ahadith* can, and have been, used to recommend the killing of those involved in same-sex acts suggests that they have contributed to the gradual cumulation of homophobic ideologies, which, as I have mentioned, became particularly important when defining the moral and legal character of the Islamic postcolonial nation in opposition to the 'permissive' West. In asserting their homophobic stances, Islamic neo-orthodox commentators have been building on, on the one hand, the internalised but seldom acknowledged influence of colonial homophobia, best illustrated in belatedly embraced colonial laws regarding homosexuality, and, on the other, on an Islamist rejection of homosexuality that relies on the ambiguities of the Qur'an and on the tendentious evidence provided by *ahadith*, while ignoring discordant voices within the *tafsir* and *fiqh* traditions, all of which have allowed for orthodox attitudes towards sexual roles to become calcified in contemporary mainstream Muslim ideologies.

I would suggest that, ultimately, it is doubtful whether a productive vindication of queer Muslims can be staged strictly on the grounds of theology or scriptural interpretation, not merely because scriptural ambiguities and complexities can easily be exploited by intolerant interpreters of the Qur'an and its attendant traditions, but also because Islamic orthodox commentators are unlikely to concede validity to arguments they automatically class as flawed, unscholarly, or simply blasphemous, merely because they threaten their moral certainties. Their dogmatic position denies Islam its due complexity, and it tries to silence centuries of Islamic interpretive and juridical debate, to the point of making the

Islamic condemnation of homosexuality seem wrongly objective and static. This authoritative – or authoritarian – appearance of consensus, Zollner (2010) and Christopher Grant Kelly (2010) compare with the more modest position of the Hanafi juridical branch of Islam, which does not believe same-sex acts should be punished, due to the lack of clear evidence of their punishment in the Qur'an. This is the kind of religious debate with which Islamic neo-orthodoxy refuses to engage by condemning homosexuality categorically. Despite such internal differences within a faith that is often constructed as monolithic, and at the risk of becoming complicit with such essentialism, it is beyond the possibilities of this study to stage an intervention into Islam that can reclaim queer Muslims merely from the field of what we have come to define as 'religion' in the West, and which scholars such as Kugle and Habib have staged so productively elsewhere. I also suspect a purely theological debate to be too narrow a framework for such a complex sociological topic and for such heterogeneous global citizens. I would suggest, instead, that the key to vindicate the positions of queer diasporic Muslims is to interrogate the crucial disjoints and overlaps in cultural expressions of homosexuality, especially by exploiting those paradoxes that can help us see through the cracks of intersecting homophobic ideologies in nationalist and diasporic discourses.

Queer diasporas, homonationalism, and micropolitical disorientation

A reclaiming of queer diasporic Muslims' perspectives should draw attention and exploit these epistemic overlaps, in order to offer a nuanced understanding of the contending sexual models informing discussions of queer desires: hence, my preference for an assembled approach to sexual orientation which attends both to constructionist and essentialist formulations of sexuality. *Queer* is also the term that can most productively bring together the various examples of non-normative desires included in this study. As we have seen, applying the term *homosexual* to all Muslims engaging in same-sex acts is problematic, especially when considering those cases where the subject in question is not sexually and emotionally orientated towards members of their own sex in an exclusive manner. I would even argue that the term *homosexuality* is too tainted by the history of Western homophobia and European colonialism, and its negative reception in many Muslim-majority countries is a symptom of discontent with such histories of colonial imposition. In turn, bisexuality has long been associated in dominant gay and lesbian discourses with fickleness, sexual indecision, and closetedness; moreover, a consideration of all Muslims as inherently bisexual merely reproduces old Orientalist tropes. The term *queer*, on the other hand, although still Western, is associated with a more polymorphous and less essentialising liberation from sexual normativity, as well as with epistemic resistance. *Homosexual*, like *gay* and *lesbian*, is formulated as an essential identity and exclusive desire, whereas *queer*, first reclaimed in the age of poststructuralism, became a tool for sexual liberation based on social and individual performance rather than on an essentialist identitarian configuration, yet, when used as an umbrella term, it has enough suppleness to include essentialist envisionings of sexuality which are not heteronormative. Seen in this light, queer can account for Islamic models of sexuality based on sexual acts and roles rather than on immanence, and to any other liminal configurations of desire.

In his Introduction to *Post-Colonial, Queer: Theoretical Intersections*, John C. Hawley quotes Annamarie Jagose on the possibilities of the term *queer*:

> queer may be used to describe an open-ended constituency, whose shared characteristic is not identity itself but an anti-normative positioning with regard to sexuality. In this way, queer may exclude lesbians and gay men whose identification with community and identity marks a relatively recent legitimacy, but include all those whose sexual identifications are not considered normal or sanctioned. (Hawley, 2001, pp. 3–4)

Jagose states that *queer* should not be understood as a fixed identity label, but as an 'anti-normative positioning', which means it can be used in a constructionist manner. As such, apart from being hospitable to the various performances of sexuality that may escape stiff categorisation, the term also strategically circumvents sensitive issues of burgeoning or non-exclusive sexual orientation. By focusing on the 'practice' of queer sexualities rather than on their configuration as an 'identity', we can avoid epistemic violence to vernacular Islamicate model of sex acts. In addition, Jagose's point avoids prescribing to those societies – such as Muslim-majority states – where the late post-imperial vindication of queer rights may be a recent phenomenon, and where individual subjects may still be tuning themselves to the cultural workings of global queer communities. In addition, the term *queer* is suitably 'open-ended'; it does not delimit a particular segment of any community or membership of any single club, but rather points to the collective social interweaving of a myriad individual cases of sexual non-normativity.

In deploying *queer* as a tool of sexual liberation applying to many global and local contexts, we need to be wary of colluding with normativity. William

Introduction

J. Spurlin highlights the self-reflexivity needed in comparative queer scholarship, arguing that a transnational queer lens should 'examine its own imperialist and homogenizing impulses made possible through globalization' (2001, p. 200). Indeed, the context of globalisation can make it too easy for those critics with a foothold in the West to glamorise queer migration and to paint it with the bright yet blinding colours of Massad's 'Gay International'. Comparative queer scholarship must divest itself of the cloak of objectivity and rationality, particularly when examining sensitive issues of faith, ethnicity, and sexual identity. We ought to see ourselves as inalienable parts of networks of desire, whose positions of knowledge invest us with authority. When dealing with the plights of queer diasporic Muslims, we must be ready to admit partial defeat when dealing with complexities outside the bounds of our linguistic or cultural competence. *Queer* constitutes a useful heuristic tool insofar as it helps us account for a multiplicity of global perspectives, but only as long as we do not relinquish the nuances of transnational human experience. In order not to collude with Western privilege and power, we must always be on the lookout for inequalities in terms of representation, visibility, or legitimisation, our eyes keen on recognising those power dynamics that are the product of (neo)colonial oppression.

Critical humility when dealing with such disparate cases of queer desire is highly necessary due to the pervading influence of Western models of sexual liberation, which can risk constructing cultures with fraught relationships with queer citizens as inferior or backward. Jasbir K. Puar (2007) has famously drawn attention to the ways in which Western LGBTIQ activism has been complicit with ongoing neocolonial attitudes, leading to the exclusion of 'Other' citizens from national and global discourses. She suggests that the accession of LGBTIQ subjects to civil rights in many European and North American countries has led to what she calls 'homonationalism': that is, a conglomeration of homosexual ideologies that dictate normative homosexual lifestyles at the expense of cultural and contextual complexities. Puar argues that Western LGBTIQ discourses are predominantly white and often intolerant towards cultures that do not unanimously accept homosexuality, a position that ignores the fact that homosexuality is not unanimously accepted or respected in all Western contexts. Puar also feels that, far from contributing towards true liberalisation, homonationalist queer ideologies exclude complex cases from normative discourses on homosexual rights, to the detriment of those queer subjects whose identification both with their non-normative sexualities *and* their ethnic identities is being wittingly or unwittingly dismissed. Exploring international representations of queer diasporic Muslims must entail an extrapolation from those forms of queer criticism that posit the West as the paragon of modernity. I reject this form of exceptionalist ideology in the knowledge that it does not foster understanding about the complex sexual and ethnic positions of queer diasporic Muslims and that, in fact, it risks strengthening Western Islamophobia.[8] This is not just a matter of liberal political correctness: affirming, against the evidence of existing debates, that Islam is inherently homophobic and that the West is exceptional because it is the best place to be homosexual is politically dangerous, for this rhetoric can easily play into the hands of Western military interventionists and their apologists, whose continued interests in Muslim-majority countries is always on the lookout for moral justification. Nonetheless, we must also ward off the most astringent claims of both Islamic conservatives and well-meaning cultural protectionists, in the hope of gauging a more flexible position that can respect the complexities of transnational queer positions.

Placing queer Muslim migrant subjects within broader discourses of diaspora should also allow us to acknowledge the ways in which sexual difference can be a crucial factor in the articulation of individual and collective migration. In *Comparing Postcolonial Diasporas*, Michelle Keown, David Murphy, and James Procter point to the belated extension of the concept's remit. Although, as they point out, the term initially referred to the 'dispersal of the Jews' (Keown *et al.*, 2009, p. 1), contemporary cultural and literary analysis has come to refer to a myriad of global migrations: Romanian, African, Asian, black, Sikh, Irish, Lebanese, Palestinian and 'Atlantic', to name but a few. The term has been globally deployed in terms of ethnicity, race, nationality, and even religion, within the various contexts of slavery, indentured labour, war, religious persecution, and poverty. However, as they suggest, '[a] corresponding expansion of diaspora's conceptual horizons has also taken place in recent years, since it has evolved to operate as a travelling metaphor associated with tropes of mobility, displacement, borders and crossings' (Keown *et al.*, 2009, p. 1). Thus configured, the term can include a plethora of individual and collective journeys in search for a place of settlement away from economic hardship or persecution. Peter Morey and Amina Yaqin concede that Muslim migration is 'now often seen as a diaspora' (2011, p. 4) because of the organisation of such migrant communities around ethnic and religious commonalities. Nonetheless, as we can easily appreciate, sexuality does not automatically figure in discussions of diaspora, and sexual non-normativity has been a generally underrated factor in the discussion of contemporary forms of migration.

A seminal examination of the concept of queer diaspora is that of Cindy Patton and Benigno Sánchez-Eppler (2000), who agree with the anti-essentialist and

Introduction

constructionist branch of queer studies when examining the conjoining of sexuality and translocation. Rather than essential, diasporic sexual identity is deemed by them as strategic and contingent, set against a backdrop of shifting material and discursive conditions. They argue that '[s]exuality is intimately and immediately felt, but publicly and internationally described and mediated. Sexuality is not only not essence, not timeless, it is also not fixed in place; sexuality is on the move' (2000, p. 2). Queer diasporic subjects must contest national and cultural borders; their sexuality is subject to ongoing negotiation within a complex framework of transcultural exchange. Patton and Eppler further observe that '[w]hen a practitioner of "homosexual acts," or a body that carries any of many queering marks moves between officially designated spaces – nation, region, metropol, neighborhood, or even culture, gender, religion, disease – intricate realignments of identity, politics, and desire take place' (2000, p. 3). These crucial realignments involve mundane challenges to those normative structures imposed by the heteronormative social majority or the state. In the instance of queer diasporic Muslims, segmentary constructions of ethnic and sexual identities which are predicated as separate in the normative public discourses of the Western 'secular' state, and of normative Islamic heteropatriarchy, suddenly become blurred, giving way to new identitarian configurations previously deemed impossible.

In constructing this argument, I am inspired by the work of Gayatri Gopinath, who lucidly argues that '[s]uturing "queer" to "diaspora" then recuperates those desires, practices, and subjectivities that are rendered impossible and unimaginable within conventional diasporic and nationalist imaginaries' (2005, p. 11). By reclaiming unheeded tensions surrounding sexuality, the study of queer diasporas can uncover previously uncharted differences with established discourses of nation, diaspora, and globalisation. These new affective maps also pose a challenge to Eurocentric LGBTIQ discourses, with a configuration of queer identities that is a combination of non-normative ethnic and sexual allegiances. Queer diasporas dissolve the linear narratives linking notions of origin and destination, home and migration, even ethnicity and sexuality. Gopinath argues that

> queer diasporic cultural forms suggests alternative forms of collectivity and communal belonging that redefine home outside of a logic of blood, purity, authenticity, and patrilineal descent. Queerness names a mode of reading, of rendering intelligible that which is unintelligible and indeed impossible within dominant diasporic and nationalist logic. (Gopinath, 2005, p. 187)

Introduction

Home, then, is no longer exclusively linked to family, community, ethnic group, patriarchal lineages, or even orthopraxy; home is redefined in representations of queer diasporas as networks of affect and desire at a remove from the heteronormative structures of the national and the diasporic communities.

Like Muhammad and his most immediate followers, queer diasporic Muslims seem empowered by the Islamic concept of *hijra*, of pilgrimage. Queer Muslim diasporas are thus crucially conditioned by an affective and physical departure from the beliefs of the social mainstream. According to Peter Mandaville (2007), this model of migration broke through ethnic barriers and united Muslims who dissented with dominant Arabian polytheism at the time of the Prophet. Although many Muslims regard their queer coreligionists and their defenders as heretics, the plight of those queer Muslims who leave their societies behind due to persecution is curiously parallel to the trajectory of Muhammad and his friends: they are searching for a place where they can live with what they perceive as their 'God-given' role. In so doing, they are severing, or at the least questioning, heteronormative familial and communitarian ties, while, in some cases, remaining loyal to their identity as Muslims. Such queer flights from the norm also result in an affective reconfiguration of Islam. In the light of such complex affiliations, the position of queer Muslims in the West is highly contingent, even equivocal, for while they may be grateful for the greater respect of their civil rights in some Western societies, they do not wish to see their ethnic or religious backgrounds abused on the grounds of their problematic treatment of homosexuals. Momin Rahman has reflected on the 'difficulties of negotiating a social world where racism, Islamophobia, and homophobia intersect' (2014, p. 27). He persuasively suggests that Islamophobia and anti-Western homophobia are engaged in a process of triangulation, whereby the more Western commentators denounce Islamic homophobia, the more Muslims respond angrily to the political and moral impositions of Western politics; these shows of animosity in turn exacerbate Western views of Islamic conservatism, and like this ad infinitum.

The very notion that queer Muslims can identify as both queer *and* Muslim must also mean that there is no inherent contradiction between sexual and ethno-religious identities; if there is tension, it is not because of their immanent conflict, but rather because of the normative social workings of Islamic heteropatriarchy and of Western homonormativity, both of which are dominant but not fully representative of 'Islam' or the 'West'. Because of the complexities added to queer Muslim identifications by the ongoing process of triangulation, Rahman proposes a model of 'intersectionality' whereby identity categories are neither

Introduction

'solid' nor 'definite' (2014, p. 13), and where different social movements can join and fight together. This relativist view of identity and its creation of inclusive social movements is inspiring. However, we must resist the temptation of singling out queer Muslims as paradigmatic of intersectionality, for this in itself is a form of exceptionalism. Due to the globalised nature of our contemporary societies and to the intersection of issues of gender, class, sexual orientation, race, and ethnicity, many contemporary citizens' predicaments are already intersectional. What queer diasporic Muslims bring to debates about nation and diaspora is not an exceptionally intersectional configuration of sexual and ethnic identities, but rather a disorganisation of normative categories at the heart of these discourses. As such, they are not the pre-eminent examples of intersectionality in otherwise normative networks of desire; rather, they constitute ideological destabilisers in societies where flights from normativity occur on a regular basis across the various social categories.

In my choice of vocabulary, I have already betrayed my indebtedness to the work of Gilles Deleuze and Félix Guattari (1996), particularly to their notion of micropolitics.[9] They suggest that the whole of Western thought is organised around the idea of the root and the tree: 'The West has a special relation to the forest and deforestation', and it favours lineages that centre around arborescent imageries; by contrast, they argue, '[t]he East presents a different figure: a relation to the steppe and the garden (or in some cases, the desert and the oasis), [...] cultivation of tubers by fragmentation of the individual' (1996, p. 18). Against the Western root, the Eastern rhizome: a complex network of subterranean tube-like connections that works horizontally, as opposed to the vertical tree-like structure of Western thought. Although too neatly cut out, and ignoring existing religious and social hierarchies in the Islamicate world, such mapping preliminarily fits the differentiation between Christian-infused secularism and political Islam: Western religious and secular authorities work through hierarchies or clan-like lineages, whereas the lack of an overarching tree-like structure in Islamic ideologies entails a myriad connections within a tribe-like rhizomic network. Nonetheless, as Deleuze and Guattari also suggest, roots and rhizomes can intersect, and there are despotic hierarchies within the rhizome – which in the case of Islam we can assign to the punctual authority of some religious figures and to pockets of extremist activity. Moreover, they argue that '[w]hat is at question at the rhizome is a relation to sexuality – but also to the animal, the vegetal, the world, politics, the book, things natural and artificial – that is totally different from the arborescent relation: all manner of "becomings"' (1996, p. 21). Queer Muslims embody such horizontal 'becomings', in a rhizome that creates dialogue between sexuality and ideology, politics, and culture. The resulting state fits the chosen image of the plateau: a space that is always in the middle, 'whose development avoids any *orientation* toward a culmination point' (Deleuze and Guattari, 1996, p. 22, emphasis added). By avoiding a final orientation in their negotiation of ethnic or sexual segments, queer diasporic Muslims inhabit a space that disorientates mainstream cultures, stopping their identities from having the chance to calcify into exceptionalist singularity.

The work of prominent current scholars, such as Puar (2007), has already benefited from Deleuze and Guattari's work, especially when she argues that 'queerness [is] not an identity nor an anti-identity, but an *assemblage* that is spatially and temporally contingent'; moreover,

> [w]hile dismantling the representational mandates of visibility identity politics that feed narratives of sexual exceptionalism, affective analyses can approach queernesses that are unknown or not cogently knowable, that are in the midst of *becoming*, that do not immediately and visibly signal themselves as insurgent, oppositional, or transcendent. (Puar, 2007, p. 204, emphasis added)

In Puar's thinking, with my emphasis on the echoes of Deleuze and Guattari, queerness is a combination of constructed categories, not, of necessity, an essence; although, as I have shown, a combination of essence and performance may be best suited to diasporic models of queer desire because of their assembled nature. In the various cases of the queer diasporic Muslims chosen for study, their assembled affective experiences should also be envisaged as different from those of visible homonormative Western queerness: their burgeoning sense of becoming can help us oppose normative views of Western sexual exceptionalism. Moreover, queer Muslims should not be positioned in a different, alternative space, at a remove from the world of macropolitics, or as paradigms of intersectional exceptionality. On the contrary, a model enabled by Deleuze and Guattari's notion of micropolitics and by the work of critics such as Puar should allow us to see queer diasporic Muslims as contributing micropolitically to the redefinition of the segmentary identity categories of heteronormative patriarchy, both Western and non-Western, without the need for a constant taking up of arms. Their challenges work at the level of mundane action and affect, leading to common views being constantly renegotiated.

Such a vision of queer diasporic Muslims as disorientating the mainstream, rather than occupying an exceptional or alternative space, is inspired by the work of Sara Ahmed (2006), whose notion of queer disorientation is highly instrumental to my study. In her work on queer phenomenology, Ahmed contends with the well-established but contentious notion of sexual orientation, which, she argues, constructs heterosexuality as the neutral sexual state and homosexuality as being a particular 'deviant' orientation. She suggests that the notion of sexual orientation is born at the same time as the figure of the homosexual, and hence homosexuals are the only subjects considered to have an orientation as such. However, instead of flatly rejecting the concept, she interrogates it and appropriates it in relation to migration and to queerness, pondering the ways in which experiences of diaspora entail a process of disorientation and reorientation in relation to the subject's shifting surroundings. Her phenomenological approach 'reminds us that spaces are not exterior to bodies; instead, spaces are like a second skin that unfolds in the folds of the body' (Ahmed, 2006, p. 9). In this mapping, queer subjects and their surroundings merge and create queer spaces that are transient yet politically insurgent.

Ahmed also intimates how queer disorientation does not merely take place in the macropolitical sphere, by asking us to consider

> how queer politics might *involve* disorientation, without legislating disorientation as a politics. It is not that disorientation is always radical. Bodies that experience disorientation can be defensive, as they reach out for support or as they search for a place to reground and reorientate their relation to the world. (Ahmed, 2006, p. 158, emphasis in original)

In Ahmed's view, disorientation does not need to be constructed in public discourse as a form of radicalism, but happens at the micropolitical level of everyday action and affect. In addition, she offers that what is important is not disorientation in and of itself, but its effect: 'The point is what we do with such moments of disorientation, as well as what such moments can do – whether they can offer us the hope of new directions, and whether new directions are reason enough for hope' (2006, p. 158). I would respond to Ahmed that the new lines drawn by queer disorientations from the micropolitical dimension are, indeed, hopeful. Queer diasporic Muslims' continued disorientation has a revulsive effect that disorganises both Western views on ethnicity and sexuality and the conservative ideologies of Islam which refuse to legitimise the various identitarian confluences. Micropolitical dynamics reminds us there is no Islam *and* the West; no secularism *and* religion; no Muslim *and* queer identities: in the realm of worldly experience, the disorientated boundaries between categories create new forms of becoming. There is hope in the fact that each micropolitical flight from normativity leaves a trace in each nation's tapestry that challenges established official discourses, and that these challenges can connect molecularly with other forms of anti-normativity within and across national borders, eventually feeding back to the macropolitical, and thus gradually contributing to the redefinition of those categories that segmentalise our contemporary world.

As cultural critics of queer diasporas, we must remain wary of those macropolitical models that construct cultures, ethnicities, or religions as hermetic, for, as the dynamics of micropolitics remind us, for every norm there is a flight from normativity that challenges the discreteness of its contours. Moreover, the work of Timothy Fitzgerald (2007) draws attention to the contradictions in Western secularism, with its claims to rationality, democracy, and free speech, and its 'authorisation' of forms of private religiosity, while opposing, also, the 'dangerous' public nature of political Islam. Fitzgerald is particularly provocative when drawing attention to the strategic but fallacious line drawn between the categories of 'religion' and 'politics'. As he suggests, 'religion is a modern invention which authorises and naturalises a form of Euro-American secular rationality. In turn, this supposed position of secular rationality constructs and authorises *its* "other", religion and religions' (2007, p. 6, emphasis in original). In other words, 'religion' has not always been a discrete category routinely extrapolated from the world of politics and law-making, but has been the object of a history of Euro-American secularisation. Before the birth of secularism, which, as Fitzgerald reminds us, was born out of religion, not the other way around, politics and religion belonged in the same public realm; there was nothing to suggest that politics could not be underpinned by theological worldviews, which were not deemed irrational or backward. In addition, religious texts, such as the Qur'an, make reference to pragmatic phenomena we would now not automatically classify as religious in the theological sense, such as inheritance laws, biology, and medicine.

Interestingly, Fitzgerald's work also helps us recognise how, despite secularism's claims to objectivity and rationality, our so-called secular Western world is still shrouded in Christian aesthetics. A cursory look at Western law easily demonstrates that Christianity is still deeply embedded in our political consciousness. Even many of the secular institutions related to the democratic state – i.e., freedom of speech, democratic elections, the pledge to a nation and its flag – are imbued with a sacrality and ritualism that Fitzgerald suggests is not dissimilar to religiosity. When considering the 'dangers' of allowing 'Islam' to enter the political realm, Western thinkers ought to realise that there is no preternatural division between 'religion' and 'politics'; that there is no incompatibility between religious belief and politics. The secularist obsession to create separate categories seems more driven by the fear of the religious 'Other' – a fear that seems to belie ethnicity rather than mere religion – and with the perception that secularism is the apogee of human development. So, in queering Islam, we should unmask Western secularism and interrogate the strategic gap it places between public politics and private religion, and ultimately between the 'secular' West and the 'religious' East.

Talad Asad argues there is a tendency in the West to see Islamic traditions as local, linked to the remote, exotic spaces of the Orient, while 'Western writers who invoke the authority of modern secular literature claim they are universal' (1993, p. 8). The view of Islamic tradition as rooted to a locality – invariably the Orient – while modern secularism is seen as universal – ignoring, in the meantime, that its global reach has more to do with Euro-American colonialism than with an 'organic' growth of secularist ideologies – further widens the gap between 'Western' and 'Muslim' perspectives, which even in my own phrasing here are mapped in two discrete localities. Morey and Yaqin suggest that the ancient presence of Muslim citizens in the West expose the lie to the familiar rhetoric of the 'clash of civilisations',[10] and expose it as a 'political strategist's daydream' (2011, p. 4). They argue that the constant framing of Muslims as extremist and retrogressive creates persistent stereotypes that only exacerbate anti-Western sentiments in Muslim communities, which in turn stereotype the West as decadent and imperialist. This model of reciprocate stereotyping 'drives a wedge between worlds that are intertwined, indeed interdependent' (Morey and Yaqin, 2011, p. 4). In other words, when approaching a contentious topic such as Islam and the West, or even Islam *in* the West, we need to remind ourselves that such discrete essentialist categories paint a false picture: the relationship between Islam and the West has for centuries been one of interrelationality despite the ontological differences still conjured in political and scholarly rhetoric. The depictions of queer diasporic Muslims that I examine in this book paint a more sympathetic picture of Muslim diasporas, which can help Western audiences begin to question the partisan pictures often painted by the Western media, and its creation of monolithic versions of the 'average' Muslim as being patriarchal, traditionalist, and violent.

In attempting to outgrow the political thrust of Western aversion towards Muslims, I take my cue from Bruce Lawrence, a respected scholar of Islam and world religions, who offers the following response when asked about how we can teach Islam after 9/11:

> Unlearn all the slogans about the red menace (communism) succeeded by the green menace (Islam), the axis of evil (mostly Muslims) overshadowing participatory democracy (almost never Muslim). Unlearn the words *shari'a* and *jihad* as catch-all categories for universal Islamic aspirations. Unlearn Islamic politics as the major reflex for Muslim social activists across the globe, whether Arab or Asian, Iranian or Turkish, African or American. In short, tell your listeners, as I have not ceased to tell my students: stop reading the headlines and the bylines that invoke Islam as the nemesis of all that is modern, Western and hopeful about the twenty-first century. (Lawrence, 2014, p. 212)

Any scholar seriously approaching Islam or Muslims should bear in mind Lawrence's powerful dictum, which addresses some of the most commonplace Western assumptions about Islam, such as the idea that it is the successor of Russia's communism as the archenemy of the democratic and liberal West. As Sadia Abbas (2014) pithily argues, such twisted political logic tends to ignore the fact that many of the West's accomplices during the Cold War were the very Muslims who are now constructed as the 'Axis of Evil' in the rhetoric of the 'War on Terror'. In addition, participatory democracy is not something often associated with Muslim-majority countries, their religiously infused autocracies being perceived as the norm, and so Western military interventionists often construct themselves as the bringers of democracy, except for those countries – such as fiercely monarchic and conservative Saudi Arabia – which are already the West's allies or oil suppliers, for which exceptions can be made. Lawrence also draws attention to a variety of Arabic terms that have become common parlance in Western media, but which are seldom understood, such as *jihad*, *Shari'a*, or *fatwa*,[11] whose frequent occurrence has turned them into almost meaningless slogans.

Perhaps most importantly, Lawrence asks us to demystify Islam as a monolithic political consciousness controlling each and every move of a heterogeneous faith community – now numbering a fast-growing 1.5 billion worldwide – which cuts through national borders, ethnicities, religious practices, and cultural traditions. By attempting to unlearn the conglomerate of negative images daily mixed by the English-speaking media, I position my work at a defiant angle from the truisms assailing Islam and Muslims in Western discourses. In so doing, I adopt a methodology that is antithetical to power, inspired by the seminal work on Islam by Edward Said. In his oft-forgotten book *Covering Islam*, Said suggests that antithetical scholars reject the notion that knowledge of Islam ought to be subservient to the government's immediate policy interests, or that it should simply feed into the media's image of Islam as supplying the world with terrifying militancy and violence, they highlight the complicity between knowledge and power. (Said, 1997, p. 168)

In so doing, Said argues, antithetical critics are trying to forge relationships with Islam that are not dictated by power, looking, putatively, for 'alternative relationships' and 'interpretative situations', which entail a 'scrupulous methodological sense' (1997, p. 168). My study is inspired by Said's postcolonial envisioning of antithetical scholars as challenging the connection between 'official' dominant knowledges and power; between the ability to represent and the power to misrepresent the political 'Other' in the eyes of the general public. The upcoming exploration of international literary and cinematic representations of queer diasporic Muslims reveals 'other interpretative situations', positions of postcolonial critical analysis that encourage Western audiences and readers to begin questioning their own assumptions about Muslims. By examining how some of these narratives challenge the tendentious images pictured in the global media, I search for 'alternative relationships' that can start breaching ontological exclusivism between 'the West' and 'the rest'. I do so by fostering the multiple and nuanced deployment of Muslim identities in the West through depictions of intersectional sexual and ethnic disorientation, often simultaneously connected to issues of gender and class, in order to gauge an understanding of the highly textured ideological assemblages at work in queer Muslim diasporas.

Notes

1 Marshall G. S. Hodgson offers a seminal definition of the 'Islamicate' which is related to yet distinctive from the term 'Islamic':

> We will require a different term for the cultural traditions of the civilization at large, when we are not restricting our reference to religion. The various peoples among whom Islam has been predominant and which have shared in the cultural traditions distinctively associated with it may be called collectively 'Islamdom' […]. The distinctive civilization of Islamdom, then, may be called 'Islamicate' (1974, p. 95).

2 The original edition of Burton's *Thousand Nights and a Night* is now freely available through the University of Adelaide's website (Burton, 2006). Its 'Terminal Essay' contains a section entitled 'Pederasty' in which this controversial issue is explicitly discussed. Burton assigns pederasty to a particular geographical location, what he calls the 'Sotadic Zone', which is 'bounded westwards by the northern shores of the Mediterranean (N. Lat. 43) and by the southern (N. Lat. 30). Thus the depth would be 780 to 800 miles including meridional France,

Introduction

the Iberian Peninsula, Italy and Greece, with the coast-regions of Africa from Morocco to Egypt' (Burton, 2006). This is a capacious yet highly specific geographical location in which pederasty allegedly occurs de facto, whereas outside of it, it is regarded as immoral: 'Within the Sotadic Zone the Vice is popular and endemic, held at the worst to be a mere peccadillo, whilst the races to the North and South of the limits here defined practice it only sporadically amid the opprobrium of their fellows who, as a rule, are physically incapable of performing the operation and look upon it with the liveliest disgust' (Burton, 2006). Although to our contemporary sensibilities such facile geographical demarcation may seem scientifically naïve, Burton also admits that tolerance of such controversial sexual practices had been gradually built into the cultures of those places within the Sotadic Zone, through the model of sexual initiation inherited from classical Greece. According to Burton, there is, furthermore, a combination of 'masculine and feminine temperaments' which makes alternative sexual arrangements more feasible. While Burton believed the Qur'an to be condemning of such acts, recounting the case of Lot's people and their attempted rape of disguised angels Gabriel, Michael and Raphael in front of their Prophet, he nonetheless recognised that the expression of homoeroticism had become commonplace in many Muslim societies, and a work such as his sexually frank version of the *Arabian Nights* simultaneously demonstrates a vernacular Muslim focus on homosexual acts and also a European exaggeration of such desires, both flying in the face of normative ideologies that forbade their expression.

3   Despite familiar Western constructs of all Muslim women as repressed victims of Islamic patriarchy, there are well-established lines of Muslim and Islamic feminist enquiry that qualify the often universalising views of Western second-wave feminism, while contesting also the masculinist thrust of mainstream Islam. Fatima Seedat (2013) mentions the seminal work in the 1990s of thinkers such as Leila Ahmed, Fatima Mernissi, and Amina Wadud, which Seedat terms 'Islamic feminism', a denomination that scholars such as Wadud have resisted because of the Western inception of the feminist movement. Seedat also points out the work of activists who apply feminist analysis to human rights frameworks, such as Ayesha Imam, Farida Shaheed, Zainah Anwar, Lily Munir, and Riffat Hassan. It is also important to mention the work of female scholars who contribute to the *tafsir* tradition, such as Shuruq Naguib, whose commentaries set out to qualify views of Islam as invariably patriarchal and query historical religious interpretation for evidence of the importance of women to Muslim societies. For instance, on feminist interpretations of menstruation in the Qur'an, see Naguib (2010). It goes without saying that a study of queer Muslim diasporas needs to engage with the specificities of female experiences of queerness, particularly given the ongoing erasure of Muslim female homosexuality from the dialogic plain (Habib, 2007).

4   Aleardo Zanghellini (2010) suggests that the Qur'an is ambiguous about same-sex practices because it was implied that its contemporaneous audience would have instantly understood the sexual references and their moral implications, without need for elucidation. This implied contextual knowledge has not travelled well down history, and therefore, through the centuries, jurists have had to grapple with the text's lack of clear explanation. Zanghellini's main argument goes against one of the main queer interventions into the Qur'an; he argues that the story of Lot's people does not merely condemn rape, and that, instead, it is explicitly meant to censure male-to-male sexual penetration. However, he ascribes this not simply to a

Introduction

condemnation of same-sex attraction, but rather to a critical view of non-egalitarian sexual practices. His persuasive historical research shows that pre-Islamic Arabic customs, in particular those of the Bedouin, imbued anal sex with issues of mastery and subordination, and the repeated references to the actions of Lot's people, particularly the misdeeds they are said to have performed among themselves in their gatherings, suggest that they do not only try to engage in sexual acts with Lot's visitors. Zhangellini's reading recruits the perspective of Kecia Ali, who also refuses the rape thesis, in favour of a narrative of sexual mastery that entailed an emasculation of the penetrated party. This view of sexual roles as being masculine/powerful and feminine/powerless depending on who does the penetrating is one that subsequently became mainstream in Islamicate cultures, and, indeed, a conflation of gender and sexual orientation still pervades the so-called 'Muslim world'.

5 Apart from the creation of a new term to designate a transgression not readily named in the original text, there are also linguistic and contextual ambiguities here. Kugle, who is a translator of classical Arabic, argues that the Arabic pronoun used to point at these women is *hunna*, but that this 'refers to a group of three or more women […] in contrast to a pair of people (represented by the pronoun *huma*)' (2010, p. 64). This linguistic construction rules out one-on-one sexual acts between women and it is arguable that it may be pointing to a different form of immorality.

6 Barbara Zollner (2010) usefully points out that classical scholar Abu Ja'afar Muhammad ibn Jarir al-Tabari, while highly concerned with denouncing anal penetration, without paying attention to rape, in the story of Lot's people, he altogether ignores same-sex acts between women, which suggests female-to-female sexuality was not considered *zina* (fornication).

7 Kugle (2010) carefully explains the structures of the *ahadith* and the process of their authentication. Each *hadith* contains two parts: information about the Prophet's speech or action (*matn*) and a narrative chain (*isnad*) that relays how this information has been passed down, which respectively gave way to *matn* and *isnad* criticism. Classical ahadith scholars tried to ascertain the reliability of each *isnad* in four ways: first, by checking that the narrative chain went all the way back to the Prophet and was not merely a claim made by one of his followers – the stronger the links, the more reliable the pronouncement; second, by testing the plausibility of the chain of narration (i.e., checking that the narrators indeed could have lived at the same time and known each other); third, by reassuring themselves about the moral status of the narrators and their lack of any suspicious agendas; fourth, by ensuring the narrators were of sound memory and intellectual ability. If a narrative passed all these tests satisfactorily, then it was considered to be a legitimate *hadith*. *Matn* criticism was somewhat overshadowed by *isnad* criticism in the classical period of Islam, mostly, according to Kugle, due to the fact scholars were unwilling to over-rationalise the purport of the Prophet's sayings. Nonetheless, classical Islamic scholarship, as well as modern interpretation, tends to suspect *matn* that 'contains information that goes against common experience, scientific observation, medical knowledge, or historical and geographical facts' (Kugle, 2010, p. 81). *Matn* scholars also assessed linguistic plausibility: if the sayings contained expressions that postdated Arabic usage of the Prophet's period, they would not be considered legitimate *ahadith*.

8   Hana Sadik el-Gallal defines the term 'Islamophobia' as the 'unexamined and deeply ingrained anxiety many Westerners experience when considering Islam and Muslim countries', pointing out that 'the term became common parlance in defining the discrimination faced by Muslims in the West' (2014, p. 105) from the 1990s onwards. Whether partly based on concrete available evidence or on internalised stereotypes handed down through history, Islamophobia constitutes an often illogical and affective aversion to all things Islamic that is not always well-founded on empirical evidence.

9   Deleuze and Guattari's concept of micropolitics (1996) is useful when envisaging the ways in which mundane flights from normativity, which they call micropolitical, routinely disorganise the solid segments imposed by societal and statist ideologies, which are labelled macropolitical. The everyday micropolitical dimension of affect, perception, and dialogue operates 'differently' from the dimension of segmentary macropolitics and destabilises its categories. Such challenges to macropolitical normative structures do not only happen in the realm or radicalism or conscious anti-systemic political action, but at the level of lived experience. According to Deleuze and Guattari, there is a cyclical and reciprocate relationship between the molar segments of macropolitics, which draw barriers between categories and highly polarise individuals, and the molecular lines of flight of micropolitics, which escape the prescribed segments, redefine them, and then feed them back to macropolitics, causing macropolitical lines to be redrawn. In this sense, queer diasporic Muslims micropolitically disorganise the macropolitical segments that define ethnicity, sexuality, nation, and diaspora. The textual and visual representations of such challenges to normativity enter the realm of macropolitics and gradually start changing public opinion, redefining sexual and ethnic categories, allowing the lines that separate identitarian allegiances to be redefined.

10 The idea of the 'clash of civilisations' has been most infamously exploited by American scholar Samuel P. Huntington in his eponymous book *The Clash of Civilizations and the Remaking of World Order* (2002), originally published in 1996. Huntington puts emphasis on a globally needed model of democracy that is persistently resisted by Muslims, which suggests, in an ethnocentric manner, that Western democracy is the only viable political model for our planet. He also asserts that '[a] civilization is thus the cultural grouping of people and the broadest level of cultural identity people have short of that which distinguishes humans from other species' (2002, p. 43). Huntington concedes that the global media is 'one of the most important contemporary manifestations of Western power' (2002, p. 59), only to add that such hegemony encourages 'populist politicians in non-Western societies to denounce Western cultural imperialism' and that Western domination of global communications is 'a major source of resentment and hostility of non-Western peoples against the West' (2002, p. 59). This argument strategically absolves the 'West' of any part in encouraging such anti-Western animosity by other means, such as undertaking military interventions in 'non-Western' countries and the coercion of their governments, which is the foremost gripe of these peoples, far and above media control and misrepresentation. Moreover, Huntington denounces the violence inherent to Islam, the 'religion of the sword' by reminding us that Muhammad was celebrated from the start as a fighter, stating '[n]o one would say this about Christ or Buddha' (2002, p. 263). Although Christ and Buddha may not have been fighting figures, Christians and Buddhists alike have become agents of violence.

Introduction

Huntington is willing to ignore historical nuance for the sake of bolstering his ethnocentric political argument.

11 The term *jihad* is often translated in Western media as 'holy war', an idiom that harkens back to the time of the Crusades and that is used in our contemporary context to account for all kinds of acts against local governments and foreign interventionists; translated literally from Arabic, it simply means 'struggle', and Peter Mandaville (2007) lists a number of different struggles, not all of which are necessarily violent: *jihad al-qalb* means 'struggle of the heart'; *jihad bil-lisan*, 'struggle by the tongue'; *jihad bil-qalam*, 'struggle by the pen' and *jihad bil-sayf*, 'struggle by the sword' (Mandaville, 2007, p. 250). To these nuances of meaning regarding the origin or nature of each particular struggle, he adds some nuances of praxis: for instance, the term *jihad bil-yad* means 'struggle by the hand', which can be interpreted either as non-violent political activism or the necessary disposal of financial resources. In addition, the term *fatwa*, long associated with the polemical death warrant issued to Salman Rushdie in 1989, does not merely mean 'death sentence', but it is a form of legally binding opinion issued by an Islamic authority; *fatwas* typically involve all kinds of rulings, and not just the dispensation of death sentences, and, arguably, they may not apply to all Muslims, let alone all humans, but to the religious followers of the particular Islamic spokesperson that has uttered them.

Part I

Queer interethnic desire

1

Of interethnic (dis)connection: queer phenomenology, and cultural and religious commodification in Hanif Kureishi's *My Beautiful Laundrette* (1985) and *The Buddha of Suburbia* (1990)

HANIF KUREISHI (b. 1954) has long been considered one of the most prominent literary figures of postcolonial Britain, particularly due to his intersecting explorations of issues of national identity, race, ethnicity, class, and sexuality. Kureishi's work has long drawn attention to the racial and sexual biases of the dominant white British majority. Although Kureishi's artistic beginnings were linked to the stage, he rose to global prominence in 1985 with his Oscar-nominated script for *My Beautiful Laundrette*, a financially modest film directed by the British director Stephen Frears. The film's international box-office success took its own makers by surprise. Set in economically challenged and racially restless London during the peak of the Thatcher era, with a young British Asian man as its main protagonist, the film came out only a few years before the publication of Salman Rushdie's *The Satanic Verses* and all its attendant controversies. These polemical events, now commonly known as the 'Rushdie Affair', have constituted the foundational moment of British Muslim identity as a political category.[1] Against such a dire watershed, *My Beautiful Laundrette* (henceforth *Laundrette*) appears a more invigorating seminal representation of the subcontinental Muslim diaspora's fortunes in Britain. The film has gradually achieved iconic status as a galvanising representation of diasporic experience in the UK. Tellingly, Gayatri Gopinath (2005) opens her study *Impossible Desires* with an analysis of *Laundrette*, and, more recently, Sadia Abbas (2014) examines *Laundrette* in the initial chapter of *At*

Freedom's Limit: Islam and the Postcolonial Predicament, focusing on Islam's role in British race relations.

Both these critical texts help to confirm the film's iconic status as a foundational narrative of South Asian diasporic and queer experience. In turn, Kureishi's debut novel, *The Buddha of Suburbia* (henceforth *Buddha*), written as a response to Rushdie's prompting that Kureishi write a novel, is often considered a seminal literary text in the representation of the first- and second-generation South Asian diaspora in Britain, although its overall stance on issues of ethnicity, race, and sexuality is more ambivalent than the more violent yet ultimately more life-affirming *Laundrette*. *Buddha* is set in London in the 1970s, and like *Laundrette*, it draws significantly from Kureishi's own experience of the racial, sexual, and cultural conundrums of the metropolis' multiethnic inhabitants. The pictures these cinematic and literary texts paint of postcolonial and multicultural Britain contain important cultural nuances that mark Kureishi's distance from Islam and his characters' ambivalent orientation towards white British culture through their embrace of youth subcultures. In *Framing Muslims: Stereotyping and Representation after 9/11*, Peter Morey and Amina Yaqin pose an urgent question:

> The crucial question being asked is whether cultural difference can be harmonized and a multicultural society created or sustained, or whether the experiment of respecting and attempting politically to include identity positions with values that may jar with those of the majority is a doomed enterprise. (Morey and Yaqin, 2011, p. 44)

I will argue in this chapter that, on the one hand, *Laundrette* attempts to answer this question affirmatively, trying to pave the way towards a multicultural understanding of Britain as a nation by pushing against socially enforced ethnic boundaries and through the strategic deployment of queerness; on the other, I suggest *Buddha* offers less optimistic, albeit similarly open-ended, conclusions about the ability of queer interethnic relationships to challenge cogently the pull of dominant white culture in the age of postmodernity. As I will show, Kureishi's work pulls between the creation of connection and disconnection across ethnic boundaries through the articulation of queerness, a queerness that, despite its initial subversion of societal mores, cannot seemingly stage a radical enough reconfiguration of Britishness alongside intersecting ethnic and sexual lines.

To begin with Kureishi's first feature film, *Laundrette* is self-consciously pitted against a series of big-budget films and TV series released in the 1980s whose chief concern was Britain's imperial past, which have been dubbed, via Rushdie, a 'Raj Revival'.[2] *Laundrette* was meant as a rebuff to, in Kureishi's own words, 'lavish films set in exotic locations' (2000, p. 5) glorifying British imperialism. However, despite its current recognition as seminal film on diasporas in Britain, it was not sympathetically received by Muslim audiences on either side of the Atlantic upon its release. Gopinath reminds us that the film 'engendered heated controversy within South Asian communities in the UK' (2005, p. 2). John Hill also notes it 'was criticized from within the Asian community both for its representation of homosexuality and [...] of Asians as money grabbing' (1999, p. 212). Additionally, Donald Weber records that 'Pakistani groups in the U.S. protested outside theaters' (1997, p. 125). Bart Moore-Gilbert cites the case of Kureishi's own aunt, who 'berated *Laundrette* for its supposedly negative vision of Pakistani immigrants and did so partly through comparing it unfavourably with [Richard Attenborough's] *Gandhi*' (2001, p. 74), which, Weber notes, earned her having one of Kureishi's lesbian agitators in Frears' *Sammy and Rosie Get Laid* named after her. Frears and Kureishi's film clearly succeeded in tickling the sensibilities of its minority Muslim audiences, whose occasional preference for aesthetically safe and politically conservative 'heritage' drama colluded ideologically with the tastes of the dominant white audience which *Laundrette* fearlessly indicts.

At heart, the problem in Kureishi and Frears' film is what Ruvani Ranasinha calls, via Kobena Mercer, 'the burden of representation': 'Namely, the assumption that minority artists speak *for* the entire community from which they come' (Ranasinha, 2002, 39, emphasis in original). Ranasinha usefully maps two camps in critical responses to *Laundrette*: on the one hand, the faction featuring Mamood Jamal and Perminder Dhillon-Kashyap, who 'perceive the role of the minority artist as necessarily didactic, so as to reduce "the imbalance caused by decades of misrepresentation and stereotyping"'; and on the other, Stuart Hall, who defends films such as *Laundrette* for their refusal to depict a monolithic representation of black experience in Britain which is 'always and only "positive"'' (Ranasinha, 2002, p. 51). I concur with the idea that Kureishi's craft transcends the pedagogic role of the minority artist, as it refuses to create any images of British Muslims – or of white Britishers – that are solely vilifying or victimising. As Jago Morrison suggests, Kureishi's texts 'are far too playful, irreverent and counter-cultural to fit into any orthodox political agenda' (2003, p. 179). Instead, Kureishi concentrates more keenly on disorientating his audience by challenging essentialist identitarian constructions of race, ethnicity, class, and sexuality. Kureishi's contemporary Kenan Malik asserts that, growing up in Britain in the 1970s, he witnessed how '"Paki-bashing" was becoming a national sport' (2010, p. 4). He argues that this polarisation was superseded in the 1980s, particularly after the 'Rushdie Affair', by new forms of collective identity: 'Radicals lost faith in secular universalism and began talking instead about multiculturalism and group rights' (Malik, 2010, p. 4). I illustrate here how a pre-Rushdie film such as *Laundrette* had already started blurring the lines between ethnic communities, strategically utilising queerness as a means of challenging the legacies of the racially turbulent 1970s and of forging interethnic connection in contemporary Britain.

Laundrette continues to aid us in the 'queering' of postcolonial London by disorganising mainstream Muslim and non-Muslim ideologies surrounding ethnicity and sexuality in a critique that should be envisaged as intersectional. In the first half of this chapter, I argue, first, that Kureishi's plot and psychological implausibilities enact a queer form of micropolitical disorientation whose effect is that of challenging the essentialist identity categories dictated by mainstream dominant ideologies. Second, I undertake queer phenomenological readings of scenes in the film that queer the diasporic body by merging it with its surrounding bodies and spaces, drawing attention to their ethnic contours. Meanwhile, I also draw attention to how female sexuality and gender non-conformity also subvert normative gendered spaces. Lastly, I delve into the topic of British interethnic connection by undertaking a queer phenomenological analysis of the film's closing scenes, where the violence suffered by queer bodies in queer spaces generates connection between different factions of British society, hence blurring the lines segmentalising ethnic communities in the multicultural nation.

To offer a brief summary of the film, *Laundrette* charts the coming of age of Omar (Gordon Warnecke), a British youth of mixed Pakistani and white British heritage. His father, Hussein (Roshan Seth), is a failed South Asian socialist journalist who has had no success in Britain: both his profession and his marriage, to a now deceased white British woman, fell victim to his inability to come to terms with British racial prejudice. Hussein begs on his phone to his enterprising brother Nasser (Saeed Jaffrey) to employ Omar in his garage for the summer months and to 'fix him with a nice girl', since he is not 'sure if his penis is in full working order' (Kureishi, 2000, p. 12). From the outset, the film's exploration of diasporic experience in Britain is attuned to sexual exploration. Omar is informally supervised by his cousin Salim (Derrick Branche), who in due course is found out to lead an affluent life through drug dealing. Not challenged enough by car washing, and inspired by keeping his uncle's accounts, Omar asks Nasser to allow him to run his dwindling laundrette, called Churchills, a name that playfully alludes to a bygone era in British history. Nasser agrees, partly because he envisages him as the heir to his businesses, through his potential marriage to his daughter Tania (Rita Wolf). While planning his takeover of the laundrette, Omar comes across his old schoolfellow Johnny (Daniel Day-Lewis), formerly a National Front supporter who, despite his devil-may-care attitude and his ongoing friendship with white supremacists, agrees to help him in his new enterprise. The film constitutes, at heart, an exploration of the burgeoning relationship between Omar and Johnny, who eventually become lovers, and who in so doing contravene, on the one hand, the strictures of Thatcherite Britain, with its discouragement of interethnic relations and homosexuality,[3] and, on the other, the diasporic Muslim community's heteronormative and familial values, both within the context, brimming with irony,[4] of ruthless Thatcherite entrepreneurship. By challenging ethnic and sexual mores, I suggest the film is hopeful about developing a connection between polarised communities, thus paving the way towards an interethnic assemblage of sociocultural perspectives.

The film refuses from the start to vindicate the position of any single ethnic grouping. Its stance is not too congratulatory of the British Muslim community's licit or illicit endeavours; nor does it completely vilify the white British contingent, with Johnny offering an antidote to the sway of white supremacism. *Laundrette* is not self-indulgent regarding the complex sociopolitical and affective positions of its characters, who queer British social relations through an investment in interethnic queer intimacy. Hill argues that 'in common with postmodern thinking, there is a strong sense of the constructedness and fluidity of social identities, and a rejection of any sense of fixed identities or "essences"' (1999, p. 207). Perhaps more crucially for our purposes here, Paul Dave suggests that 'the multiculturalism of *My Beautiful Laundrette* [...] cannot be mistaken for an uncritical liberal pluralism in which social heterogeneity is understood as the unproblematic mixing of distinct and self-coherent identities' (2006, p. 13). *Laundrette* can be seen as challenging essentialist constructions of the various social identities (i.e., ethnic, national, class-related, sexual) of multicultural British society and, crucially, the blurring of societally enforced barriers – or the ironic inversion of social expectations – contributes to a disorganisation of mainstream ideologies and the assemblage of seemingly contradictory political perspectives. Kureishi's script hence relies on disorientating its audience in order to start conciliating different political and ethnic perspectives.

Moore-Gilbert notes that *Laundrette* contains 'improbabilities at the level of plot which compromise their effectiveness as examples of critical social realism', and that the film 'is predicated on the intrinsically unlikely scenario of a young British-Asian man falling in love with a member of a vicious racist gang (and vice versa)' (2001, p. 99).[5] By contrast, Buchanan cites Vincent Canby's idea that 'characters behave in a way that has been dictated not by plausibility but [by] the *effect* it will create' (Buchanan, 2007, p. ix, emphasis added). Ranasinha concurs with Buchanan, suggesting that 'while Kureishi's portrayals are not intended as representative, we need to distinguish this from their *political effect*' (2002, p. 49, emphasis added). In light of these debates, I suggest that mimesis is not central to *Laundrette*'s concerns, and that the most pressing questions when interpreting it should not involve historical accuracy (i.e., whether Muslims routinely had sex with skinheads in the 1980s), but, rather, an appreciation of the film's 'queering' of hermetic sociopolitical positions, and the effect that such a 'strange' arrangement of human intimacy has on the audience's collective consciousness. Kureishi himself observes that '[f]or immigrants and their families, disorder and strangeness is the condition of their existence' (2002a, p. 3). In this sense, diaspora is almost always 'queer' in the extended meaning of the word; it involves unavoidable strangeness, in this case embodied by Omar and Johnny's unexpected relationship across ethnic lines, whose queerness becomes a transgressive political strategy. Kureishi and Frears are not aiming at mimesis or even realism here, but at disorientating the film's majority and minority audiences in a manner that shakes up their political complacency, by forcing them to think about the potential to create a less polarised and more multicultural society that pushes against hermetic ethnic and racial boundaries.

Such a disorientation is central to Sara Ahmed's model of queer phenomenology, especially regarding the confusion experienced by diasporic bodies and its relation to their surroundings. Ahmed observes that 'bodies that experience being out of place might need to be *orientated*, to find a place where they feel comfortable and safe in the world' (2006, p. 158, emphasis added). POWDERS, the revamped laundrette, is such a place of relative safety, where Omar can forge an affective connection with Johnny, albeit not without political complications. Disorientation and reorientation of the British Muslim subject of diasporic heritage is not self-contained; it does not involve only the individual, but also its attendant bodies and spaces, such as Johnny, POWDERS, and their local London community, the nation by metonymic extension, and even *Laundrette*'s audience, whose political perceptions are being purposefully disorientated. Crucially, Ahmed is interested in disorientation as beyond politics or, as I have suggested, as a form of micropolitics. While the disorientation created by Omar and Johnny may not be *party*-political, it does not transcend politics. As I suggested in the previous chapter, at the level of everyday lived experience and desire, micropolitical differences erode at the prescriptive categories dictated by macropolitical discourses and ideologies.

Kureishi stages such negotiation of communitarian identities within the bounds of the diasporic body, and its relationship with other bodies and spaces. This makes *Laundrette* all the more compelling as a multicultural visual narrative. Vijay Mishra suggests:

> By lifting the lid on the diaspora's own homophobic and exclusive rhetoric, by representing gay and lesbian diasporic selves, by mingling the crisis of the working class with the anxieties of diaspora, Kureishi shifts the debates to question about the diasporic body as corporeal selves within the racial economy of the nation. (Mishra 2007, p. 201)

Mishra exposes Kureishi's bravery in tackling homosexuality in *Laundrette*, a topic that remains to this day highly controversial within Britain's Muslim communities, while drawing attention to the material despair of a working class, embodied by Johnny and his white British associates, who have been turned by Thatcherite politics into an economically hard-up underclass drawn to racism and criminality through lack of opportunity. Omar's mixed-race body also challenges a monocultural, racially pure conception of Britishness, which is accentuated in intercourse with Johnny. Nonetheless, the labels 'gay' and 'homosexual' cannot encompass their complex sexual orientations, since, crucially, neither of them seems strictly attracted to the same sex. For instance, neither character staunchly rebuffs the advances of Omar's cousin Tania. They seem to fit the more polymorphous and fluid term 'queer'. Omar and Johnny's bodies become intertwined in the human tapestry of British multiculturalism, a rebellion against what Amartya Sen perceives as the threat of contemporary British 'plural monoculturalism' (2006, p. 157).

However, the queer relations between Omar's mixed-race diasporic body and Johnny's white British body do not happen in a vacuum or in an alternative heuristic space reserved for queer dissidence; rather, they intimately engage their surroundings. The revamped laundrette is named 'Powders' in wry reference to Omar and Johnny's cooption of Salim's drug dealing earnings. Through Hugo Luczyc-Wyhowski's film-set design and Oliver Stapleton's soft-focus cinematography, Powders becomes not only 'brightly painted' (Kureishi, 2000, p. 42); it shimmers, with rolling aquamarine waves painted above each washing machine. It also has '*a neon sign saying* Powders' (2000, p. 42) that further glamorises it. As Omar's Papa tells Johnny when he diffidently visits the laundrette later on: 'I thought I'd come to the wrong place. That I was suddenly in the ladies' hairdressing salon in Pinner, where one might get a pink rinse' (2000, p. 52). This camp joke is proof that the space has been constructed as purposefully queer: it could be a laundrette, but it could well be an Indian hairdressing establishment due to its flamboyancy. Omar and Johnny dress up for the occasion, discarding their ordinary daywear for a suit and bright white clothes, respectively, matching the laundrette's refurbished state. In Ahmed's thinking, 'spaces are not exterior to bodies; instead, spaces are like a second skin that unfolds in the folds of the body' (2006, p. 9). Interpreted in a phenomenological manner, POWDERS acts as a second skin to Omar and Johnny's bodies, as the queer establishment's bright new spaces merge with their own physicality.

The laundrette's grand opening is given multilayered visual and political nuance by the spatial juxtaposition of the suburban street, the laundrette's public spaces, and its back room, where the two-way mirror connotes both privacy and social surveillance, and where spaces merge with bodies.[6] Ranasinha highlights 'the one-way [sic] mirror in the laundrette, where we see two different "illicit" relationships in ironic counterpart: Nasser dancing with his lover Rachel, and Omar and Johnny having sex in the back room' (2002, p. 42). Nasser and Rachel's relationship is deemed 'illicit' not only because it is adulterous (Nasser being married to Omar's aunt Bilquis), but also because it is interethnic, contravening the Thatcherite discouragement of racial intermixing and the ethnic exclusivism of the British Muslim diaspora. The fact that Omar and Johnny are engaging in queer interracial relations simultaneously renders their 'transgression' compellingly parallel to its heterosexual counterpart, embodied by Nasser and Rachel and, *in absentia*, by Papa's wife and Omar's late mother, Mary. Moore-Gilbert reads this use of the two-way mirror as a technique Kureishi has inherited from his prior involvement in 'fringe' theatre, by 'recall[ing] the use of back-projection' (2001, p. 69), in itself a queering of genre and medium through stylistic assemblage. The two-way mirror allows for these visual superimpositions to embody an intersectional depiction of multicultural British society, creating a jointly interethnic and queer disorientation of mainstream values within Britain's assembled private and public spaces. At the centre of the action, divided but rendered parallel by the two-way mirror, Rachel and Nasser, on the one hand, and Johnny and Omar, on the other, challenge sexual and ethnic segmentalisation. Standing on each side of the laundrette's physically delineated but visually porous spaces, the film's diegetic audience (i.e., the general public eagerly watching the establishment's imminent unveiling) and its extra-diegetic audience (i.e., the audience watching the film from the other side of the screen) act as the receivers of molecular change, being wilfully exposed to interethnic and queer liaisons going against the grain of British and diasporic normative ideologies.

Far from being a solipsistic place enabling merely private liaisons, POWDERS becomes the stage where the multicultural nation's racial and sexual politics are micropolitically played out through bodily interaction. Gopinath observes that 'Omar initially acquiesces to Johnny's caresses, but he abruptly puts a halt to the seduction' (2005, p. 1), confronting his new partner (in several senses of the word) regarding his racist past:

> what were [my old friends] doing on marches through Lewisham? It was bricks and bottles and Union Jacks. It was kill us. People we knew. And it was you. [Papa] saw you marching. You saw his face, watching you. [...] Oh, such failure, such emptiness. (Kureishi, 2000, p. 43)

In Kureishi's script directions, '*JOHNNY kisses OMAR then leaves him, sitting away from him slightly. OMAR touches him, asking him to hold him*' (Kureishi, 2000, p. 43). Conversely, in the film, as Gopinath rightly notes, 'as Omar continues speaking, [Johnny] slowly reaches out to draw Omar to him and embraces Omar from behind. [...] The scene eloquently speaks to how the queer racialized body becomes a historical archive for both individuals and communities' (2005, p. 1). Omar's historically representative body is torn between intimacy with Johnny and animosity surrounding the 1977 Lewisham race riots of Omar and Johnny's early years, which demonstrates there is no neutral or apolitical merging of bodies taking place. Johnny's body wants to bridge the ideological gap created between him and Omar by his past involvement in racist marches, but he needs to become beholden to him in order to exonerate himself from his racist past. As Johnny states in a subsequent scene: 'Nothing I can say, to make it up to you. There's only things I can do to show you that I am ... with you' (Kureishi, 2000, p. 44).

Laundrette's focus on bodily action and performance, rather than on a mere discursive apology for British racism, fits a queer phenomenological interpretation of interethnic connection in the scene, whereby Omar and Johnny's queer bodies and their relation to each other micropolitically negotiate larger political tensions in the nation. This scene is followed by the official opening of POWDERS, during which the two-way mirror acquires further significance. Uncle Nasser catches Omar and Johnny hurriedly dressing after having sex, rendering his interjection to Rachel of '[w]here are those two buggers?' (Kureishi, 2000, p. 44) playfully accurate. When he sees them tucking in their shirts, he asks them: 'What the hell are you doing? Sunbathing?' (2000, p. 45), to which Omar replies, with a mixture of candour and obliqueness: 'Asleep, Uncle. We were shagged out' (2000, p. 45). Although Nasser eyes Omar disapprovingly, he does not probe him, strategically ignoring Salim's earlier suggestion that '[t]here's some things between [Omar and Johnny] I'm looking into' (2000, p. 40). Omar's British Pakistani and Muslim family is unwilling to voice the taboo of homosexuality, only referring to Omar with his self-coined soap-related but also queer nickname 'Omo' (2000, p. 40). As we will see, the Muslim family's insistence on patrilinearity and heteronormativity throws an important hurdle in the way of Omar and Johnny's relationship, one that puts a temporary stopper to the development of interethnic connection between the two men, but which is qualified by later developments in the film.

For now, the laundrette opens for the impatient multitude outside. As Omar revels in the sight of his new business from behind the two-way mirror, Johnny is proudly standing on the other side of the security mechanism, guessing, or at least partially seeing, Omar's body on the other side, and standing in the place of his reflection. For a brief moment, through Frears' inspired direction, Johnny and Omar's reflections blend together, creating a single superimposed image that gives the visual impression of an assembled identity. Although long predating the Islamist attack on New York City's Twin Towers, this assemblage is an optimistic qualification of Jasbir K. Puar's later interrogation of the 'surveillant assemblages' attending racialised bodies after 9/11, and their obsession with Muslims and brown bodies. These surveillance systems, Puar argues, 'create the sameness of population through democratization of monitoring at the same time they enable and solidify hierarchies – in other words the circuit amid profiling and racial profiling' (2007, pp. 155–6). In this case, it is Omar's mixed-race British body that is standing on the point of social surveillance, while a white British body is the one being profiled. However, the assemblage of their reflections constitutes a moment of breakdown of sociopolitical hierarchies and surveillance techniques, as Johnny wilfully stands in front of Omar and smiles at him, his body's image purposefully blending with Omar's equally beaming reflection (see Figure 1). This visual bodily assemblage is enacted following a micropolitically significant scene of interpersonal physical communion, and, together, they force the audience to confront British national identity by visually outgrowing racial profiling and monocultural exclusivism. Buchanan cites Annabel Cone's idea that 'the need for love and intimacy plays out in an indoors completely turned away from ... public spaces' (2007, p. 124, ellipsis in original). Conversely, I suggest the film creates a queer space between the public and the private, between loving intimacy and social surveillance, whose visual presentation micropolitically disorganises mainstream expectations.

Despite POWDERS' grand opening, Johnny and Omar's glory, as well as Nasser and Rachel's elation, is short-lived. Nasser commands Omar to marry

Of interethnic (dis)connection

Figure 1 *My Beautiful Laundrette* (1985), directed by Stephen Frears

Tania. Intoxicated literally by the champagne at hand and figuratively by his success, Omar strictly follows his uncle's instructions: when Tania tells Omar she will need his financial help in leaving home, he seizes the occasion to ask her whether she will marry him, to which she tartly responds: 'If you can get me some money' (Kureishi, 2000, p. 47). In popping such a question, Omar is adding heteronormativity to Thatcherite entrepreneurship, thus joining the status quo. Although Tania's financial plea is ironic (since she would merely be turning down one form of male economic support for another), such attitude helps Kureishi underline the transactional character of Omar and Tania's enforced nuptials, taking to task the family's antiquated approach to interpersonal relationships as being, above all, heterosexist and monocultural. A despondent Johnny stops cooperating, which results in Omar reminding him in a later scene of his subservient employment status. Omar has come to realise he has family obligations to fulfil:

> OMAR: I don't wanna see you for a little while. I got some big thinking to do.
> (Johnny looks regretfully at him.)
> JOHNNY: But today, it's been the best day!
> OMAR: Yeah. *Almost* the best day.
>
> (Kureishi, 2000, 51, emphasis added)

This has been *almost* the best day because it has come very close to ratifying Omar's relationship with Johnny, which has brought down ethnic and sexual barriers and has started forging affective connections across ethnic groupings. However, Omar's family has quickly put a stopper to his relationship with Johnny

43

by discouraging, in the same breath, homosexual and interethnic relationships, even when Omar's own parentage is clearly interethnic. Nasser's plan to marry Tania to Omar carries the ideological weight of Muslim patrilinearity and the clear desire to keep things 'in the family', which reveals a further conservative strand undergirding his neoliberal economic principles. These complications threaten to undo the film's burgeoning mapping of interethnic and queer connections, as the strict values of Omar's social grouping attempt to reinforce monoculturalism and heteronormative patriarchy.

Before we examine *Laundrette*'s denouement, we must focus on Tania's plight, for it is one of the main issues that has divided critical commentaries on the film. A forerunner of Karim's more vocal friend Jamila in *Buddha*, Tania's representation involves an interweaving of bodies, objects, and spaces that complements my phenomenological analysis of the film. From the outset, Tania is represented as physically forthright and, through her strategic use of her body, as rebelling against patriarchal values by moving between strictly gendered spaces. In Omar's first visit to his uncle's household in years, he is introduced to a '*selection of wives*' (Kureishi, 2000, p. 19, emphasis in original). Rahul K. Gairola lucidly observes that the living-room 'resounds a *zenana* (or part of the house reserved for women)' (2009, p. 43).[7] This gender-segregated space reconstructing South Asian spaces within Britain constitutes the most explicit Muslim aspect of Omar's extended family. Outside the door to the men's room, Tania accosts Omar physically by pushing him against the wall and asking him to see her later, stating she is 'bored with these people' (Kureishi, 2000, p. 20). Inside, Nasser welcomes Omar to the company of the other men, which includes both South Asian and white British men. Despite the multiethnic arrangement, this setting of cigars and booze is clearly a space reserved for men only. Tania then appears behind the window overlooking the garden, showing her breasts to poker-faced Omar and choking family friend Zaki. Here, Tania is impinging upon the strict South Asian and Muslim homosocial spaces of her father's home, by bringing highly coveted female sexuality to its boundaries, although only Omar, with his privileged viewing position facing the party of men, alcohol-infused Zaki, and the film's audience witness her transgression. Gairola argues that 'Tania has also managed to move between the gendered spaces, and her visibility to Omar (but not to the other men) underscores her agency as a queer subject who negotiates the terrains of her sexual desires' (2009, p. 47). Tania's ability to flout, to an extent, gender segregation demonstrates she disorganises the traditional gendered spaces of her family home with her bodily irreverence. Later, she confronts Omar again authoritatively in an empty and dark room, and takes the lead, kissing him while discussing her father's expectation of Omar's takeover of the family businesses, explaining '[h]e wouldn't think of asking me' (Kureishi, 2000, p. 22), clearly because she is a woman. While they are in the middle of discussing Nasser's affair with Rachel, during which she states 'I hate families' (2000, p. 22), her eavesdropping mother, standing by the sliding window, asks her to 'come and help' (2000, p. 22), breaking the erotic spell and consigning her, yet again, to a domestic role.

Although, according to an article on 'Asian stars' in Britain published in *India Today*, Rita Wolf, the actress playing Tania, sees the baring of her breasts as a sign of 'how little things have changed' (Chandran, 1987, para. 14), implying that the exposure of the female body on screen remains a way of commodifying it for its male and heterosexual audience, Tania's trajectory in *Laundrette* reveals a more complex queering of traditional female roles, particularly within the Muslim diasporic community in Britain, by drawing attention, through her subversive body and speech, to the limitations such roles bring to Muslim women's experience. Tania is keen on disrupting the homosocial mapping of space that protects male interests, initially by taking the lead during Omar's visit to her family home and physically mocking its gender segregation, and later by coming between Omar and Johnny, attempting to engage either's attention as a means of escaping the stifling confinement of her family home. Ranasinha suggests that, despite Inderpal Grewal's view that Kureishi 'does not do too well with feminist issues [...], [i]n his characterization of Tania as fearless, outspoken and sexually free, Kureishi contests the trope of the submissive Asian daughter and undermines stereotypes of Asian women as passive and desexualized' (Ranasinha, 2002, p. 48). Gopinath's reading of the film is less optimistic: 'The film's female diasporic character Tania, in fact, functions in a classic homosocial triangle as the conduit and foil to the desire between Johnny and Omar' (2005, p. 4). She also compellingly argues that 'all too often diasporas are narrativized through the bonds of relationality between men' (2005, p. 5). In this regard, Abbas concurs with Gopinath, suggesting that 'the world the film delineates has no space for Tania, or for a queer *female* subjectivity', albeit suggesting that 'the film is aware of this' (2014, p. 15). While it is undeniable that *Laundrette*, and Kureishi's work more generally, is more keenly focused on the interrogation of masculinities, Tania's changing material circumstances can still be interpreted as a significant rebuttal of diasporic patriarchal expectations on women. Her negotiation of space has the ability to disorganise gender policing, while making the film's audience reconsider their preconceptions about Muslim femininity.

Undeterred by Omar and Johnny's lack of interest in her erotic advances and in her plans to move out of the London suburbs, Tania refuses to be confined to a fixed, clear narrative, even stepping out of the boundaries of Kureishi's script. In the film's second-to-last scene, Tania is spotted by Nasser at Vauxhall rail station, visible across the way from her uncle Hussein's flat, only seconds after Hussein and Nasser had discussed the possibility of her marrying Omar. To Nasser's consternation, she simply disappears between passing trains, in a queering of body and space that is neither a suicide in the style of Omar's mother, Mary, nor a conventional scene in which we witness her sentimentalised departure. As Buchanan observes, Tania's disappearance constitutes 'a mysterious vanishing act which disturbs the already confused Nasser even more and is no doubt intended to show the unpredictable, fugitive nature of family relationships' (2007, p. 116). Nasser's patriarchal disposition has alienated him from three of the most important women in his life: his wife Bilquis, by wilfully ignoring her desires; his mistress Rachel, because of his failure to legitimise their relationship publicly; and his oldest daughter Tania, by refusing her enough independence to decide her own fate. Tania's final decision to flee is a micropolitical rejection of gender roles, and her trajectory is suitably predicated as open-ended, matching Annamarie Jagose's description of queerness cited in the previous chapter. By contrast, Gopinath argues that 'Kureishi's framing of the female diasporic figure makes clear the ways in which even ostensibly progressive, gay male articulations of diaspora could run the risk of stabilizing sexual and gender hierarchies' (2005, pp. 4–5). Gopinath's critique of the film as stabilising hierarchies concurs with Grewal's, who suggests that 'this disappearance seems to be the only *solution* for a feminist Asian woman' (Ranasinha, 2002, p. 48, emphasis in original). The proposal of a 'solution', however, disagrees with the film's purpose, and with Kureishi's craftsmanship more generally, since, for him, 'scepticism [is] preferable to didacticism or advocacy', since '[p]olitical or spiritual solutions render [...] the world less interesting' (Kureishi, 2002a, p. 8). *Laundrette* is not keen on providing a narrative solution to gender trouble that fits any study macropolitical positions or any form of moral didacticism. While the film remains aware of its own ideological horizons, it also creates an open-ended space for those British subjects of diasporic Muslim heritage, such as Tania, who refuse to comply with ethnic majority or minority expectations. However, seemingly aware of the unfulfilled narrative possibilities offered by a rebellious character such as Tania, Kureishi would revisit the plight of second-generation British Asian women in through Jamila, the close friend of *Buddha*'s protagonist Karim, whose more complex depiction afforded by the novel's extended medium we will investigate in due course.

Laundrette's rejection of macropolitical collusion does not mean the film does not have a political purpose, since the violent relationship between bodies and spaces finally clinches its queer micropolitical commentary on race relations in postcolonial Britain. The development of connections across ethnic lines is effected through the expiation of racist ideologies through bodily experience, in the merging of queer bodies and spaces. The tense relations between the white and the Asian communities come to their head after Salim's exercise of reverse racism, when, after stating that what Johnny's old gang needs 'is a taste of their own piss' (Kureishi, 2000, p. 61), he drives over gang member Moose's foot. Following this incident, Johnny explicitly refuses to engage further with Salim, and Genghis and his gang of racists start patrolling POWDERS' environs, watching out for Salim. Eventually, they start destroying Salim's car while he is inside the laundrette, in a visually powerful scene in which the stillness inside contrasts with the aggressive movements of the skinhead gang destroying the car on the other side of the laundrette's window. This can be interpreted as an attack on Salim's privileged economic status in Britain. Ahmed suggests that '[b]odies tend toward some objects more than others given their tendencies' (2006, p. 58). Given the economic precariousness of much of Thatcherite Britain, both the financially deprived racist gang and affluent Salim are suitably driven towards the symbol of wealth, the car becoming an extension of Salim's body, which is also beaten up when he comes out of the laundrette to confront the white attackers. While Salim is being hit by the whole gang, Johnny publicly crosses the ethnic line to defend him, antagonising his former clan and effectively siding with the diasporic South Asian community, in a moment of high political significance for the film that begins incepting interethnic connection.

In the footage, Johnny tells Genghis that he does not want to fight; nonetheless, like Salim, he also gets beaten up, before Omar comes to his rescue. It is at this moment that we witness a decisive phenomenological merging of bodies, objects, and space. While Omar is picking up Johnny's distressed body – his face now fully covered in blood – from beside the destroyed car, Genghis runs behind both of them, holding up a rubbish bin and shouting. For a second, it looks as if he is going to hit both Omar and Johnny with the metal container; instead, he turns away at the last moment and puts the bin through the laundrette's window. It is significant that Omar and Johnny's queer bodies become aligned with the troubled queer spaces of their smashed up laundrette, as bodies and space are folded over and acquire micropolitical significance. The violence that Johnny receives from his former friends is what is necessary in order to atone for his racist past: his bodily sufferance starts to develop an interethnic connection: Omar seems reassured by this act, and appears visibly elated by Johnny's heroism, telling him, in the soothing spaces of POWDERS' back room: 'You're dirty. You're beautiful. […] I'm going to give you a wash' (Kureishi, 2000, p. 68), which suggests an assemblage of broken bodies and places. After Tania's departure, and while we watch POWDERS' shattered spaces, in the back room Omar and Johnny are washing each other, their bodily actions blending with the laundrette's main function, in a moment of ethnic and sexual assemblage that has come out of the renegotiation and expiation of Britain's racist history, and that finds in the blending of queer and ethnically plural bodies the best hope for Britain as a multicultural nation.

While Johnny and Omar splash each other amidst laughter, the door closes in on us, acting as a theatre curtain, in playful reference to Kureishi's own theatrical beginnings. Gayatri Spivak is not convinced by the film's ending; she argues that 'the two boys had been kept in the same place; the development of the solution to racial problems', and deems this optimistic denouement too overtly 'didactic' (1993, p. 249). Conversely, Vinh Nguyen argues that

> The two men coming together can be seen as a temporary but not insubstantial relation, an attachment that is always in negotiation. Omar and Johnny occupy a queer impasse in which there is a holding out for something as yet undetermined, where pleasure does not cancel violence and 'together' does not mean 'one.' (Nguyen, 2017, p. 157)

Conceptually drawing on the work of Lauren Berlant, Nguyen interprets this impasse at the film's closing not as a moment of political foreclosure or offering an impossible ideal of unity, but as a queer moment of open futurity that does not do away with the legacies of the colonial past and does not ignore the effects of violence. In other words, Omar and Johnny's relationship does not obviate the phenomenological journeys they have undertaken and experienced through their checked bodies and surroundings.

I would add that Omar and Johnny's relationship has been presented as complex and multilayered, first through the inversion and subversion of power structures inherited from colonialism and rekindled by Thatcherite neoliberalism, and through the aforementioned superimposition of bodies and spaces and their eventual micropolitical merging in intersectional ethnic and sexual debates, which refuse to ring with any morally glib or macropolitical rhetoric. In fact, the film's final blending of blood and water could be interpreted as a queer reconfiguration of inherited racist discourse, particularly that of Enoch Powell's incendiary 'Rivers of Blood' speech, in which he warned the British nation that 'the black man would have the whip hand over [the white British population]' (Gilroy, 1987, p. 48). Quoting it in the seminal study of British race relations, *"There Ain't*

No Black in the Union Jack": The Cultural Politics of Race and Nation, Gilroy draws critical attention to Powell's highly polarising political rhetoric, arguing that Powell's ethnocentric position constructs 'black presence [...] as a problem or threat against which a homogenous, white, national "we" could be unified' (1987, p. 48). In 'The Rainbow Sign', Kureishi (2002a) himself confesses the revulsive effect that Powell's speeches had on him as a teenager, which made him feel ashamed of his South Asian heritage. *Laundrette* constitutes Kureishi's own response to this racist discourse. Blood has indeed been spilled because of racial unrest, within a context where the 'black man' (i.e., Omar) has occasionally had the economic 'whip' over the white man (i.e., Johnny), but this fact has been ostensibly qualified by Johnny's wilful rejection of his involvement with the National Front and his joint physical and moral expiation of his racist past. It has also been checked by Omar's final embrace of Johnny, cancelling their hierarchical professional relationship and leading to a cathartic moment of assembled intimacy, of interethnic connection, whereby brown and white bodies wash each other in materially checked but affectively strengthened queer spaces. The role that Islam plays in Kureishi's sensibility in this film remains relatively marginal, restricted as it is to a configuration of gendered spaces that can be interpreted as both religious and cultural, and a general contravention of South Asian and British heteronormativity, yet the intersection of ethnicity and sexuality is a useful line of flight from normative ideologies surrounding ethnic exclusivism and monoculturalism.

Kureishi's other main text dealing with diasporic queerness in the multicultural metropolis is his first and highly popular novel *The Buddha of Suburbia*, which avoids the alleged didacticism denounced by Spivak in *Laundrette* by constructing characters who are more visibly queer, particularly in terms of their sexual fluidity, but who, like Uncle Nasser – and Omar before his change of heart – also become the pawns of neoliberal ideology, while eventually opting for publicly heteronormative lifestyles, thus betraying the subversive elements of their initial queerness. *Buddha* paints a less violent but also less optimistic picture of racial and sexual relations in 1970s London and the suburbs. In this text, I argue, religion is depicted as the commodified pastime of the white British middle class, divorced from any form of ethnic filiation, and interethnic queer relations, far from leading to interethnic understanding, only seem to exacerbate disconnection. *Buddha* contains important thematic and structural parallelisms with *Laundrette*: both narratives feature a protagonist of mixed British and Pakistani heritage, in this case the British Asian actor Karim Amir, who famously introduces himself as 'an Englishman born and bred, almost' (Kureishi, 1999,

p. 3); the film and the novel also concern themselves with queer relationships across ethnic divides, Karim being infatuated with the diffidently queer Charlie Hero, his father's white lover Eva's son and hence his new stepbrother, while being simultaneously attracted to British Asian family friend Jamila and the white British characters Helen and fellow actress Eleanor. Unlike Omar, who despite enjoying his cousin Tania's attention is mostly erotically orientated towards Johnny, Karim remains queer, orientated towards both men and women, with no exclusive penchant for either gender, clearly infatuated with Charlie yet often emotionally drawn to Jamila. As he tells us:

> It was unusual, I knew, the way I wanted to sleep with boys as well as girls. I liked strong bodies and the backs of boys' necks. I liked being handled by men, their fists pulling me; and I liked objects – the ends of brushes, pens, fingers – up my arse. But I liked cunts and breasts, all of women's softness, long smooth legs and the way women dressed. I felt it would be heart-breaking to have to choose one or the other. (Kureishi, 1999, p. 55)

Karim does not define his sexual orientation here as bisexuality, yet its relentless fluidity and his remark about its 'unusual' character seems to point towards queerness rather than towards an essentialist conception of sexuality. Moreover, his focus on the performance of masculinity and femininity through bodily acts and dress belies a constructionist approach to sexual orientation which is also in keeping with queerness. Such fluidity remains, however, the extent of Karim's sexual disorientation of societal conventionality, with the rest of the narrative being a charting of his attempt at becoming normative through an assimilation into white British culture. The characters of *Buddha* are also invested in challenging the familial and cultural stagnation of the suburbs, as opposed to the presumed vibrancy offered by the city. As I demonstrate, however, Charlie's reorientation towards youth musical subcultures, first in London and subsequently in New York City, belies the betrayal of his class position and his ethnic heritage, something of which Karim becomes conscious when his fascination with Charlie starts waning.

If Omar and Johnny's relationship entailed the rekindling of an interethnic connection severed by Johnny's racist past, as well as the subversion of both the colonial relationship and Thatcherite colour-blind entrepreneurial neoliberalism, then the relationship between Karim and Charlie is conversely marked by ongoing tension and inequality, and by Karim's desire for assimilation into white British middle-class society. Karim intimates:

> My love for [Charlie] was unusual [...]: it was not generous. I admired him more than anyone but I didn't wish him well. [...] I preferred him to me and wanted to be him. I coveted his talents, face, style. I wanted to wake up with them all transferred to me. (Kureishi, 1999, p. 15)

There is no mutual edification, no interethnic merging or assemblage here, but an envious desire to become someone else, revealing cultural and racial self-denial. Consequently, Karim makes himself subservient to Charlie, and in their only extended moment of sexual intimacy, it is invariably Karim who gratifies Charlie, while Charlie remains the receptor of Karim's touch: 'I tried to kiss him. He avoided my lips by turning his head to one side. But when he came in my hand it was, I swear, one of the preeminent moments of my earlyish life' (Kureishi, 1999, p. 17). Whereas Karim's young persona interprets Charlie's slight 'twitch[ing]' (1999, p. 17) as a sign of interpersonal connection, stating that '[t]hrough such human electricity we understood each other' (1999, p. 17), the affair remains remarkably one-sided, with Karim pleasuring Charlie, even ingesting Charlie's sperm, while Charlie simply allows him to do it. Kureishi's depiction of this sexual scene lends a sense that Karim's and Charlie's queerness are not commensurate; that Karim is orientated towards Charlie but that Charlie's desire is not fully aligned with Karim's.

Karim's initial fascination with Charlie begins to unravel once he becomes attuned to Charlie's artificial cultural posturing, which is expressed through the idiom of popular music. Kureishi's personal penchant for 1960s and 1970s rock and pop music does not cloud his judgement regarding the pitfalls of subcultural forms of youthful resistance becoming culturally appropriated and commodified. During a punk gig both characters attend together in London, we are told:

> [T]he carrot-haired kid cursed us to death. He seemed to be yelling direct at Charlie and me. I could feel Charlie getting tense beside me. I knew London was killing us as I heard, 'Fuck off, all you smelly old hippies! You fucking slags! You ugly fart-breaths! Fuck off to hell!' he shouted at us. [...]
>
> Charlie was excited. 'That's it, that's it,' he said as we strolled. 'That's fucking it.' His voice was squeaking with rapture. 'The sixties have been given notice tonight. Those kids we have seen have assassinated all hope. They're the fucking future.'
>
> 'Yeah, maybe, but we can't follow them,' I said casually.
>
> 'Why not?'

> 'Obviously we can't wear rubber and safety-pins and all. What would we look like? Sure, Charlie.'
>
> 'Why not, Karim? Why not, man?'
>
> 'It's not us.'
>
> 'But we've got to change. What are you saying? We shouldn't keep up? That suburban boys like us always know where it's at?'
>
> 'It would be artificial,' I said. 'We're not like them. We don't hate the way they do. We've got no reason to. We're not from the estates. We haven't been through what they have.'
>
> He turned on me with one of his nastiest looks.
>
> 'You're not going anywhere, Karim. You're not doing anything with your life because as usual you're facing in the wrong direction and going the wrong way.'
>
> (Kureishi, 1999, pp. 131–2)

Unlike Karim, Charlie is willing to become reorientated, to turn away from his middle-class hippy self incepted in the 1960s and towards the working-class 1970s punk movement, but Karim is conscious of insurmountable class differences between themselves and the punk movement. As he admonishes to Charlie, such a move would be 'artificial': a strategic and inauthentic put-on that betrays their social origins. Kureishi deals here with the tensions between 'filiation' and 'affiliation' that Edward Said explored in *The World, the Text, and the Critic*. Despite Karim's queerness, which remains fluid and hence in keeping with constructionism, Kureishi seems aware that class and cultural allegiances must be filiative to remain culturally authentic, and that strategic affiliation creates false personas at a remove from one's cultural background.

As a consequence of their tense conversation, Charlie takes flight and he and Karim go their different ways. The next time they meet, Karim does not recognise Charlie at first due to his transformation into a punk artist. He avers that

> Charlie was magnificent in his venom, his manufactured rage, his anger, his defiance. [...] He was brilliant: he'd assembled all the right elements. It was a wonderful trick and disguise. The one flaw, I giggled to myself, was his milky and healthy white teeth, which, to me, betrayed everything else. (Kureishi, 1999, p. 154)

By 'everything else', Karim is implying, once more, Charlie's middle-class origins, which remain at odds with his 'manufactured' and artificially assembled punk persona, which later acquires silver hair and starts resembling Kureishi's idol David Bowie, a cultural icon of ambiguous sexuality and subversive gender performance. Berkem Gürenci Sa Ğlam suggests that '[w]hile not strictly punk, Charlie resembles a Ziggy Stardust-era David Bowie, whom Karim also mentions as having gone to their high school several years earlier (as did Billy Idol to Kureishi's school)' (2014, p. 559). Sa Ğlam had also argued that 'although [Kureishi] views both the hippies and punks as superfluous and too willing to sell out their values for the consumption of mainstream society, he does make a distinction between the genuine member of a counterculture and the fake imitator' (2014, p. 555). Charlie is deemed such a 'fake imitator', talentless as regards music itself, yet adept at creating personas that bring him success with the mainstream public. Similarly to the way the postcolonial diasporic citizen's attempt to move from the margins to the centre has been deemed an effort to join dominant white British culture, the commodification of punk and its joining of the mainstream betrays its countercultural impetus and renders it normative. Kureishi's text suggests that for cultures, ethnicities, and sexualities to remain countercultural, they must struggle with their place in the margins and forfeit the privilege that comes from becoming mainstream.

Religion is another element that, like music, becomes commodified in British culture, and *Buddha* critiques the double standards and hypocrisy that underpin religious conservatism in its negotiation with Western modernity. Said suggests that an 'alternative for the critic is to recognize the difference between instinctual filiation and social affiliation' (1983, p. 24). An example of instinctual filiation and social affiliation is provided by Karim's father, Haroon, a South Asian Muslim émigré who abandons his familial Islam and socially embraces Buddhism in Britain, albeit remaining censorious of same-sex relations in a manner that reveals his deep-seated instinctual filiation to Islamic orthodoxy. Haroon preaches to Karim's love-interests Helen and Jamila: 'We live in an age of doubt and uncertainty. The old religions under which people lived for ninety-nine point nine per cent of human history have decayed or are irrelevant. Our problem is secularism. We have replaced our spiritual values and wisdom with materialism' (Kureishi, 1999, p. 76). Haroon announces here the debunking of the 'old' religions, such as Christianity and Islam, and the victory of materialism, the byproduct of secular capitalism. However, paradoxically, Haroon makes money through his self-Orientalisation: he becomes a yogi, despite being a Muslim, and coaches white British middle-class hippies interested in Oriental mysticism without beliefs. As Karim inwardly ponders after he catches his father and his mistress having loud sex: 'Was I conceived like this, I wondered, in the suburban night air, to the wailing of Christian curses from the mouth of a renegade Muslim masquerading as a Buddhist?' (Kureishi, 1999, p. 16) As the titular 'Buddha of Suburbia', Haroon commodifies Buddhism through social affiliation, choosing a faith popular with Westerners and exploiting his racial and ethnic profile as a brown-skinned Oriental man in order to bypass his ethnic heritage.

Nonetheless, despite Haroon being a 'renegade Muslim masquerading as a Buddhist', while also having an extramarital affair in contravention of Islamic doctrine, Haroon is mortified when he witnesses Karim's same-sex affair with Charlie and confronts him about it:

'What the hell were you doing?'
  'Shut up!' I said, as quietly as I could.
  'I saw you, Karim. My God, you're a bloody pure shitter! A bum-banger! My own son – how did it transpire?'
  He was disappointed in me. He jumped up and down in anguish as if he'd just heard the whole house had been burned to the ground. I didn't know what to do. So I started to imitate the voice he'd used earlier with the advertisers and Eva.
  'Relax, Dad. Relax your whole body from your fingers to your toes and send your mind to a quiet garden where –'
  'I'll send you to a fucking doctor to have your balls examined!'
(Kureishi, 1999, p. 18)

Kureishi depicts here the internalised homophobia Haroon still professes, despite his having abandoned his familial Islam; in order to deflate him, Karim satirises his father's meditation discourse and cadences, only to be subsequently medicalised in a playful nineteenth-century fashion, which reveals the colonial dimensions of Haroon's deep-seated homophobia, which I cited in the Introduction. Despite the fact Karim can see through his father's cultural put-ons and prejudices, he is affected by his father's censure and henceforth prioritises his liaisons with women. As Karim tells us later, his relationship with the actress Eleanor was a 'relief' to Haroon, who 'was so terrified that [Karim] might turn out to be gay that he could never bring himself to mention the matter' (Kureishi, 1999, p. 174). Karim goes on to suggest that '[i]n his [father's] Muslim mind it was bad enough being a woman; being a man and denying your male sex was perverse and self-destructive' (1999, p. 174). Karim's assessment of his father chimes with the Islamic conflation of homosexuality and emasculation. Kureishi's novel suggests that Haroon cannot completely outgrow his filiative inheritance of Islamic orthodoxy despite his social affiliation to Buddhism – he still possesses 'a Muslim mind' with all its patriarchal baggage – and his son must do everything in his power to favour relationships with women that will make him appear duly heteronormative.

Karim's close friend and occasional lover, Jamila, is also the victim of her father's first-generation migrant Muslim patriarchal expectations, whose selective application further exemplifies the gap between filiative Islamic principles and the realities of living in the diaspora. Jamila's father, Anwar, insists on Jamila going through the marriage arranged by her family in India. As Karim narrates,

> Anwar's brother in Bombay had fixed up Jamila with a boy eager to come and live in London as Jamila's husband. [...] As a dowry, the ageing boy had demanded a warm winter overcoat from Moss Bros., a colour television and, mysteriously, an edition of the complete works of Conan Doyle. (Kureishi, 1999, p. 57)

Jamila resists being married off to this unknown colonial mimic, but in order to convince her of his seriousness, Anwar emulates, paradoxically enough, the hunger strike of Mahatma Gandhi, not a Muslim model figure but a Hindu revivalist. Karim attempts to intervene, telling Anwar that 'it's old-fashioned, Uncle, out of date [...]. No one does that kind of thing now. They just marry the person they're into', to which Anwar staunchly responds: 'That is not our way, boy. Our way is firm. She must do what I say or I will die' (Kureishi, 1999, p. 60). There is a cleavage here between first-generation adherence to their inherited religious and cultural principles and the second-generation diasporic subscription to Western modernity. Moreover, Karim sees through Anwar's dogged insistence on Muslim tradition: 'It was certainly bizarre, Uncle Anwar behaving like a Muslim. I'd never known him believe in anything before, so it was an amazing novelty to find him literally shaking his life on the principle of absolute patriarchal control. [...] Anwar even scoffed pork pies' (1999, p. 64). According to Kureishi's text, there is inconsistency and strategic selection in Anwar's approach to Islam, and his own patchy investment in his faith does not seem to match his stubborn insistence on his patriarchal authority regarding Jamila's marriage.

In his reading of *Buddha*, Moore-Gilbert suggests that this is not so much a religious as a patriarchal dilemma derived from Anwar's South Asian cosmology:

> That the issue is not properly one of religion, but of patriarchal rights, is suggested by Anwar's personal hypocrisy. While he takes a hard-line attitude towards Haroon's relationship with Eva, Anwar himself has been involved with 'the prostitutes who hung around Hyde Park' and, while he deems Haroon's interest in pop music to be a sign of the latter's decadence, he still continues to smoke and drink alcohol long after his readopting of an apparently strict Islamic identity. (Moore-Gilbert, 2001, p. 134)

According to this, although Anwar is quick to criticise his close friend Haroon's extramarital affair with a white British woman and the hedonistic influence of Western pop music, he himself is not impervious to the 'temptations' of a 'Western' lifestyle: he frequents prostitutes and he drinks, smokes, and, as Karim reminds us, he sometimes eats pork, all in contravention of his Islamic faith. His strictness when it comes to the issue of marriage, then, constitutes not so much an item of the Islamic faith as of the resilience of patriarchal values. Indeed, Ruth Maxey highlights 'the unbending patriarchy which Kureishi's first-generation men perpetuate in Britain: they cling increasingly to the security of perceived homeland values as they become less able to control the external circumstances of their lives' (2006, p. 18). In other words, the first-generation diaspora that is orientated to 'homeland values' (i.e., Indian, Muslim) cannot escape the disorientation and reorientation experienced by living in the 'West', and their mundane realities gradually erode South Asian and Islamic orthodoxies.

It is ironically fitting that the arranged marriage to which Jamila finally agrees ends up providing the most prominent outlet in the novel for resisting heteronormativity and inherited Islamic values, in contrast with Karim and Charlie's – as well as Haroon and Eva's – conforming to social normativity. At the end of *Buddha*, Haroon announces his and Eva's upcoming nuptials, which mark a purposeful reorientation of their relationship towards social respectability. Although Karim's predicament is left open-ended, Karim and Charlie make an appearance in Kureishi's later novel *Gabriel's Gift*. In this text, the titular adolescent Gabriel bumps into the two local pseudo-celebrities while he is in a bar with his father. When the bar owner, Speedy, strikes a conversation with Charlie about Karim, Charlie tells him that '[h]e's good at the moment. [...] [H]e's got a son now – Haroon, he's called, known as Harry. Then he's getting married' (Kureishi, 2002b, p. 125). What follows this boasting of conventionality is indicative of the ongoing rivalry between Karim and Charlie, as Charlie entreats Speedy to send a waitress to him, ask him for his autograph, and give him a kiss while purposefully ignoring Karim. Charlie's attention-seeking ploy demonstrates his ongoing sexual tension with Karim; it works, since 'Karim got up and left the table' (2002b, p. 126), in apparent jealousy. It is significant that these sexual power games take place furtively, while the personas the characters publicly project remain ultimately heteronormative. Neither Karim nor Charlie are radical enough to channel their queerness into a fight against inherited values, and their personal quests for success as an actor and a musician, respectively, demonstrate their complicity with the 'Establishment' and their affiliation to neoliberal individualistic values. Indeed, to add to these characters' dispiriting absorption into dominant society, Rehana Ahmed lucidly observes the reoccurrence of *Laundrette*'s Omar in Kureishi's novel *Something to Tell You*, where he has become 'a wealthy middle-aged businessman as well as a "stalwart of the anti-racist industry" and a Labour peer [who] supports the post-9/11 British bombings of Iraq, voicing the neb-imperial rhetoric of "civilisation" as his rationale' (Ahmed, 2015, p. 118). Kureishi's narratives seem to suggest that queerness is not, in and of itself, enough to challenge the status quo, and his characters' cooption into mainstream British society and politics reveals their gradual 'ascent' into power and normativity.

By contrast, the seemingly submissive Jamila, who ends up ruefully marrying Changez, the satirically depicted Indian husband her uncle finds for her, manages to reorient her conventional family in a way that suits her rebellious queer outlook. Despite being tutored in feminism by a religious missionary, Miss Cutmore, whom she eventually rejects because of the colonial inception of her views, Jamila is forced to submit to her father's wishes. However, once she is married, she refashions her union with Changez and forges a model of family that simultaneously defies bloodlines and the nuclear, patrilineal, and heterosexual nature of traditional families. Changez initially objects to Jamila's sexual and moral independence:

[Changez had] railed at Jamila and accused her of adultery, incest, betrayal, whoredom, deceit, lesbianism, husband-hatred, frigidity, lying and callousness, as well as the usual things. Jamila was equally fine and fierce that day, explaining just who her damned body belonged to. And anyway, it was none of his business: didn't he have a regular fuck? He could shove his hypocrisy up his fat arse! Changez, being at heart a traditional Muslim, explained the teachings of the Koran on this subjects to her, and then, when words were not sufficient to convince her, he tried to give her a whack. But Jamila was not whackable. She gave Changez a considerable backhander across his wobbling chops, which shut his mouth for a fortnight. (Kureishi, 1999, pp. 134–5)

Kureishi's text creates conflict in the Indian man's Anglophilic yet resiliently Muslim worldview, which, however traditional, contains double standards: he objects to his wife's extramarital same-sex affairs while he regularly has sex with his Japanese lady-friend Chinko. Changez piles up on Jamila accusations according to the alleged teachings of Islam, to which Jamila defiantly responds by claiming ownership over her own body, and by responding to his patriarchal violence with a reciprocated blow. Jamila's untameable nature forces Changez to adapt his worldviews gradually, to partly reorient himself so as to accommodate her queerness. She eventually has a child with another man and has a relationship with a woman, even suggesting to Changez the possibility of living in a queer commune. Touchingly, Changez becomes devoted to Jamila's baby, whom he treats as his own child. In welcoming such an unusual, queer arrangement, Jamila and Changez's polyamorous and matrilineal family flies in the face of heteronormativity and conventional conceptions of the nuclear family. Jamila's queer polyamory also turns on its head the Islamic permission of heterosexual male polygamy and its curtailment of female equality in marriage. Changez, Jamila, and their respective lovers inhabit the margins of both the novel and of 'respectable society' as a whole, and I suggest they remain, together with the lesbian agitators of Kureishi's second penned film, *Sammy and Rosie Get Laid*, released in 1987, the most transgressively queer characters in Kureishi's work, precisely because of their marginality. In their lack of ambition to affiliate to mainstream white British culture and in their challenge to the South Asian diaspora's filiative Islamic values, Jamila and her associates remain insurgently queer, eroding, in a micropolitical and mundane manner, the sturdy identitarian segments built by national and diasporic ideologies.

Kureishi's cinematic and literary texts offer no clear resolution to the race and national identity debates. Nonetheless, *Laundrette*'s hopeful denouement brings a suitably happy ending to a film that is playfully anarchic and non-partisan, and which subverts normative ideologies by making strategic recourse to queerness. As I have shown, instead of subscribing to a totalising macropolitical worldview, Kureishi allows *Laundrette* to function micropolitically, affectively eroding at the heteronormative and monocultural biases of mainstream nationalist and diasporic ideologies in Britain, in a way that presciently anticipates some of the political turmoil surrounding the publication of *The Satanic Verses*, but which retains hope for the ability of normative ideologies, whether of majority or minority ethnic groups, to be gradually qualified. Thirty years on from its original release, *Laundrette*'s intersectional approach still has the power to tease and disorientate its audience, drawing attention to the stiff segmentalisation of British social groupings, and suggesting the assemblage of various discourses of emancipation – i.e., queer, feminist, ethnic, class-related – as the best hope for Britain as a truly multicultural nation, albeit offering a belated caveat in *Something to Tell You* about the risks of becoming normative. Together with *Buddha* and *Gabriel's Gift*, these novels illustrate Kureishi's queer characters' gradual progression into normativity, which constitutes the seemingly unavoidable result of class privilege and sexual conformism. As I have illustrated, both Haroon and Karim become normative, as they choose to marry women and have children, and Omar becomes a Labour peer who becomes politically complicit in the Iraq War. Islam plays no discernible role in their evolving identities as first- and second-generation diasporic Muslims. Kureishi's texts suggest that the only way to be properly queer is to live in the margins of society. In my reading of Jamila and Changez's family, they are rendered marginal characters who disorientate both Muslim and non-Muslim ideologies. On the other hand, Karim and Charlie's move to the centre in pursuance of success entails buying into neoliberalism, which Omar's entrepreneurial trajectory had warned us about in *Laundrette* as being complicit with the status quo, and which he himself failed to escape in Kureishi's later work. Kureishi's vision holds little hope for the influence of Islam in the carving on new and benign forms of Britishness, yet in its contravention of the dominant ideologies of both the white British majority and the South Asian diaspora in Britain, Kureishi's work remains subversive and countercultural, despite his lack of proper engagement with Islam and his characters' dispiriting cooption into positions of power.

Notes

1   The polemic surrounding *The Satanic Verses* has left a clear imprint on Kureishi's work. In *The Word and the Bomb*, Kureishi asserts that '[t]he Rushdie case remains instructive. In the end it is Islam itself which suffers from the repudiation of more sensual and dissident ideas of itself' (2005, p. 11). Kureishi's second novel, *The Black Album*, set in London in 1989, follows the movements of the diffident British Muslim Shahid Hasan, who becomes involved, and eventually disenchanted, with a group of politically active Muslims who condemn the publication of Rushdie's novel. Kureishi's narrative features its own book-burning scene mirroring similar historical events involving *The Satanic Verses*. 'Bradford' (2005, pp. 75–80) features Kureishi's visit to the northern English city, and what he perceived as a hub of Islamist sentiment subsequently informed his post-Rushdie and post-Gulf War short story 'My Son the Fanatic' (Kureishi, 2010, p. 116–27) and his adaptation of it to film released in 1997. As a self-declared atheist of Muslim ethnic heritage, Kureishi's relationship with Islam remains ambivalent: he can passionately defend freedom of speech against Islamic offence and condemn Islamic fundamentalism, while castigating racial profiling of

Muslims and Western interventionism in Muslim-majority countries. Due to his British upbringing and his distance from Muslim ideologies, Kureishi's cultural position can be a double-edged sword most sharply deployed in his creative work, while his essays betray a not too sophisticated understanding of Islam and an uncritical eagerness to embrace the legacies of Enlightenment. For a perceptive analysis of Kureishi's essays that pays attention to the ideological and cultural slippages in Kureishi's use of personal pronouns, see Dave Gunning (2015).

2   These include David Lean's adaptation of E. M. Forster's *A Passage to India*, the film version of M. M. Kaye's *The Far Pavilions*, and ITV's grand adaptation of Paul Scott's *The Raj Quartet*, *The Jewel in the Crown*. Despite Kureishi's alleged chagrin about these films, there is some aesthetic kinship in the representation of colonial and postcolonial homoeroticism, which I have explored in my comparative reading of Forster's *A Passage to India*, Lean's adaptation of Forster's novel and *Laundrette* (Fernández Carbajal, 2017a.) Rushdie's astringent reservations about films and TV series produced in the 1980s and set in the Indian colonial past are given vent in his famous essay 'Outside the Whale', collected in *Imaginary Homelands*, where he observes that 'the British Raj, after three and a half decades in retirement, has been making a sort of comeback' (Rushdie, 1992, p. 87). Bart Moore-Gilbert offers a perceptive reading of *Laundrette* as a response to this Raj Revivalist cultural trend and to the popular genre of 'heritage film', although such analysis is sometimes undertaken at the expense of oversimplifying the work of other independent production companies, such as Merchant Ivory. The equally independently produced and class-conscious *A Room with a View*, produced by the postcolonial team of Ismail Merchant, James Ivory, and Ruth Prawer Jhabvala, released in the same year as *Laundrette*, also features Daniel Day-Lewis, in a critique of the biases and exclusions of the British class system during the Edwardian period.

3   According to Moore-Gilbert, Kureishi's films aim to 'counter a more specific manifestation of the New Right's assault on "permisiveness", its desire to curb homosexuality' (2001, p. 87), and he lists Thatcher's failure, fuelled by the AIDS crisis, to bring homosexual age of consent to par with its heterosexual counterpart and the discouragement of discussions of homosexuality enforced through the gagging Section 28, part of the Local Governments Act of 1988, which forbad the public 'promotion' of homosexuality.

4   Kureishi's use of irony ensures that his critique is neither too acerbic or victimising. His most salient use of irony in *Laundrette* involves an inversion of imperialism. John Hill argues that 'a part of the film's strategy is to use the business success of the Asian characters to invert old imperial power relations' (1999, p. 210). In addition, Bradley Buchanan suggests that '[i]rony is Kureishi's most reliable trope, and he evinces scepticism about the capacity of any group or ideology to effect lasting or meaningful change' (2007, p. 14).

5   One of the film's original American reviewers, Rita Kempley, concurs with those critics who question the film's veracity, when she observes that '[t]he two men fall in love in this heady atmosphere of suds and soap; their heads spin like the clothes in a tub. It all seems to come *out of nowhere*' (1986, p. 25, emphasis added). According to Kempley and other like-minded commentators, the relationship between Omar, a mixed-race British man, and Johnny, a white Britisher who formerly supported the National Front, would seem, at best,

unexpected, and, at worst, improbable. However, their liaison mirrors that of Kureishi himself with one of his friends earlier in life, 'who became Johnny in *My Beautiful Laundrette*' (Kureishi, 2002a, p. 26), with an added element of 'wishing'. In an interview with Susie Thomas, Kureishi declares: 'You might say that one of the most important parts of you is your wishing, your desire, and in your writing there might be a lot of wishing' (Thomas, 2007, p. 11). However, as I propose above, the film's intentions reach beyond mimesis and social realism.

6 Rahul. K. Gairola's analysis of this scene is particularly insightful: 'This scene is especially significant if we consider its framing. Frears situates the two men in the foreground of a one-way mirror looking out into the laundrette, where Nasser and his mistress Rachel are dancing to a waltz. Behind Rachel and Nasser, a crowd of working class locals eagerly awaits the laundrette's grand opening. Frears maps out the boys in the foreground having sex in the backroom upon the image of Nasser and Rachel kissing on the other side of the one-way mirror. This shooting technique not only humanizes both couples using close ups and soft colours, but suggests that both modes of eroticism are equally transgressive in the face of the heteronormativity that drives Thatcher's economic liberalism' (2009, p. 45).

7 Gairola usefully notes that '[i]n South Asian culture, the term "aunty" does not literally denote one's blood-aunt. Rather, it is a gentile colloquialism used to address elder women who are family friends or to express a respectful familiarity' (2009, p. 53n).

2

'Are we on the same wavelength?': Interstitial queerness and the Ismaili diaspora in Ian Iqbal Rashid's poetry and films

THE WORK of Canadian poet, screenwriter, and film director Ian Iqbal Rashid follows in the footsteps of Hanif Kureishi's *My Beautiful Laundrette* and *The Buddha of Suburbia*, explored in the previous chapter. Here, I undertake a combined exploration of Rashid's poetry and film work, since both media articulate overlapping themes of diaspora, ethnicity, faith, and sexuality in fictionalised but also autobiographical ways, with a keen emphasis on the realignment of allegiance and desire involved in queer Muslim diasporas. Rashid utilises the medium of film as a site of conjoined ethnic and sexual resistance, in awareness of Kureishi's status as his most direct artistic precursor. South Asian diaspora scholar Jigna Desai is quoted by Claudia Sternberg during her analysis of Rashid's debut short film, *Surviving Sabu*, where she corroborates Kureishi's lasting imprint on South Asian diasporic imaginaries: 'As brown bodies trespassed the spaces of colonial anthropology and history to spaces marked as the present, I experienced a return and a rupture simultaneously' (Sternberg, 2010). Rashid's film work, which undertakes a similar 'return and rupture', extends the debates started by Kureishi, with its exploration of interethnic and diasporic queerness, the legacies of colonial and postcolonial modernities, and intergenerational ideological disparity in the Muslim diaspora. Rashid's poetry is highly aware of queer desire's entanglement with power struggles that belong in the continuum of colonial and postcolonial history, which is also articulated in his films.

Yet, whereas *Laundrette* made accessible to a global audience its art-house and countercultural visual aesthetic, Rashid's first feature film, *Touch of Pink*, performs a feat that is significantly different: it queers the heteronormative mainstream genre of the Hollywood romantic comedy, appropriating and experimenting with its techniques while focusing on a previously underrepresented ethnic community, namely the East African Ismaili diaspora in Canada and its offshoots in Britain, which mirrors Rashid's familial and personal trajectory. As he himself confesses during an interview, 'the themes that run through much of my work are concerned with the effects of migration on immigrant families' (*IndieWire*, 2007). Indeed, families are central to Rashid's Ismaili imaginary, yet his work is also highly concerned with issues of individual desire, especially when it comes to the intersection of queerness, ethnicity, and Muslim identities. In the closing of *Touch of Pink* (2004), white British Giles asks his Canadian Ismaili partner: 'Alim, are we on the same wavelength?' Rashid's whole oeuvre is invested in exploring how characters and poetic personae need to tune themselves to the different wavelengths provided by diasporic and global histories, to the disorientations and reorientations involved in queer relationships across ethnic divides. It is these connections across ethnic and generational lines that will claim our attention in the forthcoming pages.

Rashid was born in Dar es Salaam, Tanzania, in 1965 to Ismaili Muslim parents of Indian heritage. His family left Tanzania in 1970, unsuccessfully seeking asylum in London. They eventually settled in Canada. Rashid grew up in a majority white and violent suburb of inner-city Toronto (*Sher Vancouver*, n.d.). These were the days before the current institutional celebration of Canadian multiculturalism, and Rashid found this environment challenging as a member of an ethno-religious minority. Rashid's initial artistic calling was as a poet, with his award-winning debut collection, *Black Markets White Boyfriends and Other Acts of Elision* (henceforth *Black Markets*), published in 1991, followed by the poetry chapbook *Song of Sabu* in 1993, which is included in full in Rashid's second full-length volume on poetry, *The Heat Yesterday*, published in 1995. Rashid's poetry collections were all published in Canada. However, his poems have also appeared in the British postcolonial journal and literary magazine *Wasafiri* (Rashid, 2007), and they have been anthologised in *The Redbeck Anthology of British South Asian Poetry*, in *Making a Difference: Canadian Multicultural Literature*, and, more recently, in *Seminal: The Anthology of Canada's Gay Male Poets*, among other publications. Smaro Kamboureli describes Rashid's first poetry collection as being 'concerned with racial difference and sexuality, and how these constructs affect power within personal relationships', while his second volume deals with 'issues of memory and mourning, especially mourning in the age of AIDS, and addresses, once again, the concept of belonging' (1996, p. 503). Indeed, *Black*

Markets is most keenly focused on issues of queer interethnic relationships, whereas *The Heat Yesterday*, while still steeped in interethnic same-sex desire, is more visibly invested in the themes of family and diaspora.

Rashid's poetry has been equally praised by postcolonial and queer critics. For instance, 'of the less familiar works [in *The Redbeck Anthology*]', writes Ashok Bery, 'Rashid's poems are worth a mention' (2001, p. 75). In the 'Gay literature' entry for *The Oxford Companion to Canadian Literature*, Robert K. Martin asserts that 'Rashid reminds us that the body is social as well as personal', while observing that his 'work evokes the doubleness of subjectivity, [...] in which desire for a culture and desire for a man seem dangerously entangled' (Toye and Benson, 1997, p. 454). The subjective doubleness of desire and cultural affiliation, the collision between the personal and the political, as well as issues of belonging and racial difference, are all a constant in Rashid's oeuvre, including his films, which embody, in their colourful complexity, the dilemmas of living in the diaspora as a queer citizen of Ismaili heritage.

Rashid's transcontinental familial and personal journeys demonstrates just how queer diasporas can be, featuring collective and individual migrations from India to East Africa, then Canada, and finally to Britain, where Rashid relocated in the early 1990s, initially to Bristol and subsequently to London, where he currently lives with his Australian male partner. In 1994, and following his partner's submission of one of Rashid's stories to a public competition, Rashid was selected from more than 800 applicants for a BBC drama screenwriting development course (*V Tape*, n.d.), where a first draft of the script for *Touch of Pink* was written. For a while, Rashid concentrated on his script and short fiction writing. At around the turn of the twenty-first century, Rashid started to direct his own scripts, initially in the shape of short films, such as *Surviving Sabu*, funded by the English Arts Council, and *Stag*, produced by BBC Films, eventually leading to his first feature film, the British-Canadian co-production *Touch of Pink*, which was more than a decade in the making. These three films' semi-autobiographical dealings with Muslim identity, interethnic desire, and queerness are interwoven here with a critical examination of Rashid's poetry, which highlights the overlapping concerns of Rashid's variegated work. Despite garnering positive reviews, Rashid's poetry has not yet merited critical assessment, so it will be illuminating to put his poems in dialogue with his more easily accessible film work. Since the production of his main full-length film, *Touch of Pink*, Rashid has continued writing for television and film.

For Rashid, being Muslim is inseparable from being part of the diasporic Ismaili community in Canada, so we must pay due heed to his particular positionality. In an early study published before their collective departure from Tanzania, Robert J. Bocock states the uniqueness of the Ismailis and their subscription to Shia Islam, the branch of the faith that believes in the hereditary nature of religious leadership. He observes that 'Shias believe that spiritual authority continues to be with man in the Imam, but today the Ismailis are the only group left who still think that the Imam is known and identifiable' (Bocock, 1971, p. 366).[1] Moreover, the Imam encourages loyalty to the countries where Ismailis have settled. This allegiance must be honoured regardless of whether these nations have a Muslim majority or a Muslim minority, and whether the largest Islamic group is Sunni or Shia. However, there is an inherent paradox in the Ismailis' ability socially to 'integrate' while clinging to a sense of cultural and religious distinctiveness. As Rashid himself has remarked:

> We do work well in the west. We do kind of assimilate better than a lot of other South Asian and Muslim communities who have migrated and yet we are very community minded. Family is so important and the community is so insular as well. (Meherali, 2004)

Peter B. Clarke observes that '[t]here is a "givenness" about community in Ismailism. It stems from being born into this particular religious community', adding that 'East African Ismailis tend to form together a group, and loyalty to and kinship among East African Ismailis accounts for some of the strength of the associational and communal bonds' (1976, pp. 490, 492). This distinct combination of integration, modernity, and tradition entails an often fraught relationship with issues of sexual liberation that are shared with other Muslims in the diaspora but which are distinctly articulated and with different outcomes.

As regards Canadian Muslims, Amir Hussain has pointed out they are clustered in cities like Toronto, Ottawa, Montreal, and Vancouver, with smaller communities in Calgary, Edmonton, Winnipeg, Saskatoon, Windsor, and Halifax. Although the large majority of Canadian Muslims is Sunni, there are important groups of Shia Muslims – Twelver and Ismaili – in Canada. However, as he clearly states regarding their perceptions of homosexuality:

> Traditional Islam recognizes the validity of only the heterosexual relationship. A number of Muslim groups and leaders have spoken out against homosexuality. However, there are Muslims who self-identify as gay/lesbian/bisexual/transgendered/intersex/questioning (GLBTIQ) [...] In talking with a member of Min al-Alaq [a Canadian LGBTIQ support

group for Muslims whose Qur'anic name means 'from the same cloth'], I was reminded of the tremendous religious isolation that comes with being a gay Muslim in Toronto. (Hussain, 2004, p. 372)

Membership of a religious community such as the Ismailis, who embrace modernity and social betterment, while risking collusion with neoliberalism, yet who steadfastly hold on to traditional religious values, creates a rupture in the sense of identification of queer Ismailis, who are forced to attune their sensibilities to the various wavelengths of alleged Western sexual exceptionalism, resilient colonial forms of racism – both external and internalised – and Muslim heteronormativity. As Karim H. Karim suggests, the Ismailis' 'search for balance between tradition and modernity extends into interaction with the postmodern'; he argues that the ongoing struggle to find balance is dependent on life's changing circumstances and contexts, and that 'experience unfolds unendingly in the intervening spaces – the interstices – between tradition, modernity and postmodernity' (Karim, 2010, p. 267). Here, I examine Rashid's literary and film work as being placed at these interstices, constantly attempting to strike a balance between the exigencies of Ismaili and Muslim traditionalism, colonial and postcolonial modernity, and diasporic postmodernity.

Rashid's first two short films as screenwriter and director, *Surviving Sabu* and *Stag*, preliminarily enact some of the diasporic themes and political issues that are fledged out in Rashid's first full-length feature film, *Touch of Pink*. We will first examine *Stag*, a film around nine minutes long whose depiction of queerness and interethnic relationships shares important resonances with Rashid's poetry. This short piece commissioned by the BBC features two characters, British Asian bridegroom Sammi (Nitin Ganatra) and white British best man Luke (Stuart Laing). The film opens with photographic evidence of Sammi's stag party, hence the name of the film, with extra-diegetic sound of the celebrations. We are witness here to a homosocial space of partly naked men with their arms round their shoulders. These Polaroid photographs, which already show intimacy between Sammi and Luke, are intercalated with images of Sammi and Luke sharing the same bed. Following this opening, a new scene shows us Luke embracing Sammi in his sleep. They are both lying naked. The seemingly extra-diegetic sound of David Gray's song 'Babylon' turns out to be the alarm clock; when Sammi's arm reaches out to turn it off, he realises with a start that he is next to Luke and gets out of bed in a panic. It takes both men a little while to recollect the significance of what happened the previous night, which allegedly leaves Luke 'speechless' (*Stag*, 2002). The rest of the film constitutes an examination of the different ways in which both men attempt to reconcile their perspectives on their homoerotic encounter and its implications for Sammi's imminent wedding to his fiancée, Yasmin. The minimalism of Rashid's script, closely focused on the two characters, allows him to dissect their queer relationship and its cultural and political underpinnings.

I would argue the relationship between Sammi and Luke is deeply imbricated in existing structures of sexual and political domination historically linked not only to British imperialism, but also to classical Islamic and ancient Greek civilizations. Crucially, Luke never lets Sammi forget, either explicitly or through indirect allusion, that it was he who penetrated Sammi. Sammi's distaste for Luke's boasting angers him to the point of cultural disavowal, as he rebelliously states: 'My culture didn't descend from the fucking Greeks like your lot' (*Stag*, 2002), which is historically inaccurate. As we saw in the Introduction, the work of Khaled El-Rouayheb links Islamicate and Greek homoeroticism, revealing that the Islamicate focus on active and passive anal penetration is drawn from classical Greek civilisation. As he observes, '[i]t was the *ma'būn* or *mukhannath* who was viewed as a pathological case. The Arabic medical tradition, following the Greek, tended to regard the male who desires to be anally penetrated as being afflicted with a disease – *ubnah*' (El-Rouayheb, 2005, p. 19). Sammi refuses to be placed in the subservient position connected in his Muslim imaginary to disease and subservience, demonstrating that his sensibility is more indebted to his Greek-inspired Islamicate cultural legacy than he himself would want to admit.

However, the political reverberations of Luke and Sammi's sexual encounter have more recent and pressing connotations. When Sammi asks Luke how it came to happen that Luke became the dominant party, Luke nonchalantly responds that 'it's just how these things happen, I suppose', to which Sammi insurgently retorts: 'Yeah, for 300 years' (*Stag*, 2002) In Gayatri Gopinath's reading of *Laundrette* referenced previously, 'the barely submerged histories of colonialism and racism erupt into the present at the very moment when queer sexuality is being articulated' (2005, p. 2). The interpersonal relations in *Stag* are also a clear indictment of colonial racial hierarchies that become manifest with the articulation of queerness. Sammi finally unmasks Luke's persistence and shows it for what it is: a continued desire to be dominant, which is connected to the long history of British colonialism. As the men are about to leave Sammi's house, Luke descends the stairs and plants a passionate kiss on Sammi's mouth, stating afterwards: 'I don't wanna lose you, Sammi', to which Sammi lucidly responds: 'You just don't wanna lose. […] You've always hated losing', which this time leaves Luke truly speechless. Instead of submitting to Luke's emotional demands, with his persistent hints that

Sammi should postpone the wedding, Sammi in fact honours his commitment to his bride. It is significant that Rashid's film articulates a model of queerness whereby characters are not forced into an essentialist gay/straight paradigm. In fact, neither character identifies as 'gay', with Sammi reminding Luke about all the girls he is known to have seduced. The film's main act of political defiance is refusing to collude with homonormative expectations about the need for Muslims to 'come out' and thus to join modernity. In *Stag*, the act of fulfilling so-called 'tradition' – i.e., honouring a heterosexual union through matrimony – becomes an act of political defiance, posited against the emotional demands of a white British citizen who is unable to come to terms with his loss of personal and political preponderance. Instead of a submission to Westernisation and so-called 'modernity', *Stag* constitutes a pithy critique of the colonial inception of the power struggle between the former colonisers and the formerly colonised.

This exploration of sociopolitical hierarchies and interethnic desire chimes with Rashid's poetry, particularly 'An/other Country', the opening poem of *Black Markets*, where Rashid's poetic persona watches his white male lover watching the 1980s ITV series *The Jewel in the Crown*:

> Now I watch you watch Sergeant Merrick watch poor Hari Kumar.
> And follow as the white man's desire is twisted,
> manipulated into a brutal beating.
> You are affected by the actor's brown sweating
> body supple under punishment. What moves you?
> The pain within the geometry of the body bent?
> The dignity willed in the motions of refusal?
> A private fantasy promised, exploding
> within every bead of sweat?
> Or is it the knowledge of later:
> how my body will become supple
> for you, will curve and bow to your wishes
> as yours can never quite bend to mine.
> What moves you then?
> My beauty is branded onto the colour of my skin,
> my strands of hair thick as snakes,
> damp with the lushness of all the tropics,
> My humble penis cheated by the imperial wealth of yours.
> Hari's corporal punishment, mine corporeal:
> Yet this is also part of my desire.

> Even stroking myself against your absence
> I must close my eyes and think of England.
>
> (Rashid, 1991, pp. 3–4)

Rashid's poem is invested in interrogating issues of the gaze, colonial sexual and physical paramountcy, and the exoticisation of the 'Other', which is already implicit in the title of the poem, 'An/other Country'. Nevertheless, and despite the poetic voice's self-consciousness about his racial 'Othering' – with references to the colour of his skin, his hair, and his being a metonym for 'the lushness of all the tropics' – there is also an ambivalent submission to these colonial imageries. The numerous rhetorical questions in Rashid's poem allow him to overlay the uneven colonial relationship between Merrick and Kumar in the popular TV adaptation of Paul Scott's *The Raj Quartet* and his own relationship with his white male lover, which foregrounds overlapping issues of desire and objectification, subservience and domination. At the heart of this literary disquisition is the poet's own troubled desire, which becomes entangled with that of his lover and which simultaneously fetishises and scrutinises the colonial relationship.

The joint critique of colonialism and the acknowledgement of homoerotic desire is at the root of what Martin calls the 'doubleness of subjectivity' (Toye and Benson, 1997, p. 454) evoked in Rashid's work, which blurs the boundaries between the personal and the political. Indeed, a fellow Canadian of South Asian heritage, Himani Bannerji, responds to Rashid's questions with some of her own in her epistolary preface to *Black Markets*: 'Does Hari Kumar create the Constable of the Raj even as he is unmade by him […]? How much do you create the white male lover of your dualist duels who holds you, puzzled, in thrall? Are such things even permissible to talk about?' (Rashid, 1991, p. x). She answers some of her own questions, telling Rashid that '[i]t seems you speak of much that is not "correct," not comfortable to linear psyches' (Rashid, 1991, p. x). Bannerji productively highlights issues of reciprocated gazing and the fetishisation of the 'Other' and the self, while appreciating the polemical character of Rashid's queer interethnic desire: just as Kumar and the poetic persona are deemed the objects of white male supremacy, Merrick and the poet's male lover are also wilfully fetishised through the poet's dualistic gaze, torn as it is between resistance and desire, between the pain of ongoing colonial sociopolitical structures and the pleasures sought in queer diasporic desire. Much of what Rashid's poetry examines disorganises the expectations of dominant white, South Asian, and postcolonial readers alike, dealing as it does with the overlapping of sex and dominance across racial and ethnic lines between members of the same sex. As Bannerji rightly suggests, such an epistemic overlap is not 'linear': I argue it is the subject of an ideological and affective assemblage which is the result of Rashid's diasporic condition, torn between his filiation to his South Asian heritage and his affiliation to same-sex interethnic desire, which is the product of global modernity.

Rashid's investment in interethnic same-sex desire and his simultaneous problematisation and embrace of relationships placed in the continuum of colonial and postcolonial histories does not altogether cancel his political awareness about the appropriation and objectification of brown bodies and the downsides of living in the diaspora. Rashid's debut short film, *Surviving Sabu*, contributes its own critique of British and American cultural imperialism. Rashid has long been interested in the figure of the Indian film star Sabu Dastagir (1924–1963), known in the West as 'Sabu', the 'exotic' actor in a series of British and American films, who met an early death after the dwindling of his film career. Sabu was the main subject of Rashid's second poetry book, *Song of Sabu*, published in 1993. From the outset, Rashid's reconstruction of Sabu's voice draws attention to issues of objectification and desire:

> I was born under a Banyan tree. Later I was found. Discovered. *A little devil with a wonderful smile*. Junglee, then a jungle boy. Then a star. I am the most famous Indian in all of the movies. Still. I was chosen. […]
>
> They chose me, they loved me. Men who love only women remarked on the beauty of my body. My skin. Rich and wet like mud in the studio heat. And such dark eyes, they said. […] The edgeless shimmer of my hair. On and on and on in the lights. Floating. Without borders. (Rashid, 1995, p. 11, emphasis in original)

The diasporic borderlessness metonymically embodied by Sabu's shimmering black hair cannot overwrite the acts of exoticisation and desire implied in the poem's opening. Sabu is found, or discovered, an inveterate act of colonial exploration and exploitation. He is wilfully represented according to a Western gaze in the italicised passage '*A little devil with a wonderful smile*', which is later channelled through Sabu's own voice. Sabu's poetic persona realises that heterosexual men – like Sadru, a character in *Surviving Sabu* – feel a certain attraction towards his body because of its Indian beauty. Sabu internalises this Western gaze, when he states 'such dark eyes, *they said*' (emphasis added). Sabu is allegedly 'loved', even by heterosexual men, which at first seems a positive occurrence, but which eventually reveals the insidious workings of Euro-American cultural imperialism, which, joined by Hollywood-style capitalism, enshrine and subsequently dispose of Sabu. Such disposability seems to have led to his untimely death, which the character of Amin in *Surviving Sabu* interprets as the ruthless exploitation of the 'Other' by Western powers.

Sabu's exploitation and the audience's troubled fascination are the subject of the short film *Surviving Sabu*, which also explores the relationship between a Pakistani father, Sadru (Suresh Oberoi), and his British son, Amin (Navin Chowdhry), as tested by their shooting of Amin's first film, a documentary about Sabu. Priya Jaikumar observes that, beyond the uppermost layer of the colonial gaze, Sabu's framing conceals deeper meanings for a variety of audiences: '[Sabu's] body is effeminised, made sexually ambiguous with its attributes of over- or under-dress, yielding his figure to a range of desires outside those ruled by the conventions of heterosexuality, patriarchy and empire' (2012, p. 64). However, Sadru and Amin clash over their disparate perceptions of Sabu. For Sadru, Sabu is an example of an Indian who met success in the West and an embodiment of ideal Indian masculinity. As Claudia Sternberg suggests, 'Sabu's presence on the screen marks a certain moment in film history that provided migrant and diasporic audiences of earlier generations with the pleasure of recognition, seeing black or brown bodies at the heart of popular (if problematic) cinematic narratives' (2010, p. 269). To Sadru's migrant 'pleasure of recognition', Rashid's film adds Amin's qualified viewpoint. As a second-generation diasporic citizen of South Asian Muslim heritage who was born and brought up in Britain, Sadru's son is more politically aware of the camera's exoticising gaze. Whereas Sadru idolises Sabu and wants to lionise him in his son's film, Amin is keen on tackling Sabu's downfall and juxtaposing it with his father's failed attempt at becoming a policeman in 1970s London. Amin's ultimate aim is to critique American and British racism, which enshrined and exploited Sabu from the 1930s until his death, and which also crushed his father's ambitions. Nonetheless, and for all of Amin's anti-colonial impetus, he is also sensually drawn towards Sabu. Indeed, the film goes as far as implying that Sadru's fascination with Sabu's physicality may have influenced his son's attraction to men.

Amin's homosexuality and Sadru's troubled Muslim perception of it are at the centre of Rashid's film, interwoven with issues of the gaze, spectatorship, and filmmaking. Incensed by Amin's negative portrayal of Sabu's fate and by his fatalistic perspective on his own fortunes in Britain, Sadru orders the filmmakers out of the house. Subsequently, and as the trigger of their reconciliation, Rashid offers us two intercalated soliloquies which reveal how both father and son attempt to tune themselves to each other's wavelength. Amin tells the camera: 'he left Uganda with no money; started from scratch; he rebuilt his life. That's *courage*' (*Surviving Sabu*, 1998, emphasis added). Amin tells the audience

'I remember when I first told him I was gay. I remember his face. In that moment, I imagined if he could, he'd swap me for anyone; anyone else's son.' Amin's perception of his father's disapproval of his homosexuality contrasts with his father's reflection. In Sadru's monologue, he states: 'On the night he told us, he stayed over. That took *courage*. He knew we were upset. He wanted us to be alright' (*Surviving Sabu*, 1998, emphasis added). What Sadru and Amin require to trigger their reconciliation is the recognition of each other's 'courage': Sadru's daring in starting afresh in the racially hostile Britain of the 1970s; Amin's bravery in looking beyond his own feelings and considering his parents' initial disappointment about his same-sex desire.

Despite Sadru's alleged lack of political insight into the ideological workings of Sabu's films, his defiance of his son's overarching interpretation also provides a lesson about the continued exoticisation of the racial 'Other'. When Amin accuses Sadru earlier in the film of being complicit with Sabu's colonialist objectification, Sadru searingly responds: 'And those white boys you take up with, how do they look at you?' (*Surviving Sabu*, 1998). Although the comment hurts Amin, it also forces him – and the film's implied multiethnic audiences – to consider the complex interweaving of ethnic objectification and desire that constitute the legacies of colonial social hierarchies. Indeed, in spite of Amin's British accent, dress, and manner, Sadru implies how his son's white lovers may be attracted to him because they perceive him as an ethnic 'Other'.

The resolution of *Surviving Sabu* rehearses an optimistic building of bridges between two generations of migrants that complicate constructions of the 'good Muslim' and which acknowledge the multifaceted nature of diasporic film fandom. In one of the film's last scenes, Amin catches his father watching the Sabu-starring 1942 British-American film *The Jungle Book*. Father and son smoke together for the first time. To Amin's playful quip that 'I thought good Muslims don't drink or smoke', Sadru responds: 'don't teach me about good Muslims' (*Surviving Sabu*, 1998), before they start reciting the lines from the film in unison. Gopinath suggests that 'this scene is Rashid's film speaks to an intergenerational queer diasporic desire between fathers and sons that is produced through and against dominant culture' (2005, p. 68). Sadru then offers to fund the rest of Amin's documentary about Sabu. Amin thanks his father by showing him clips of Sabu in his back garden, which reminds the middle-aged man about being 'back home' in Uganda. Jaikumar writes:

> The son's rejection of Sabu's body as purely constructed through the colonial gaze is nullified by the end of the film when, together and with a

sense of rapprochement, the two of them view *The Thief of Baghdad* as it is projected on the back wall of Sadru's house. Sabu is thus redeemed from the imperial gaze in an exchange about the alternative possibilities of his image for the queer and diasporic gaze. (Jaikumar, 2012, p. 62)

During this moment of intergenerational diasporic communion, Sadru asks Amin about his boyfriend, which takes his son pleasantly by surprise, and which signifies parental acceptance. Rashid's film illustrates the ideological disorientation and reorientation that are part and parcel of living in the diaspora, as well as the ability of film to create a connection between different generations of diasporic viewers. Sadru and Amin's reconciliation involves a shared enjoyment of Sabu's films that encompasses both first-generation diasporic nostalgic identification and second-generation queer diasporic desire, extending the use of Sabu's image above and beyond the imperial gaze, albeit in a manner that is self-consciously laden with what Gopinath calls 'disidentification' (2005, p. 68). This is a nuanced political perspective afforded by Rashid's distinct queer diasporic worldview, which is highly conscious of ongoing issues of racial and sexual objectification of the 'Other', yet which is also aware of overlapping issues of identification and desire that cannot be constructed as simply complicit with imperialism.

Rashid's first short film is reasonably taken to task by Gopinath for eliding the depiction of Amin's mother, who remains off-camera, hence perpetuating queer diaspora's concern with the relationships between fathers and sons already interrogated in *Laundrette*. Rashid's first full-length feature film, *Touch of Pink*, redresses this gender imbalance by focusing on a diasporic mother-and-son relationship. *Touch of Pink* premiered at the Sundance Film Festival in 2004 and was eventually distributed worldwide by Sony Pictures, hence delivering the film to global audiences. It unites the examination of colonial power relations and queer desires across racial divides of *Stag* – and, earlier, of *Laundrette* – as well as the metafilmic style, the debates on intergenerational ideological differences, and the critique of metropolitan racism of *Surviving Sabu*. To these issues, *Touch of Pink* adds a more rounded gendered depiction of Muslim diasporas, chiefly through a Canadian Ismaili man's relationship with his first-generation diasporic mother from East Africa. Due in part to its semi-autobiographical nature, which charts explicitly and implicitly its protagonist's and his family's collective migration from Kenya to Canada and then his own individual journey to Britain, *Touch of Pink* illustrates queer diasporic Muslims' arduous existence at the interstices between Muslim traditionalism, colonial modernity, and diasporic postmodernity. As I will show now, if Rashid's short films are more intent on exploring issues of

Muslim diasporic masculinity, *Touch of Pink* is also concerned with the motivations and internal dilemmas of diasporic Muslim women, who are represented as less imperviously traditional than the younger generation of Muslims brought up in the West would want to believe, and who are not immune to the competing values of tradition and modernity.

The film is a romantic comedy with explicit references to the Hollywood of the 'Golden Age': Rashid mobilises his aesthetic penchant for films featuring Cary Grant, Katharine Hepburn, and Doris Day in order to comment on the pitfalls of postmodernity, particularly on characters' overreliance on Western culture to dictate the scripts of their lives. However, by self-consciously deploying the techniques of classic romantic comedies in a narrative that is zoomed in on a diasporic Ismaili community coming to terms with sexual non-normativity, I argue that Rashid is queering and diversifying the cinematic mainstream. The film's protagonist is Alim (Jimi Mistry), a Canadian young man of Ismaili Kenyan heritage living in London with his partner Giles (Kris Holden-Ried), a white British man, without the knowledge of his Ismaili community in North America. As we gradually find out during the course of the film, Alim's childhood trauma surrounding his homosexuality, his father's untimely death, and his mother's subsequent individual move to London, all drove him to the creation of an imaginary friend, the spirit of Cary Grant (Kyle MacLachlan), who constantly advises him on sentimental and family relationships and who feeds his escapist obsession with old Hollywood films. The film's title,[2] a pun on the Cary Grant and Doris Day 1962 romantic comedy *That Touch of Mink*, and Cary Grant's camera-facing opening monologue, both set the narrative's metafilmic tone as well as its investment in classic Hollywood tropes and aesthetics.

The film's main premise is the visit of Alim's mother Nuru (Suleka Mathew) to London to convince Alim to attend his cousin Khaled's (Raoul Bhaneja) traditional Ismaili wedding, which she uses as an attempt to lure him into a heteronormative Ismaili lifestyle back in Canada. The film explores Alim's difficulty in 'coming out' to his mother, which he repeatedly avoids in consultation with Cary Grant's interfering ghost, as well as his mother's inner and social dilemmas once she learns about his homosexuality. Alim's relationships with Giles and with Nuru are tested by his emotional stumbling block, which is the result of his assumptions about Nuru's Ismaili traditionalism and his related inability to reconcile such ethno-religious ideology with modernity, and with his own postmodern worldview in the diaspora. Nuru, whose growing intimacy with Giles is cut short by Alim's coming out, leaves London in anger about her son and Giles' deception and about their same-sex relationship. Giles then temporarily leaves Alim for white swimmer

Alisdair Keith (Dean McDermott), alienated both by Alim's 'closetedness' and by his heavy-handed dealings with his mother. Alim follows Nuru to Toronto, where he attends Khaled's wedding preparations, thus rekindling his connection with his Ismaili family. He is eventually joined by Giles, whose presence prompts their joint 'coming out' to Alim's whole community, including Nuru's public sanctioning of their same-sex and interethnic relationship.

Such a conventional narrative arc and predictable happy ending do not do full justice to Rashid's formal and thematic adventurousness, particularly when it comes to dealing with the different emotional and ideological wavelengths to which his characters need to tune themselves, as well as with the tensions surrounding moral and social propriety in his own ethno-religious community. Thomas Waugh hails the film as an 'excellent queer subversion of the oppressively heterocentric diasporic wedding cycle of the 1990s and 2000s. *Pink* is an intercontinental, intercultural couple comedy-romance and family melodrama' (2006, p. 495). As such, it has garnered polarised responses from the international Ismaili community. According to Kamal Al-Solaylee (2004), Naaznin Rajani and a movie-going friend felt 'thoroughly humiliated, very insulted, ashamed of ourselves as to how our Ismailis are being portrayed', including being depicted as 'racist as well, not building bridges with *dhorias* [white people]' and focused on material gain and social climbing through education. Despite the fact that Nuru does indeed build a bridge with Giles, it would seem her approval of his relationship with her son is not fully representative of Ismaili communitarian sentiments about their sexuality. As Zahra Meherali observes:

> The film was criticized for its 'deliberate "exposing" of aberration' in the community. By having a homosexual protagonist who is ultimately accepted by his mother, the movie's message was deemed 'tantamount to going against the will of majority, which creates nothing but "division and dissension".' (Meherali, 2004)

Such responses to Rashid's film need to be framed within the context of Ismaili community cohesion and dissent in the diaspora. On the one hand, Clarke argues that criticism within the Ismaili community 'is always made in private [...] One reason why this is so is the social stigma attached to being branded a critic' (1976, p. 487). On the other hand, commenting on sexual diversity in Muslim communities in North America, Momin Rahman and Amir Hussain affirm that '[d]iasporic communities in the large urban centres of the West have openings for those raising critical questions about traditional religious and cultural ideas' (2014, p. 262).

Dissenting Muslim voices either remove themselves from their ethno-religious communities, as illustrated by Alim's initial predicament in *Touch of Pink*, or attempt to change attitudes from within, as becomes the case later on in the film during Khaled's wedding. Rahman and Hussain explain the persistence of Islamic traditionalist values by observing that

> social traditionalism may well be strengthened by the relatively recent migration of the great majority of Muslims to both Canada and the United States as well as by the starkly conservative norms relating to gender and sexuality that prevail in the countries from which they migrated. (Rahman and Hussain, 2014, p. 263)

Nonetheless, values are shown to be constantly on the move, and Rashid's film is testament to the ways in which diasporic Ismaili citizens often have to juggle the conflicting demands of their community's traditionalism and of global modernity.

The blind spot of Alim's predicament is his lack of self-awareness in regarding his mother as nothing but a strict traditionalist bound to East African colonial values. Encouraged by Cary Grant's spirit into believing that Nuru is a 'Muslim from the Third World' and that 'she would not understand' (*Touch of Pink*, 2004) about his sexual orientation, he forces himself to adapt his lifestyle to her expectations, for instance by ridding his flat, with Grant's ghost's help, of any books and photographs that could be interpreted as 'gay', and by evicting Giles to the spare room, thus pretending they are mere 'roommates'. Nuru is initially disappointed by Alim's choice of a non-Muslim housemate. As she sarcastically tells her son in Kutchi, the main language spoken by the Ismaili community, after being introduced to Giles: 'What? There aren't any nice Ismaili boys that need a place to live?' (*Touch of Pink*, 2004). This scene parodically illustrates the ethnic insularity of the Ismailis, which is fledged out in a later scene in the film, in which Alim avoids coming out by pretending to be engaged to Giles' sister Delia (Liisa Repo-Martell).

The scene of Alim's surprise announcement to his mother of his non-existent engagement to Delia posits an ethnic understanding of being 'in the closet' that is metafilmically articulated through techniques appropriated from classic Hollywood romantic comedies. Nuru is by now steadily pressurising Alim into moving back to Toronto, telling him that he could work for his uncle Hassan (Brian George) and that he could have his own home there. When Alim replies that he already has a home, Nuru asks him how he expects to 'attract a nice professional girl when [he is] living with a lodger' (*Touch of Pink*, 2004). Alim retorts

'Are we on the same wavelength?'

that he lives with Giles because he wants to, and finally caves in, revealing that he is in a relationship. When Giles and Delia suddenly arrive in mid-conversation, Giles gleefully assumes that Alim has told Nuru about their same-sex relationship. In this moment of confusion, which already resembles classic comedies' misunderstandings based on characters' partial knowledge, Giles embraces Alim and tells Nuru they were 'concerned about how [she] would handle it', to which Nuru retorts: 'Who could this frightening creature be I can't handle?' (*Touch of Pink*, 2004). At this point, Cary Grant's spirit, who is thoroughly enjoying the scene, motions towards Delia to hesitant Alim, who swiftly calls her name and kisses her on the cheek, announcing that they are engaged, to Delia's and Giles' astonishment, and to the delight of Cary Grant's ghost, who approves of this game of Hollywood-style identity swapping (see Figure 2).

Here, Rashid metafilmically references the identity swap device of one of his main intertexts, the 1940 romantic comedy *The Philadelphia Story*, directed by George Cukor and starring Katharine Hepburn, Cary Grant, and James Stewart, in which the identity of Hepburn's character's father and uncle are swapped in order to avoid social scandal. In *Touch of Pink*, this technique is self-consciously deployed in order to signal the unresolved tensions between Alim's ethno-religious identity and his sexual orientation. While avoiding 'coming out' to his mother, he rebels against her qualms about Delia not being a Muslim by stating that he is no longer a Muslim, ironically adding that he is not going to pretend. Nuru is dismayed by the revelation, which Alim attempts to downplay by stating, even more problematically that: 'I just mean I don't believe in God' (*Touch of Pink*, 2004). This pronouncement indexes an understanding of Muslim identity

Figure 2 *Touch of Pink* (2004), directed by Ian Iqbal Rashid

as a set of cultural traits and not just an issue of faith, but Alim's timing mars the proceedings. Rashid mobilises 'religion' here as a substitute for a debate about sexual orientation that Alim is not yet ready to face: it reveals that he needs to come out to himself as both being a Muslim and a homosexual before he can fully reconcile himself with his multifaceted personality.

In her reading of Rashid's film, Shamira Meghani proposes that queer Muslim narratives posit the closet as a resolutely ethnic space:

> the coming-out narrative is one of religion and ethnicity that needs to be overcome, in order for the closet to reopen. It is not sexual identity that needs to be discovered, but rather religion and ethnicity that stand in the way of what is already known. [...] *Touch of Pink* presents religion and ethnicity as ideas that have become overdetermined and that can be undone. (Meghani, 2014, p. 183)

Meghani rightly suggests that, in the case of queer diasporic Muslims like Alim, while homosexuality has already been internally accepted and externally acknowledged in select social situations, it is faith and ethnicity that preclude the 'closet' from reopening, which is exacerbated, meanwhile, by a diminished sense of self-worth and by internalised racism – what Rashid calls an 'inferiority complex' (Meherali, 2004) – that constitute the lingering legacies of colonial structural imbalances. Alim's problematic 'coming out' as a 'heathen', as Cary Grant's spirit labels it, alienates both his mother and his partner. By self-consciously deploying identity game techniques from classic Hollywood romantic comedies in the exploration of the ethno-religious underpinnings of the closet, Rashid is queering the cinematic mainstream in order to present the moral and social quandaries of an underrepresented religious community and its arduous dealings with issues of sexual non-normativity.

Nuru's bias against Giles and Delia, as non-Muslims in general and non-Ismailis specifically, could be interpreted as being ironic, given her gradual acknowledgement of the hurdles she has encountered in her own life as a woman of South Asian and East African ethnicity in the West. Following her disagreement with Alim over his faith, Nuru becomes more intimate with Giles, who takes her out sightseeing in London and who persuades her to buy a two-piece suit that reminds her of her favourite film in her youth, *That Touch of Mink*. This episode of interethnic bonding starts revealing Nuru's life story and her own experience of metropolitan racism and modernity. In a manner similar to Sadru, the father figure in *Surviving Sabu*, Nuru experienced the insidious workings of

British racism as a young woman in 1970s London. Later in the film, in the wake of a heart-to-heart with Alim about his relationship with Giles, and while personally adapting her late husband's suit for Alim to wear at Khaled's wedding, Nuru dwells on her life story. She ponders how she 'went to London to be Doris Day'. After Alim's father unexpectedly passed away, Nuru tells Alim:

> For weeks I just felt nothing. Then, one afternoon, I went to a film. Suddenly there was a way out. Suddenly, I could be Doris Day, flying off to a new life in London. Trouble is, London wasn't interested in any Indian Doris Days. Then or now. (*Touch of Pink*, 2004)

I would suggest that the Hollywood films that Nuru has taught Alim to love do not offer either of them a suitable script to deal with the difficulties of their lives as diasporic South Asians from East Africa and Canada. Nuru's encounter with Western modernity entails both negative and positive lessons, which involve a gradual detachment from Islamicate traditionalism. As she comically tells Alim, 'I'm not completely backwards. I know about men with men. I subscribe to *Reader's Digest* [...]. I didn't know about you and Giles. I didn't know that you had such feelings for him.' Nuru's lack of a word for same-sex desire demonstrates, as Rashid tells Al-Solaylee, that 'there's no word for homosexual in Kutchi' (*Touch of Pink*, 2004), or at least a non-derogatory or euphemistic one, which indexes the lingering invisibility of queerness within the Ismaili community. Nonetheless, Nuru's gradual acceptance of Alim and Giles' same-sex relationship is symptomatic of her own experience as a woman at the interstices between tradition and modernity, between the heteronormativity of her Ismaili community and the variegated knowledges and values attained in the diaspora.

Like his short films, *Touch of Pink* also extends debates started in Rashid's poetry, in this case surrounding motherhood and sexual orientation. In the second section of the prose poem 'Bastards in the Diaspora', from *The Heat Yesterday*, Rashid explores his own coming out to his mother and their respective dealings with the disorientation and reorientation entailed in diasporic experience:

> *If you are Muslim, you can not be what your* [sic] *are*, she says her sari falling into perfect lines around her as she moves. How can her certainty wound me so much? Me, manoeuvring in my bigger world, such a big world. [...] I suddenly know what to say. *You were not this when we met before, in another place.* The surprise is returned. She has heard all the questions

before but this one. She recovers her head, moves forward, whether to jostle or embrace oblivion, I cannot be sure. I hear the charge of fabric as she walks by me. But the rustle whispers to me: *survival*. My indignation tramples over me in retreat: *Sssssurvival*. (Rashid, 1995, p. 32, emphasis in original)

Rashid captures here the ideological tensions involved in navigating Muslim values and global modernity. The poetic persona's mother's italicised speech reveals an unwavering religious position: Muslim identity is deemed incompatible with homosexuality. This categorical religious pronouncement remains in keeping with her traditional dress, the sari that stands for her South Asian ethnic background and her insistent upholding of its heteronormative traditions. Like *Touch of Pink*'s protagonist, Rashid's poetic persona assumes that his world is bigger than his mother's, that his subsequent migrations entail a more arduous entanglement with global modernity. Similarly to Alim, the poetic persona is consigning his mother to a place of circumscribed traditionalism. However, in a moment of epiphany, he sees through her cultural posturings and disarms her: like him, she is also a diasporic citizen whose values have been tried and tested by colonial and global modernities. Her apparent attempt not to see her son's viewpoint and his homosexuality is undergirded by the shared theme of survival: the sari itself reveals her own dealings with the difficulties of living in the diaspora, which affects both mother and son.

Rashid's poetic and cinematic characters are forced to 'see', to recognise the realities involved in their diasporic experience. In other words, they need to attune themselves to each other's wavelengths in order to understand each other. The emotional conversation between Nuru and Alim in *Touch of Pink* is prompted by her exposure to the duplicity of her nephew Khaled, which Alim himself had attempted to probe in order to gauge whether, by marrying his fiancée Nina, he would be following his personal desires or merely honouring his family's expectations. When he is about to go home for the night, Alim asks Khaled whether he is happy; the latter responds: 'Sure. [...] I'm doing what's expected of me; what I expect of myself' (*Touch of Pink*, 2004). Khaled is a well-regarded member of his Ismaili community because he has qualified as a dentist and he has bought his parents an opulent home where they all live together, and where his future wife will join them. *Touch of Pink*'s stress on education and on its characters' obsession with qualifications and financial betterment is in keeping with ongoing developments in the Ismaili community. As Farhad Daftary (2010) observes, the present spiritual leader of the Ismaili, the fourth Aga Khan, who was educated at Harvard University, has extended his father's modernisation plans, founding learning programmes and institutions which generally benefit all Muslims and so-called Third World countries.³ However, this educational and economic embrace of global modernity, which could be interrogated in terms of its collusion with neoliberalism, still needs to wrestle with religious traditionalism, and *Touch of Pink*'s characters demonstrate their struggle with this ideological inheritance. After Khaled's stag party, as he is drunkenly rummaging through cupboards looking for alcohol, he makes a sexual pass on Alim, who rejects his advances, alleging he is in love with someone else, not the female brain surgeon Nuru has been boasting about, but Giles. Khaled dismisses Alim and Giles' relationship: 'You're in love with a guy? You don't love men, Alim. Fuck 'em, by all means. Hey, he's just in it for the squirt. I bet he doesn't love you. [...] It's just not normal,' to which Alim retorts: 'Hey, if you're normal, count me out. Look at you: a closet drunk, closet queer. Name a closet. You're hanging there' (*Touch of Pink*, 2004). This is a closet in which Muslims drink alcohol and in which they engage in clandestine same-sex practices while upholding a public heteronormative façade. Khaled is incensed by Alim's indictment, telling him not to play 'high and mighty with me. [...] You ever think of your mother?' However, eavesdropping Nuru has been privy to the encounter. When she makes her presence known, Khaled backtracks in a panic: 'Auntie, it's not what you were imagining', to which she responds: 'I'm not imagining. I'm seeing' (*Touch of Pink*, 2004).

What Nuru's eyes have become open to is the doubleness of some Muslims' lives: their internalised homophobia and their attempt to conform to familial ideas of social propriety, which can mask but not fully eradicate their queer desires, as they wrestle with traditionalism and modernity. Sometimes, the need to accommodate oneself to these societal mores involves, like a Hollywood romantic comedy, the ability to pretend. Crucially, Khaled's closeted queerness is disguised not only by himself, but also by his family: when Nuru's sister Dolly (Veena Sood) notices during her son's wedding that Nuru is troubled, she comically tells her:

> It's all right, Nuru. I know. [...] About Alim. Our room used to be next to Khaled's and your boy's got quite a set of lungs. [...] I've always given Khaled his freedom. He's given me all this. [...] Look, I want grandchildren and ice sculptures and place cards. And so do you, Nuru, don't pretend. But if Khaled can do his duty, there's no reason why Alim can't. (*Touch of Pink*, 2004)

Dolly's confession demonstrates that, despite her knowledge of Khaled and Alim's queerness, discovered while they were in their adolescence, when Nuru was in London and Alim was left with Dolly's family, her social aspirations require her son to kowtow to the heteronormativity of their Ismaili community. This sexual normativity is constructed as Khaled's 'duty' to his family, which Alim is also expected to fulfil. As John Esposito suggests, 'Muslim minority communities have faced many hurdles in making the transition [between countries]; other hurdles continue to exist. Muslims and non-Muslim citizens and communities alike face the challenges of living in a pluralistic society' (2002, p. viii). The acceptance of homosexuality is one such stumbling block that still needs to be overcome, as is, I would argue, the acknowledgement of different ideological hurdles for queer citizens of different ethnicities.

While Alim's Ismaili community needs to become attuned to his queerness, his partner Giles also needs to tune himself, crucially, to the different sociocultural demands placed on Alim as a member of an ethno-religious minority plunged into global modernity but which clings on to Islamic traditionalism as a way of reaffirming their group identity. Moreover, the case of Giles' British family demonstrates that queer Muslims are not the only ones dealing with intergenerational ideological differences, and that insidious forms of homophobia also exist within the spaces of the allegedly 'liberal' West. As Meghani declares, '[t]hat religion coheres with race as ethnicity in public discrimination is a key issue in the critical debate about "Muslim homophobia". Its premise is that Muslims are inherently anti-gay, while non-Muslim antagonism towards LGBT people is assumed to be unusual' (2014, p. 173). This view of Muslims as invariably homophobic and of Westerners as usually accepting is qualified by Rashid's depiction of Giles' family. In the scene early on in the film in which Alim and Giles are thrown a surprise anniversary party, Giles' mother (Linda Thorson) and father (Andrew Gillies) appear awkwardly out of place, showing their displeasure about celebrating their son's anniversary in a gay club, which makes Alim equally uncomfortable. As Alim says to Cary Grant's spirit: 'Can you imagine Giles' mother at the Ramrod? Imagine my mum here' (*Touch of Pink*, 2004). Although Alim is disparaging about Nuru, a pre-empting of her unwavering views that, as we have seen, is interrogated elsewhere in the film, this scene evinces how awkwardness about queer spaces is not exclusive to Muslims, but also includes non-Muslims. Although Alim needs to learn to qualify his views on his Ismaili mother's intolerance of homosexuality, *Touch of Pink* avoids the pitfall of constructing all Muslims as uniformly homophobic, and all Western communities as embracing Western sexual exceptionalism.

In addition to the already explored tensions between tradition and modernity, Alim's diasporic predicament as a global citizen also requires his self-effacing negotiation of postmodernity. The ready availability of Western cultural artefacts, such as old Hollywood films, cannot cogently encompass the complexity of his subjective position as a queer diasporic Muslim. Karim suggests:

> The eclectic consumption of the products of many cultures in a way that negates the distinctiveness of each and all is [...] viewed as a feature of postmodernism. Muslims participate along with other people in a global consumerism that has served to rearrange relationships that were constructed by both tradition and modernity. (Karim, 2010, p. 275)

Whereas the negation of distinctiveness is clearly one of the legacies of Hollywood film in Alim's sensibility, the rearranging of his relationships in light of postmodern capitalist culture does not entail a positive lesson, but a prescriptive script of self-negation. The tell-tale sign in *Touch of Pink* of Alim's final liberation, after 'coming out' to his ethno-religious community during Khaled's wedding, is how he overgrows the influence of the paternalistic, colonial, and closeted figure of Cary Grant. Meghani observes that '[t]he coming-out story is subtended by the imaginary friendship Alim has with the film star Cary Grant, whose sexuality has been the subject of contentious debate since his death', adding that 'Cary Grant functions as his closet-gay closet-coach' (2014, p. 180), one that, as a white male surrogate father figure, provides both camp comic relief and the perpetuation of racist colonial ideologies.

Meghani argues that Alim's relationship with the spirit of Cary Grant constitutes an externalisation of what Frantz Fanon calls 'third person consciousness', which is 'productive of non-belonging' (Meghani, 2014, p. 182). Apart from the fuelling of a sense of non-belonging and of ethnic inferiority, Cary Grant's spirit encourages social heteronormativity and private homosexual transgression, as he favours pretence over truthfulness and constantly advises Alim not to tell Nuru about his relationship with Giles. The final drop in Alim and Cary Grant's relationship is the ghost's donning of a conspicuous Gunga Din outfit for Khaled's wedding, which signifies the persistence of colonial imageries inherited from Hollywood. When it eventually dawns on him that Alim is trying to bid him farewell, Cary Grant's spirit finally relents and confesses: 'I envy you. Live every moment of it. Live it for me. [...] Be happy, my little samosa' (*Touch of Pink*, 2004). The spirit is envious of Alim because he is finally out of the closet, unlike the real Cary Grant, who never came out during his lifetime, and because he has a chance to live his own life in the open, as a queer diasporic Muslim of South Asian and East African Ismaili heritage. In finally accepting all facets of his complex personality, Alim learns to negotiate the highs and the lows of postmodernity.

In the end, Alim's shedding of his investment in Hollywood film's glamorous signifier as the ultimate 'message', together with Giles' reconciliation with the personal and cultural distinctiveness of Alim's experience, allows for their relationship to be rekindled, not before one last moment of Hollywood-style misunderstanding: when Alim tells Giles 'there's been another man', meaning Cary Grant, Giles assumes he is referring to Alisdair Keith, the swimmer with whom he has had an affair while Alim was busy reconnecting with his family in Toronto. Seeing his confusion, Giles looks into Alim's eyes and asks: 'Alim, are we on the same wavelength?', to which Alim smiles back and responds: 'We are now' (*Touch of Pink*, 2004). The couple embraces in a balcony overlooking misty Toronto, suitably fading to pink. I would suggest Alim and Giles are finally on the same wavelength due to the interethnic negotiation of their competing ideological demands; in other words, they have acknowledged their culturally distinctive experiences as coloured and white queer citizens, and they have also interrogated the legacies of colonial social hierarchies and Western cultural hegemonies.

Rashid's poetry and films ultimately illustrate the complications of living in the interstices, which involves an awareness of resilient colonial racial hierarchies, as well as of the ideological entanglements entailed in the fraught tensions between ethnic tradition, global modernity, and diasporic postmodernity. Rashid's work ostensibly demonstrates that the only way to overcome the segmentalisation encouraged by discrete ethnic groupings – i.e., white British, Canadian Ismaili – is by becoming aware of issues of interstitiality. In other words, Rashid's poetic personae and cinematic characters need to become attuned to the possibility of being both queer and Muslim, both ethnically South Asian, Muslim, and Western by virtue of their diasporic condition, and of 'Other' citizens, queer or not, to be critical of their ideological inheritance. Rashid's interstitial queerness does not constitute either a witting or an unwitting complicity with imperialism: Rashid's poetry and all of his films, particularly his short films, constitute pithy critiques of the power struggles involved in interethnic relationships, whereby the white British are instilled with a lingering sense of political and personal preponderance over brown bodies.

Rashid's oeuvre is testament, instead, to the inexorable workings of queer diasporic desire, which resists political fixity and demands a recognition of ideological overlaps, contradictions, and assemblage. Rashid's work suggests that the Ismaili community's imbrication in global modernity entails a disorientation and gradual reorientation towards new ways of being that can encompass both Muslim identities and non-heteronormative desires. Whereas Kureishi's work illustrates the dangers of sexual and social conformism and the pitfalls of a strategic cooption into the mainstream, Rashid's work, conversely, carves its own niche within the mainstream, queering its spaces by drawing attention to queer interethnic desire from a Muslim perspective within a cinematic idiom that can appeal to a variety of implied audiences, albeit most visibly geared towards Western audiences familiar with the genre of the romantic comedy. However, the Westernised model of 'coming out' depicted in *Touch of Pink* is not posited as an uncomplicated liberating gesture: it requires arduous negotiation both by Muslims and by their non-Muslim partners, paying due attention to fraught cultural negotiation and the necessary self-effacement about the different positionalities that are involved in forging productive queer interethnic relations. The film's persuasion, nonetheless, does not ultimately reside in its avant-gardism but in its aesthetic familiarity, which, despite its glossy and seductive exterior, reveals ethnic, religious, and sexual complexities tugging at the sturdy segmentalisation of Muslims' identities in the diaspora.

Notes

1   According to Bocock, the Imam, like the Catholic Pope, is infallible; he is also free of sin, and although mainly a religious authority, he can advise on the material aspects of life. According to Farhad Daftary (2010), and by contrast with Sunni Muslims, Ismailis do not participate in the compiling of *ahadith* or in the exegetical tradition of the *tafsir*, since the living Imam and his associates provide all necessary spiritual guidance derived from their interpretation of the Qur'an. According to this, this should make them less easily persuaded by the various homophobic *ahadith* and *tafasir* mobilised in order to castigate queer Muslims throughout history.

2   Veronika Koller undertakes a useful analysis of the use of pink in visual cultures. She observes: 'the cultural status of pink as a femininity marker is such a commonplace that it regularly surfaces in popular culture [.]... The stereotypical association also gives rise to parody as, for instance, in the queer-themed films *Pink Flamingos* (John Waters, 1972), *Ma Vie en Rose/My Life in Pink* (Alan Berliner, 1997), *But I'm a Cheerleader* (Jamie Babbit, 1999) and *A Touch of Pink* (Ian Iqbal Rashid, 2004)' (Koller, 2008, p. 402). In light of this, Rashid would be using pink as a parodic take on Hollywood romantic comedies, as a means of subverting their heteronormativity with a colour-coded reference to dominant camp visualities. Koller further argues that 'the functions of pink in gay culture are an illustration of the double-edged nature of ironic recontextualization, which always both destabilizes and re-instantiates dominant meanings' (2008, p. 415). This use of pink seems to fit not only

Rashid's own deployment of this particular colour in his film's lighting and its final 'fade to pink', but his own destabilisation and re-instantiation of the techniques of Hollywood romantic comedies, which demonstrates his aesthetic indebtedness but also his wish to subvert their whiteness and their heteronormativity.

3   This includes the London-based Institute of Ismaili Studies, now called the Institute for the Study of Muslim Civilisations, and the Aga Khan University, unveiled in Karachi in 1985, and which now has other international branches.

3

Queering Orientalism, Ottoman homoeroticism, and Turkishness in Ferzan Özpetek's *Hamam: The Turkish Bath* (1997)

THE LAST film explored in the 'Queer interethnic desire' section, Ferzan Özpetek's cinematic debut, *Hamam: The Turkish Bath*, released in 1997, contains numerous thematic parallels with the two main works previously analysed, which also happen to be their creators' first feature films. Like Kureishi and Frears' *My Beautiful Laundrette*, Özpetek's narrative is concerned with water and the act of cleansing. Whereas a laundromat was the most highly symbolic location in Kureishi's script, a *hamam*, or Turkish bath, is one of the central spaces in Özpetek's film. Such a focus on aquatic imageries renders their spaces metonymic of queer fluidity. Furthermore, in a vein similar to Ian Iqbal Rashid's *Touch of Pink*, *Hamam* also constitutes a return journey for its diasporic creator – if not for its protagonist – resembling Alim's trip to Toronto to reconnect with his family and his ethnic community. However, in this case, the protagonist is an Italian man visiting Turkey for the first time. Elisabetta Girelli remarks in her critique of *Hamam* that 'Özpetek's return to his point of origin is thus not accomplished directly, being instead heavily mediated by an Italian point of view and an Orientalist vision' (2007, p. 32). One could argue that *Hamam*'s Italian protagonist becomes a cypher of the Italian side of Özpetek's diasporic sensibility, as the filmmaker undertakes an imaginative return to his native city, after years of living in Italy, which is also remarkably different from the Istanbul where he was raised. This journey through the eyes of a foreign focaliser allows Özpetek's Western audiences to empathise with the character and with his tested assumptions about European and Near Eastern sexualities. Simultaneously, the filmmaker's Turkish inception enables his challenge to dominant Islamist and Kemalist homophobia in contemporary Turkey. This double orientation towards Western and Eastern audiences is most subversively articulated in a derelict Turkish bath and the family house containing it, where private and public spaces are queered, and where personal and communal discourses and desires are visibly confronted, particularly the systemic character of Turkish homophobia. I undertake here a rereading of *Hamam* that qualifies some of the most astringent critiques of the film which ascribe it a Westernised Orientalist aesthetic complicit with foreign representations of Turkey.

In her study of the decline and redevelopment of bathing culture in Istanbul, Nina Cichocki observes that, alongside foreign visitors, 'modernizing Turks who have previously shunned these Ottoman institutions are also rediscovering *hamams*, but they do it as a result of what [Mary Louise] Pratt has called "autoethnography" and in a manner that can be called internal tourism' (2005, p. 107). Through his film, Özpetek visually rediscovers *hamams*, but his perspective gains authority by merging internal and external perspectives, becoming a form of 'native informant', whereby the vantage point of an Italian outsider, and his interethnic relationships in late twentieth-century Turkey, is deployed in order to reimagine Özpetek's place of origin from his diasporic perspective. I argue here that, instead of subscribing solely to a Western and Orientalist perspective, Özpetek's imaginative revisitation of Turkey's bathing culture arises not so much from his wish to embrace Western discourses of modernity as from his conservationist interest in recovering the Ottoman homoerotic past, which was disavowed by the Westernising impetus of nineteenth-century Ottoman and twentieth-century Kemalist modernities. However, Özpetek's excavation of Ottoman homoeroticism also updates it for contemporary sensibilities and makes it more in keeping with culturally assembled contemporary queerness.

Some film reviewers and critics have pointed out there is a certain element of nostalgia in *Hamam* (Onaran, 1997; Anderlini-D'Onofrio, 2007; Girelli, 2007), but this is not so much nostalgia for a place, since Özpetek still visits his native city on a regular basis, but for Istanbul at a particular *moment* in history when same-sex practices were an intrinsic part of the city's life. I wish to demonstrate that, whereas the seductive Orientalism articulated in Özpetek's cinematic narrative seems, on a superficial level, to align him with old-fashioned Orientalists who bolstered a picture of Turkey as a place of base hedonism, he does so in a way that productively excavates a repressed aspect of the Ottoman past against the constraints, as I illustrate, of dominant Kemalist modernity and Islamist homophobia, and in response to the destructive urban redevelopment spurred on by neoliberalism and globalisation. In addition, I henceforth argue that the recovery of historical homoeroticism does not constitute retrogressive complicity with outdated models of sexuality, but a micropolitical assemblage of Ottoman homoeroticism and contemporary queerness which qualifies earlier versions of same-sex desire while also resisting the Western notion of *homosexuality*.

In the *Directory of World Cinema: Italy*, Daniel Hipkins describes Özpetek as 'a rare example of a high-profile foreign film director working in Italy' (2014, p. 94). Born in Istanbul in 1959, Özpetek left Turkey when he was twenty years old to study film in Italy, where he has worked and lived ever since. A foreign-born presence within Italy's predominantly white film industry, Özpetek is often singled out as one of the country's important 'ethnic' directors, albeit often in a tokenistic and perfunctory manner. To offer two separate examples, in the essay collection *Queer Italia: Same-Sex Desire in Italian Literature and Film*, editor Gary Cestaro asserts that '[s]ome of the most successful Italian films of recent years involving same-sex desire are by the Turkish-born Ferzan Özpetek' (2004, p. 17). This assessment takes place in the last endnote of Cestaro's introduction to an essay collection dealing chiefly with the work of white Italian filmmakers. Furthermore, in an essay on the past in present-day Europe, Rosalind Galt observes in one of her endnotes:

> Since the 1990s, a series of transnational-themed films have been released in Europe that have dealt with questions of immigration, ethnicity, and nation. Examples include *Beautiful People* (Jazmin Dizdar, 1999), *Steam: The Turkish Bath* (*Hamam*, Ferzan Ozpetek, 1997), and *Last Resort* (Pawel Pawlikowski, 2000). However, these films are overwhelmingly contemporary in setting and narrative, seeking to document recent cultural change rather than to reread the past. (Galt, 2005, p. 19)

Galt's misjudged assessment of Özpetek's film, which, despite being set in the present is highly concerned with ways of rereading and recovering the Ottoman past, demonstrates persistent issues of ethnic visibility in critical assessments of queer Italian cinema, possibly because of Özpetek's celebrated yet also complicated status as a 'transnational' filmmaker (Girelli, 2007; Galt, 2005, 2013; Boschi, 2015), which signals ambiguous national and political allegiances. Hipkins describes Özpetek's films as 'family melodramas with a queer twist' (2014, p. 94). As another early example of Özpetek's focus on the Ottoman past and on contemporary queerness, Özpetek's second film, *Harem Suare* revisits the female homosociality of the Ottoman Empire's last *harem* before the abolition of the Caliphate, concentrating on the diminished fortunes of the Sultan's wives and concubines, in particular that of the Sultana Safiye and her romantic relationship with her attendant, the eunuch Nadir. In turn, *His Secret Life*, released in Italian as *Le Fate Ignoranti* (Ignorant Faeries), Özpetek's third film as writer and director, deals with how an Italian man's widow, Antonia, deals with her late husband's queerness by striking a friendship with his male lover, Michele, and with his queer flatmates in contemporary Rome, including a Turkish rape victim called Serra. In *Le Cuore Sacro* (Sacred Heart), Özpetek continues the critique of modern urban development through an Italian female protagonist, a rich real-estate entrepreneur whose eyes gradually become more open to the needs of others, particularly Italy's poor. My analysis here concentrates chiefly on *Hamam* because of its explicit focus on queer interethnic relations, and due to its constituting Özpetek's most prominent depiction of queerness in contemporary Istanbul from his perspective as a diasporic filmmaker.

Despite its intermittent cooption into Turkish and Italian cinema, *Hamam* is an Italian, Turkish, and Spanish co-production, which means the film cannot be wholly claimed by any national project, belonging instead to the elusive realm of transnational or diasporic cinema. *Hamam* opens with the sudden death of the protagonist's aunt, Anita,[1] read in voiceover by Ludovica Modugno when Francesco peruses her letters addressed to her estranged sister Giuliana. Her body is discovered off-screen in the film's opening scene by one of her carers and long-time companions, Perran (Serif Sezer), a middle-aged Turkish woman, who loudly announces it to her husband Osman (Halil Ergün) through the window. This scene is offered in Turkish with no subtitles, placing the Western viewer in a position of cultural and linguistic alienation; the scene constitutes, according to Girelli, 'Özpetek's act of self-inscription as a Turk in the filmic text, expressing knowledge and control from an insider's position' (2007, p. 34). After conveying the official written communication of Anita's death to her remaining family in Italy, the film cuts to the Italian capital, where Anita's heir, Francesco (Alessandro Gassman) and his wife Marta (Francesca d'Aloja) lead an affluent but loveless life as interior designers. After a heated confrontation about who must deal with the situation and who ought to stay behind to manage their business, the film presents Francesco's physical and spiritual journey as he heads to Istanbul to sell off his estranged aunt's property. There, he eventually meets his aunt's 'adoptive' Turkish family, composed of Perran, her husband Osman, their young daughter Fusun (Basak Köklükaya), who soon becomes subtly infatuated with Francesco, and their young son Mehmet (Mehmet Günsür), who later becomes Francesco's lover. Francesco's initial coldness and diffidence towards Turkey, and his patent wish to be swiftly rid of all of his aunt's possessions, are gradually superseded by irresistible curiosity about the place and its inhabitants.

Francesco's growing attraction towards Turkey and Turkish people is first incepted in his initial visit to an old *hamam*. Encountering a frail old man in need of a glass of water, Francesco escorts him to a nearby Turkish bath, where the Italian man – and, by extension, Özpetek – encounters a previously unknown aspect of the city's culture. In his reading of the scene, Joseph Allen Boon observes:

> in an exchange of reverse shots, Francesco finds himself the object of a bather's intense gaze and looks back – the first indication of male-male attraction in the film – then accepts the older man's invitation to bathe: entering its world of steam, he finds himself transported. (Boon, 2015, p. 156)

Francesco is 'transported' to an earlier period of Ottoman bathing, before the onset of modernity and the general availability of instant hot water at home. This cleansing space, Francesco finds, is steaming with latent same-sex desire. His cultural and sexual curiosity is spurred on by the subsequent discovery that his aunt's house also contains a shut-up traditional Turkish bath. Francesco lies to Mehmet in front of the boy's family, when he says he has never been to a *hamam*, either wary of opening up too swiftly to his rather overfamiliar hosts, or hoping for an introduction to Turkish bathing culture from the younger man. The haunting proximity of Anita's old Turkish bath, *Aynali Sultan Hamami* – diegetically translated as 'the *hamam* of the Sultan of the Mirrors' – kindles both Francesco's restorative instincts as an interior designer and his latent queer desire, following the wake of the tantalising homosociality experienced in the Cimili *hamam*.

Although Francesco is at first tempted by his contact Zozo (Zozo Toledo) to sell the building to an ambitious female developer, played by Zerrin Arbaş, Francesco's look at the model of the shopping centre and leisure complex intended for the area brings home to him the stark realisation that the steely eyed developer has plans to flatten the whole neighbourhood. He refuses to sign the papers and decides, instead, to restore his aunt's *hamam* to its former glory, during which he becomes erotically involved with his hosts' son, Mehmet. When Francesco's wife, Marta, travels to Istanbul to tell her husband about her relationship with their business partner, Paolo, and about her wish to divorce him, Francesco appears to her remarkably transfigured into a much more relaxed and less self-centred, materialistic person. Unable to find the privacy in the busy family home

Figure 3 *Hamam: The Turkish Bath* (1997), directed by Ferzan Özpetek

to make her feelings known to him, she discovers his affair with Mehmet during a nocturnal visit to the family's *hamam*, which is connected to the house through a passageway. She spies both men bathing shirtless in loincloths, with Mehmet casually reclining on Francesco while sharing a roll-up cigarette presumably filled with marihuana. Marta seems to consider joining them, as she checks her physical appearance. However, when she looks again, almost ready to make her presence known, she witnesses Francesco and Mehmet kissing passionately (see Figure 3), a moment intensified by the extra-diegetic music,[2] after which she silently backs away and retreats to the bedroom. Marta repeatedly tries to confront Francesco about this nocturnal revelation, but Francesco is too engrossed in the restoration of the *hamam* and in his relationship with Mehmet, and the family's communal spaces are always too busy for a private heart-to-heart.

Marta's bottled-up internal conflict about her husband's homosexual affair eventually manifests itself when she becomes intoxicated at Fusun's engagement dinner. Perhaps intuiting Francesco and Mehmet's affair and the former's lack of erotic interest in her, Fusun had rashly decided to become engaged to a previously unsuccessful suitor, a union that Marta helps reverse later. Emboldened by wine, Marta tells the whole party that she and Paolo have been having an affair for several years behind Francesco's back, listing all the places where they have had sex. Embarrassed by his wife's drunkenness and her scandalous public confession, Francesco takes her away from the restaurant and, in the heated confrontation that follows, they argue about Francesco's real motivations in Turkey. An incensed Marta tells him that she does not believe his 'laid back, mister nice family guy' persona and that he does not 'give a shit about Turkey', adding that she thinks he is 'taking advantage of the situation' to do 'what [he was] afraid to do in Rome' (*Hamam*, 1997). Here, Marta is ostensibly accusing Francesco of being an Orientalist sex tourist, and that Turkey merely provides a welcome release from the heteronormativity and Catholic-infused homophobia of their native Italy. The argument continues back in the house, where Francesco hits back, affirming that Marta has no right to judge, since she started having her affair with Paolo long before his trip to Turkey. When Marta states '[i]t's not the same thing. [...] I betrayed you with a man', Francesco bluntly responds '[s]o did I', which brings a smile to their faces, almost despite themselves.

Unable to fathom a full reconciliation, the couple agree to separate. However, before departing from Turkey, after a fond farewell to Perran and a perfunctory, and reciprocated, 'good luck' wish to Mehmet, Marta calls in on a family friend who used to know Anita, Oscar (Carlo Cecchi), where she discusses her lingering love for the transformed Francesco. Marta confesses that, whereas she was ready to divorce Francesco on her way to Istanbul, now that the divorce papers have been signed, she cannot deny she finds his personality attractive once again. However, this intimate scene is juxtaposed with the scene where Francesco is knifed and killed on the doorstep of his aunt's house by an anonymous assassin, who is supposedly linked to the frustrated urban developer, although I suggest this scene invites a double reading. After the hospital scene in which Marta and Mehmet embrace in mourning surrounded by almost the whole neighbourhood, and in which she puts on Francesco's wedding band, the film's final scene, offering a view of Istanbul's iconic skyline, reveals Marta has taken over the restoration of the *hamam* in a voiceover that is part of an affectionate letter to her 'dear' Mehmet. Francesco's lover has left his neighbourhood in order to pursue his studies and, perhaps, also to escape the despondency following Francesco's death and his native city's systemic homophobia. Smoking a cigarette encased in Anita's metal cigarette holder shown earlier in the film, Marta has picked up Anita and Francesco's lead, bearing the torch of interethnic connection and urban preservation in contemporary Istanbul. As Marta tells Mehmet, '[a]lmost every afternoon, I go down to the *hamam*. All the work is finished now.' Although this may seem a conventional melodramatic plot involving a journey to an exotic location in need of foreign aid and a tragic 'coming out' story, the film's visual encoding of homoeroticism and its Orientalist yet queering approach provide a complex assemblage of cultural sensibilities which restores Ottoman homoeroticism, while resisting sturdy dominant ideologies of Turkish and Italian capitalist modernities. The film offers implicit challenges to the Catholic homophobia of Francesco and

Marta's native Rome, to the homophobia of the Kemalist national project, and to resilient Islamicate homophobia still underpinning Turkish culture.

Hamam is eminently intersectional in its interweaving of issues of sexual orientation, interethnic relations, gender, and urban development, rendering it not a 'single issue' film merely dealing with its subjects' sexualities, although their unsettling power is meant to bolster the film's critique of Turkish and Italian modernities. William Hope suggests that no viewer of Özpetek's film will 'emerge without having had the fundamental tenets of their existence – their career, their lifestyle, and the nature of the interpersonal relations – challenged to the core'; he also adds that, although the film 'in no way constitutes politicized art, […] it demands a complete reappraisal of the values that has come to characterise Western capitalist society' (2005, p. 13). In other words, Özpetek does not adopt Francesco's viewpoint simply to paint a picture of Istanbul from a perspective akin to that of his implied Western audiences, but utilises Francesco and Marta's Italian inception to critique the pernicious materialism of contemporary Italy, which is not inverted in Turkey, as 'classical' Orientalism would have it, but is mirrored in the recurrent threat of capitalist urban development embodied by Francesco's would-be buyer and his eventual murderer. Francesco could be interpreted, as Girelli (2007) suggests, as the Orientalist hero, the white saviour who travels to Turkey to save the helpless country from itself. Indeed, after he refuses to sign the deal with the cunning Turkish developer, Perran embraces him, telling him that he did the right thing, and calling him a 'brave boy' (*Hamam*, 1997). It could be assumed that the precious *hamam* would have never been saved had it not been for his – and his aunt's – enterprising Western influence.

Nonetheless, Francesco's confrontation with his aunt's Turkish caretakers forces him to mend his initial business-like ways, and he cannot be deemed just a foreign capitalist looking for financial gain in a backward country, or a sex tourist seeking mere erotic satisfaction: a deep change happens within Francesco that shakes up his whole worldview, distancing him from Italian capitalist modernity and homophobia through his close intimacy with his Turkish hosts. The civilising or beneficent role of the Italian characters in the film is complicated in a visually compelling and highly symbolic fashion by two mirrored scenes. In one of his first forays into Istanbul, Francesco comes across a dilapidated building with a sign that reads, in Turkish: 'This building was built in 1921 by Italian architect Carlo Zanichelli' (my translation), which he enters and ogles at silently. Later in the film, Marta undertakes a similar lone exploration of the city, after discovering Francesco and Mehmet's affair. Seeking shelter from the pouring rain, Marta walks into the building designed by the Italian architect, where she finds an old woman smoking. Marta smiles at her and the woman reciprocates. Marta then takes off her wedding band and gives it to her, without exchanging any words, in a moment of emotional liberation from her failed heterosexual marriage and of female interethnic communion. The silent and eerie nature of these two scenes almost invites a psychosocial reading, whereby a ruined building stands for the outdated yet resilient civilising role of foreign benefactors in Turkey. The bequest of a wedding band epitomises the only possible act of communication, restricted to a material act of charity – ultimately, a gesture of capitalist moral self-appeasement. Whereas Francesco's reciprocated relationship with Mehmet reaches beyond such materialism, Marta is still restricted to a material and potentially colonialist understanding of her role in Istanbul, which still requires a more productive connection with Turkey.

Hamam's deployment of exterior and interior spaces and their interweaving of personal affect and collective ideologies is similar to the queer overlaying of private and public spaces in Kureishi and Frears' *My Beautiful Laundrette*. In Özpetek's case, the film offers a 'visual language of doors, crossings, interiors, and spaces within spaces – simultaneously mysterious, beckoning, self-revelatory' (Boone, 2015, p. 157). The Turkish bath where homoeroticism finally breaks into the surface is at the centre of this interplay of thresholds and spaces. In order to appreciate Özpetek's recovery of Ottoman homoeroticism, it is necessary to consider Turkish baths' historical relationship with homosociality. Boone observes, via the work of Abdelwahab Bouhdiba, that

> the hamam [is] a transitional zone that links religiously mandated purification rituals, the latent eroticism of single-sex world, and, for every boy, memories of his banishment from the comforting realm of the female bath on reaching puberty and simultaneous initiation into the competitive realities of male homosociality. (Boone, 2015, p. 78)

In light of this historical perspective, *hamams* constitute spaces where Islamic religious ablutions used to take place, but also where the religiously infused enforcement of gender segregation provided an avenue for unorthodox sexualities. The allegedly timeless homoeroticism afforded by this recovered homosocial space has been charged with conforming to an Orientalist construction of Turkey as a place of decadence and stasis. Girelli supports this view by pointing out that '[t]he hamam also serves a prime function in the film's overt Orientalist plot, allowing the "Western" Francesco and Marta, like the aunt before them, to assist the preservation of traditional Turkishness' (2007, p. 29). In Girelli's assessment, foreigners are constructed as benefactors in a country in need of foreign intervention. However, Turkishness is essentialised here and posited as the backbone of Turkish tradition and history, which evinces the ideological seductiveness of modern Turkishness. Girelli's argument fails to account for the multiethnic nuances of the Ottoman past Özpetek excavates. I would argue that what is being preserved in Özpetek's film is not 'traditional Turkishness'. Turkishness was only one element of Ottoman identity, and not the dominant one it is in contemporary Turkey. What Özpetek's film advocates is Ottoman multiculturalism and its investment in multifaith communities and homosociality.

Ussama Makdisi defines Ottoman Orientalism as 'a complex of Ottoman attitudes produced by a nineteenth-century age of Ottoman reform that implicitly and explicitly acknowledged the West to be the home of progress and the East, writ large, to be a *present* theater of backwardness' (2002, p. 769, emphasis in original). In Makdisi's view, the Ottoman Empire's agents became aware of the Empire's decadence, submitting to the European narrative of being 'the sick man of Europe', and embracing an idea of Western superiority that constructed the Ottoman present as a time of backwardness in urgent need of modernisation. In addition, Katarina Dalacoura observes, via the work of Ali Shariati, that '[i]n modern day Turkey Kemalists and Islamists share equally negative responses to homosexuality but "the former [Kemalists] are probably more hateful because it threatens the essence and principles of the Republic"' (2014, p. 1295). Moreover, Tarik Bereket and Barryd Adam underline the ongoing dominance of Islamic groups within the allegedly secular republic: 'it is a country with a Muslim majority (99%), where Islam maintains a strong influence on values and norms (Müftüler-Bac, 1999), and where an Islamist political party, the Justice and Development Party, came to power in 2003' (2008, p. 205). The narratives of late Ottoman, Kemalist, and Islamist heteronormative modernities are crucially subverted in Özpetek's film. Although supposedly Orientalist and nostalgic for the Ottoman past, Francesco and Mehmet's same-sex affair in the *hamam* becomes, in itself, an inversion and subversion of the traditional Ottoman same-sex dynamic. Bereket and Adam acknowledge how 'Stephen Murray's extensive discussion of age-structured homosexualities during the Ottoman Empire, in which the "boy" is sexually subordinant to an older man who takes responsibility for mentoring him in becoming a masculine adult warrior, shows that this form of homosexual bonding was once institutionalized' (2008, p. 210). In opposition to the dominant Ottoman pederastic model in which an older man grooms a beardless pubescent boy, Özpetek offers us a different homoerotic relationship: in *Hamam*, it is the younger Mehmet who initiates the older Francesco into the bath's homoerotics. In a scene where intermittent close-ups of Mehmet and Francesco in a *hamam* build up an intimate visual tone, Mehmet recalls his own initiation into the pleasures of the Turkish bath. Mehmet looks at Francesco meaningfully as he tells him about the physical techniques used to 'relieve the spirit' (*Hamam*, 1997). Although in the scene where Francesco and Mehmet kiss within Marta's view, Francesco takes the lead and physically towers over Mehmet, it is significant that Mehmet is the one who first initiates Francesco. In addition, while Mehmet may be younger than his Italian lover, the age gap between the two men is not intergenerational, hence their qualification of age-structured Ottoman homoeroticism.

Özpetek's articulation of homoeroticism can be interpreted as not just a mere replication of Ottoman same-sex hierarchies, but as an assemblage of 'classical' Ottoman bathing homoeroticism and contemporary age-egalitarian sexuality, whereby lovers are deemed equal in the relationship and of mutual affective benefit to each other. As Francesco later tells Marta, 'Mehmet encourages me a lot, listens to me; he understands. I'm good with him' (*Hamam*, 1997). In light of this mutual understanding, the film does not encourage the traditional Islamicate sexual binary of dominance versus subservience. Indeed, the film does not elucidate who takes the active and passive role — it does not even clarify whether Francesco and Mehmet engage in penetrative sex at all. The narrative purposefully forecloses sexual categorisation according to traditional sexual roles, favouring, instead, an open-ended form of queer fluidity. Moreover, Mehmet seemingly attempts to communicate, indirectly, that he does not wish to stand between Francesco and his wife, stating that he likes her, and observing, with salacious camaraderie tinged with male homosexual misogyny, that 'she even has nice tits' (*Hamam*, 1997), which makes Francesco smile. Here, Özpetek's narrative flouts the binary opposition of heterosexuality and homosexuality, allowing their characters to thrive in unfettered queerness. Nonetheless, a counter-reading is also possible here, since the film predates Özpetek's public 'coming out' and his recent marriage to Simone Pontesilli in 2016.

Kılıçbay quotes Özpetek's response to a journalist's question about the film's homosexual theme: 'I don't approve of such a concept as homosexuality. I think sexuality shouldn't have boundaries. I could fall in love either with a man or a woman' (2008, p. 118). According to Griffiths' account,

> He goes on to argue that the Italian protagonist, mesmerized by both Istanbul and the wonderful hospitality of the Turkish family, could well have fallen in love with a female member of the family, like the daughter or even the mother. The same line is parroted by Mehmet Günsür, who

played Mehmet, the son who seduced Francesco in the hamam [...], and by Alessandro Gassman [...] who played Francesco. (Kılıçbay, 2008, p. 118)

In avoiding the concept of *homosexuality*, both the filmmaker and the actors may be protecting their masculinities while unwittingly enacting their own internalised homophobia. In a recent study, Cenk Özbay suggests '[g]ay men in Istanbul have an increasing obsession with the "straight-acting" and "straight-looking" self-presentation, which demands a certain degree of heterosexual masculinity for erotic engagement' (2010, p. 650). A demeanour akin to heterosexuality is shown as being desired in Özpetek's film, with neither Francesco nor Mehmet conforming to the traits of femininity and delicacy often associated with homosexuality in Islamicate and non-Islamicate cultures alike. Nonetheless, whereas Francesco *could* have fallen in love with Fusun or Perran, it is significant that he does so with Mehmet instead. The choice is not arbitrary and is ultimately one of the most subversive aspects of Özpetek's cinematic narrative.

On the one hand, and in light of the filmmaker and actors' unwillingness to concede to *homosexuality*, the character of Mehmet may feel compelled to present himself as interested in women in order to protect his own masculinity in a heteronormative society such as modern Turkey. On the other, the film may be proposing a queer model, since, according to Serena Anderlini-D'Onofrio, 'Özpetek's bicultural diegetic spaces are hospitable to multiple mechanisms of suture. For example, in [*Hamam*], the central character starts monosexual and becomes bisexual in the course of the story. This allows both straight and gay viewers to identify with him' (2007, p. 123). She also proposes that 'Özpetek's films present ludic structures that play with people's latent or denied bisexual desires to model an ethic of care, respect, and emotional sustainability' (Anderlini-D'Onofrio, 2007, p. 125). In addition, James S. Williams suggests that 'the film itself is more interested in the bounds and physical spaces of homosociality than in homosexuality. Indeed, no name is given to the men's homoerotic desire, which takes place quite naturally in a society that is still sexually segregated' (2010, p. 208). Although the real gender segregation in the film is arguable, it is true that *Hamam* and its maker do not provide any sexual labels, including *bisexual*. However, homoeroticism remains a catalyst in the film. As one of the narrative's main focalisers, Francesco constitutes the blueprint of the film's implied spectator: a sexually corseted subject ruled by society's heteronormativity who needs to become attuned to queer sexual fluidity.

It is also significant that the relationship between Francesco and Mehmet is interethnic, for this constitutes part of Özpetek's queering of Ottoman

Orientalism. Whereas Ottoman nineteenth-century modernising impulses, and subsequently also Kemalist modernity, decided to turn its back against seemingly decadent and old-fashioned Ottomanness, giving Turkishness a more prominent guiding role in the modern national project, Özpetek's film favours a more multiethnic and multifaith envisioning of the nation, in the spirit of the Ottoman Empire. Stephen O. Murray cites Lord Kinross' idea that

> the Ottoman Empire was 'in no sense a national[ist], but [rather] a dynastic and multiracial empire, whose varied populations, whether Turkic or otherwise, Moslem or Christian or Jewish, were above all else Ottomans, members of a single body politic which transcended such conceptions as nationhood, religion, and race'. (Murray, 2007, p. 102)

This historical interpretation is supported by Kevin Robins and Asu Aksoy, who suggest that '[t]he Lebanese historian, Georges Corm, has characterised the Ottoman Empire in terms of an astonishing complexity of identity – multicultural, multi-confessional, multi-lingual' (2000, p. 192). The character of Mehmet, and by extension his family, makes no differentiation between himself and Francesco, or his aunt Anita, regardless of their being Muslims or Christians of different ethnicities and nationalities. This inclusivity makes reference to a model of Ottoman citizenship that sidestepped man-made barriers and encouraged the merging of ethnicities and religions. Hence, while queering Ottoman homoeroticism by updating it and making it more in keeping with contemporary queerness, Özpetek's film also adopts the ethos of Ottomanness as a plural and multicultural identity, in defiance, by extension, of the Turkish monoculturalism encouraged by the contemporary Turkish Republic and its repression of non-Turkish ethnic groups. Seen in this light, I would suggest that the homoerotic and interethnic relations microcosmically encapsulated in the *hamam* excavate and transform prior sites of Ottoman homoeroticism and multiculturalism against the onset of homogenising Turkish modernity.

Özpetek's approach to homoeroticism must also be regarded in relation to his distinctive vision as a diasporic filmmaker, for *Hamam* bears the imprint of the legacies of Ottoman and Roman homoeroticism. Analysing the film's echoes of Roman mythology, Angela Tumini proposes:

> Ozpetek's intention is to reconstruct a *locus amoenus* for his protagonist, which is reminiscent of the tradition set by classical poetry and mythology, thus adding a legendary flavour to the scenes. In *Metamorphoses*,

for example, Ovid weaves the tale of Narcissus [...]. Like a spellbound Narcissus, Francesco wanders around the floating waters of the Turkish bath awakening his senses and his desire to confront a different culture. (Tumini, 2009, p. 52)

Tumini suggests that Ovid's *Metamorphoses* is one of Özpetek's intertexts in the film, and that the theme of transformation that features in Roman mythology is redeployed in Özpetek's film most manifestly through the character of Francesco. Francesco requires a *locus amoenus* – an amenable place – in this case his aunt's old *hamam*, for his personal transformation to occur.

In addition to this diasporic assemblage of Roman and Ottoman cultural references and sensibilities, on a larger scale, there is also an aesthetic and spatial link to the more recent Italian past in the film's representation of contemporary Istanbul. Anderlini-D'Onofrio lucidly observes that 'in [*Hamam*], there is an emphasis on Istanbul as a run-down, but mysteriously charming city which is reminiscent of an older Italy – the Italy of neorealismo before the economic boom turned the country into a Mecca of style, design, and consumerism' (2007, p. 123). As it turns out, Özpetek's cinematic style constitutes an aesthetic tribute to an older style of Italian filmmaking, which demonstrates his film provides a simultaneous critique of Turkish and Italian modernities. Aesthetically speaking, Özpetek's Istanbul is not so much a retrogressive return to a premodern version of the Turkish city, but a visual tribute to an earlier cinematic envisioning of postwar Italy, the country he came to know and love as a diasporic filmmaker in Rome. Hence, this vision of Istanbul constitutes an aesthetic assemblage of the Turkish and Italian dimensions of Özpetek's diasporic sensibility.

While Özpetek is keen on excavating and transforming repressed sites of homoerotic desire and multicultural citizenship against the ravages of rampant Turkish and Italian modernities, which are still charged with Islamic and Christian homophobia, he cannot help signalling his characters' lingering stumbling blocks with regard to forming viable same-sex relationships. Crucially, the relationship between Francesco and Mehmet is carefully kept under wraps, and only Marta knows about their erotic liaison because of her nocturnal visit to the Turkish bath. In the film, family life is visually organised around the dining table. In her study on queer phenomenology, Sara Ahmed ponders, '[t]he dining table is a table around which a "we" gathers. [...] The dining table is a table around which bodies gather, cohering as a group through the "mediation" of its surface, sharing the food and drink that is "on" the table' (2006, p. 80). The dining table is where Francesco is given his proper welcome by Perran and Osman's family, with a Turkish feast, and where he is welcomed into their family; it is also where life stories – about Anita, about his own life – are shared, like food. As he gradually 'coheres' with the Turkish family group, Francesco is eventually joined by Marta, who looks visibly incommoded by Perran's entreaties to eat more of her food; at another point, around the coffee table, she tries to hide her consternation at Perran's accurate reading of the coffee grinds in Marta's cup, which point to there being potentially two men in her life: Francesco and Paolo; or, in an alternative reading, Francesco and Mehmet. While the Turkish family dining table constitutes a site of hospitality and coherence, it also remains a space of shared normative values, for the objects and ideas that are shared are only the ones that, as Ahmed intimates, are readily available 'on' the table. The silence surrounding Francesco and Mehmet's same-sex affair demonstrates their affection could not possibly be shared around the dining table, which reminds us it remains a considerable taboo in modern Turkey. As Jürgen Gerhards surveys, '[o]wing to the fact that Turkey is a secular republic, homosexuality is not illegal. But despite this legal protection, public expressions or displays of homosexuality remain largely taboo in the general public' (2010, p. 16–17). Francesco and Mehmet's visual presentation and manner around the dining table are suitably heteronormative: no telling sign of affection is ever passed between dishes, and they tend not to sit in close proximity to each other, as though trying to avoid familial conjecture. Once Marta has found out about their relationship, she also does not dare to bring up the topic around the dining table, in front of the whole family, and she continuously attempts, unsuccessfully, to have a heart-to-heart with her husband, which eventually takes place on the street in the midst of Fusun's engagement party. I would argue that the Turkish table thus remains the site of heteronormative familial performance, metonymic of Kemalist modernity.

In attempting to resolve this complicated love triangle, Özpetek opts for a tragic outcome for his 'hero'. Called to the front door by the doorbell, Francesco encounters a strange man, who asks him whether he is Francesco, the Italian. Francesco answers in the affirmative, and after a short hesitation, the nameless individual takes out a knife and plunges it into Francesco's abdomen before running away. This fatal scene welcomes a double reading: at a superficial, more materialist level, it could reasonably be surmised that Francesco has been killed by the ambitious urban developer's envoy for thwarting her plans to modernise the neighbourhood; at a deeper, more ideological one, he could have also been punished for his controversial homosexual affair with Mehmet. Whether the former is the most manifest and the latter the more latent political burdens on Francesco, he still meets the same tragic end, and Mehmet eventually abandons his native Istanbul in search of more amenable and, as the letter Marta writes to him seems to imply, less homophobic surroundings. Özpetek's reclamation and reconfiguration of Ottoman homoeroticism constitutes, thus, a careful approach to the subject that does not ring with too much optimism about Turkish modernity and the acceptance of homosexuality. In a recent sociological study, Berrin Eylen Özyurt and Veli Duyan argue that 'Turkey is endeavoring to become "westernized," with steps being taken toward modernization. Social values, attitudes, and beliefs are slowly changing. Despite these changes, having a lesbian or gay sexual identity is not acceptable in Turkish society' (2017, p. 2).

It could be argued that the Westernisation encouraged by Ottoman Orientalist and Kemalist modernities still contains a strong element of homophobia derived from mainstream Islamicate values and from the European homophobic discourses that became the global norm in the nineteenth century. Indeed, the Turkish state's disavowal of the film itself evinces this residual homophobia. Elena Boschi cites several critical sources when she recalls 'how the Turkish Ministry of Culture's selection committee reacted after *Hamam* was tentatively put forward as a candidate for Best Foreign Film for the American Academy Awards. The committee chose another movie, because *Hamam* "does not represent Turkish culture"' (2015, p. 250). In a review contemporaneous with the film, Yalman Onaran stated:

> Turks are lining up for blocks to see the tale of two men who fall in love in a Turkish bath, a film nominated to represent the nation at the 1998 Academy Awards. But 'Hamam' won't get a shot at the Oscar: Turkey's Culture Ministry overruled the independent film board, choosing a traditional romantic drama. (Onaran, 1997)

Although the Turkish Culture Ministry did not really provide any reasons for not choosing *Hamam* to represent the country at the Oscars, its silence regarding the same-sex relations depicted on screen belies their unwillingness to be charged with homophobia and to be therefore placed outside the precincts of European modernity, which reinforces the idea that, while homosexuality may be not criminalised in Turkey, Turkish homophobia still works clandestinely; it is this systemic form of homophobia, I argue, that still stands in the way of same-sex relationships such as Francesco and Mehmet's in *Hamam*.

Despite the fact that Özpetek's film was overlooked by Turkish cultural authorities and that it was denounced by some Turkish bath owners as depicting a 'perverted' view of the *hamams*' daily routines, other commentators have regarded *Hamam* as an ideal conduit for modern-day tourism. Indeed, Arzu Öztürkmen regrets that the success of Özpetek's film was not deemed a suitable opportunity for attracting foreign visitors:

> Turkish members of the tourism sector often touch upon the view that state censorship blunts myriad promotion opportunities. For instance, according to numerous members of the tourism sector, the movie 'Hamam' that had not been nominated for the Oscars from Turkey on the basis that it incorporated elements of homosexuality, was actually a film that could have presented portraits of ordinary, gentle, and amicable Turkish individuals to wide audiences. (Öztürkmen, 2005, p. 612)

Although, according to Öztürkmen, the zealotry of the Turkish Government could have harmed promotional opportunities for the country, Cichocki notes the rise in the late twentieth century of foreign interest in Ottoman culture in general, and in *hamams* in particular, observing how 'tourists in search of the exotic and erotic provided the Çemberlitaş *Hamam* and other well-known bathhouses with a new source of income' (2005, p. 106). She regards *Hamam* as a cultural text fostering this foreign and local interest in Ottoman revivalism. However, despite the blatant similarities between this model of latter-day Ottoman tourism and the sexual and sensual Orientalism famous since the eighteenth century, Özpetek's film is contributing to a conservationist form of modern tourism that recovers the Ottoman past, as opposed to a developmental view of the city that would modernise it at the expense of losing its Ottoman cultural heritage. Girelli argues that critics often passionately defend Özpetek's work against charges of conservatism, citing the contested assessment offered by G. Gairazzo, who argued that 'Özpetek's films do not defy received knowledge, but at best compromise between old and new' (Girelli, 2007, p. 25). While *Hamam* may not offer a revolutionary departure from received forms of knowledge, its excavation of the Ottoman past and its 'compromise between old and new', between older forms of Ottoman homoeroticism and multiculturalism and contemporary queerness is, in itself, a productive form of micropolitical resistance against the homogenising and homophobic forces of Turkish modernity.

The three film directors whose work we have examined in Part I have been closely focused on interethnic relationships between Muslim and non-Muslim men, to the relative detriment, according to some critics, of their female characters and of the representation of women more generally. As we saw in Chapter 1, Kureishi was taken to task for not delving deeper into Tania's plight in *Laundrette*, and for concentrating more keenly on the relationship between his male protagonists, Omar and Johnny. Rashid's first short film, *Surviving Sabu*, explored in Chapter 2, was singled out by Gopinath (2005) as an example of the persistent marginalisation of women's voices in the exploration of diasporas and of the usual focus on father-and-son relationships. However, Rashid's first feature film, *Touch of Pink*, ameliorated this gender imbalance by exploring Nuru's diasporic subjectivity. Özpetek has been similarly criticised for his circumscribed representation of women: according to Hipkins, 'critics have overlooked the tendency of this new kind of male melodrama to privilege male sexual agency and to construct women as bearers of an abstract and idealized femininity' (2014, p. 94). He substantiates his argument by noting:

> It is a vengeful Westernized woman, in the form of an entrepreneur who wishes to modernize the area, who stands behind the killing: the castrating female, and the dark side of the *hamam*'s protective womb. Female characters are maternal (traditional), vengeful (modern), or neutered and neutralized, like Francesco's wife. (Hipkins, 2014, p. 95)

Hipkins' provocative critique of the film sees femininity as an idealised and abstracted category that either protects or obstructs the male characters' progression, while being excluded from their erotic activities and from a self-empowering role in the films' denouements. While it is difficult imagining such a point being made about films exploring female same-sex desire at the comparative expense of male characters' erotic subjectivity, it is undeniable that Özpetek is most materially and erotically invested in the exploration of male homoeroticism and masculinity, and that women often constitute mere facilitators of such intimacy.

Anita's voiceover in *Hamam* reveals how she relished the idea of facilitating same-sex practices in the Turkish bath she is thinking of restoring. As she tells her sister Giuliana in one of her unsent letters, which Francesco peruses: 'I have many friends who would be grateful if I offered them a discreet and welcome shelter for certain indulgences. And I, as you know, can hardly resist the opportunity of making a man happy' (*Hamam*, 1997). Here, Anita's codified language implies her male friends would welcome a space where they could bond with other men in ways frowned upon by mainstream Turkish society. As a female figure who realises the rarity of her position, being 'the first western madame in this city of omnipotent heads of families' (*Hamam*, 1997), she becomes a facilitator of anti-normative male sexualities, while remaining visually out of the frame. However, Anderlini-D'Onofrio offers a different reading of Anita's sensibility. As she unceremoniously puts it, 'Madame fits the stereotype of the fag hag in traditional gay lingo, a woman who lives her sexuality vicariously through the eroticism of gay men. However, as I have claimed elsewhere, a fag hag is often a repressed bisexual woman' (Anderlini-D'Onofrio, 2007, p. 126). In light of this interpretation, the men's activities in the *hamam*, which are mirrored in its (unseen) parallel female spaces, provide an indirect outlet for Anita's latent queerness, evinced by her interest in facilitating homosocial spaces where unorthodox erotic bonding can take place. In addition, Marta discovers Francesco and Mehmet's affair as she seems about to join them in the *hamam*: she herself would have been subverting the bath's homosociality in order, potentially, to quench her own desires. Nonetheless, it is difficult to deny that Anita's and Marta's desires are ultimately subservient to those of her male patrons and her estranged husband, respectively, and their own potential queerness is never fully explored in the film. However, Özpetek's second film, *Harem Suare*, is closely focused on female homosocial spaces, including female *hamams*, during the fall of the Ottoman Empire, and his subsequent films often have central female characters. In addition, two of the narratives explored in the next section of this book, *I Can't Think Straight* and *Three Veils*, are zoomed in on Muslim women's sexualities and gender performances.

Although Anita and Marta certainly grant more visibility to male homoeroticism, they are recipients of a reified model of femininity that renders them subversive figures in modern Turkish society. In the Turkish republican past evoked in her letters, Anita remarks how '*Hamams* are *strange* places, where the steam relaxes customs together with bodies' (*Hamam*, 1997, emphasis added). Anita enjoys being able to relax the customs of Turkish and Islamicate heteronormativity by encouraging the strange dreaminess of Turkish baths. In addition, in the film's last scene, Marta tells Mehmet in voiceover about her work in the *hamam*, whose restoration has been completed, and about her feelings: 'I get melancholy, but then suddenly this cool breeze rises and takes it far away. It is a *strange* wind, like no other I have ever felt. A light breeze, and it loves me' (*Hamam*, 1997, emphasis added). Withstanding, for now, the lyrical image of the love-pregnant wind evoked in pre-Islamic and Islamic poetry, the strangeness – or queerness – felt and encouraged by Marta and Anita provides a running thread through Özpetek's highly suggestive visual narrative: a sensual and erotic strangeness that is connected to the micropolitical and mundanely subversive queer act of disorientating the binarist heteronormative and homophobic impulses of Ottoman, Kemalist, and Islamicate modernities.

Notes

1. We encounter Anita in Özpetek's second film, *Harem Suare*, in which, played by Valeria Golino, she meets the old Italian-born Sultana Safiye (Lucía Bosé), who tells her the story of the end of the Ottoman Empire, the dissolution of the Sultan's *harem*, and her subsequent life as a performing artist pandering to the European thirst for the exotic Orient. As it transpires in this film, Anita's reason for leaving Italy was her love affair with her sister's husband, which she needed to break off in order to preserve her sister's marriage, although this entails severing ties with her family and relocating to Turkey. A love triangle, hence, also features in the ambiguous past of *Hamam*'s storyline, creating an parallel that is queerly re-enacted in *Hamam*'s diegetic present.

2. Elena Boschi offers a compelling and persuasive analysis of the use of music in Özpetek's films. She illustrates Özpetek's regular use of fusion music to score key moments in his films, such as the scene where Francesco and Mehmet kiss in the *hamam*. Bosch argues: 'Where the music's hybridity becomes audible, visible, or is known by certain audiences, these songs can effectively bring their musical fusions to a narrative where cultural fusion thus becomes not only visible but also audible. However, the music's hybridity often does not surface and generically non-Italian music might well be what most Italians will hear' (Boschi, 2015, pp. 248–9). In Boschi's thinking, hybrid music blending Italian and Turkish elements can be misperceived by Italian – and generally Western – audiences as merely exotic Turkish music, which strengthens an Orientalist perception of the film. However, Özpetek's stealthy deployment of hybridised art forms evince his true engagement with intercultural assemblage in a way which qualifies overarching interpretations of his work as Orientalist or as merely pandering to Western preconceptions.

Part II

Negotiating Islamic gender

4

Countermemories of desire: exploring gender, anti-racism, and homonormativity in Shamim Sarif's *The World Unseen* (2001) and *I Can't Think Straight* (2008)

Queer diasporic writers and filmmakers of Muslim heritage, as well as the scholars examining their work, regularly have to contend with sturdy Western ideologies when approaching the topic of gender in Islam. Like *homosexuality*, perceptions of how 'Islam' reputedly 'does' gender has become a touchstone of contemporary identity politics and it has been mobilised as the ideological undergirding of Euro-American geopolitical imperialism. As Jasmin Zine lucidly points out:

> In the post-9/11 era, Muslim women navigate between both racialized and gendered politics that variously script the ways their bodies and identities are narrated, defined, and regulated. Located within this dialectical dynamic, the rhetoric of Muslim women's liberation is all too often caught up in the vast undercurrents of ideological extremism, on the one hand, and racism and Islamiphobia [sic], on the other. (Zine, 2004, p. 168)

In the light of Zine's work, Muslim women are simultaneously caught up between Islamist patriarchal traditionalism, on the one hand, and Western Islamophobia and racism, on the other, including the problematic discourses of white feminists who routinely 'otherise' them. Hence, queer Muslim women are forced to navigate the muddy waters of Western gender discourses in an attempt to define their distinctive gender orientations, and in their own terms, with the added difficulties that diasporic experience and its attendant ideological assemblages entail. I would add that a critical examination of Islamic gender must extend beyond femininity, so in this book section I also consider the construction of Islamic masculinities, albeit focusing on the ways narratives by queer diasporic *women* of Muslim heritage explore these gender vicissitudes.

The first author and filmmaker whose work I examine in this book section is Shamim Sarif. Born in 1969, Sarif is a British woman of diasporic South Asian Muslim heritage: her Muslim family originally migrated from colonial India to South Africa several generations ago, eventually settling in Britain after the onset of apartheid. Sarif grew up in Britain and was a novelist before she became a filmmaker.[1] Her debut novel, *The World Unseen*, first published in 2001, constitutes an exploration of racial tensions and Muslim homosexuality during South African apartheid, and as such it is partly inspired by Sarif's diasporic family history. Sarif's literary efforts are eminently intersectional, invested as she is in taking to task the racist imperative as well as the attendant homophobia of South African apartheid and of the nation's white and coloured communities.

Although a generation removed from Sarif's personal experience, *The World Unseen* is materially rooted in the South Africa of the 1950s. As Chantal Zabus observes, the narrative 'is set against the tormented canvas of the 1946 Indian Congress protests against the Ghetto Bill, the 1949 Mixed Marriages Act, and the Group Areas Act of 1950' (2013, p. 208). These polemical pieces of legislation segregated the South Asian communities in South Africa, prohibited interethnic marriages across all racial lines, and officially discouraged contact and collaboration between white, coloured, and black communities. This fraught racial backdrop is one against which Sarif's characters routinely struggle, testing the boundaries of officially designated spaces with anti-racist intent, which intersects with issues of female same-sex desire.

This chapter offers a combined examination of the conjoined anti-racist, anti-homophobic, and feminist stance of Sarif's first novel with that of Sarif's own screen adaptation of it, released in 2008, the same year as Sarif's film debut, *I Can't Think Straight*, and the literary version of the story that was created in conjunction with it. Unlike *The World Unseen*, *I Can't Think Straight* is set chiefly in contemporary Britain and Amman, Jordan's capital city, hence exploring the third diasporic phase of Sarif's family history. The film and novel versions of the story offer a semi-autobiographical account of the development of Sarif's relationship with her civil partner, Hanan Kattan, a Palestinian-Jordanian woman of Christian Arab heritage who regularly acts as Sarif's film producer. The story deals with the cultural and familial obstacles a female same-sex couple must overcome in the national and diasporic spaces of contemporary Britain and Jordan.

The relationship between the literary and cinematic versions of *I Can't Think Straight* is a symbiotic one: interviewed by Regina Marler, Sarif reveals that she had finished a first draft of the novel by the time she started preparing the film, whose script was written in collaboration with screenwriter Kelly Moss. After the film's completion, Sarif returned to the novel. In the book's acknowledgements, she candidly states that she 'managed to shamelessly appropriate some of the best lines that Kelly wrote for the film and use them in this book' (Marler, 2008, p. 4), yet she also admits that '[s]ome scenes are coming out very different!' (Marler, 2008, p. 57).

Ronnie Scheib argues that '[i]n both cases, Sharif's [sic] novels have suffered in translation to the screen, with detail and subtlety sacrificed to point-making exposition and broad caricature' (2008, p. 37). The literary versions of *The World Unseen* and *I Can't Think Straight* are best suited to capture Sarif's characters' interiority and their innermost dilemmas about race, gender, and sexuality, whereas the films are partly limited by the generic conventions of the period drama and the romantic comedy, respectively. For instance, as we shall see, *The World Unseen* sometimes relies on tropes, situations, and themes inherited from Western representations of racial segregation and female queerness in prior literature and film. (I am thinking specifically of Fannie Flagg's American novel *Fried Green Tomatoes at the Whistle Stop Cafe*, published in 1987, and the film adaptation released in 1991.) In turn, *I Can't Think Straight* offers caricatured character representations that can be deemed problematic. For example, the comically vindictive Indian housemaid, Rani (Nina Wadia), often spits into the various drinks made for her snobbish Palestinian mistress, Reema (Antonia Frering), whose arch materialism perpetuates the stereotype of the rich cosmopolitan Arab. In her own defence, Sarif explains that her cinematic efforts 'aren't meant to be traditional art house or experimental films' and that she is 'definitely looking for strong story arcs and characterizations' (Oumano, 2010, p. 99). In subscribing to dominant cinematic styles, Sarif is ultimately queering the mainstream, making previously unheard stories intelligible through a popular medium that is accessible to both queer viewers and wider global audiences.

This chapter constitutes the first extended critical examination of Sarif's novel and film versions of *I Can't Think Straight*[2] and one of the first dealing with *The World Unseen*. In the forthcoming pages, I explore afresh the ways in which Sarif's narratives undertake a critique of intersecting issues of gender, race, faith, and sexuality, albeit critiquing their ideological and cultural limitations. I propose that Sarif's narratives help us undertake a triangular critique of diasporic British monoculturalism and South African apartheid, Muslim homophobia, and Western Islamophobia. In an interwoven examination of *The World Unseen* and *I Can't Think Straight*, I analyse, first, how the diasporic women's negotiation of the societal and familial expectations placed on them challenge Western stereotypes of the pious and domesticated Muslim and Arab woman, while confirming the persistence of marriage as an issue of sociocultural containment. Second, I explore apartheid's casual homophobia and the clandestine existence of female homosexuality in South Africa, which is posited as analogous, if not synonymous, with racial segregation. Moreover, in Sarif's literary and cinematic narratives, some South Asian characters are deemed as racist and dehumanising as their white counterparts. Third, I explore Sarif's characters' subscription to assembled religious and medical discourses about homosexuality in *I Can't Think Straight*. Fourth, I interrogate Sarif's configuration of same-sex desire in relation to Western cultural models and the ideological limitations this poses on her creative achievements. I suggest that Sarif's *The World Unseen* is largely indebted to received American models of sexual dissidence and gender performance, albeit extending their debates by making female homosexuality more prominent and visible. In addition, I argue that Sarif's Western 'coming out' model in *I Can't Think Straight* constitutes an example of homonormativity.[3] Conversely, I also argue that the subscription to Western models of sexual liberation and gender self-styling is due to the absence in Sarif's British upbringing of an Islamicate cultural archive of same-sex desire. In response to this absence, I offer a queer reading that identifies Sarif's deployment of queer female entrepreneurship in the South African past, and of intertwined queer bodies in the British present, as forging what Gayatri Gopinath calls, via Joseph Roach, 'clandestine countermemories' (Gopinath, 2005, p. 4) challenging the discursive erasure of Muslim female homosexuality in Western and diasporic communities.

The World Unseen explores the relationship between South Asian Muslims Miriam, a café owner, and Amina, a housewife and shopkeeper. As I have already noted, Gopinath suggests that 'all too often diasporas are narrativised through the bonds of relationality between men' (2005, p. 5). Conversely, Sarif gives prevalence to the dialectic relationship between diasporic and cosmopolitan women in 1950s South Africa and in contemporary Britain. In both her literary and cinematic narratives, women are torn between their desire to be financially and professionally independent and their subjugation to societal and familial domestic roles. In the novel version of *The World Unseen*, Amina's way of forging a safe place of same-sex intimacy with her lover Miriam is to invite her to cook in her Pretoria café, a transgressive establishment where Amina is clandestinely allowed by her police contact to serve both blacks and coloureds. In turn, according to Cheryl Stobie, Miriam constitutes 'the epitome of the obedient and docile woman, who unthinkingly accepts an arranged marriage, which becomes increasingly unhappy, to the point of physical violence from her husband' (2003, p. 125). Although Miriam may at first seem to conform to Western expectations of Muslim women's submissiveness, her burgeoning relationship with the unconventional Amina begins to unravel her 'docile' personality. Miriam is initially reluctant to accept Amina's professional yet personally transgressive proposition, visibly limited by her heteropatriarchal domestic arrangement: ' "I can't go with you. [...] I have a husband and three children and a shop to look after." [...] "I'm offering the job to you, not your husband" (Sarif, 2011b, pp. 241, 243). Amina explicitly appeals to Miriam's personal desire and not to her husband's dictates, to which Miriam soon relents in a preliminary but important show of female emancipation.

Miriam's husband Omar constitutes an almost archetypical version of the modern Muslim patriarch: Westernised and sleek in his two-piece suit, yet ultimately conservative in his Muslim values carried on from South Asia, which are reinforced in his collusion with South African apartheid. Sarif's construction of Omar as aggressively patriarchal and in cahoots with officialdom signals the risky complicity of Sarif's early work with stereotyped Western versions of Muslim masculinity, which she qualifies in *I Can't Think Straight*. To Omar's physical restraint of Miriam, we should add his displeasure about her request to work at Amina's café three mornings a week: ' "You will not be my wife and work!" he shouted, slamming his hand instead against the wall. [...] "I don't like it," he said, quietly, almost to himself. "If I don't like it, that should be enough" ' (Sarif, 2011b, pp. 312–13). Sarif ensures her readership and audience understand that Omar is not simply being a seemingly pious Muslim but an agent of patriarchal tyranny. At this point, the film and novel versions of the story slightly diverge: whereas the literary version of *The World Unseen* ends with Miriam's professionally worded letter to Amina accepting her job offer, the film shows Miriam arriving at the café by car, on her own, and surprising Amina, which signals more prominently her growing independence from her husband, and offers a more hopeful glimpse of Amina and Miriam's professional and personal future together. In 1950s South Africa, Miriam may not be confident enough to leave her husband, and her same-sex relationship with Miriam has to be kept under the guise of a professional arrangement, yet this paves the way for more self-empowered versions of Muslim femininity in Sarif's work.

Before we move on to examine *I Can't Think Straight*, which remains more interesting for our purposes here as an exploration of queer Muslim diasporas because it is based more closely on Sarif's own material experiences, it is important to point out the intersectional aspects of *The World Unseen*. If the novel and film are visibly indebted to American narratives of female queer intimacy, they are also inspired by the American fight against racial segregation which it transposes to the even more aggressively segregated South African past and which, as Zabus (2013) argues, it firmly roots in the South African context. Even at the risk of rendering the character of Omar an archetype of Muslim masculinity and a colonial mimic, in keeping with Western expectations of Islamic patriarchy and Muslim colonial identity, Sarif is daring enough to portray his cooption into apartheid ideologies and the intermediary role of some members of South Asian communities in upholding black subservience to other racial minorities. As Omar unceremoniously warns his wife about the 'kuffar', the Islamic term for non-believers, which in Africa invariably came to refer to the black population: 'You must not be friendly with them [...]. If they think you are soft, they will take advantage. Make them work. That is what they are there for' (Sarif, 2011b, p. 28). Here, Sarif makes Omar the blatant accomplice of South African apartheid, an aspect of his identity that is developed later in the novel, and which his wife Miriam wilfully resists.

Miriam's gradual defiance of the values imposed by apartheid through her husband includes rebelling against both white and South Asian racism, inspired by Amina's example. When one of their black servants is run over by a white farmer of Afrikaans heritage, she secretly goes in his rescue:

> A man is knocked down – a *kaffir*, a black man, but a man, just the same, and the man who hit him, together with the man whom she was married to, and who was the father of her children, were outside worrying about the dent in the car. [...] With a sense of resolution, though, and with, for some reason, a fleeting thought of Amina Harjan, she started purposefully down the track. (Sarif, 2011b, pp. 200, 201)

Sarif's narrative maps the complicity between South Asian Omar and the white Afrikaans farmer, while Miriam's consciousness dwells on the common humanity of the injured black servant. It is not fortuitous, however, that she has 'a fleeting thought' of Amina. Amina's active opposition to apartheid, embodied by her subversively interracial business endeavour, chiefly her café in Pretoria, inspires Miriam's anti-racism. Her action will be found out by her husband and she will be consequently beaten up for it, but her compassionate interracial deed has planted the seed of her intersectional social consciousness: Amina and Miriam, as characters who jointly oppose Islamic patriarchy and white supremacy, are testament to the need for intersectionality, by simultaneously opposing apartheid's racism and South African and Islamic heteropatriarchy. Sarif's narrative does not pose queers and blacks as synonymous but as analogous, as marginalised social groupings whose liberation, according to Sarif's diasporic sensibility, should go hand in hand.

I Can't Think Straight tells, in turn, the love story of Tala, a young Palestinian-Jordanian businesswoman spending her time between Amman and London, and Leyla, a young British writer of South Asian heritage based in suburban London. If *The World Unseen* gives us a perspective of women as becoming gradually emancipated materially and morally from the strictures of heterosexual marriage, in *I Can't Think Straight*, young women of South Asian and Arab heritage are not merely confined to domestic spaces or expected to depend financially on men, yet they are often coopted into their fathers' businesses, which demonstrates they are still the subjects of patriarchal familial expectations. For instance, budding writer Leyla continually refuses her father's entreaties to take a more active role in his life insurance firm, and Tala has started her own trading business selling Palestinian products in the West. As she tells her fiancé, Hani: 'I have to make it work. My father's already pressing me to come back to the family business' (Sarif, 2008, p. 11).[4] Sarif's diasporic and cosmopolitan women are defiant of familial strictures, offering a positive challenge to gender roles in diasporic Muslim and cosmopolitan Arab communities in Britain, while unsettling the image, often conjured up in the West, of the repressed and domesticated Muslim or Middle Eastern woman. Marriage is still, nonetheless, the ultimate destination for Sarif's two female protagonists, at least in their families' views, and not just any form of heterosexual legal union, but one that remains within strict ethno-religious boundaries and is financially advantageous.

Tala's mother, Reema, throws a lavish engagement party for her eldest daughter in order 'to ensure that nobody missed the fact that this final fiancé outshone even the three wealthy heirs she had previously been promised to, because Hani was handsome and articulate, as well as Palestinian, Christian and rich' (Sarif, 2008, p. 18). In Reema's assessment, Hani's physical and intellectual attributes only help complement the circumstances that really matter: his ethnicity, religion, and economic status. Tala defends her choice while speaking to her uncle when he tells her: 'Of course you love him. He's Christian and he's rich', to which she responds: 'He's kind and honest and forward-thinking. And handsome' (Sarif, 2008, p. 19). Tala's emphasis falls on personal qualities, yet when she later discusses relationships with Leyla, she cannot help making manifest her internalised societal and familial expectations: ' "The third [fiancé] ticked all the boxes – good family, Christian Arab, intelligent, handsome. But it just didn't click". She looked to Leyla for understanding and received it in the glance back' (Sarif, 2008, p. 58). Sarif's narrator highlights Leyla's sympathy for Tala because she herself has internalised the culturally enforced necessity to find a prospective life partner that 'ticked all the boxes'. Her current boyfriend, Ali, is the person who introduces her to Tala and her family. At their initial meeting in Tala's second family home in London, Leyla is probed by Tala's mother about their two-month relationship. Reema's intrusive cross-questioning forces Leyla to assess the foundations of their relationship, expressed more fully in the novel's exploration of Leyla's thoughts: 'And since she came from the same religious background as he, and since he had the advantage of money, business acumen and charm it would have been inconceivable for her to turn him down when he asked for a date' (Sarif, 2008, p. 30). As a young British Muslim woman, Leyla feels socially conditioned to accept the advances of suitors of her same religious background.

Sarif's narratives suggest that, as regards marriage, British Muslim and cosmopolitan Arab communities are too religiously exclusive and that they foster monoculturalism rather than multicultural exchange, although they show how this is not just a symptom of a crisis in British multiculturalism, but that it also affects Christian families based in both Britain and the Middle East. The culturally hermetic character of ethno-religious unions does not chiefly affect Christian Tala and Muslim Leyla, who, as we shall see, are sometimes at loggerheads regarding the provenance of their values, but also Tala's 'good' and 'bad' sisters, sensitive Zina (Kimberly Jaraj) and materialistic Lamia (Anya Lahiri). In a scene of sisterly intimacy depicted in both the novel and the film, Zina confides to Tala that her Jewish boyfriend has broken up with her because she is of Palestinian Christian heritage: 'He can't imagine being married to a non-Jew [...] he wants Jewish kids and Hannakah and Passover ... it would be impossible' (Sarif, 2008, pp. 117–18). Conversely, we find out in the novel that materialistic Lamia, who is jealous of her family's continuous investment in Tala's relationships, has previously been romantically entangled with a Muslim boy working in her father's business. Apart from being of lesser class status, which was not a totally insurmountable fact, 'he was also Muslim, and that, Lamia knew, was nothing less than impossible. He told her that his family would not accept her if she remained a Christian, and she knew that hers would never countenance a conversion to Islam' (Sarif, 2008, p. 85). Lamia makes the mistake of confessing her relationship to her mother, who pats her daughter's back reassuringly before immediately laying him off. Reema's upholding of religious exclusivism shows to what an extent religious identity is not a matter of free choice, but of familial and cultural inheritance.

Tariq Modood argues that British liberal secularists believe gender, sexuality and race 'are not chosen, whereas religion is something one can walk away from' (2010, p. 42). Although Sarif's characters gradually walk away from organised religion, her narratives confirm Modood's assertion that '[n]o one chooses to be or not to be born into a Muslim family' (2010, p. 42). In fact, in Tala and Leyla's initial meeting at Tala's family's London home, Tala wrestles with the identitarian religious model and teases both her mother and later Leyla herself about religious conditioning when one is born into a British Muslim family. She later questions Leyla's beliefs, a playful quip on issues of filiation and affiliation: 'But did you prefer Islam? Or do you prefer it because you were brought up with it? How would your parents feel if you "preferred" Judaism?' (Sarif, 2008, p. 38). At first, Leyla is unsettled by Tala's pointed questions, yet at their second meeting, Leyla confesses that Tala has made her think '[a]bout why we follow certain paths. Is it just expectation? Or conditioning?' (Sarif, 2008, p. 53). Sara Ahmed suggests that subjects 'inherit the proximity of certain objects [...]. These objects are not only material: they are values, capital, aspirations, projects, and styles' (2006, p. 86). Sarif's narratives construct familial religious conditioning as a negative influence that circumscribes the social and romantic prospects of British Muslims and cosmopolitan Arabs, since they are expected to remain within the boundaries of their ethno-religious communities, a preliminary hurdle even before queerness is broached.

In Leyla's case, her identity as a second-generation diasporic British citizen is in tension with the values and aspirations of her Muslim family, and she resists following the lines of traditional religious practice, illustrating her ideological struggle with her religious inheritance. In a conversation with her father, Sam, about missing Friday prayers at the mosque, Leyla mildly reassures him: 'Dad, I believe in our religion. You know I do. I just don't like to go when everyone else does', to which he retorts, half-jokingly: 'If you don't go with everyone else, how will they know you're a good Muslim?' (Sarif, 2008, pp. 27–28). The issue here, echoed later by Leyla's mother, seems to be not so much with either moral or spiritual orthodoxy, but with *orthopraxy*, or adherence to 'correct' religious performance. For Leyla's family, religious observance involves a collective performance that sits awkwardly with Leyla's second-generation diasporic perspective in Britain. Sarif's narratives suggest that religion is not a matter of choice for those born into particular religious communities, and that the expected adherence to religious tradition involves a struggle for British-born diasporic subjects.

Crucially, the exploration of Muslim and Arab communities' monocultural biases runs alongside Sarif's critique of their equally prescriptive heteronormativity. Elena Oumano declares that 'sexual preference is largely irrelevant to [Sarif's] films. Sarif's paramount concern is exploring the issue of "finding one's own place within the culture and family that one is born into, something most people grapple with as they mature"' (2010, p. 266). Conversely, I would argue that sexual orientation is of the utmost centrality to *I Can't Think Straight*, since the film focuses on how sexual non-normativity contravenes the overlapping cultural and religious values of Leyla's British Muslim and Tala's cosmopolitan Arab families. Tala and Leyla – played in the film by Canadian-Indian Lisa Ray, the star of Deepa Mehta's *Water*, and American-Indian Sheetal Sheth, who play Miriam and Amina, respectively, in the film version of *The World Unseen* – begin their romantic relationship in the quintessentially English spaces of Oxford, on a shopping trip covertly used to get to know each other better. The queer presence of a British Muslim and a Christian Arab same-sex female couple in the seat of English higher education constitutes an antidote to what Gopinath calls 'the unthinkability of a queer female subject position within various mappings of nation and diaspora' (2005, p. 15). However, their erotic sojourn is cut short by an enforcement of compulsory heterosexuality. Tala's jealous sister, Lamia, who accompanies the two women, suspects their intimate bond and drops enough clues for their mother to find out about their liaison. Alarmed, Reema quickly manufactures a plot to bring Tala's fiancé, Hani, on a surprise trip to London that will discourage Tala's homosexual tendencies. Reema and Hani catch Tala and Leyla *in flagrante* just as they return from their trip to Oxford. Reema intently looks on the scene while Tala and Hani greet each other with a passionate kiss, as she also watches the effect of this heterosexual gesture on Leyla. According to Sara Ahmed,

> We can reconsider how one 'becomes straight' by reflecting on how an orientation, as a direction (taken) towards objects and others, is made compulsory. In other words, subjects are *required* to 'tend toward' some objects and not others as a condition of familial as well as social love. (Ahmed, 2006, p. 85, emphasis in original)

In Ahmed's consideration of sexual orientation, she ponders how subjects are made to 'become straight' by being socially and family conditioned to tend towards some objects – heterosexual partners – and not others – homosexual ones. In the scene described above, Tala's mother purposefully throws Tala towards Hani and away from Leyla, in a way that makes her heterosexuality compulsory. After this incident, conditioned by familial and social versions of love, Tala chooses to honour her publicly sanctioned relationship with Hani and is forced to leave Leyla.

However, Leyla's eyes have been opened by her affair with Tala to the inexorability of her same-sex desire and she sees no way back to Ali or to pretending to be heterosexual. She decides to 'come out' to her family, and will eventually persuade Tala to do the same, as an immoveable condition of their relationship. Familial responses to their homosexuality constitute a typical assemblage of mainstream religious dogma and internalised Western homophobia. Leyla stuns her mother, Maya, by proclaiming: 'I'm gay!' Leyla's father, Sam, joins their conversation in the kitchen. After Leyla repeats her confession, he retorts, with perfect comic timing: 'But I've only been gone two hours' (Sarif, 2008, p. 147). Maya's rage escalates in the following argument:

> 'First you stop coming to mosque, now you are up to your neck in sin!'
> 'It's not a sin.'
> 'It's a huge sin.'
> 'According to who?' Leyla was close to tears now.
> 'According to God!' Maya yelled.
> 'What kind of a God is that? I don't accept it!' Leyla yelled back.
> 'Then you will burn in hell,' stated Maya [...].
> 'That's enough.' Sam's firm voice cut through the thick air and brought Maya to a stop.
>
> (Sarif, 2008, p. 148)

This dialogue features Maya's mainstream Muslim reaction to Leyla's alleged 'deviance'. It is believed by many Muslims that homosexuality is a sin explicitly censured by God, despite historical debates surrounding same-sex relations, indexed in the Introduction, that counteract the alleged objectivity of this dogma. Sam comes to their daughter's rescue. Leyla subsequently tells him: 'If I could help it, I would, [...] [b]ut I can't'. He responds, soothingly: 'I know, [...]. I know' (Sarif, 2008, p. 149). In the film, father and daughter embrace at this point. Here, Sarif opposes dominant Western Islamophobia, particularly the stereotype of the conservative and homophobic Muslim patriarch, while disorganising dominant gendered narrative structures.

Gopinath argues that 'the oedipal relations between fathers and sons [often serve] as a central and recurring feature within diasporic narratives' (2005, p. 5). *I Can't Think Straight* extends British diasporic gender debates often focused on fathers and sons, while qualifying Western notions of Islamic patriarchy, by depicting the supportive relationship between a Muslim father and his homosexual daughter, hence opposing mainstream Western conceptions of Muslim men as universally homophobic and misogynistic. These popular images of intolerant and oppressive Muslim fathers have been circulated routinely in the West since 9/11, and have contributed to discourses of justification for military intervention in Muslim-majority countries.

Nonetheless, Sarif's queer mirroring of Oedipal relations is partly undertaken at the expense of the other women in her work. Sarif's depiction of the censorious Muslim and Arab matriarch is somewhat redolent, for instance, of some of Salman Rushdie's ferocious female characters.[5] Yet, despite Sarif's exaggerated construction of Reema as the epitome of maternal ruthlessness, she is also keen to dissect Maya's religious zeal, her homophobia shown, not unsympathetically, as being culturally conditioned. Whereas Maya's initial condemnation of homosexuality invokes God's censure, her qualms about her daughter's sexual orientation gradually intersect with Western medical discourses, demonstrating how Muslim homophobia is not purely Islamic but intermingles with Western models of homophobia. When Leyla's supportive sister Yasmin jokes about the fact that Leyla 'can't think straight at all', Maya surmises that 'it had something to do with Leyla and her *affliction*' (Sarif, 2008, p. 165, emphasis added). She later offers, 'What do two women do together? […] It's *not natural*' (2008, p. 167, emphasis added). Analysing the current collusion of Islamist and Western homophobic discourses, Olivier Roy suggests that '[e]ven when the mainstream Muslim approach in the West is very conservative (towards homosexuality or abortion, for example), it is usually expressed in line with the position of the Catholic Church or Christian Right' (2004, p. 32), which reveals not a 'pure' Islamic conception of sexuality, but an assemblage of various models of homophobia. In fact, Maya's medicalised perspective on her daughter's homosexuality has much in common with the Christian perspective of Tala's mother, who ponders: 'she would have to find a way to *cure* Tala of this' (Sarif, 2008, p. 194, emphasis added). We can perceive here the intersection of Muslim and Christian religious dogmas with a medical view of homosexuality as a disease, which constitutes the legacy of nineteenth-century Western homophobia and of historical Islamicate perspectives on same-sex desire as an *ubnah*, or disease. Moreover, although Maya's initial outrage seemed provoked by Leyla's spiritual degeneration, the novel's exploration of her interiority illustrates that her discontent is more linked to cultural practice than to religious orthodoxy: 'Without [Leyla's marriage], without the preparations and shopping and congratulations and general elevation of status amongst her peers at the mosque, she could not imagine what else could be left for her' (Sarif, 2008, p. 167). Instead of referring to any scriptural traditions, Maya's main concern is with social perception, and with her own status within her ethnic community. Sarif's depiction of Maya's social anxiety, which is not dissimilar to her husband's opinion on Leyla's scant mosque attendance, suggests that some British Muslims are not as troubled by homosexuality as a moral transgression as by its being a deterrent to their social status in Britain's Muslim communities.

As regards Leyla's and Tala's journeys towards sexual liberation and away from compulsory heterosexuality, Sarif's various texts are visibly drawn to a Western model of sexuality and a lesbian cultural archive, exposing the limitations of her intersectional critique. In both *The World Unseen* and *I Can't Think Straight*, Sarif demonstrates that her British Muslim sensibility contains a central absence: a lack of a homoerotic archive and vocabulary which are inspired by historical versions of Islamicate same-sex desire. Tellingly, *The World Unseen* cannot help revealing a Westernised conception of gender performance and its indebtedness to prior Western stories exploring female queerness. Some of the central tropes of Sarif's literary and cinematic narrative are manifestly drawn from a popular intersectional exploration of race and queerness set in the American South of the past, namely Fannie Flagg's novel *Fried Green Tomatoes at the Whistle Stop Cafe*, originally published in 1987, and the subsequent film version of the story, directed by Jon Avnet, written by Flagg herself and Carol Sobieski, and released in 1991. Sarif's Amina is described by Stobie as an 'unconventional young woman who, contrary to custom, lives apart from her family, wears trousers, co-owns a restaurant with a "coloured" man, scoffs at the thought of an arranged marriage, and to top it all is a lesbian' (2003, p. 124). In her attributes, Amina highly resembles Idgie Threadgoode, the tomboyish and independently spirited heroine of Flagg's novel, played by Mary Stuart Masterson in the film. Idgie also wears purportedly 'masculine' clothes, she employs black workers who are, indeed, also her friends, and she equally embarks on a professional venture, the eponymous Whistle Stop Cafe, with her assumed same-sex lover Ruth Jamison, her dead brother's sweetheart. In turn, Miriam is seemingly moulded after the character of Ruth, played by Mary-Louise Parker in the film version of the story, a seemingly heterosexual character who marries the abusive Frank Bennett, the forerunner of Sarif's Omar, whom she leaves in pursuit of her life with Idgie. Sarif's narratives are less forthcoming in terms of Miriam and Amina's professional and personal ventures, since Miriam does not leave her violent husband in order to become Amina's business partner. However, Sarif develops more explicitly the homoerotic elements of her narrative. The novel version of Flagg's story hints at the homoerotic relationship between Ruth, who is implicitly queer or at least a 'femme', and Idgie, who is more visibly a 'butch' lesbian, tropes that Sarif's literary and cinematic narratives take on[6] (see Figure 4). However, the film version of the story altogether elides Idgie and Ruth's sentimental relationship, potentially on account of the filmmakers' desire to market it to heterosexual audiences, rendering it a close friendship. In this regard, Sarif's novel and film, although visibly moulded on prior Western narratives of same-sex desire and anti-racism, are more daring in their explicit approach to queer relations, giving them more visibility without pandering to heteronormative audiences.

Sarif's vision, however, is partly compromised by her reliance on Westernised conceptions of gender performance and on inherited tropes. By turning Amina into the 'butch' half to the homosexual couple and Miriam into the 'femme' one, she is assimilating them too complacently into Western sexual and gender taxonomies, without any sense of their sexualities having been a part, at any point in history, of any cultural conversations regarding Islam and Muslim identities. In addition, in allowing her main intertext to be a novel set in the American South, she reveals a lack of cultural engagement with South African homosexualities, a feat potentially exacerbated by her having accessed the South African past via familial narratives and her own literary imagination. Sarif's adherence to established Western tropes is continued in *I Can't Think Straight*. Leyla's British

Figure 4 *The World Unseen* (2008), directed by Shamim Sarif

and middle-class liberal embrace of Western lesbian icons and of 'coming out' as the only possible option for queer citizens either in Britain, or elsewhere, constitutes a problematic example of homonormativity, which reproduces Western exceptionalism at the expense of cultural difference.

In both the novel and the film, Leyla's perceptive sister Yasmin (Amber Rose Revah) visits Leyla's attic bedsit in their family home, where she realises her older sister may be struggling with her sexual orientation: 'Yasmin recalled that Leyla has been playing the new kd lang CD almost non stop recently' (Sarif, 2008, p. 65). Both the novel and film versions of *I Can't Think Straight* also refer to popular representations of female homosexuality on American TV: when, later in the narrative, Yasmin questions Ali's naivety about Tala and Leyla's relationship, she says: 'Listen, did you ever see the TV show, "The L Word"?' (Sarif, 2008, p. 178). However, the film is more emphatic than the novel about Leyla's lesbian cultural archive. Sarif's shot of Leyla's room offers a candid view of it in the shape of a significant tower of books, containing the short story collection *A Haunted House*, by first-wave feminist Virginia Woolf; lesbian tennis player Martina Navratilova's autobiography *Being Myself*; Jeanette Winterson's edited collection of lesbian short fiction *Passion Fruit* and her popular autobiographical novel *Oranges Are Not the Only Fruit*; Sarah Waters' neo-Victorian revisionist lesbian novel *Fingersmith*; and lastly, tentatively placed at the bottom, Sarif's second novel *Despite the Falling Snow* (see Figure 5). In this *mise en scène*, Sarif places her work in line with a Western and decidedly Anglophone lesbian canon, while establishing her position as a minority ethnic pioneer of sexual dissidence, for hers is the only contribution of any writer of Muslim heritage. Nonetheless,

Figure 5 *I Can't Think Straight* (2008), directed by Shamim Sarif

her embrace of a Western lesbian canon and model of sexual liberation also entails a narrow subscription to Western liberal values and a lack of commensurability of other cultures.

For instance, although Tala breaks up with Hani on the morning of their wedding, Leyla will not give her relationship with her a second chance unless she follows her example and 'comes out' to her Middle Eastern family, in a manner that obviates ideological as well as cultural differences. Palestinian-Jordanian Tala is highly conscious of social censure, and bluntly tells Leyla after their first night together: 'This is not a way to live [...] It's not easy. It's not acceptable', to which Leyla responds with homonationalist aplomb: 'You live in the West now' (Sarif, 2008, pp. 93, 94). Although Jasbir K. Puar (2007) focuses on American forms of homonormativity, her assessment of the ways in which the US propounds its exceptionalism at the expense of constructing 'Other' nations and citizens as inferior is applicable to Sarif's British depiction of other countries and cultures. Sarif's characters often describe the Middle East as a place of ideological stasis – as Hani tells Tala: 'Amman was the same, [...], nothing ever changed' (Sarif, 2008, p. 78). When Leyla presses Tala to be honest with her family about her sexual orientation, the latter is pessimistic about Jordanian tolerance of homosexuality: 'Look, Leyla, you don't understand. The Middle East is an unforgiving place. And my parents have a strong presence in that world, and it's a culture that doesn't change' (Sarif, 2008, p. 186–7). As a privileged middle-class Britisher, Leyla admittedly does not 'understand' the position of those outside her ethnicity, nationality, and class.

Sarif's potentially Orientalising depiction of the Middle East as culturally and ideologically static, as opposed to the West's implied social progress, does little to conceal Sarif's biased perspective as a British writer and filmmaker. Leyla ultimately triumphs, and Tala comes out to her parents, after which she tellingly takes refuge in London, this being the prerogative of her affluent middle-class position. Sarif's texts construct Britain as the place of sexual exceptionalism, and 'coming out' as the only tenable model of sexual liberation. In favouring such a dominant model, Sarif is ostensibly siding with what Joseph Massad (2007) calls the 'Gay International', occluding British and other global cases in which 'coming out' may be materially and socially unadvisable or dangerous, and failing to countenance any other forms of sexual liberation. Yet, for all the epistemic violence inherent to this embrace of one single form of sexual emancipation, Samar Habib reminds us that 'life for individuals with non-normative sexuality in the Arab and Muslim world may be lived inside a culturally unique closet, but a closet is still a closet' (2010, p. xxix), meaning that keeping one's homosexuality a secret, despite different cultural codifications, remains at heart a universal condition for which the closet is simply 'another trope' (Habib, 2010, p. xxx). Habib's judiciousness about the arbitrariness of nomenclatures and her highlighting of commonalities across geographical borders and cultural predicaments helps us overlook the more homonormative tones of some of Sarif's characters and to appreciate the visibility it bestows on queer characters whose stories would have otherwise been easily elided, particularly given the precariousness of discussions of female homosexuality in Muslim and Arabic contexts and their diasporic counterparts.

As a British citizen of South Asian Muslim heritage, Sarif and her self-fashioned character, Leyla, have been brought up in a diasporic Muslim community in Britain whose uprooting from South Asia and rerooting in the West involves her family's subscription to global Islamic values. Amanullah De Sondy (2014) points out the persisting influence in South Asia, as well as globally, of Syed Abul A'la Mawdudi's anti-colonial interpretation of Islam, arguing that much of the tenor of global mainstream Islam regarding women's roles and sexual 'deviance' harkens back to his work. This astringent interpretation of Islam includes a dismissal of centuries' worth of Muslim non-normativity, including an Islamicate homoerotic archive. In light of such glaring absence, Sarif utilises Tala and Leyla to forge her own version of same-sex desire, their bodies becoming an antidote to the current silencing of Islamicate female homoeroticism.

Sarif is more adept and experienced a novelist than a filmmaker at depicting her characters' sensations and interactions, in ways that chime with Sara Ahmed's consideration of queer phenomenology. Ahmed surmises:

> We are turned towards things. [...] We perceive them insofar as they are near to us, insofar as we share a residence with them. Perception hence involves orientation; what is perceived depends on where we are located, which gives us a certain take on things. (Ahmed, 2006, p. 27)

Location and perception are both central to orientation, and sensorial proximity can affect queer subjects' perspective on themselves and others, which is significant for Sarif's forging of interpersonal connections in multicultural Britain. For Tala and Leyla, interaction with each other involves a positive reorientation in terms of desire. In Tala and Leyla's first intimate scene in their hotel room in Oxford, they do not talk, but let their instinctive movements speak for themselves, their kissing 'arousing a desire [Tala] had denied at every moment' (Sarif, 2008, p. 90), which suggests an excavation of feelings previously repressed, both ideologically and culturally. This is followed by a significant homoerotic moment: 'Now Leyla gave an audible sigh, an intake of breath as Tala reached the centre of her, and together they began to move against each other *in a rhythm that neither had to search for*' (Sarif, 2008, p. 90, emphasis added). Sarif constructs her protagonists' same-sex desire as manifesting itself instinctively. Habib reminds us that these same-sex acts have a definite place in Islamicate cultures:

> For female homosexual behaviour, the term most commonly used in both past and present Arab-speaking cultures is *suḥaq* ['grinding'] [...]. Anatomically speaking, the word 'grinding' is in reference to the rubbing of clitorises against each other, or presumably, against the lover's or beloved's body parts. (Habib, 2007, p. 17)

Tala and Leyla find a shared homoerotic rhythm that has been discursively silenced by dominant heteropatriarchal versions of Islam, yet not empirically eradicated, and which allows them to connect with each other phenomenologically. Despite Sarif's novel's lack of access to a cultural archive that can give her characters an Islamicate homoerotic language, her depiction of interpersonal physical communion restores suppressed female same-sex desire through firsthand bodily interaction, fruitfully acting as a material corrective to Islamist discursive erasure.

In addition, Tala and Leyla are reinscribing female homosexuality onto Muslim and Arab cultures while simultaneously contesting diasporic normativity in Britain. Gopinath asserts that '[q]ueer diasporic cultural forms [...] enact what [Joseph] Roach terms "clandestine countermemories" that bring into the present those pasts that are deliberately forgotten within conventional nationalist or diasporic scripts' (2005, p. 5). Although Gopinath is referring to forgetfulness about the colonial past, her point can be extrapolated to the current Islamist erasure of homoeroticism in the collective Islamicate past. Tala and Leyla's interfaith homosexual affair challenges the conservatism of traditional diasporic communities in Britain, which deny both interethnic intimacy and the historicity of Islamicate homosexuality. The reciprocated 'unthinkable' desire of a Christian Jordanian woman towards a British Muslim woman is given due visibility in Sarif's queer narrative. In the final sex scene described in the book, Leyla and Tala's bodies become an assemblage of identities previously deemed incompatible by normative nationalist and diasporic ideologies: 'Shaking, [Leyla] slid down on top of Tala, who held her close against her own skin, their bodies fused together, so that, in the indefinable world revealed by her heightened senses, Leyla could not tell where hers ended and Tala's began' (Sarif, 2008, p. 202). Here, Leyla's senses, erotically oriented towards Tala, create a symbiosis between her and Tala's bodies, forging, through reciprocated homoeroticism, a clandestine countermemory that challenges dominant ethno-religious exclusivism and homophobia, incepting, meanwhile, a new homosexual *and* female archive assembling various national and ethnic positions in Britain's diasporic spaces.

Nevertheless, this assemblage of queer Muslim diasporic and cosmopolitan Arab perspectives is ultimately tenable because of the economically privileged position of Sarif's protagonists. When Tala breaks up with Hani, she can feasibly escape to London, with the film offering footage of a plane leaving Amman. After Leyla's mother's negative reaction to Leyla's coming out, her father mentions the possibility of arranging a flat for Leyla, a sympathetic financial gesture mentioned only in the film version of the story. Sarif seems partially aware of her characters' circumscribed class positions, yet unable to surmount their experiential constrains. For instance, when discussing the conflict between Israel and Palestine, Kareem, Lamia's husband, responds hotly to Hani's diplomatic gestures: 'You and I have never suffered like our Palestinian countrymen. [...] You and I have never held a dying baby in our arms because an Israeli gun shot him in response to stone-throwing. You and I have never watched our children crying from hunger.' Tala inwardly admits, '[i]t was a stirring piece of rhetoric, but Tala was willing to wager that Kareem himself had never placed his perfectly polished shoes within miles of a refugee camp' (Sarif, 2008, pp. 137, 138). In spite of Tala's cynicism, Kareem's rhetoric becomes unwittingly metonymic of Sarif's empirical limitations, since her focus never goes beyond her privileged characters' environs. In the novel's acknowledgements, Sarif mentions a research trip to Amman to prepare for the book, featuring a visit to a 'refugee camp' (Sarif, 2008, p. 4). Palestinian refugees' harrowing material realities do not feature directly in the cinematic or literary versions of Sarif's story. Instead, the film shows how, when Tala's wedding is suddenly called off, her sympathetic father, Omar (Dalip Tahil), orders all the food to be taken to the 'camps', probably meaning the Palestinian refugee camps in Jordan, although the link is left for the audience to make. The film's narrow class vistas ultimately demonstrate the significant limitations of Sarif's British middle-class perspective on her financially privileged characters.

These class limitations should not altogether diminish, however, our estimation of the power of Sarif's intersectional exploration of female homosexuality in British and South African contexts. As a whole, her queer diasporic narratives act as instruments of gradual ideological change and ethnic resistance. Culturally and ideologically rooted in Britain, Sarif chooses the vehicle of a romantic comedy and a period drama to start revealing the contours of mainstream nationalist and diasporic expectations, offering us: ethnic minorities in dialogue with each other despite dominant monoculturalism and state-enforced racial segregation; significant representations of Muslim and Arab characters post-9/11 who, despite residual patriarchal values, are not universally repressive or homophobic; and a focus on female homoeroticism challenging both the Islamist censorship of historical debates surrounding same-sex desire and Western normative ideologies that fail to include the perspectives of queer citizens from ethnic minorities.

Although Sarif's British, liberal, and middle-class perspective, as I have suggested, poses limitations regarding class positions and homoerotic cultural archives, indebted as she is to a Western lesbian canon, while also prizing 'coming out' as the only tenable model of sexual liberation, her work still forges clandestine countermemories, whose urgency constitutes a necessary antidote to the continued neglect of non-normative female sexuality in local and global contexts. It is a pity that Sarif's stories end at the beginning – that is, both the narrative arcs of *The World Unseen* and *I Can't Think Straight* finish with the proper inception of their queer relationships, with not much intimation of how they may be more fully lived out in terms of faith and anti-normative sexualities. Despite the fact that Sarif's dissident characters in *I Can't Think Straight*, as well as their counterparts in real life, Sarif and Kattan, gradually abandon both Islam and Christianity in search of more self-affirming worldviews – neither Tala nor Leyla ever return to the topic of 'religion' once their initial debate is over – and in spite of the reliance of *The World Unseen* on narratives of gender performance, sexual liberation, and racial segregation inherited second-hand, their defiance of British and South African nationalist and diasporic mainstream values offers counter-discourses disorganising compulsory heterosexuality and ethno-religious exclusivism. Moreover, Sarif's literary and audiovisual texts foreground the queer experiences of women of Arab and South Asian Muslim heritage, hence giving overdue visibility to issues that affect queer Muslim women, and queer women of colour more generally.

Notes

1 Sarif is a versatile artist, with each of her novels and films exploring a different genre. It is notable that most of her fiction contains a queer or lesbian element or plot twist. Her other works include the Cold War spy novel *Despite the Falling Snow*, published in 2004 and turned into an eponymous film in 2016, and a documentary about Palestinian and Israeli women entitled *The House of Tomorrow* after the poetry of Khalil Gibran, released in 2011.

Sarif's first Young Adult novel, *The Athena Protocol*, is due to be published in 2019. She and her civil partner Hanan Kattan are the owners of the independent British production company Enlightenment Productions, which has so far produced all of Sarif's films, and which has a literary imprint called Enlightenment Press, which has reissued and published Sarif's novels.

2   A shorter version of this article, dealing only with *I Can't Think Straight*, was previously published in *The Journal of Commonwealth Literature*. See Preface and Acknowledgements section.

3   Linking homonormativity – i.e., homosexual normativity in line with heteronormative values – to the even more astringent homonationalism, Jasbir K. Puar argues that 'this brand of homosexuality operates as a regulatory script not only of normative gayness, queerness, or homosexuality, but also of the racial and national norms that reinforce these sexual subjects' (2007, p. 2). In other words, Western sexual taxonomies – which Puar argues are ultimately white – regulate homosexuality and normativise it by favouring specific sexual identifications and processes; I suggest this includes the uncritical prizing of the 'coming out' scenario as the most tenable model for sexual liberation, regardless of ethnic, religious, or political contexts.

4   Reem M. Abu Hassan observes that Jordanian women's status is going through a 'historic transition', with women having the same rights as men to 'health care, education, political participation, and employment' (2005, p. 106). However, she also states that family laws and social security benefits still discriminate against women, and legal protection against gender violence is not yet completely satisfactory.

5   Rushdie's women often embody popular cultural models of femininity handed down through the ages. For instance, the historical characters of Ayesha and Hind in *The Satanic Verses*, both powerful and cruel women, seem to belong in an Arabic and Orientalist archive including one of Rushdie's favourite intertexts, *The Arabian Nights*. Nicole Thiara argues that Rushdie's acerbic deployment of women is a deliberate strategy to reveal the workings of patriarchy: 'One of the purposes of Saleem's monstrosity-bestowing description of Indian women [in *Midnight's Children*] is criticism of those strategies which make women appear monstrous in the first place whenever they violate the essentialist image of feminine nature and demeanour' (2009, p. 76). I must thank Rehana Ahmed for alerting me to the problematic depiction of Muslim matriarchal figures in Sarif's work.

6   Michelle Gibson and Deborah Meem usefully chart the history of the 'butch' and 'femme' dichotomy in lesbian history. The observe that the codification of butch and femme lesbian identities was well established in the USA by the time of WWII, after which its prominence waxed and waned. According to them: 'The advent of second-wave feminism in the late 1960s and 1970s drove many butches and femmes underground, as the new movement scorned butch-femme as an unhealthy, not to mention politically incorrect, imitation of sexist male-female power relations. After a decade or so of invisibility, butch-femme gender roles resurfaced as part of the "lesbian sex wars" of the 1980s. This time, however, lesbian gender was academically theorized as feminist theory, deconstruction, and postmodernism merged to produce queer theory. The pioneering work of Sue-Ellen Case, Judith Butler, and others introduced the concept of butch-femme gender as lesbian erotic play' (Gibson

and Meem, 2002, p. 4). So, whereas the 1960s and 1970s second-wave – and invariably heterosexist – feminism critiqued the butch–femme dichotomy as imitating the masculine and feminine roles of patriarchy, the queer activists and theorists of the 1980s and 1990s reclaimed such performances of gender and sexual orientation as queering the contours of heteronormative aesthetics. However, it is arguable that such a configuration of female same-sex identities has become its own kind of normativity, and its prominence has allowed artists such as Sarif to place it at the centre of *The World Unseen* following the example of mainstream American depictions of female same-sex intimacy.

5

Between gang and family: queering ethnicity and British Muslim masculinities in Sally El Hosaini's *My Brother the Devil* (2012)

S O FAR, our exploration of Shamim Sarif's literary and film work has provided us with one viewpoint on the negotiation of sexual non-normativity within diasporic Muslim communities in Britain in in the first decade of the twenty-first century. Sarif's films and novels, *The World Unseen* and *I Can't Think Straight*, focus specifically on the plight of sexually dissident Muslim and Arab women. I have argued that, as the work of a British citizen of South African and South Asian Muslim heritage with no direct access to an Islamicate female homoerotic archive, Sarif's work creates a form of queer countermemory through intimate personal bonding which qualifies the erasure of female homosexuality in normative Islamic discourses, while partly challenging dominant Western views on Arab and Muslim men's conservatism and homophobia.

The work of film director and screenwriter Sally El Hosaini offers both a departure from and a continuation of Sarif's efforts to bring queer disorientation to the forefront of intersecting debates on Britishness, gender, and sexuality in contemporary British cinema. Hosaini's debut feature film, *My Brother the Devil*, released in 2012, complicates those debates undertaken by her predecessors, such as Sarif and Hanif Kureishi, and is even more probing in her critique of the prescriptions of gender and sexuality, with a keen yet undidactic focus on sexual fluidity and class disenfranchisement. She chooses the London Borough of Hackney as her main setting, and youth male gangs as her protagonists; yet, far from constructing racially segregated groupings, her multiethnic gangs share a rooted and localised diasporic sense of belonging. In addition, as opposed to

Kureishi's and Sarif's more circumstantial and familial – and altogether less direct – articulation of Muslim religious sensibilities, El Hosaini allows the Islamic faith to have a more tangible position in her characters' ideological makeup by giving it a role in their moral conundrums and in their grappling for a relational sense of cultural identity.

The ethos of El Hosaini's depiction of Islam is at once transnational and localised, rooted within its specific locality in contemporary multicultural London. In this chapter's exploration of *My Brother the Devil* (henceforth *My Brother*), I suggest that the racially pitted gangs of Kureishi's depiction of Thatcherite Britain have evolved into multiethnic gangs organised around London's postcodes, which involves a sometimes problematic distancing from the values of first-generation migrants, as well as a queering of masculinity which disorientates nationalist and diasporic normativity. However, far from undertaking a stringent critique of Islam, El Hosaini enacts micropolitical disorientations, for instance, through the incisive representation of Muslim girlhood challenging persistent stereotypes about helpless and repressed Muslim women. In fact, El Hosaini's Muslim women, as we shall see, instil a sense of morality onto disaffected Muslim boys who are coopted into drug dealing.

El Hosaini is a British screenwriter and filmmaker of mixed Welsh and Egyptian heritage. As she relays in an interview with Liz Hoggard (2013), her parents met while they were at university in Liverpool in the 1960s. Although El Hosaini was born in Swansea (Wales), she grew up in Cairo and attended a United World College in South Wales from the age of sixteen. El Hosaini ascribes her empathy with people of various ethnic, national, and class backgrounds to her college's ability to 'foster intercultural understanding' (Hoggard, 2013). She went on to study Arabic and Middle Eastern Politics at Durham University. It was at this time that she realised she should have studied film. After graduating, she became an apprentice in the UK Arts International foundation, and then was involved in the production of Middle Eastern war documentaries, including on-site coverage of the Euro-American invasion of Iraq in 2003. Her experiences began to show her that the filmmaking environment was highly controlled by Western company superiors, who were preventing complex perspectives on the conflict to arise. Disenchanted with these political biases (McCrum, 2013), El Hosaini became involved in the production of fictional feature films, most notably the British-Yemeni romantic comedy *A New Day In Old Sana'a*. She then became a script editor for BBC drama before moving on to produce her own scripts and films, which are often concerned with the silenced or the disenfranchised. In her own words: 'I'm interested in people on the margins of society; outsiders and outcasts. Being Welsh-Egyptian – half from one place, half from another – you always see both sides of everything' (Hoggard, 2013). This dual cultural heritage lends El Hosaini's work both its ideological complexity and its compassion for the perspectives of the dismissed or the persecuted, providing her with the ideological tools to critique diasporic ethnic communities from within, while also qualifying Western stereotypes about the ethnic 'Other'.

El Hosaini's work often forfeits clean-cut ideological positions and rejects monolithic cultural affiliations, as it strives to tell the stories of those who do not conform to dominant ideas of citizenship, often in more ways than one. In her case, this multivalent lack of conformity intersects with issues of sexual non-normativity. El Hosaini's first short film as a screenwriter and director, *Henna Night*, released in 2009, refers in its title to the traditional ritual of decorating a bride's hands and feet with henna before her nuptials. The narrative depicts female same-sex desire in a British Muslim context of compulsory heterosexuality, showing the emotional despair of a character called Amina, portrayed by Amber Rose Revah (who also played Sheetal Sheth's sister in Sarif's *I Can't Think Straight* and her grandmother in *The World Unseen*). Amina is a young British Muslim who locks herself in the bathroom on the day before her wedding and refuses to come out. She is eventually persuaded by the almost incantatory cook of her bachelorette party, her friend Nour (Beatriz Romilly), who intermittently consults her handwritten Arabic book for recipes to 'enchant a heart', and to 'distract the stubborn mind' (*Henna Night*, 2009). As it turns out, Nour is Amina's female lover, and the main reason why she is lately questioning her marriage to her fiancé, Bilal. Nour prompts Amina to cancel the wedding and to leave with her, but Amina believes it is too late: it would 'kill them', meaning her family, or they would 'kill us', a proleptic yet ironic reference to the film's denouement. During Amina's henna night, Nour, who is visibly distraught, decides, according to her voiceover, to brew a concoction that will 'bond eternal love when all hope disappears' (*Henna Night*, 2009). After the party, Amina's mother (Badria Timimi) leaves both girls in Amina's room, where they inconspicuously share a bed, highlighting the invisibility to normative society of female same-sex desire. Nour then offers Amina a glass containing her 'magical' potion; after Amina has tasted it, Nour tells her that she loves her, to which Amina responds with 'I know'; Nour then drinks the remaining contents. When dawn breaks, their bodies are framed pale and inert: Amina presents a nosebleed, while Nour's unblinking body stares into her lover's face. The trope of lovers' fatal poisoning fits within an British canonical cultural tradition, best embodied in William Shakespeare's *Romeo and Juliet*, yet El Hosaini queers it by drawing attention to the problematic heteronormativity inherent to the Muslim diasporic communities in Britain. The short film finishes with a single poignant shot of the empty bed after Amina's and Nour's bodies have been taken away, which acts a silent indictment of the strictures placed on queer Muslim desire. El Hosaini's short film contrasts significantly with Sarif's life-affirming examination of female homosexuality in a British multicultural context, offering the tragic flip-side of Muslim same-sex desire: whereas Sarif's protagonists rebelled and distanced themselves from their families' dogmatic positions on homosexuality, El Hosaini's short film offers a more pessimistic resolution, showing the limited range of options offered to those Muslims who refuse to conform to their diasporic community's societal and familial expectations.

El Hosaini's first full-length cinematic effort as a writer and director, *My Brother*, is more optimistic in terms of the fate of Muslim subjects embracing same-sex desire, yet it is also markedly different from her initial examination of queerness, for instead of focusing on female homoerotic desire, it dwells more intently on the performance of British Muslim masculinities. In the film's context, same-sex desire, a revulsive intended to shock both the film's characters and different sectors of its audience, risks appearing a mere ideological conduit, yet one that still micropolitically erodes identitarian expectations. The film is inspired by El Hosaini's community in Hackney, East London, where she had lived for more than a decade before shooting the film. According to her, she researched and wrote the film script by falling back on her 'documentary roots': she 'embedded [her]self within gangs in Hackney, Highbury and Brixton' (Dawson, 2013), which taught her their particular language, lending the film its sense of cultural authenticity. In her own words: 'What I discovered is that there's a young disenfranchised generation emerging, but it's much more intelligent, thinking, and feeling than most people or the media give it credit for. It was during this research phase that I contemplated the concept of masculinity' (Dawson, 2013). In El Hosaini's cinematic depiction of East London, performances of masculinity are contingent upon peer pressure from other members of youth gangs, with an emphasis on inter-gang assertiveness and aggression, as well as upon patriarchal ideals inherited from the diasporic family grouping, all set against an unsentimental social backdrop of class disenfranchisement. Although we must remain wary of conflating the filmmaker's and her subjects' particular politics of location, Stuart Hall reminds us in his essay 'Cultural Identity and Diaspora' that cinema is not a mere mirror held up to reality, but 'a form of representation which is able to constitute us as new kinds of subjects, and thereby enable us to discover places from which to speak' (1990, pp. 236–7). In *My Brother*, El Hosaini attempts to forge a new way of representing British diasporic identity in a manner that disorientates normative positions about diasporic youth.

El Hosaini remains aware of the media's persistent construction of British youth either as anti-social hooligans or as radicalised terrorists waiting to strike and thus failing to offer ideological nuance or to garner sympathy for their material plights. Crucially, the film's production commenced on the day riots broke out in Hackney, in August 2011, which confirmed to El Hosaini the urgent need to make an 'honest' film about discriminated British youth (Hoggard, 2013). In addition, and crucially to our concerns here, she affirms that '[a]fter the 7/7 tube bombings I was tired of media reports that painted all British Arab youth as potential terror threats' (*Indiewire*, 2012). Disorganising the Islamophobic idea that all British Muslims of Arab descent are potential terrorists is central to El Hosaini's work, since she expresses no doubt about the Britishness of the male gangs she represents in *My Brother*. Influenced by her own mixed cultural background, she focuses on British youth of Arab heritage, but their confederates, as she observes, are of Nigerian, Somali, Turkish, Jamaican, British, and often mixed ethnic heritage, which leads her to exclaim: 'This racially mixed, youth subculture fascinates me because this is real London! These are British boys' (Dawson, 2013). In the ensuing pages, I examine El Hosaini's depiction of multi-ethnic London as challenging nationalist ethnic absolutism and diasporic relativism: I argue that, far from demonstrating an extrapolation from, or a rejection of, Britishness, London youth's granulated sense of space avoids nostalgia for a lost homeland and cements a highly located sense of belonging in the multicultural metropolis. In addition, I suggest, via the work of Fatima El Tayeb (2011), that the film contributes to queering ethnicity by constructing her characters as legitimately British and, moreover, also European, through association with other diasporic Muslims from other European locales. I also undertake a critical exploration of Islam in the film as offering competing versions of masculinity which eventually relinquish violence and prize affective empathy. I interrogate, as well, intergenerational differences in the film's central British Arab family, and how such disparities are important for the articulation of the British Muslim diasporic citizen. El Hosaini's representation of British diasporic and cosmopolitan Muslims, I suggest, challenges both Western commonplaces about Muslim masculinities and views on Muslim women that construct them as invariably repressed and gender-segregated. Finally, the film's dealings with queerness are analysed as a means of challenging normative constructions of masculinity and as a rejection of homonationalist models of sexual orientation prescribing cultural assimilation and sexual fixity to the West's constructed 'Others'.

My Brother follows the trajectories of two British brothers of Egyptian heritage living in a council estate in Hackney: Mohammed (Fady Elsayed), commonly known as Mo, a teenager interested in hip-hop poetry and 'grime',[1] and Rashid (James Floyd), usually shortened to Rash, the older brother whom Mo idolises, and who happens to be one of the leaders of the local DGM ('Drugs, Guns, and Money') youth gang, albeit a gradually more diffident member. El Hosaini observes that the interwoven strands of the two brothers' experiences was her guiding image while writing the script: 'Each brother was a strand of the helix and their lives twisted and spiralled around each other; on separate paths, but forever connected' (Dawson, 2013). Although mentally structuring the film around a genetic image may suggest an investment in bloodlines, or in biological forms of heritage and belonging, the two strands of DNA also denote a certain duality, both in terms of the film's intermittent exploration of each brother's viewpoint and of their assembled cultural identity. Both Rash and Mo are self-admittedly British and Hackney is their home, yet they are also Muslim and of Egyptian heritage, and precariously living in a council estate, all of which complicates their cultural and political affiliations. In fact, their parents' North African provenance renders them an ethnic minority within Britain's Muslim minority. As Nasar Meer (2010) points out, according to a recent census of Britain's Muslim constituencies, 42.5 per cent of British Muslims are of Pakistani heritage; 16.8 per cent, Bangladeshi; 8.5 per cent, Indian; and 7.5 per cent, 'White Other', which refers to those citizens with Turkish, Arabic, and North African ethnic links. Due to their Egyptian heritage, Rashid and Mohammed would seem to belong to this last small group of British Muslims who are not considered part of an ethnic minority. The central household in El Hosaini's film is one where Arabic and English freely intermingle, rather than, say, English and Punjabi. El Hosaini thus offers us an ethnic minority within an ethno-religious minority, disorganising the conflation of British Muslim identities and the South Asian diaspora.

By contrast, global disquisitions of Islam offer an inverted mirroring of debates about British Muslims. Amanullah De Sondy (2014) lucidly observes that, due to Islam's inception in Arabia, general global discussions about Muslims often tend to focus on the 'Arab world', while South Asian Muslims are often relegated to the periphery, which, we could add, they share with other 'marginal', stateless forms of Muslim identity, such as Kurdishness. However, by contrast, and due to Britain's particular histories of colonialism and postcolonial migration, the category 'British Muslim' is most often associated with British citizens of South Asian heritage, as illustrated so far in this study by the British Asian Muslims in *My Beautiful Laundrette* and one of the two main families in

Sarif's *I Can't Think Straight*. Meer suggests that it is 'understandable – if a little misleading – that British Muslims are associated first and foremost with a South-Asian background, especially since those with this background make up roughly 68 per cent of the British Muslim population' (2010, p. 91). In addition, as Humayun Ansari summarises: 'In this heavy ethnic mix, religious affiliations intersect in many ways with age-group, gender and socio-economic status, as well as with the specific circumstances of immigrant settlement experience in Britain' (2004, p. 3). *My Brother* thus serves to disorganise the category of 'British Muslim' by drawing the audience's attention to the diversity of Muslims' trajectories: for instance, Mohammed and Rashid are of Egyptian heritage, their parents hailing from Cairo and Mansura, and Mo's new friend and platonic love interest, Aisha (Letitia Wright), is a Muslim girl who has recently moved to their council estate in Hackney from Ejere in Ethiopia. (Aisha's depiction also brings into the frame an often underrepresented black perspective to issues of Muslim identity.) On the one hand, El Hosaini's characters visibly subsume their minority ethnic status in Britain and attempt to transcend ethnocentric constructions of Britishness by claiming membership of communities that are multiethnic yet firmly located and belonging in London; on the other, their simultaneous identification with Islam provides them with an internationalist vantage point that bypasses national borders and allows them to search for commonalities without obviating cultural differences and national perspectives. So, while belonging in multicultural Britain is of great importance to El Hosaini's protagonists, who are used to claiming ownership of their neighbourhood in London – if not, perhaps, as we shall see, of the whole of Britain – some of her characters also learn to look beyond their most immediate sociocultural milieux, forging a more transcultural and less orthodox form of Muslim identity that queers normative constructions of diasporic masculinities.

From Mohammed and Rashid's second-generation diasporic perspectives as British citizens, London is undeniably their home, and they have no strong feelings invested in Egypt as an ancestral homeland. For example, when Rashid first meets the French Arab Sayyid (Saïd Taghmaoui), a professional photographer and his best friend Izzi's (Anthony Welsh) marihuana-buying client, Rash is visibly discomfited by Sayyid's probing about his nationality. When Sayyid asks him where he is from, Rashid bluntly gives him the Hackney postcode: 'Right here, *bruv*: E9.' Sayyid insists: 'No, originally', to which Rash flippantly responds: 'Egypt'. 'Do you speak Arabic?', questions the French Arab. Rash retorts with one word: '*Shwaya*' ('a little bit') (*My Brother*, 2012). This episode replays an established trope in British representations of second-generation diasporic citizens, or the familiar question of 'where you *really* from?' To Sayyid's probing of his place of origin, Rashid answers by positioning himself firmly in Hackney, yet after Izzi's brutal murder by rival gang leader, Demon (Leemore Marrett Jr.), he pursues the friendship with the French Arab, suggesting, I would argue, a transnational kinship between diasporic Muslim subjects.

Rashid is eventually employed by Sayyid in his photography studio, after which Sayyid is invited to Rashid and Mohammed's family home for a traditional Egyptian meal cooked by their mother, Hanan (Amira Ghazalla). Here, the film's historical backdrop comes again into play, since its production coincided not only with the London riots of 2011, but also with the Egyptian Revolution against president Hosni Mubarak, part of the extended social movement popularly known as the 'Arab Spring'. Rash and Mo's father, Abdul-Aziz (Nasser Memarzia), is enthused by the political dissent in Egypt, which reminds him of the heyday of Egyptian anti-colonial nationalism in 1952. He states: 'I didn't sleep for the entire eighteen days. The Revolution brought out the true Egyptian, the Egyptian we didn't see since Nasser' (*My Brother*, 2012).[2] When Sayyid asks Abdul-Aziz whether he ever thinks of going back to Egypt, he admits that there is nothing awaiting their return, to which Sayyid responds that 'we' – a pronoun in which he seems to include all Arabs – need to be more involved in 'the democratic process', otherwise 'why else did we end up here?' After Sayyid's expression of his idealistic yearning to be more politically involved in North Africa, young Mo cannot contain himself any more, angrily responding that 'we didn't end up here; we was *born* here' (*My Brother*, 2012). He then pronounces all politicians 'liars' before storming out of the dining room. According to Ansari, 'Britishness is often described [by British Muslims] in terms of citizenship, a *birthright*, but not really a deeply-held emotional and cultural bond shared with the white, secular or Christian majority' (2004, p. 17, emphasis added). Although it is Mo who is being more vocal about his Britishness as a birth right, neither he nor Rashid subscribe to ethnocentric constructions of British national identity. In addition, London is their home due to their birth, and not Egypt, their parents' country of origin. Unlike the French Arab Sayyid, who has forcefully fled the racially volatile French Republic and therefore subscribes to the ideal of 'lost origins', the two brothers do not make manifest any nostalgia for an ancestral homeland. Yet, in Rashid's case, his friendship and eventual romantic relationship with Sayyid belies a thirst for a more transnational sense of belonging as diasporic and cosmopolitan Arabs in Europe.

Mohammed's localised sense of belonging, which is shared with other diasporic characters in the film, does not entail a nationalist allegiance to 'king and country', but is linked to their most immediate environs in multicultural London. In her study on young Muslims in the postcolonial metropolis, Louise Ryan suggests that '[d]ay-to-day experiences of place are mainly rooted in the local – the neighbourhood environments where people live, work, study, socialize and worship' (2012, p. 102). Ryan's anthropological study suggests that 'while Britain was often perceived [by young British Muslims] as not inclusive of their identities, London was regarded much more positively as a place of possibilities' (2012, pp. 105–6). Moreover, while the city 'does not belong to any one particular group', it can 'accommodate notions of "home" for a wide range of people' (Ryan, 2012, p 108). El Hosaini's film deftly captures this localised reclaiming of London as a diasporic 'home'. According to James Procter, '[t]ravelling rhetorics tend to underplay the extent to which diaspora is also an issue of *settlement* and a constant battle over territories' (2003, p. 22, emphasis in original). El Hosaini shows us how diasporic youth wilfully appropriate urban space, offering intermittent shots of Mo composing hip-hop poetry in the council estate's balconies, green areas, and kids' playground, where he 'hangs out' with his best friends, Ethiopia-born Aisha and white British Jamie (Aaron Ishmael). Within this mapping of the city, Islam acts as a community-building catalyst: Izzi's visibly Muslim funeral constitutes a communal experience of mourning for the whole neighbourhood, constructing a multiethnic form of togetherness that illustrates the cultural synergies within diasporic communities between the transnational – Islam as a unifying worldview – and the local – Hackney as a place of settlement.

The council estate's ruling DGM gang is also multiethnic, with members who are visibly of Arab, South Asian, African, and Caribbean heritage, but who do not draw attention to any ethnic differences, often addressing each other as 'fam', 'bruv', and 'cuz' (youth slang for 'family', 'brother', and 'cousin'). This colloquial use of modified familial language and the general homeliness of the gang's premises, overseen by the pseudo-maternal figure of Sonya (Yusra Warsama), an occasional drug addict whose biological child has been taken away by Social Services, illustrates El Hosaini's interest in exploring the 'gang as a surrogate family' (Hoggard, 2013). The gang acts as a space of freedom from familial expectations and constraints, since, according to Ansari, 'the extended social networks based on caste, clan and tribal and regional loyalties, which loom large in the perceptions of the older generations, have little relevance for [younger Muslims] in the British context' (2004, p. 20). I would suggest that the diasporic youth of El Hosaini's film visibly steer away from the values of first-generation migrants and seek their own space where they can forge new ways of belonging that are multiethnic and diasporic, with more emphasis on settlement and rerooting than on dislocation.

The gang's premises constitute in some ways an embodiment of Avtar Brah's influential definition of 'diaspora space' as 'decentr[ing] the subject position of "native", "immigrant", "migrant", the in/outsider' (1996, p. 242), whereby all diasporic subjects become natives in a relational sense within a multiethnic locale. However, their activities are underpinned by a more problematic subscription to a model of masculinity organised around violence and criminality. From the start, *My Brother* visibly constructs masculinity as synonymous with machismo. For instance, in the opening sequence, Rashid is shown boxing intensively at the gym, which sports a telling sign reading 'NO GUTS NO GLORY' (*My Brother*, 2012; see Figure 6). His careful attention to his physical fitness is meant to bolster the hypermasculine persona he has created for his role in the DGM gang, a violent team whose territoriality and masculinist posturing ultimately demonstrates, in El Hosaini's words, 'how much pressure these boys put on themselves "to be men"' (Dawson, 2013). In addition, Peter Cherry observes that '[f]or the men who join the gang, violence (hetero)sexual conquest, and crime become an opportunity to transcend the limited opportunities afforded by their class, race, and cultural background as well as an important resource for reaffirming their claims to (masculine) power' (2017, p. 7). Mo's grappling with his identity involves moving away from his PlayStation and towards the cultural expression of his teenage male disaffection, namely composing hip-hop poetry emulating the cadences of the black performers he has seen outside school, which is in itself also a diaspora space of commonality.

The film's opening shots of Mo and Rashid are interspersed with black-and-white photographs from Simon Wheatley's *Don't Call Me Urban! The Time of Grime*, a photography book published in 2010 whose multimodal digital edition

Figure 6 *My Brother the Devil* (2012), directed by Sally El Hosaini

is billed as 'convey[ing] the hopes and frustrations of an apolitical generation locked into London's decaying housing estates' (www.dontcallmeurban.com). As El Hosaini's film shows, music and poetry are affirmative means of expressing dissent and togetherness, although Mo's intermittent writing of his 'bars' can at times appear an adolescent pastime removed from his most immediate material surroundings, and hence he is gradually more sensually drawn towards the attractive sociability of his older brother's youth gang.

While the multiethnic youth community in *My Brother* seems to have adopted the tones of black youth subcultures, El Hosaini's narrative also attempts to disorganise systematic – and systemic – conflations of blackness and criminality, something of which she is particularly conscious in the wake of the 2011 London riots. Her critique is framed within a context in which the historian and polemicist David Starkey problematically claimed on national television that '[t]he whites have become black. A particular sort of violent destructive, nihilistic gangster culture has become the fashion and black and white boys and girls operate in this language together' (Quinn, 2011). Initially, the troubling monolithic construction of black gangsterism is adopted by some of El Hosaini's Arab characters: for instance, when Rashid, aided by his best friend, Izzi, arrives home with a new TV set, a reward for Mohammed's improving performance at school, his father, Abdul-Aziz, first assumes that the item was cheap 'because it's stolen', before telling his wife, in a clearly audible aside, that he is 'sick of [Rashid] hanging around with these black boys' (*My Brother*, 2012). Abdul-Aziz's remark implies that Izzi is a bad influence on his son because he is black, although he is mixed race; he misidentifies him as a monolith of blackness. Nonetheless, it is Izzi who begins extricating himself from street culture and who ultimately inspires Rashid's break from drug dealing. Smartly dressed and accompanied by Rashid on his way to a job interview, Izzi states: 'I need this job. I'm a flippin' dad' (*My Brother*, 2012), which Rash ridicules, confidently stating that he makes more 'dough' on the road dealing drugs than his father earns driving a bus. Despite Rashid's flippancy, rival gang-leader Demon's stabbing of Izzi during a fortuitous inter-gang street brawl acts as a catalyst for Rashid's change of heart. Following the fatal stabbing, as Kramer and El Hosaini jointly describe, 'El Hosaini created a moment of calm and stillness in the film to show what she called "that moment when their masks dropped and they are children and they are scared"' (Kramer, 2013). Izzi's death begins to unravel Rashid's gang-style masculinity, proving to him and to El Hosaini's audience that, that for all his mastering of drug dealing, penknives, and street slang, when confronted with fatal violence, his emotional response of running away and huddling under a railway bridge is that of a helpless child: a clear check to his hypermasculine gang persona. I would argue Izzi's death triggers Rashid's search for a model of masculinity that is removed from drug dealing and violence, but that still retains its more transgressive homosocial dimensions.

Intermingled with the DGM gang's construction of brazen masculinity, there is a certain level of homosocial bonding in the gang's diaspora space that starts revealing the fault lines of heteronormative diasporic masculinity. In fact, there is a paradox inherent to the gang's intersecting of homophobia and homosociality. As El Hosaini observes, '[gang members] are extremely homophobic and yet constantly flirting with one another. All men, and constantly hugging around the neck, touching heads' (Kramer, 2013). In Mohammed's initial visit to the gang's premises, he is visibly amused by the way Rash puts his arm around Izzi's neck in seemingly innocent comradeship. Despite such camaraderie, this homosociality creates a mood of same-sex intimacy that El Hosaini is keen to probe further from Rashid's viewpoint. When prowling the streets in search of customers, Rashid's subjective point of view, located in the car gang member Aj (Arnold Oceng) routinely borrows from his uncle, reveals his curiosity about Izzi's dealings with Sayyid, after the pair openly embrace in the street. Rash's gaze lingers on the two men and then retreats, subtly yet tellingly teased by their physical gesture, as he seemingly attempts to ascertain if the embrace constitutes just a sign of male-to-male friendship or a deeper homoerotic bond. Following Izzi's traumatic death, Rashid's state of mourning draws him instinctively towards Sayyid, who becomes Izzi's emotional stand-in. As we will see now, the two Arab men's burgeoning relationship forges a new model of diasporic masculinity that constitutes a simultaneous assemblage of competing models of Muslim masculinities and queerness, which micropolitically disorientates diasporic familial constructions of Islamic masculinity and the hypermasculine gang model.

Rashid's and Aziz's initial bonding after Izzi's death is, in fact, facilitated by their Muslim cultural backgrounds, which despite being distinctly different – Rashid being British of Egyptian heritage and Sayyid being French with ethnic links to the Maghreb – nonetheless draw them to each other due to the transnational nature of Islam and the universalist ethos of the Islamic *ummah*. However, their self-fashioning, embodying different ways of being a Muslim man, is complicated by the lack of a cohesive model of Islamic masculinity. As De Sondy suggests in *The Crisis of Islamic Masculinities*, the prophets of Islam are supposed to be examples for all humans – Muhammad being often billed, most famously by Ibn Arabi, as 'the perfect man' – however, as De Sondy proposes, '[t]heir lives tell us much about ethics and morality but little about a uniform

Islamic masculinity' (2014, p. 118). He stresses that, in opposition to the disparity and heterogeneity offered by Islamic prophets, the major commentators of the Qur'an have interpreted the holy scripture in such a way that particular gender roles, often formulated around the family unit, are singled out for social reinforcement, hence perpetuating gender inequalities and a seemingly 'traditional' understanding of masculinity and femininity. In fact, in the absence of a widely accepted or centralised model of Islamic masculinity, De Sondy observes that many Muslim boys are being 'bombarded with masculine role models to emulate' in order to become '"acceptably" male', including a socioculturally 'dominant mode [...] associated with heterosexuality, toughness, power, and authority, competitiveness and the subordination of gay men' (2014, p. 9). According to De Sondy's argument, it would seem this heteronormative and homophobic model of masculinity is not configured in direct relation to Islam, but that it remains culturally linked to Muslim heteropatriarchal values ossified through centuries of male and heterosexual preponderance. Nonetheless, it is the lack of a consensual image of Islamic masculinity that renders Rashid's and Sayyid's worldviews productively dissident; their disparity draws attention to the lack of a dominant form of Islamic masculinity that can fully encompass them, and this triggers their assemblage of a queer diasporic Muslim masculinity posited at a remove from heteronormativity.

When discussing Izzi's murder, Rashid's and Sayyid's recourse to Islam evinces radically different viewpoints arising from their particular life experiences and their differing understanding of Islam's traditions. After Rashid chances upon a photograph of Sayyid posing with his brothers, it is revealed that he was raised in Seine-Saint-Denis, a French neighbourhood with a large Muslim population, situated in the suburbs of Paris and colloquially referred to by Sayyid as 'neuf trois' ('nine three' in French, which reflects the locality's administrative number: 93). Sayyid then dispassionately points out that his two brothers are in jail, although it is never ascertained on what grounds they have been incarcerated. A surprised Rashid asks him whether his siblings' imprisonment was his central motivation for leaving France, to which Sayyid evasively answers: 'yeah, and other reasons' (*My Brother*, 2012), subtly indexing the sexual non-normativity that will become manifest in his later romantic involvement with Rashid. Sayyid's experience of violence involving his family has visibly influenced his current ideological standpoint. Rash partly blames himself for Izzi's death, stating that he used to believe himself untouchable, yet he remains adamant about how the culprits need to 'pay for this'. As Sayyid tries to comfort Rashid about Izzi's murder while appeasing his thirst for revenge, he quotes his deceased father's invocation of Prophet Muhammad's words: 'The strong man is the one who can controls himself when he's angry [...]. It's from the *hadith*' (*My Brother*, 2012). Sayyid's reference is to a saying of the Prophet Muhammad compiled in *Saḥīḥ Al-Bukhari*.³ In Book 78, dealing with '*Al-Adab* (Good Manners)', the Prophet's *hadith* number 6114 reports: 'The strong is not the one who overcomes the people by his strength, but the strong is the one who controls himself while in anger' (Khan, 1997, p. 83). Sayyid makes recourse to Prophet Muhammad's *Sunnah* for a moral standpoint on anger that can help him reflect on past violent misdeeds and discourage further violence. Sayyid has experienced aggression himself, his personal history being illustrated later during the first erotic encounter with Rashid by an old scar cutting through his abdomen. This unexplained wound illustrates the hard material way in which Sayyid has had to learn to control his emotions, which he justifies by invoking Prophet Muhammad's words on the need to control one's anger. Sayyid uses Islamic doctrinal wisdom in order to access a form of masculinity that transcends anger and aggression, showing that strength is not merely a matter of masculine physical prowess, but a mental, even spiritual, trait, involving even-temperedness in the face of injustice and adversity.

Sayyid's pacifist stance, which is the result of his own troubled experience of violence in France and of his personal understanding of Islam, contrasts with Rashid's fatalistic comeback, which attempts to assert itself by dismissing Sayyid's quoted *hadith* and purposefully 'returning' to the Qur'an. As he somewhat derisively asserts: 'Yeah, but in the Qur'an it says everything is *maktoob* [Arabic for "written"], so if it's all written from before, then what difference does it make? If shit's gonna happen, then it's gonna happen, innit?' (*My Brother*, 2012). This statement goes unchallenged by a dispirited-looking Sayyid. The concept of fate that Rashid invokes is more fully explained in *sura* 57, *ayat* 22 of the Qur'an: 'No misfortune can happen, either in the earth or in yourselves, that was not set down in writing before We brought it into being – that is easy for God – so you need not grieve for what you miss or gloat over what you gain' (Abdel Haleem, 2005, p. 368). Rashid dismisses Sayyid's request for temperance and peaceful resolution by drawing attention to the concept of predetermination: everything about a person's destiny has already been written; hence, Izzi's murder, as well as Rashid's vengeful retaliation, would have always been a part of God's masterplan. This view renders human free will inconsequential, a nihilistic position that Rashid authorises with reference to the Qur'an, and in defiance of any subsequent scriptural or intellectual elaborations on God's message.

El Hosaini's construction of Rashid's youthful nihilism and exclusive reliance on the Qur'an fits existing debates about Muslim diasporic youth and their embrace of Salafi-style literalist understandings of Islam that will not be 'perverted' by undue reinterpretation or by making recourse to the *ahadith* or the *Sunnah*, let alone the *tafsir* and *fiqh* traditions. Peter Mandaville asserts that Salafism 'aims to rid Islam of anything that has entered the faith through contact with various local, "cultural" beliefs and practices', which entails young Muslims' alienation from their parents' understanding of Islam; according to him, Muslim diasporic youths face the challenges of being Muslim in a global world, 'caught between two senses of identity' (Mandaville, 2007, p. 262): being citizens of Western nations and being Muslims. In addition, Ahmad and Sardar's study of British Muslim youth states that most of their research participants 'referred to the Qur'an as the source of their knowledge and understanding of Islam, undiluted by cultural practices' (2012, p. 111). Rashid's youthful perspective disqualifies any traditions following the Qur'an, making the sacred text the only script informing his understanding of Islam. Moreover, Rashid's understanding of the Qur'an through raw anger and emotion, as opposed to Sayyid's pacifist and intellectual approach, belies what Olivier Roy describes as 'a widespread anti-intellectualism that favours a more emotional religiosity, linked with individualism and with the crisis of intellectual authority' (2004, p. 31). Rashid has no qualms about subscribing to a literalist and potentially totalitarian perspective on his faith which dismisses all cultural negotiations of Islam, for the sake of justifying his ongoing emotional investment in inter-gang wars and their violent configuration of masculinity. As Roy also points out, there is a 'growing generation gap' (2004, p. 139) between first-generation Muslim migrants and their second-generation descendants in the West: elders no longer have much intellectual or ideological authority over their children, as partly illustrated by Abdul-Aziz's material preponderance but also by his lack of moral prowess in his male-dominated household, where there is no control over his children's activities. All of this illustrates Rashid's peculiar position as a second-generation diasporic Muslim in Britain: he embraces the Qur'an and disqualifies later cultural traditions; he dismisses the perspective of his parents' generation as old-fashioned and out of touch with the plight of the global contemporary world; he embraces Islam from a highly individualistic perspective that relies on emotion and affect, but which also deactivates a more critical and intellectual understanding of his faith.

For all of Rashid's bravado when discussing Islamic debates on anger with Sayyid, he cannot ultimately drive himself to kill Izzi's murderer, Demon, the leader of the rival gang. Present at the scene in a tattoo parlour is the young character simply known as 'Demon's Boy' (McKell Celaschi-David), who smiles at Rashid as he is about to pull his gun, while innocently dangling his feet. He is incidentally wearing the sneakers stolen earlier from his brother Mo, together with the DGM gang's marihuana. I would argue that the parallelism of Demon/Rashid, Demon's Boy/Mohammed created by the white trainers brings home to Rashid the irrevocable and centrifugal nature of murder, whose breaching of 'honour' could eventually involve Rashid's little brother after killing Demon. Something in Rashid's resolve, I would suggest, changes in this scene, so that when Mo tells Rashid upon his return to their shared bedroom: 'you'll get him next time, *bruv*', Rashid responds: 'There ain't gonna be a next time. Death is real, *bruv*. It ain't a fucking game. Once you're dead, you ain't coming back. *Halas*. [Arabic: "Done."]'. Mo retorts, with a naïve sense of clan loyalty: 'But if we don't body [slang for "kill"] Demon, then we lose and they win', to which Rashid responds: 'But we all lose in a sense' (*My Brother*, 2012), implying that it is not only the victims of murder and their loved ones that are affected by murder, but also its perpetrators, who have to live with the consequences of their acts. As it turns out, Rashid's gradual withdrawal from the inter-gang wars, which challenges the aggressive configuration of Muslim diasporic masculinities, becomes intimately linked with the queering of dominant diasporic masculinities and its challenge to mainstream homophobia of both gang and family. In addition, I would argue that El Hosaini has chosen to focus on Rashid's eventual reciprocation of Sayyid's homoerotic advances in order to disorientate her potential audiences with a salient instance of queer micropolitics that is transnational and, because of the affective links between Muslim European identities, also, to an extent, post-national. El Hosaini's unexpected tackling of queer Muslim desire does not merely target global Western audiences unused to fathoming the existence of queer Muslims in multiethnic working-class communities, but also the various implied diasporic audiences whose homophobia and restricting masculine models still need to be critically checked.

The intersecting in *My Brother* of ethnicity and sexuality contributes in great measure to the queering of ethnocentric ideas of European identity, and it is crucial that El Hosaini's critique is undertaken via Muslim characters, since Islam plays such an important role in the ethnic policing of Europeanness. As Fatima El Tayeb suggests, 'the trope of the Muslim as Other offers an apparently easy and unambiguous means to divide Europeans and migrants'; however, diasporic citizens, she argues, often create their own forms of belonging through the constant 'reassessment of the relationship between community, space, and identity in a postethnic and translocal context' (El Tayeb, 2011, p. xxx). In *My Brother*, such forms of collective diasporic belonging are best exemplified by Mo's aforementioned penchant for hip-hop poetry, which cuts molecularly through ethnic categories and articulates multiethnic youth's disaffection. However, Europeanness is more forcefully queered by the unexpected and disorientating liaison between Rashid and Sayyid, a translocal homoerotic connection between Muslims from London and Paris which is based on their shared second-generation European Muslim identities, despite their parents', and their own, different nationalities. The emphasis within diasporic communities, El Tayeb observes, is in 'producing a queering of ethnicity that is increasingly transformed into an active process of cultural resistance primarily located in the continent's urban centers' (2011, p. xxxii). However, such cultural resistance, which disorganises the identity categories segmentalising Europe into white native 'selves' and Muslim 'Others', must also confront the monolithic construction of Muslim diasporic masculinities as invariably heteronormative, which does not necessarily always make recourse to Islamic religious doctrine, but which is crucially underpinned by models of masculinity enforced by both gang and family.

I would advance the idea that Mo's reaction to his older brother's same-sex relationship with Sayyid has much to do with the perpetuation of internalised normative forms of masculinity, and the web of deceit Mo builds around Rashid's lifestyle in order to avoid telling the truth and potentially shaming his family makes him subscribe to the Western stereotype of the radicalised Muslim youth. Teased by Rash's time-consuming relationship with Sayyid, which is taking him away from their family home, Mo follows him and climbs the scaffolding outside Sayyid's apartment. Perched on it, he spies Sayyid's half-naked body as he drinks some water, and he listens into the couple's intimate activities. In a manner not dissimilar to the framing of queer bodies in *My Beautiful Laundrette*, the glass window acts as an explicit framing device, making us privy to Mohammed's subjective point of view, superimposing the perspectives of character and audience. Visibly disturbed by the realisation of his brother's homosexual relationship, Mo flees in a panic, struggling to discuss the matter with anyone. His attempt at telling his two closest friends, Aisha and Jamie, results in the false confession that Rashid is involved in 'terrorist shit' (*My Brother*, 2012). Peter Morey and Amina Yaqin highlight 'those features that are used again and again [in Western representation of Muslims], becoming a default signifier for the mistrusted Muslim' (2011, p. 19); this includes the stereotypical figure of the young Muslim terrorist born and bred in the West, or the so-called 'enemy within'. El Hosaini's film relies on irony here, for there is nothing about Rashid or any of his confederates' activities that is remotely linked to Islamic terrorism, and the false accusation of terrorism serves the indirect purpose of disorganising the culturally dominant stereotype of the Muslim terrorist whose values are thought to differ from those of the Western nation of his birth.

As it turns out, Rashid is not a Muslim terrorist, but a queer Muslim 'terrorising' his own cultural community, a figure contravening received and policed notions of Islamic masculinity. In this view, he is rather a different form of political agitator. As rumours of his own non-existent terror activities reach Rashid's ears, he prompts Mo to tell him why he has been calling him a terrorist. Mo states: ''cause that's what I wish you was. I'd rather have a brother who's a bomber – than a homo. You make me sick, Rash. You know, I wish you was never my brother' (*My Brother*, 2012). In Mo's configuration of masculinity, violence denotes male dominance, whereas homosexuality involves an emasculation. Rashid's response to his younger brother's rejection of him is to state his intent to leave the family home after killing Demon, which would exonerate both brothers from further involvement with the DGM gang. Despite his masculinist posturing in front of Rashid, the following scene portrays Mo breaking down and consuming the drugs he still possesses after being expelled, following Rashid's critical intervention, from the DGM gang. Mo's emotional response to his unsympathetic conversation with Rashid suggests a far more conflicted and guilt-ridden perspective on his brother's sexual orientation. By this point Mo, who has been seemingly failed by his idolised older brother, thrown out of his gang, and rejected by his love interest, Aisha, is having a crisis of confidence in his own manliness and in his social standing in his community.

Challenging once again mainstream Western expectations of Islamic gender politics, El Hosaini renders the female character of Aisha, the Ethiopian Muslim girl who rejects Mo's invitations to drink alcohol and to smoke, and who voluntarily wears the *hijab*, as the initial trigger of Mohammed's gradual moral 'reformation'. Her headscarf is a source of both fascination and respect: Mo is clearly impressed by her appearance when she first arrives in the council estate; her subscription to Islam also singles her out as a clearly discernible cultural ally. Sadia Abbas emphatically argues: 'The Muslim woman is object of imperial rescue, justification of imperial warfare, Orientalist cipher, target of jihadist violence, and, increasingly, the discursive site on which the central preoccupation of our time – how do you free yourself from freedom? – is worked out' (2014, p. 45). In addition, Roy argues that '[t]he stress on chastity, accompanying the voluntary wearing of the headscarf as a way of being respected by gangs of boys in poor neighbourhoods, says more about the crisis of traditional values and family structures than about the pervasiveness of traditional imported values' (2004, p. 141). In contravention of ongoing Western debates about this marker of Islamic identity, El Hosaini's most prominent young female Muslim in *My Brother* does not need to be rescued; she is not restricted to gender segregated spaces; and she is allowed to socialise with her local friends while upholding her religious principles, which includes the wearing of the *hijab*, which is not deemed a kowtowing to Islamic patriarchy.

El Hosaini does not construct Aisha as wearing the *hijab* to protect herself from young males in her council estate, for her headdress predates her move to the area, and she has a healthy and mutually respectful relationship with Mo and Jaime. In depicting a Muslim girl who is neither the object of Islamophobia nor the victim of Muslim patriarchy, El Hosaini is disorganising mainstream Western expectations of Muslim feminine subjugation and of Muslim patriarchal dominance and tutelage. Tellingly, Aisha is the character who begins to question the intergenerational gap between first- and second-generation diasporic subjects and who takes a position of moral responsibility by questioning Mo's involvement in the DGM gang's criminal activities. When an enthused Mo purchases a golden necklace for her with the proceeds of his drug dealing, she refuses it regretfully but constructively: she cannot accept it because she knows 'how [he] got the dough'; she also questions his problematic involvement with the gang: to Mohammed's assertion that '[t]hey're my *fam*', she responds with: 'I think Rashid's your *fam*. So is your mum and dad' (*My Brother*, 2012). Aisha may be illustrating here what Roy calls 'the crisis of traditional values and family structures' (2004, p. 141), yet this is does not take the form of her own submission to patriarchy; instead, it constitutes a warning to young Muslim men whose drastic steering away from their families is not opening them up to more just or more cosmopolitan worldviews, but is perpetuating, instead, models of British diasporic masculinity organised around dominance and violence that perpetuate drug addiction and social inequality.

Aisha is the character who initially prompts Mohammed's self-questioning, which eventually leads him to his rescue his brother from death. Rashid's relationship with Sayyid becomes publicly known, following Mo's confession to Rash's once-girlfriend Vanessa (Elarica Gallacher), who in turns tells members of DGM gang. The plot to assassinate Izzi's murderer, Demon, headed by Rashid, who is hoping to use this final act as an end to his involvement with the gang, becomes a stratagem to kill Rashid himself. Following the unsuccessful murder of Demon in an inconclusive night-time scene which is interrupted by Sayyid's arrival in his motorbike, Repo (Aymen Hamdouchi) and another gang member approach Mo the following morning and tell him they are looking for Rashid, who they say was wounded the previous night. Mo agrees to take them to Sayyid's apartment, but his suspicion mounts as he spots a latex glove in Repo's trouser pocket. In a manner reminiscent of the spilling of blood in *My Beautiful*

Laundrette, Mohammed must encounter the possibility of losing his brother in order to become reconciled with his difference, and in so doing he risks his own life, for he becomes the human shield standing between Rashid and Repo, as the latter attempts to shoot him. It is Mo who gets shot while trying to save Rashid, leading to screaming and to a profuse spurting of blood.

El Hosaini renders this scene of violence micropolitically significant, by turning it into an mundane indictment of masculinist homophobia which initially checks but which will ultimately strengthen affective ties within the second generation of a Muslim diasporic family. In the film's last sequence, Rashid is smoking outside the hospital where Mo is convalescing after surgical intervention on his shoulder. He is in intensive care but fortunately out of danger. Rash walks up to his parents as they come out of hospital and explain to him Mo's stable situation, while he attempts to hide the motorbike helmet he is holding, which stands metonymically for his relationship with Sayyid, with whom he now lives. Cherry suggests that 'Rash's parents are also uncomfortable with their son's sexuality, choosing to eject him from the family home' (2017, p. 9). However, due to the time lapse in the narrative, it is unclear whether Rashid has been banished or whether he has voluntarily moved in with Sayyid. Abdul-Aziz begs Rashid to 'come home now' and, looking at the helmet, asks him to put 'all this' behind him (*My Brother*, 2012), implying his 'illicit' same-sex relationship with Sayyid, but Rashid turns the offer down and chooses to honour his queer liaison. This is the film's illustration of Rashid's ideological extrapolation from his family's traditional values regarding sexuality, which complements the role of queerness in removing him materially and morally from both the violent masculinity of his former gang and received familial values. His mother, Hanan, poignantly embraces him in tears, but he reassures her that he is alright and has money, and that he will be 'in touch' (*My Brother*, 2012). She quietly acquiesces and smiles at him; in fact it is she, and not Abdul-Aziz, who looks back to Rashid in the parting shot where the couple is shown walking away from the hospital, which suggests an unsevered affective link with the family. According to film critic Alex Heeney (2015) and to El Hosaini herself, walking away is a recurrent visual motif in the narrative, illustrated in this departure, which marks the growing distance between first-generation diasporic Muslim normativity and second-generation queer diasporic dissidence. The motif is corroborated in the subsequent separation between Rashid and Mo in the film's last scene, set in the council estate, which, as El Hosaini tells Heeney, came first as she was devising the film: 'That kind of goodbye to childhood, or goodbye to the phases of your life, that transition was where I wanted to end the movie' (Heeney, 2015). The visual trope of walking away marks an important evolution in her characters, who need to come to terms with the plurality of British diasporic masculinities.

Mo's general worldview has changed dramatically after confronting the possibility of losing his brother and following his close encounter with death. He finally tells Rashid that he is 'cool' and that he can leave without regret. Despite the cast on Mo's left shoulder, the two brothers rehearse a final embrace, an affectionate gesture El Hosaini's direction suffuses with pent-up masculine emotion. Rashid then walks away, while Mo looks onto his straddling figure with what seems a mixture of self-sufficiency and emotional yearning. The film's last scene illustrates Mohammed's transition between childhood and adulthood, and it involves his learning to accept Rashid's queerness, which, as I have shown, is simultaneously at a remove from the normative masculinity upheld by their Muslim familial background and from the aggressive heteronormativity of their local youth gang. Mo and Rash must separate, for safety, yet the film's denouement seems to be one of hope for the understanding of human plurality.

Sexual difference, however, is not posited as invariably Westernised, and in fact both Rashid and Sayyid refuse to describe themselves in terms of exclusive sexual categories, such as *homosexual*, *gay*, or *bisexual*. As the actor who plays Rashid, James Floyd, observes, *My Brother* 'is not a coming out film' (Kramer, 2013), which is echoed later by El Hosaini, who wishes 'there weren't all these boxes and labels people try to put people in' (Kramer, 2013). In avoiding fixed sexual categorisation according to Western taxonomies, El Hosaini forfeits a homonormative – and potentially homonationalist – interpretation of her film, which does not set out to castigate Islamic normativity, but which critiques in a more nuanced manner the intersection between different dominant models of diasporic masculinity in postcolonial Britain.

Despite the forfeiture of a narrative arc that forces characters to 'come out' in Western fashion; despite a configuration of Islamic masculinities that decouples Muslim masculinity and aggression; and despite Rashid's family's troubled yet gradual acceptance of his queerness, the existing scholarship available on the film considers El Hosaini's sensibility to be homonationalist and as creating irreconcilable tensions between gayness – despite the characters never being labelled as exclusively homosexual – and Muslim identity. Cherry argues that the film exploits the binaries of homonationalism, buying into the Western discourses that construct all Muslims as homophobic and queer Muslims as unable to surmount familial and communitarian homophobia while remaining Muslims. Cherry suggests, specifically, that the pitting of Rash and Sayyid against the homophobia of the DGM gang is an example of homonationalism, alleging that 'a binary is employed between the prosperous, liberal, homosexual character of Sayid, whose appearance and lifestyle closely resemble homonormative scripts, and the gang who are portrayed as the homophobic "other"' (2017, p. 6). It must be pointed out that Sayyid may be relatively prosperous and indeed liberal, yet these conditions are not born out of privilege, but are earned, since he is deliberately shown as hailing from humble origins in Seine-Saint-Denis, and nothing about his lifestyle shown in the film seems to suggest he is homonormative. The gang is never presented, either, as a separate 'Other': rather, Rash is torn between hypermasculine gang culture and living life more ethically with another Muslim. The homophobia of the gang, in addition, is not solely a Muslim problem and it can be ascribed to a form of hypermasculinity that is culturally embedded in multiethnic communities with links to colonial and postcolonial forms of homophobia. It would seem that the main reason why El Hosaini's film is castigated for being homonationalist is for her depiction of Muslims and characters of other ethnicities as homophobic, in line with dominant Western ideologies. However, in spite of the depiction of this ongoing plight of many queer Muslims, El Hosaini does not predicate Islam and queerness as being mutually exclusive: both Rash and Sayyid are constructed as making recourse to the teachings of Islam in order to dwell on their lives' moral conundrums, which means they do not need to forfeit their Muslim identities in order to be queer: they simply need to find 'a place where they feel comfortable and safe in the world' (Ahmed, 2006, p. 158), and this, for now, means a temporary distance from both gang and family.

While rejecting gang criminality and familial heteronormativity, El Hosaini's film favours the possibility of an affectively engaged form of fraternity which can start micropolitically eroding both familial and social expectations placed on young British Muslims to be 'properly' male, namely aggressively dominant and heterosexual. What her debut feature film seems to suggest, I would argue, is that the multiethnic and unruly nature of the social groupings of contemporary London is not enough to challenge social normativity. The real challenge to societal mores lies in the disorganisation of dominant forms of masculinity, since both family and gang give a narrow range of options to British Muslim youth. Queerness, although allegedly incidental to the film's agenda, remains at the heart of El Hosaini's critique of postcolonial Britain. *My Brother* finds richness in heterogeneity, prizing unfixed sexual orientations and narrative open-endedness over a monolithic understanding of identities and personal histories. Surrounding and connecting with queerness, there is the challenge to Islamophobic constructions of all Muslim youth as potential terrorists and as universally homophobic and patriarchal, since ideological transformations such as Mo's are deemed possible.

In opposing dominant Western views, El Hosaini addresses her implicit majority- and minority-ethnic audiences with a keen disorganising intent that attempts to shake up their complacency. She forces all of 'us' – global and local audiences, majority and minority ethnic groupings – to confront our preconceptions about Muslim youth and their sexual orientation in contemporary Britain and Europe, begging us to consider Islam as a form of transnational interpersonal connection instilling disenfranchised Muslim youth with a sense of relational cultural identity that can be pacifist, anti-masculinist, and also queer.

Notes

1 Simon Wheatley, the author of *Don't Call Me Urban! The Time of Grime*, usefully defines 'grime' in the book's website: 'Grime, an angst-ridden and confrontational sound, has been the most significant and controversial musical expression to emerge from the UK since punk. Essentially an authentic response to hip hop, it conveyed the hopes and frustrations of an apolitical generation locked into London's decaying housing estates' (www.dontcallmeurban.com/info.html). Because of the lack of a party-political approach, grime may be considered a micropolitical response to older forms of black counterculture, such as hip hop, and arising culturally from the direct experiences of London's council estate inhabitants; hence, it is molecular and localised, rather than being a publicly organised macropolitical response to social disenfranchisement. In addition, in an interview with Kieran Yates for *The Guardian*, Wheatley observes that 'I could see there was a definite shift in the way young people were behaving, and the attitudes towards older people' (Yates, 2015). Such framing of British youth's extrication from their elders' values is depicted more specifically within El Hosaini's film as an ideological reorganisation around gangs.

2 Abdul-Aziz is full of enthusiasm for the 'Arab Spring', yet he cannot predict its multifarious descent into various sectarian clashes between the original revolutionaries and contending Islamic extremists in various Middle Eastern nations, leading to civil wars and to the rise of totalitarian forms of Islamism. The editors of *Democracy and Reform in the Middle East and Asia: Social Protest and Authoritarian Rule after the Arab Spring* observe: 'There is not much evidence that Islamic radicalism is driving these uprisings, although this could change, especially during the political game of electing new governments. If there was a sense of nationalism, it is not the old-fashioned Arabism but the nationalism that is entwined with a craving for political change. It is not a purely visceral cultural nationalism. There is also the demographic factor behind these political uprisings, with huge numbers of unemployed youth becoming increasingly frustrated with their governments and taking to protest' (Saikal and Acharya, 2014, p. 3). Although many of the young people involved in the so-called 'Arab Spring' are Muslim, it is assumed here that they had no Islamist agenda, but articulated, instead, a general disaffection with the status quo. Instead, Islamic extremists have coopted Islam for their own political ends, and they have led to the discursive pitting of non-religious, or allegedly secular, revolutionaries, against religious fanatics, which fails

to account for cultural complexities, particularly in relation to Muslim ethno-religious identities. In fact, for all of Abdul-Aziz's nostalgia in *My Brother* for Egyptian president Gamal Abdel Nasser, who visibly opposed the religious revivalism of the Muslim Brotherhood, his family still shows features of Islamicate culture, not least his wife's *hijab*.

3   Muhammad Zubayr Siddiqi calls Al-Bukhari's compilation the most important of all *hadith* collections: 'loved in places as far apart as Balkh, Merv, Nīsabūr, the Ḥijāz, Egypt and Iraq' (Siddiqi, 1993, p. 53). Jonathan Brown (2007) has charted the process of canonisation of Al-Bukhari's particular collection, and ascribes its rise to prominence to Nizam Al-Mulk, vizier of the Seljuk Empire in the eleventh century. His gathering of Muslims for readings of Al-Bukhari's *Sahih* 'reinforc[ed] a sense of Sunni communalism, [...] inculcating [it] as a touchstone of Sunni identity in the impressionable young minds of the next generation' (Brown, 2007, p. 4).

6

The Good, the bad, and the ugly? Unveiling American Muslim women in Rolla Selbak's *Three Veils* (2011)

As we have seen in the previous two chapters of this section on 'Negotiating Islamic gender', cinematic and literary narratives crafted by queer diasporic Muslim women micropolitically challenge commonplace images of Islamic gender, particularly mainstream Western expectations of Muslim masculinity and femininity, as well as dominant Muslim diasporic gender normativity. Moreover, they adhere to – in the case of Sarif's *I Can't Think Straight* – or subvert – in El Hosaini's *My Brother the Devil* – Western 'coming out' narrative arcs that assimilate queer Muslims by invoking or circumventing the notion of the 'closet' and attendant issues of social visibility. As we have seen, Sarif's visual and textual narratives privilege 'coming out' as the only tenable means of sexual liberation for her British Muslim and Christian Arab protagonists, asserting this seemingly indispensable form of living out one's sexuality while placing the Middle East in a position of inexorable ideological stasis.

Whereas Sarif's story of female and inter-religious homosexuality rings with some homonationalist overtones, El Hosaini's film has been seen to achieve the opposite: El Hosaini's cinematic tale of queer Muslim masculinities foregoes any attempt at making her Muslim characters 'come out', allowing their unorthodox homoerotic liaison to exist both outside compulsory heterosexuality and homonormativity, in a space of sexual fluidity that simultaneously bypasses Western sexual taxonomies and Islamic traditionalism. Sarif and El Hosaini seem to grapple with an essentialist and a constructionist envisioning of human sexuality, respectively, with El Hosaini, as a British citizen who grew up in Egypt, remaining more overtly conscious of the hegemony of imperial epistemologies and of the pitfalls of Western sexual exceptionalism, whereas, as a British-born woman of South Asian and South African Muslim heritage, Sarif is more attuned to a Westernised essentialist configuration of sexuality.

In turn, Rolla Selbak's film *Three Veils*, released in 2011, which depicts the experiences of three diasporic Arab women of Muslim heritage in the USA, combines essentialist and constructionist models of sexual orientation while probing different versions of Muslim femininity in America. In articulating her distinct vision of Arab Muslim Americans, Selbak, an American filmmaker of Palestinian heritage, whose family settled for a time in Abu Dhabi after the onset of the Gulf War (1990–91), but who has spent most of her adult life in the US, has had to contend with sturdy American representations of Muslims and Islam, especially in the decade following 9/11. As Rubina Ramji observes in her study of post-9/11 depictions of Muslims: 'The Arab Muslim male is portrayed as a backward and undeveloped heathen. American film, in its projection of Arabs, consistently associates "Arab" with "Islam"' (2016, p. 2). Ramji argues this conflation of Arabness and Islam homogenises America's variegated migrant – and native – Muslim populations. Jack G. Shaheen points out that 'prior to World War I, nearly all the Arabs immigrating to America were Christians: Lebanese, Palestinians, and Syrians. Today, the majority of the United States' Arab-American population is also Christian; about 40 percent are Muslim' (2001, p. 3). He highlights how only 12 per cent of the world's Muslim population is actually Arab. However, American cinema's obsession with Arab Muslims since, at least, the Iranian Revolution of 1979 has created its own mythology: 'Hollywood's celluloid mythology dominates the culture. No doubt about it, Hollywood's rendition of Arabs frame stereotypes in viewers' minds. The problem is peculiarly American' (Shaheen, 2001, p. 4). Being the world's largest exporter of film and television, Hollywood's stereotypes of Arab Muslims have had a global negative impact, built on top of several centuries' worth of European Orientalism.

By comparison, in Western imaginaries Muslim women are often positioned at the receiving end of Muslim men's aggressive Islamic patriarchy. According to Sofia Sjo, 'Muslim women are usually represented as subjugated and invisible in public, a situation from which only the white or the westernized man would seem to be able to save them' (2013, p. 6). As a joint antidote to the appropriation of Muslim women's causes by Western interventionists and to their continued invisibility in mainstream Western media, *Three Veils* reclaims, first-hand, the stories and perspectives of the Arab Muslim women of America. Ramji notes how Shaheen has singled out Selbak's work alongside that of Annemarie Jacir, Jackie Salloum, Alain Zaloum, Ahmad Zahra, and Cherien Dabis, as 'offering diverse and crucial representations of Islam in film' (2016, p. 8). Although Selbak's film tackles controversial topics as a direct response to mainstream concerns about Islam and Muslim men and women – such as arranged marriages, rape, homophobia, child abuse, and gender violence – Selbak does not perpetuate 'War on Terror' discourses, in an apparent attempt to depolemicise her subjects. Her Muslim characters are given centre stage and they never come under fire from the white Christian majority of European descent, which is mostly absent from the film. There is also no mention of Islamic terrorism or of 9/11. Selbak's characters are constructed as an ordinary section of multicultural American society, and as such, Selbak depicts Muslim women and their families as they go about their everyday lives. While zooming in on a trio of Arab Muslim families may lay Selbak open to the criticism that, like most mainstream media outlets, she automatically conflates Arabness with Islam, she portrays women of Muslim heritage in order to show the variety of their experiences of Muslim and Arab femininities, complicating Western stereotypes about Islam. This chapter, which constitutes the first academic engagement with Selbak's film, specifically explores its grappling with the idea of the 'good Muslim woman'.

Three Veils is Selbak's first professionally produced film, following her amateur debut fiction feature, *Making Maya*, released in 2003, a story about a young American lesbian with ambitions of becoming a professional basketball player. Selbak's debut garnered the attention of cinema production and distribution company Zahra Pictures, which went on to produce and distribute *Three Veils*, and which specialises on stories featuring Arab characters in America and the Middle East. Selbak has directed several fiction and non-fiction short films. She has also written and directed the web series *Kiss Her I'm Famous*. Selbak is a committed advocate of LGBTIQ, Muslim, and feminist issues. She has shot a popular web documentary called *A Day with a Muslim: Trump Supporters* in the lead-up to the USA's presidential election of 2016, which aimed to show how personal contact between ethnic communities can challenge prejudice. She is also a contributor on various topics for progressive publications such as the *Huffington Post*, for which she wrote an article entitled 'Coming Out to a Muslim Family'. In addition, she leads the feminist online initiative *Grrl's Guide to Filmmaking*, which offers pithy filmmaking advice for women in a highly male-dominated industry. Here, I will concentrate chiefly on *Three Veils* due to its rare foregrounding of Muslim female homosexuality and for its critique of Muslim gender roles, and since it is so far Selbak's only extensive fictional exploration of Arab Muslim subjectivities.

Three Veils was shot on a very modest budget. As she told her audience at a special screening of the film I hosted at the University of Leicester in 2017, Selbak self-confessedly had a difficult time raising funds for the film, given its controversial themes and its depiction of an American ethno-religious minority. The film charts the interwoven stories of three young Arab women in contemporary suburban California: Leila (Mercedes Mason), an American middle-class girl whose Middle Eastern parents have arranged her upcoming marriage to the seemingly pious Ali (Sammy Sheik); Amira (Angela Zahra), a young working-class Egyptian woman experiencing religiously repressed homosexual attraction; and Nikki (Sheetal Sheth), a young woman born in Iran to an Afghani father and a Persian mother who travelled to the USA in search of their fortunes. The film is told in three individual vignettes, subsequently dealing with Leila, Amira, and Nikki's stories. However, each section of the film covers roughly the same chronological events from each character's point of view, with extra sequences examining Amira and Nikki's childhoods in flashback. A coda ties together, through Nikki's perspective, the strands of the film's three plots.

The veil, which is explicitly referenced in film's title, acts as the narrative's central metaphor about Muslim femininity, a somewhat predictable yet semiotically significant one. The veil remains chiefly a metaphor because none of the film's protagonists actively wear the veil in public, so I would suggest Selbak self-consciously chose a catchy title that fitted Western expectations of Muslim femininity to then have them overturned. Even pious Amira only covers herself when she prays at home and invariably takes head cover off when her rituals are finished. The only women in the film who publicly wear the *hijab* are Leila's mother, Mrs Qasim (Salwa Shaker), and Nikki's mother, Farridah (Anne Bedian), both Middle Eastern women whose donning of the headscarf may be interpreted as culturally inflected, which chimes with ongoing global discussions about traditional Muslim gender roles and Islamic notions of modesty.[1] Katherine Bullock makes a crucial distinction between the 'veil', which only leaves the eyes uncovered, and the *hijab*, which covers the hair and neck and which is commonly referred to as a 'headscarf'. She intimates that 'Muslim women who wear a headscarf (and the minority in North America who wear a face veil) are targets every time they step out into public space in a way that most Muslim men are not' (2005, p. xvii). A decade after 9/11 and the ensuing 'War on Terror', which promised to liberate Muslim women from Muslim men, Leila Ahmed observes: 'It is still even today a rare week when some issue or other relating to women, Islam, and/or the hijab or burka does not make headlines in Western media' (2011, p. 15). Saba Mahmood further argues: 'The veil, more than any other Islamic practice, has become the symbol and evidence of the violence Islam has inflicted upon women' (2005, p. 195).

For many feminists and non-feminists alike, the veil's sole ideological purpose is the subjugation of Muslim women. However, what such simplistic

The good, the bad, and the ugly?

Figure 7 *Three Veils* (2011), directed by Rolla Selbak

understanding of the veil's purpose effectively obscures is the political, cultural, and religious complexities surrounding the wearing of the headscarf, especially when the garment is voluntarily taken up, and most particularly so in the West. As Megan MacDonald asserts, 'the veil always already works beyond the simple binary in which to be veiled is to be oppressed and to be unveiled is to be liberated and modern at the same time' (2014, p. 26). Ostensibly, for Muslim women, the choice of wearing the *hijab* honours different personal instincts and political strategies. Ashraf Zahedi suggests that Muslim American women have been 'eclipsed by two opposing discourses on Muslim women, Orientalism and Islamic fundamentalism, which essentialize the image and meaning of Muslim womanhood' (2011, p. 184). In *Three Veils*, Amira's home use of a full-body praying dress, or female *ihram* (see Figure 7),which leaves only the face uncovered, is used as a symbol of her modesty in her submission to God. However, Selbak does not use the 'veil' as a material political tool of anti-imperialist resistance, but rather as an overarching metaphor with a double purpose: the film's 'three veils' simultaneously embody the patriarchal shroud constraining Muslim women and the invisibility of their ordinary experiences in mainstream American culture. Selbak's main aim in her film, which will be my focus here, is to 'unveil' her female characters, in a manner that extricates them from both Western Orientalism and Islamic traditionalism.

Selbak's depiction of Leila, Amira, and Nikki confronts the idea of the 'good', the 'bad', and the 'deviant' Muslim woman, and the pressures the sociocultural ideal of Islamic womanhood exerts on their femininities. The title of this chapter is playfully drawn from Sergio Leone's 1966 'Spaghetti western' *The Good, The Bad and the Ugly*, whose title allows us to focus, instead, on Selbak's trio of women. Their struggle to live as Arab and Muslim women is given complexity by their living in the diaspora, which causes values to be negotiated across generational and national borders. As Nadine Naber observes in an anthropological study of Arab American women,

> concepts of 'good Arab girls' operated as a marker of community boundaries and the notion of a morally superior 'Arab culture' in comparison to concepts of 'American girls' and 'American culture.' Idealized concepts of femininity are connected to idealized notions of family and an idealized concept of heterosexual marriage. (Naber, 2012, p. 8)

Naber observes that Arabness is often posited in Arab American households as good, as an 'ideal', while Americanness is perceived as bad. Naber recognises the sway of both classical Orientalism, which aggrandises the West while belittling the Orient, and of Occidentalism, which champions Arab values in the face of Western 'decadence'. Arab women thus become the bearers of a reified version of femininity, which is predicated as the direct opposite of licentious and immoral American femininity. In light of their symbolic responsibilities, Selbak's protagonists constantly come up against sociocultural and familial expectations. As I propose in my systematic critical exploration of each vignette, Leila can be considered the 'good' Muslim, the dutiful daughter who precariously tries to accept the marriage arranged by her Middle Eastern parents; Amira constitutes the 'ugly' Muslim, a girl with 'deviant' homosexual tendencies that contravene Islamic and Arab values; and Nikki appears to be the 'bad' Muslim, as she drinks alcohol, smokes, and has promiscuous sex, a lifestyle deemed at a remove from Islamic notions of feminine modesty. In making the film gravitate around these three young women and their individual yet enmeshed perspectives, Selbak explores different challenges assailing Muslim women in the diaspora.

Leila's vignette charts the events in her life leading up to her forthcoming wedding to Ali, dwelling on the patriarchal institution of the arranged marriage, on coveted Muslim virginity, which still renders Arab American women the bearers of family honour, and on sexual violence against Arab women. The film opens with a clear demarcation of gender roles and expectations. We witness the formal enactment of Leila and Ali's engagement, with the men 'doing business' downstairs, while the women watch from the balcony above, an enforcement of gender segregation that preliminarily reveals the insidious workings of Arab patriarchy, even in the diaspora. Ali's private courtship of Leila, which takes place mostly in Ali's car – a place that bypasses family surveillance – reveals the lack of a genuine erotic connection between them, despite Leila's best intentions to like Ali and to be sensually drawn to him. Leila continually attempts to justify her upcoming marriage to Ali, stating to her best friend Nikki that he is a 'good guy' (*Three Veils*, 2011). She only begins to perceive the darker side of Ali's personality when she becomes entangled with Jamal (Garen Boyajian), Amira's handsome brother. Her attraction to Jamal signals her repressed sexual desire and her internalisation of the idea of the 'good Muslim woman'. Her inner conflict as an American Muslim becomes manifest in her divided allegiances to the life arranged for her by her family, embodied in her engagement to Ali, and to her own individual desires, in the shape of her frustrated relationship with Jamal. As Sarah Abboud, Loretta Jemmott, and Marilyn Sommers remark in their study of Arab American women, their young respondents 'portrayed an image of a "good Arab girl" that they were socialized to preserve. For the majority of participants, the "good Arab girl" image was a virgin and an educated woman who followed assigned traditional gender roles' (Abboud *et al.*, 2015, p. 725). Selbak constructs Leila as a character visibly attempting to fit this image of the 'good Arab girl', as she is a diligent student wilfully preserving her virginity and acting modestly, although her desire pulls her in a different direction.

Leila is not visibly religious, which seems to indicate that her internalisation of patriarchal values about marriage and female virginity is cultural rather than spiritual. For instance, she is impressed by Ali's piety when he tells her he has donated $30,000 towards the building of a new mosque in the area, and she calls his devotion to God 'admirable', yet she is self-confessedly not sure about the necessity of building more mosques. This confession is followed by Ali's first expression of jealousy, as he questions Leila's gazing at Jamal. Leila tries to laugh the episode off, but Ali chastises her, telling her that 'this is about *decency*. You remember what we talked about before, how we're always gonna act like we're married?' (*Three Veils*, 2011, emphasis added). Leila does not take well to this unsolicited lecture on Islamic morality. As she attempts to leave the car, she is physically restrained by Ali, who firmly holds her arm, only to change tactic and apologise for his rashness, which I would suggest encapsulates the manipulative behaviour of an abuser. Somewhat ironically, Ali's jealousy about Leila's mere glance at Jamal is what propels her sensually towards the latter, as the direct opposite of Ali's toxic surveillance. Jamal is a young amateur painter who likes to paint portraits, smoke, and drink, three occupations that, as a Muslim, set him apart not only from Ali but also from his somewhat traditional Egyptian family. Leila seems as seduced by his apparent 'Americanisation' as by his philosophically carefree attitude towards life, which show him as unfettered by Arab societal expectations.

When Leila is upset by a heated argument with Nikki, it is Jamal she runs to for sympathy. He lets her into the house and she automatically runs to his room, where she lies down on the bed and pulls his arm around her. She cries even more disconsolately when he tells her that he is moving to Egypt the following morning. He candidly asks her whether she loves Ali. She evasively responds 'that's not the point'. She tells him that she does not 'know what to do' and that she wants someone 'to tell [her] what to do', but before he has a chance to respond, she lunges forward and kisses him, triggering the beginning of a love scene. Leila's voice states off-camera: 'You know those moments nobody ever finds about? [...] [T]hey're deeply hidden. That was my moment. Looking back I know it wouldn't have worked with Jamal, but I loved how he made me feel: happy' (*Three Veils*, 2011). Despite the personal chemistry between them, Leila changes her mind in mid-scene and runs out of the room. This scene serves to 'unveil' Leila's 'deeply hidden' desires, an intimate event in her life to which only the film audience is privy. Here, Leila is shown to confront the image of the 'good Muslim girl' which she has been trying to uphold, and she appears morally conflicted. Seemingly plagued by guilt, sex between them is never consummated. In preserving her virginity, Leila's actions match the experience of Abboud *et al.*'s correspondents, for whom 'to embody virginity was to live it as an Arab or an Arab American woman; it also meant to live with the socially constructed meanings of virginity that many participants internalized at certain phases in their lives' (2015, p. 734). Leila is forced to 'embody virginity' as an Arab American woman, as she has internalised her community's constructed – and constricting – meanings about the value of her chastity, which curtail her attraction to partners who are not legally sanctified.

I would argue Leila's vignette offers a double critique of Arab Muslim patriarchy which qualifies dominant Western views of Muslim women's oppression. First, her arranged marriage to Ali makes her relationship with Jamal impossible, although strategic events in Jamal's life – in the shape of his imminent move to Egypt – already constitute a serious enough deterrent. The frustrated attraction between Leila and Jamal serves as an illustration of the limitations imposed on Arab American women by traditional forms of Arab marriage and parental control. In the face of this patriarchal institution, however, it is the father figure of Mr Qasim (Erick Avari) who starts questioning the feasibility of Ali and Leila's match. Leila's father is shown trying to tell his wife that their daughter 'is not happy about this whole marriage thing', to which the mother bombastically responds: 'Of course she's happy. She's getting married very soon. He's a great guy. He's from a good family. We all agreed on him, remember?'

(*Three Veils*, 2011). In this scene, Selbak offers a qualified view of Islamic patriarchy in which women are also visibly implicated. In a manner similar to that of Sarif's *I Can't Think Straight*, mothers are constructed as reinforcing patriarchal institutions. In offering a sympathetic father and an unwavering mother, Selbak offers a micropolitical challenge to dominant Orientalist constructions of tyrannical Islamist men and oppressed Muslim women; in so doing, she does not deny Islamic patriarchy, but predicates it, instead, as a worldview sustained by both men and women, although this is undertaken at the expense of Orientalising the first-generation diasporic women who are shown as clinging on to seemingly old-fashioned ideas about gender roles.

The second, and most prominent, critique of Arab male domination of women in the first section of *Three Veils* is Ali's treatment of Leila. From the outset, he is shown as policing Leila's femininity. After her first visit to Jamal's house, during which he shows her his paintings and lets her have one of his cigarettes, Ali questions her about smelling of cigarette smoke, which is anathema to his traditional Islamic values. Later in the film, after Leila's intimate scene with Jamal, Ali picks up on the clue of their relationship – i.e., her abandoned mobile phone – and brings it up as Leila tries to tell him that she does not 'think this is working out' (*Three Veils*, 2011). Pre-empting that Leila is about to suggest postponing their wedding, Ali interrupts her and tells her he wants to surprise her, taking her to a hotel room by the sea, where he kneels down and offers her a white rose, telling her how he cannot wait for them to be married, before jumping on her. Leila is incommoded by Ali's behaviour and tries to stop him, telling him this premarital sexual encounter is something they had not discussed. Ali then questions Leila about her virginity, urging her to tell him whether she has slept with someone else, to which she reacts by smacking him. Seemingly unaffected by her response, he forces himself on her and rapes her. The scene fades to black, marking the end of Leila's vignette. Here, Selbak denounces the control that Ali, as a seemingly pious Muslim, exerts on Leila, ensuring he 'owns' her virginity before they are officially married, hence compromising her and ensuring she will not be able to abandon the plans for their upcoming wedding. In this scene, Selbak brings to the surface a scene of sexual violence that critiques the ongoing sexual violence and control practised by Muslim men. It is worth considering whether portraying a Muslim man in this negative light is effectively Orientalising, whether it provides yet more ammunition for Western Islamophobes. Selbak's more optimistic depiction of other Muslim men in the film would suggest she is neither criticising *all* Muslim men, nor painting a purely positive picture of Arab Muslim life in America: her work simply encompasses difficult topics that remain relevant to the experiences of Muslim American women.

Indeed, *Three Veils* shows that sexual violence against women is still a problem in Muslim communities, but Selbak goes to some lengths to denounce such violence as un-Islamic, and to depict familial and social sympathy towards Leila as the victim of rape, which attempts to curb micropolitically the Western stereotype of all Muslim communities as invariably patriarchal. The film's coda offers a resolution of Leila's plot through Nikki's voiceover:

> Despite the scandal Leila could have created, she told everyone what Ali had done. And, to her surprise, her family and community were completely supportive of her. After all, he had committed one of the biggest and most unforgivable *crimes* in Islam: forcing a woman against her will. Even the mosque he'd donated so much money to gave the money back. This of course meant she'd admitted she was damaged goods, but she didn't care. A year later, she met and married a wonderful Moroccan man named Kader, and they had their first baby. They named him Jamal.
> (*Three Veils*, 2011, emphasis added)

Leila is surprised by her family and community's supportive response to her rape because she has visibly internalised patriarchal values about women's responsibility as repositories of family honour. Nikki's speech overlays a shot of Mrs Qasim comforting Leila and a shot of Ali, visibly upset, walking away from the mosque. The mosque's rejection of Ali's monetary gift is highly symbolic: Ali's donation is tainted by his immoral treatment of Leila, which is not merely un-Islamic on the count of being outside a legally sanctioned relationship – thus constituting *zina*, or fornication, – but because it is non-consensual. Selbak's script explicitly frames rape as a 'crime', not as a sin, which demonstrates a granulated knowledge of Islam that takes into consideration not just religious scripture and doctrine, but the attendant traditions of the *tafsir* and the *fiqh*. The resolution of Leila's story may seem at once orthodox and optimistic: she ends up marrying another Muslim, albeit a Maghrebi, and the picture-perfect framing of her family life, including a little baby purposefully called Jamal, is not mindful enough of the trauma of sexual violence. In addition, this denouement is perhaps too naïvely hopeful in its invariably supportive depiction of Leila's plight.[2] Arguably, an Arab American community might have forced her to marry Ali and to put family honour before women's rights. However, Selbak's fictional gesture advocates a growing sensitivity towards the plights of women, while challenging Western perspectives on Muslim communities which label them as inexorably patriarchal. Selbak thus attempts to strike a representational balance, enacting a critique of Islamic patriarchal attitudes while challenging calcified Western views on Islam and Muslims.

I would suggest Selbak's narrative choices demonstrate a forward-thinking understanding of Islam. According to Kecia Ali, the *tafsir* tradition has long tried to probe and qualify the Qur'an's gender imbalance: 'The scholarly tradition is one significant source of knowledge and wisdom; much is lost when Muslims – Qur'an-only feminists or pro-hadith Salafis – choose to bypass it for a literalist approach to source texts' (2006, p. xx). To this, we can add the *fiqh*, which sought to interpret the Qur'an and the *Sunnah* according to the specific needs of their contemporaneous societies. It is important to note that the rape of women is not once mentioned in the Qur'an. The Qur'an also sanctions forms of non-consensual sex between men and women, such as between a free Muslim man and his female slaves. The work of Azman Mohd Noor demonstrates that classical Islamic jurists attempted to redress the sacred text's lack of reference to women's sexual rights: 'Rape is translated in Arabic as *ightisāb* or *zinā bi al-ikrāh*, which literally can be translated back to English as forcible unlawful sexual intercourse. The word *ightisāb*, or its root *ghasb* literally means: usurpation, illegal seizure, coercion, ravishing, violation and rape' (2010, p. 427). Rape has been considered non-consensual fornication and jurists denounced it as such centuries ago. Noor also notes how the three main classical Islamic juridical schools all criminalised the use of sexual violence on women. Whereas the crime of fornication (*zina*) required four witnesses to be legally recognised, this stipulation was not necessary in the case of rape. In addition, 'the victim of rape is not held liable as it is a case of *zinā*' (Noor, 2010, p. 430), which means the survivors of rape are not tainted. In framing Leila's case as an un-Islamic 'crime', and in showing community and familial support, Selbak puts forward an understanding of Islam that goes beyond the Qur'an and which, wittingly or unwittingly, takes its tone from the nuances of the scholarly and juridical traditions, which wilfully tried to redress the alleged patriarchal biases of both the Qur'an and of Islamicate communities. So, while Leila's narrative arc may be deemed too idealistic, it remains a hopeful gesture towards a juster understanding of Muslim women's sexual rights.

In the film's second vignette, we witness Amira's narrative: she is the 'ugly' Muslim of the trio, unattractively single and friendless because she is sexually 'deviant'. In her initial voiceover, she tells us, as she despondently washes her face:

All my life, I felt left out. God was the only one who understood me. We left Egypt when I was thirteen and moved to America. This made me feel even more out of place. The other kids didn't seem to like me, so I got used to being alone. (*Three Veils*, 2011)

In her loneliness, Amira comes to represent not just diasporic alienation, but also the isolation of most Muslims who live with immanent homosexual orientation. Amira's plight also illustrates the tensions between Arab and American values in an Egyptian family living in America. *Three Veils* was conceived and shot before the onset of the 'Arab Spring' in Egypt, already referenced in the previous chapter. However, while Amira's case might have been fruitfully complicated by the popular uprising that started on the year of the film's release, her case helpfully hints towards the Islamisation of Egyptian values by the Muslim Brotherhood,[3] which affects even those citizens living in the diaspora.

Selbak's film shows how Amira's homosexuality is checked by her family from an early age, offered to us in flashback. As the teenage version of Amira (Lexi Greene) becomes close to her school friend Shoshana (Chelsea Gray), Amira's mother, Samira (Madline Tabar), discovers them when they are about to kiss for the first time. Samira expels Shoshana from the house immediately. Amira's voice-over tells us she never saw the girl again. Samira's ensuing words are simple but emphatic: 'And you. What's this? [...] Your father will kill you when he finds out' (*Three Veils*, 2011). Samira's severity ostensibly veils Islam's complex relationship with homosexuality. Aside from the fact female homosexuality is never explicitly mentioned in the Qur'an, Samar Habib candidly tells the audience of the Palestinian Lesbian Organisation (*Aswat*) that 'the prophet never officially punished homosexuality in his lifetime' (2009, p. 18). This fact alone demonstrates that, while affirmative *tafsir* and *fiqh* can arrive at emancipatory interpretations and rulings, the disquisitions of various *ahadith*, reported by the Prophet's heteropatriarchal followers, have swayed Islamicate values towards the categorical condemnation of male and female homosexuality. While feminist and queer interpretations of Islam have gradually and inexorably carved a niche for pluralistic understandings of the faith, women and queers have had to contend with contextually bound heteropatriarchal visions of Islam with grandiose claims to universality.

Amira's parents' response to their daughter's incipient homosexuality is a traditionalist one. Although we never get to see Amira's father and it is her mother who represents the heteropatriarchal values of the diasporic Egyptian household, Amira's voiceover tells us:

That's when my parents made me take religion classes three times a day. At first, I hated it. I cried every day. But soon I wasn't able to imagine my life without it. Despite what people might think, the Qur'an has so much wisdom in it. It has verses about smiling, giving, and compassion, about patience, loyalty, and freedom, and when I read it, it made everything good again. (*Three Veils*, 2011)

Similarly to Leila's case, Selbak incepts a double critique here: on the one hand, she maps the resilient homophobia of Muslim communities, which prescribe religious classes to those deviating from heteronormative behaviours and identities; on the other, Amira's monologue seems to address an implicit Western audience that may harbour negative views on Islam as a religion of violence and oppression. That said, Rachel Shatto succinctly describes Amira as a character 'whose shame over her lesbianism leads her to bury her feelings in religion' (2013, p. 30). In this case, Islamic traditionalism becomes the veil shrouding Amira and rendering her life visibly heteronormative. Although Amira's faith provides some comfort in the face of her loneliness, the Qur'an as a guiding text cannot fully contain her, as someone not attracted to heterosexual marriage. In the lack of emotional satisfaction, her daily prayers become a substitute for her erotic self-fulfilment. Selbak's film remains carefully Islamophilic yet also critical of mainstream heteropatriarchal Muslim values. Despite her effort at painting a pacifist – but ultimately also pacifying – understanding of Islam, this may not be deemed committed enough by queer Muslims who are engaged in LGBTIQ liberation theology. In other words, depicting Islam as a faith that is successfully mobilised to repress Amira's same-sex desire may not altogether ameliorate simplistic Western understandings of Islam that deem it incompatible with queerness.

Nonetheless, Selbak's depiction of Amira's household highlights the cultural conundrums of an Egyptian family living in the diaspora in America. Whereas Amira's deviance is 'treated' with religious orthodoxy, she does not take up the *hijab* to signify her Muslim identity, and her mother, who is not a *hijabi* either, wears makeup and Western clothing; her father and her brother are starting a computer business in Egypt, which points to the technological modernity borne out of globalisation, although it is telling that it is only the men in the family who carry out this enterprise. In the realm of fashion and occupation, Amira's clan is not a fully traditional Muslim family, but a relatively modern one still dependent on traditionally designated gender roles. Amira is still expected to uphold their Arab and Islamic identity, conforming to the idea of the 'good Muslim' and the 'good Arab' girl. As regards Western dress and not donning the *hijab*, Yvonne Yazbeck Haddad, Jane I. Smith, and Kathleen M. Moore observe: 'The majority of Muslim women in America choose not to wear garb that would distinguish them from the rest of society for a variety of reasons' (2006, p. 18), which includes their not wishing to stand out as Muslims. Neither Samira nor Amira feel the need to let their clothes embody their Muslim identity, yet they are both still subject to Arab and Islamic patriarchal values: Samira in her perpetuation of Arab women's domestic roles; Amira in the subjection to her mother's inherited patriarchal values and in the repression of her same-sex desire.

Samira makes it clear, during a conversation in which she tries to pair up her daughter with a male Egyptian suitor, that there is a cleavage between Arab and American values. After asking why she should not be allowed to stay in the USA on her own to finish her studies, Amira is told by her mother that America is not a good influence on her. As Naber states:

> the ideal of Arabness as family with 'good Arab women' forecloses the possibility of homosexuality. Within this logic, the survival of an imagined Arab community depends upon a good Arab family, which requires good women within the construct of heterosexual marriage. These demands, and the articulation of homosexuality as distinctly Western, operate as markers that distinguish good Arabs from bad Americans. (Naber, 2012, p. 84)

Amira can be interpreted as the victim of these inherited ideas. Amira's incipient homosexuality is interpreted by her family as a sign of her unwelcome Americanisation, which is actively repressed through religious indoctrination, and Samira's persistence in wanting to marry her daughter off perpetuates the heteropatriarchal idea of Arab women as the carriers of Arab identity. Abboud, Jemmott and Sommers observe 'how parental control and pressure to preserve the Arab identity contributed to intergenerational tensions as well as a conflict among young adults between Arab and American cultures' (2015, p. 732). Amira's identity is purposefully fractured: she can be either a 'good Arab' or a 'bad American', with no possibility of a hyphenated, let alone assembled, identity. Furthermore, the anthropologists quoted above point out their participants' 'tension with parents, specifically mothers' (Abboud *et al.*, 2015, p. 732), which closely matches Amira's difficult relationship with her mother and the mother's active policing of her daughter's femininity, which is only allowed to be heterosexual. In this regard, Selbak's film usefully tackles intergenerational differences and the tensions between American and Arab-Islamic discourses regarding female sexuality.

Nonetheless, Amira's fortuitous relationship with Nikki demonstrates the former's attempt to live out her Muslim identity and Nikki's accommodation of Amira's faith. Amira's attraction to Nikki is not merely a symptom of her emotional and sexual attraction to the same sex, but also the manifestation of her charitable instincts as a Muslim. Amira's piety drives her to help Nikki, with no value attached to her good deed. When Nikki shows up at her house unannounced, Amira gives her shelter, even though an altercation takes place between them because of Nikki's prodding of Amira's faith. Nikki casually calls the Qur'an resting on Amira's bedside table 'all that stuff' and nonchalantly flicks through the volume. She also mockingly questions Amira about her religious rituals, asking her whether she prays every day, bends down, and does 'aerobics and all that' (*Three Veils*, 2011). Amira cannot stand Nikki's irreverence towards her faith and asks her to leave. When it becomes apparent that Nikki has nowhere to go, Amira relents and allows her to stay.

Amira's wish to console Nikki makes her compromise on some aspects of her religious identity, particularly surrounding her perceptions of Islamic modesty. Amira finds out Nikki is heartbroken about Leila's refusal to take part in the bachelorette party she has arranged for her. Amira then offers to stand in for Leila and to let Nikki take her out for the night. What follows is a series of compromises between Amira's faith and Leila's apparent faithlessness. Nikki takes Amira to a dance club managed by her black male friend Wes (Desmond Faison). When a waiter comes to their table to take their order, Nikki glances coyly at the menu and states that neither of them will be drinking. Nikki's refusal of alcohol is a meaningful gesture towards Amira's Muslim abstention. In turn, Amira is persuaded to join Nikki on the dance floor. There, Nikki and Amira's bodies become sensually intertwined through dance, as Nikki keeps rolling into Amira's arms. This highly sensual homosocial dance, redolent of Leyla and Tala's dance in the film version of Sarif's *I Can't Think Straight*, constitutes Amira's compromise on her Islamic modesty. In the next scene, Nikki expresses her gratitude to Amira: 'I know it's not easy for you to be around someone like me, so thank you for doing it', to which Amira replies: 'It's nothing. I'm happy to' (*Three Veils*, 2011), before she lunges forward and kisses Nikki on the lips. The latter does not recoil from this homoerotic advance, but the scene is interrupted by Wes' appearance and his invitation to join him in his place. Amira declines but Nikki takes up the offer, and the heterosexual couple leave the disappointed Amira behind. Back in her bed, Amira pleas to God in Arabic, guiltily rubbing Nikki's lipstick off her mouth. There is a visible conflict here between Amira's well-meaning attraction to Nikki and her relationship with God and her adherence to Islamic ideas of feminine modesty.

These scenes illustrate how Amira and Nikki are constructed by Selbak as different forms of Muslim women driven to compromise on their divergent outlooks in order to forge an imperfect yet burgeoning interpersonal homoerotic connection with each other. Amira's goodwill towards Nikki makes her adapt her attitude and appearance, and Nikki's appreciation of her friend's gesture results in her own behavioural change. However, their emotional and sexual liaison is the feat that most powerfully disorganises their respective performances of Muslim femininity. In a subsequent scene, Nikki enters Amira's bedroom through the window in the middle of the night, announcing that she is running away and that she has come to say goodbye to Amira. Amira begs Nikki to take her with her, which is followed by a love-making scene, in which Nikki progressively kisses Amira on the forehead, cheek, and mouth. The women caress each other's faces, before Amira kisses and licks Nikki's stomach. Selbak's directorial treatment of the scene is remarkably chaste: while Amira appears considerably less experienced, she nonetheless quenches her attraction for Nikki, as both women's bodies become orientated towards each other through kissing, licking, and caressing.

In the scene set the following morning, Nikki writes the address of their meeting point in the palm of Amira's hand. However, Amira does not discover it until after her mother has woken her up and pressurised her into helping her clean the flat. Realising Nikki wants her to run away with her, Amira undertakes her own line of flight and leaves her family home, but she never finds Nikki. Amira's voiceover intimates:

> There's a moment in a person's life when her heart changes, when it breaks for the first time. It feels like it changes shape; it changes colour. You don't mean to let it happen, but it does, and your old heart stays hidden, *veiled*, and it never goes back to the way it used to be. (*Three Veils*, 2011, emphasis added)

Selbak deploys once again in Amira's monologue the trope of the veil. Here, it signifies the shroud around Amira's broken heart, as it is screened off from her family, and which crucially contains unfulfilled homoerotic desire. As a queer couple constituted by two vastly different Muslim women, Amira and Nikki best embody the struggle of Muslim diasporic women to come to terms with the gender roles dictated by Islamicate heteropatriarchy. Despite her piety, Amira's attraction to Nikki sets her at an angle from the dominant values of her faith, but most importantly, from those of her family, which deem a domestic and heterosexual role as her only possible destination. Ali reminds us that 'in making value judgments, people are influenced not only by religious texts and teachings but also by their own social, cultural, and religious backgrounds' (2006, p. xxvi). Amira's conditioning is thus not only religious but sociocultural, shaped by the inheritance of her family's traditional values about Arab femininity. Similarly, Nikki is circumscribed by expectations of Muslim women to be chaste and to forego hedonistic habits such as drinking alcohol and smoking, which are only compounded by her queerness. Naber suggests queer Arabs 'have confronted a [...] schema that defines Arabness in terms of heterosexuality and Americanness in terms of sexual transgression and promiscuity' (2012, p. 83). Amira and Nikki challenge the idea of the 'good Muslim', as their homoerotic desires and habits contravene the values of the Muslim diaspora, but heteronormativity ultimately prevails.

In the film's coda, Amira is shown to have given up on her homosexual desire and to have devoted herself, instead, to 'religion'. Over footage that shows us Amira wearing the *hijab*, Nikki's voiceover states:

> Amira eventually left home and went to school in Boston. She got her Masters in Theology and moved to Jordan to teach religion at an all-girls school. She told me she doesn't think she'll ever get married, because it's easier to deal with God than with love. (*Three Veils*, 2011)

Shatto suggests that '[w]hile the ending may leave some disappointed [*Three Veils*] [i]s an interesting film that breaks from the painfully narrow representation Arab women typically receive in films' (2013, p. 30). Selbak surrenders the idea of a 'happy' ending for Amira and Nikki, despite the implied queer audience's potential disappointment, because of the persistent homophobia of some contemporary Muslim communities. Selbak's film wilfully treads a culturally sensitive line that does not construct Islam as uniformly repressive or all Arab and Muslim men as invariably patriarchal, while still giving visual expression to everyday situations of female sexual repression that are still rife in some Muslim communities. Amira manages to flee the encroaching conventional family home and to make a life for herself in Jordan, yet she is unable to give in to her immanent homosexual desire. Haddad, Smith and Moore admit the risks for Muslims of leading an openly homosexual life, observing how 'those who admit to such an orientation may well find themselves ostracized from their families and communities' (2006, p. 138), a risk that Amira is clearly not ready to take, hence refusing to be openly homosexual. Susan Marshall and Jen'an Ghazal Read point out that when there are conflicting identities in Muslim women, there tends to be 'dominance of one identity over the others in salience and loyalty. In some settings it appears to be religion, since religious traditions and institutions are among the most stable of cultural forms, providing secure anchors of meaning in an environment of social change' (2003, p. 877). These sociologists argue that gender and sexual orientation become subservient, in effect, to ethno-religious affiliations. Selbak's construction of Amira can be deemed to conform to the sociological conditions of Muslim women who choose one identity – as Muslims – over more peripheral or seemingly problematic identities – as homosexuals – in order to avoid social ostracism from their ethno-religious communities.

Nevertheless, Selbak's narrative remains conscious of the possibility of misjudging or oversimplifying Muslim women's perspectives, especially in societies swayed by patriarchal values that overdetermine women's symbolic function. Explored in the film's last vignette, Nikki's predicament proves to be the most complex one, forcing viewers to reconsider their assumptions about the girl's seemingly faithless and hedonistic persona. Behind this protective 'veil', the audience finds a traumatic history of child abuse, family bereavement, and domestic violence. Encouraged by her mother, who is the source of spiritual guidance missing later in her life, young Nikki reads the Qur'an and raises it to her lips and forehead before putting it down, a visual reference to her early religious upbringing. Despite her mother's tutelage, she cannot save Nikki from male abuse, as she cannot save herself from the constricting expectations of Muslim femininity. In a bedtime scene, Nikki's mother, Farridah, and father, Mehdi (Christopher Maleki), discuss the upcoming visit of Nikki's uncle Hafiz (Andrew J. Ferranti). Mehdi observes how that will keep Farridah occupied. Farridah suggests getting a part-time job that she can combine with her household and childcare duties, but Medhi is adamant that she does not need to work, adding that 'a woman needs her life' (*Three Veils*, 2011), to which Farridah responds that she has a life. Hailing from Afghanistan, Mehdi holds on to patriarchal Muslim values that consign women to the domestic space. Contemporary Islamic feminists such as Amina Wadud challenge the patriarchal values underpinning Muslim societies, arguing that such division of labour is not originally found in the Qur'an:

> Each social context divides the labour between the male and the female in such a way as to allow for the optimal function of that society. The Qur'an does not divide the labour and establish a monolithic order for every social system which completely disregards the natural variations in society. (Wadud, 1999, p. 61)

According to Wadud, Islam's sacred scripture does not stipulate the occupations that are reserved for men and women. However, Mehdi has internalised patriarchal values which, calcified through the years, construct men as breadwinners and women as housekeepers. Even before any of the problematic child abuse and intergenerational violence surfaces, Nikki's mother's existence is already shown as constricted by women's patriarchally assigned domestic roles.

Upon his arrival, Uncle Hafiz showers both young Nikki (Andria Carpenter) and Farridah with compliments and money. Farridah is depicted as unable to refuse this financial gesture, given their precarity as recent migrants to America. As the main housekeeper and child carer, Farridah is sometimes obliged to leave Nikki under Hafiz's supervision. In a crucial scene, she dons the *hijab* and leaves the house to run some errands, only to panic and return to the house to check up on them. She discovers them playing innocently, yet Nikki's voiceover confirms that her mother's concerns about her safety were warranted: '[Hafiz] babysat me for the rest of that summer. I couldn't tell my mother what he was doing to me. He said if I did he would do the same to her' (*Three Veils*, 2011). Uncle Hafiz will die a year later, yet as the family prepares to move house in the wake of Mehdi's professional success, Farridah discovers a pair of Nikki's panties concealed within the bedsheet used by Hafiz. Mehdi returns from work and finds Farridah in tears holding Nikki by her side. All Farridah can pronounce is his brother's name. Mehdi asks Nikki what Hafiz did to her, only to then turn against his wife, demanding: 'Where were you? Answer me.' (*Three Veils*, 2011) Here, Selbak depicts the responsibilities in the Muslim family home as resting on the shoulders of women, as they are expected to tend to it both physically and morally. Overwhelmed by her apparent failure as a mother and wife, Farridah shuts herself in the bathroom, where, despite Mehdi's apology and entreaties to open the door, she commits self-harm, leading to her death sometime in the unspecified future.

So far, Nikki's life conceals sexual abuse during her childhood and her mother's death. To this, we must add her father's alcoholism following his wife's death, which renders him unable to carry out his parental duties, and which forces the young woman to become her father's diffident carer. As a girl who has suffered abuse, Nikki's sporadic relationships with men, which she recounts to Leila and Amira, hint towards a lingering psychosexual trauma she cannot overcome. Witnessing her mother's demise and her father's subsequent descent into alcoholism propel her in the direction of the whisky her father consumes. Mehdi's constant state of inebriation and his violent outburst when Nikki draws attention to their dysfunctional family life force her to stay away from the family home, often seeking shelter in Leila's – and later Amira's – house. Leila's mother is the main character in the film who vocally questions Nikki's lifestyle, which she interprets as being immoral. When, after a fight with Mehdi, Nikki needs a refuge for the night, Mrs Qasim does not allow her to pass through her door. As Nikki overhears across the slammed door: 'This is a respectable house, not a whore house for a hussy' (*Three Veils*, 2011). This rejection drives Nikki to drink alcohol in the streets before desperately calling Amira. *Three Veils*' first two vignettes gave us only partial visions of Nikki's life: she was shown as a pleasure-seeking girl who drank irresponsibly and who had carefree sexual relations with men. This third vignette constitutes Selbak's 'unveiling' of Nikki's complex predicament. She is socially labelled as a 'bad Muslim' (i.e., a whore, a hussy), whereas she simply does not benefit from spiritual or practical guidance, and she is indeed the victim of sexual abuse and parental violence, two stark sets of familial circumstances buried under a façade of hedonism and licentiousness.

The theme of gender violence is central to Selbak's endeavours in *Three Veils*. It is brave of Selbak to explore such a painful topic, since, in reclaiming the perspectives of abused Muslim women, her work could be interpreted as attacking the whole Islamic community. As Sara Ahmed observes in *Living a Feminist Life*: 'We must tell these stories of violence because of how quickly that violence is concealed and reproduced. We must always tell them with care. But it is risky: when they are taken out of hands, they can become another form of beating' (2017, p. 72). Selbak's commitment is to telling stories of violence which would otherwise remain hidden, but in so doing she is treating her stories 'with care', in order to avoid tarnishing the whole of the Arab and Muslim diaspora in America. Selbak ensures this is the case by redeeming the father figures in her film. As we have seen, Leila's father, Mr Qasim, is duly concerned about his daughter's happiness and welfare. Similarly, after Nikki runs away from home and she takes a near-fatal drug overdose, her father comforts her in hospital. They both confess to each other that they feel lost, but he reassures her that they both have each other. Although there is an element of melodrama in Selbak's narrative arcs, they constitute, nonetheless, a serious attempt at complicating Western views that might construct all Muslim males as inherently patriarchal and unsympathetic towards the plight of women. Like Sarif in *I Can't Think Straight*, Selbak redeems Muslim men by rendering mothers the unwitting reproducers of patriarchal values, with Mrs Qasim and Samira enforcing the institutions of arranged marriage and of women's necessary domesticity within heterosexual marriage.

The only refuge Nikki finds away from the glaring absences in her life after her mother's death is Amira, who cares about her and becomes homoerotically entangled with her. This is a jointly feminist and queer refuge. For the two women, their queer liaison becomes a shelter from sturdy societal and familial expectations about their compulsory heterosexuality, chastity, and modesty. Their diasporic Muslim communities are shown as offering challenges that far outstrip the characters' moral responsibilities. Thus, Selbak's film could be seen as critiquing the symbolic burden placed on Muslim women simply for the biological fact of being women. In Selbak's cinematic narrative, the two girls come to embody different Muslim configurations of same-sex desire which are not locked in battle, but which demonstrate the overlapping and coexistence of different models of sexual orientation. Amira is constructed as having immanent homosexual tendencies that are deeply ingrained. In turn, Nikki's unlabelled sexual orientation is posited as queer: her desire towards men and women is fluid, and her representation avoids a polarised understanding of sexuality. In combining such disparate configurations of female desire, Selbak debunks Occidentalist charges against homosexuality as being Westernised, for Amira's attraction to women does not seem inspired by any Western cultural traits. Selbak also opposes entrenched Arab perceptions of homosexuality as being the result of 'religious prohibition and inadequate heterosexual relations' (Habib, 2007, p. 11). Nikki does not reject men, which suggests she is not merely attracted to women because of her experience of male sexual violence. *Three Veils* thus attests to the possibility of having overlapping essentialist and constructionist articulations of Islamicate sexualities, which micropolitically challenge the idea that all immanent models of homosexuality are simply Westernised and that Arab same-sex desire is merely the symptom of inadequate heterosexual relationships.

With the intertwined stories of three ordinary Muslim women in America, one a 'good' dutiful Muslim girl, another 'bad' in her seemingly hedonistic habits, and the other 'ugly' in her homosexuality, Selbak singles out controversial topics, yet she does not attempt to sensationalise but to humanise her characters and to foreground their often elided perspectives. Her attempt to bring the stories of queer Muslim women, and of Arab women more generally, to mainstream Western culture has led her to be accused by Rosalind Galt and Karl Schoonover, alongside other minority-ethnic queer filmmakers, of adopting a 'neoliberal optic' (2016, p. 210). In their assessment of so-called 'queer middlebrow cinema', these critics see these films

> as attempting to cross over from the queer cinematic ghetto to a mainstream cultural space, whether that journey is from queer to mixed audiences, from festival to general release, or from a radical to a liberal vision of queer culture. [...] These crossover films cross borders and become crowdpleasers that promise a liberal and cosmopolitan vision of queer worldliness. (Galt and Schoonover, 2016, p. 210)

It is contentious that Galt and Schoonover uncritically equate 'liberal' with 'neoliberal', the latter implying a celebration of globalisation and affluent cosmopolitanism. None of Selbak's characters is particularly well-off or benefits too highly from the 'perks' of cosmopolitanism; on the contrary, they demonstrate the arduous ideological and practical negotiations undertaken by queer Muslims in the diaspora. In addition, despite offering Leila a happy ending after her traumatic experience of rape, neither Nikki nor Amira afford a 'crowd-pleasing' denouement: Nikki finally finds a voice and writes hers and her friends' stories, duly entitled *Three Veils*, yet we are not privy to any romantic fulfilment, and Amira has discarded her homosexuality in favour of her ethno-religious identity. There is no embrace here of a facile or simplified version of sexual liberation in the 'liberal' West, in acknowledgement of the precariousness of many Muslim women who still struggle with imposed societal and familial expectations about their femininity and their sexual orientation.

It seems that any minority-ethnic narratives that do not subscribe to a preordained political programme are to be interpreted as inherently complicit with the status quo. *Three Veils* may not subscribe to any single political agenda, prizing, instead, women's individual perspectives. If individualism is to be considered the main symptom of neoliberalism, then we are consigned to ignore the perspectives of those individuals whose first-hand perspectives are often elided in macropolitical discourses, such as those of Arab Muslim women. I would argue Selbak ultimately honours the motto of second-wave feminism recalled by Sara Ahmed: 'the personal is political' (2017, p. 3). However, Selbak remains wary of bolstering a homonationalist understanding of Muslim sexualities: the West's alleged sexual exceptionalism is not posited as being at loggerheads with backwards Islam; rather, Selbak gives a granulated vision of Muslim communities as steeped in patriarchal values, but also as gradually becoming more attuned to women's plights. In that sense, Selbak's artistic perspective is certainly that of a feminist of colour: she is conscious of issues of cultural difference while fiercely critiquing ongoing conditions of Islamic heteropatriarchal oppression. Denouncing such oppression does not automatically render her an Orientalist or an Islamophobe, but simply a critical member of her community, and she cannot be made fully responsible of the ends to which her representation may be put by her implicit audiences. I suggest *Three Veils* simultaneously de-essentialises Muslims against the continued clout of Orientalism, while raising awareness about persistent issues of gender and sexual inequality in Muslim communities, hence also challenging Islamic traditionalism. The film may not offer easy solutions to gender trouble or stage a queer revolution, yet it constitutes a timely contribution to a gradually growing body of queer diasporic depictions simultaneously challenging Western Islamophobia and Arab and Islamicate heteropatriarchal values about gender and sexuality.

Notes

1 Explorations of Muslim veil and all its different variations (i.e., the *hijab*, *niqab*, *burqa*, etc.) have been gathering momentum with the sway of global identity politics, and especially in the wake of the 'War on Terror', which has brought to the forefront, once again, the visual presentation of Muslim women around the world. Anybody approaching the topic for the first time should start with Fatima Mernissi's seminal book *Beyond the Veil: Male–Female Dynamics in Modern Muslim Society*, originally published in 1975. One of the most prominent recent examinations of the veil is Saba Mahmood's *Politics of Piety: The Islamic Revival and the Feminist Subject*. As Mahmood writes in response to categorical interpretations of the veil as a symbol of women's subjugation: 'I am often struck by my audience's lack of curiosity about what else the veil might perform in the world beyond its violation of women' (2005, p. 195). Within the American context, there is Katherine Bullock's edited collection of essays, *Muslim Women Activists in North America: Speaking for Ourselves*, including the personal reflections of *hijab*-wearing activists, and Yvonne Yazbeck Haddad, Jane I. Smith, and Kathleen M. Moore's *Muslim Women in America: The Challenge of Islamic Identity Today*. A recent sociological study is Smeeta Mishra and Faegheh Shirazi's (2010). For more recent contributions to the debate, see Sadia Abbas (2014) and Lisa K. Taylor and Jasmine Zine's edited collection (2014).
2 I must thank Ebtihal Mahadeen for her insightful personal reading of this section of the film, which contrasts with her research about the treatment of virginity in Jordan society and Jordanian media. See her forthcoming book chapter, Mahadeen (2018).
3 Although Amira's family's Egyptian provenance is not thoroughly examined, it is not altogether felicitous that the film's most prominent example of Islamic indoctrination takes place in a family linked to Egypt, a country where women became highly Islamised in the aftermath of Nasser's Government, via the Muslim Brotherhood and the legacies of the Islamic women's activist Zaynab Al-Ghazali. For a detailed discussion of Islam in colonial and postcolonial Egypt, see Mahmood (2005).

Part III

Narrating the self in queer time and place

7

A postcolonial queer melancholia: matrilinearity, Sufism, and *l'errance* in the autofictional works of Abdellah Taïa

FROM THE disquisition of gender and sexuality in the literary and film work of Shamim Sarif, Sally El Hosaini, and Rolla Selbak, I now move on to interrogate the interaction of the queer self with Islamicate ideologies and cultures as located in time and place. In the story 'From Jenih to Genet', originally published in Abdellah Taïa's *Le rouge du tarbouche* (The red of the fez) in 2005, the author's young autobiographical counterpart is taken by his distant cousin Ali on a pilgrimage to the Moroccan city of Larache. Taïa's first two books do not explicitly reference homosexuality, yet his desire for his cousin is palpably homoerotic from the start. As he intimates: 'Of course, I liked Ali a lot. I watched him discreetly, sneakily adoring him with my eyes, and in my heart I held a strong desire to be with him' (Taïa, 2017a, p. 96). In Larache, they visit the tomb of a 'saint' his mother's cousin Malika distinctly calls 'Jenih', who turns out to be none other than Jean Genet, one of the most famous writers of autofiction in the French language.

The visit to the celebrated French writer's grave usefully encapsulates some of the central concerns of Taïa's work: Genet is, like Taïa, thoroughly working class; he is a migrant who lives away from his own kind; he is queer. He connects with the people of Morocco and is in turn appropriated by them. Ralph Heyndels observes:

> Ici s'effectue une substitution qui n'est pas un effacement, car le *Jenih* de la mère d'Ali demeure, telle une autre manière de dire *Genet*; et celle-ci reste associée mentalement à *une forme de sainteté*: 'Genet était la bonne prononciation, *mais je préférais Jenih, comme Malika, c'était plus marocain*

> *ainsi, plus proche de moi'. Le français d'Ali est certes fascinant, mais son amoureux ne vent [sic] cependant pas renoncer au Maroc.* (Here a substitution is undertaken that is not a deletion, since the *Jenih* of Ali's mother remains just another way of saying *Genet*; and it remains mentally associated with *a form of saintliness*: 'Genet was the right pronunciation, *but I preferred Jenih, like Malika, it was more Moroccan like this, closer to me.*' Ali's French is certainly fascinating, *but his loving admirer, however, will not give up Morocco*. (Heyndels, 2009, p. 474, emphasis in original)

French literature acts here as a catalyst of Abdellah's attraction to the same sex: Ali's beauty and his knowledge of sexually unorthodox French writers allow for the flourishing of homoeroticism in Taïa. Nonetheless, his penchant for French culture mediated by his fascination with Ali does not imply a uncritical submission to the cultural legacies of French colonialism in Morocco: the young Abdellah embraces a specifically Moroccan vernacular that transforms the canonised *Genet* into the Moroccan *Jenih*, a phonetic and cultural reconfiguration that feels closer to the author's autofictional self. As Taïa has related to me in interview, 'French is a language that separates people in Morocco' (Fernández Carbajal, 2017b, p. 497); it carries the indelible imprint of colonial history, hence Taïa's need to transform it to reflect his position in life and art from his postcolonial diasporic perspective.

However, far from 'writing back' to Genet from a contrapuntal postcolonial perspective, Taïa's work is keen to maintain the sainthood of this queer and diasporic French writer who loved Morocco as much as Moroccans. According to Heyndels, Taïa pays tribute to

> ce 'saint' qui a abandoné son pays, sa terre [et] qui s'est converti à l'amour de l'autre, et a sa culture, en partie même à sa langue et à sa religion, corps et esprit confondus, et qui repose là face à la mere, au Maroc. (Heyndels, 2009, p. 475)
>
> (this 'saint' who has abandoned his country, his land [and] who has converted to the love of the other, and to his culture, as well as to his language and his religion, body and mind confounded, and who rests facing the sea in Morocco.)

Alessandro Badin concurs with Heyndels, and describes Genet as 'a tutelary figure' (2016, p. 112). To Taïa, regardless of Genet's French nationality, there is an admirable self-effacement in his queer and migrant experiences in Morocco.

As Edmund White reminds us, Genet befriended 'several Arab writers, including the leading Moroccan novelist Tahar Ben Jelloun' – one of Taïa's literary precursors – moreover, '[h]is last lover was Moroccan and Genet is buried in his town, Larache' (1994, p. xli). *Jenih*'s life and art have some echoes in Taïa's fiction, which I probe forthwith. In this chapter, I examine Taïa's autofictional literary work, with due reference to his debut film, *Salvation Army*, released in 2013, by analysing, first, Taïa's chosen genre of autofiction and its relationship with issues of embodiment. I subsequently link the writing of the self's body to Taïa's postcolonial queer melancholia, and to the theme of *l'errance* – errancy or wandering – in *An Arab Melancholia*, which performs a queer assemblage of cultures and temporalities validating his position as a gay, Moroccan, Muslim, Arab man. Moroccan society's negation of the homosexual citizen, I suggest, triggers religious doubt in Taïa's autobiographical self and a desperate embrace of matrilineal and Sufi versions of Islam posited at a remove from mainstream Islamicate normativity. Despite his repeated gestures towards interethnic homo-eroticism, which chimes with the work of Hanif Kureishi, Ian Iqbal Rashid, and Ferzan Özpetek explored in Part I, I examine Taïa's critique of residual colonial social hierarchies in contemporary sexual tourism, as depicted in both the literary and cinematic versions of *Salvation Army*. I argue that Taïa's most hopeful episode of homoerotic connection is enacted in the representation of queer diasporas in the literary version of *Salvation Army*, where same-sex desire experienced in transit dissolves geographical and personal borders. I finally propose that episodes of productive interpersonal connection, however inspirational, are ephemeral in Taïa's work, and that the queer Muslim diasporic self's endless wandering is linked to ongoing social inequalities and to the unending search for the beloved.

Abdellah Taïa, born in 1973 in Rabat, the capital city of Morocco, but raised in the coastal town of Salé, is the second contemporary Moroccan writer – after Rachid O. – to write about his homosexuality autobiographically, and the first modern Arab writer to publicly assume it without the protection of pseudonymity.[1] Living in Paris as a gay[2] Moroccan in the diaspora, Taïa becomes concerned with the urgent issue of constructing his own self narratively. His first four works of fiction, *Mon Maroc* (My Morocco), *Le rouge du tarbouche* (The red of the fez) – two short fiction collections whose stories have been selected and translated into English in *Another Morocco* – *Salvation Army*, and *An Arab Melancholia*, all published in French in the first decade of the twenty-first century, deal in more or less direct ways with the textual embodiment of the self.[3] Arnaud Genon (2013) defines this form of autobiographical literature as *autofiction*, observing that, despite the homonymity between the writer, narrator, and character of these texts, the works are written and commercialised primarily as fiction. There is in autofiction an autobiographical intent to relay the self's experiences, but it is written in a manner that remains aesthetically unfettered. In other words, autofiction's aim is not to represent reality mimetically, but to convey the self's subjectivity creatively, thus blurring the boundaries between autobiography and fiction. This discursive assemblage renders the self a literary construct. Gibson Ncube asserts that '[a] symbiotic relationship exists between the written word and the body and this in turn plays a pivotal role in the creation and fortification of [Taïa's] queer identity' (2014, p. 93). Ncube's point is supported by René de Ceccatty's preface to *Mon Maroc*, where he writes that

> [l]e livre devient corps, le corps devient livre. Il n'y a pas, en lui, de conflit entre le corps et le livre. Il a une façon naturelle d'évoquer toutes les sensations de son existence où la sexualité a une part importante. (Taïa, 2009a, p. 11)
>
> (The book becomes a body, the body becomes a book. There is no conflict in him between the body and the book. He has a natural way of evoking the sensations of his life, where sexuality plays an important part.)

I would suggest that Taïa's urgency to 'become a book' is linked to his traumatic experience as a gay man in Morocco, and to the lack of a 'real' geographical space where his homosexuality can be freely discussed with fellow Moroccans. Taïa's autofictional literature and film provide the safe space where he can directly confront his sexuality and fashion himself according to his particular queer and diasporic sensibility, without the immediate risk of societal or religious retribution.

Taïa's work has important micropolitical implications arising from his approach to writing the queer diasporic self. As Valérie K. Orlando asserts, the writing of the first-person singular of a postcolonial queer Moroccan citizen – and a diasporic one living in France, at that – cannot be construed as anything *but* political:

> In general, using 'I' for third generation [postcolonial] male and female authors, gay or straight, is equivalent to 'un acte politique.' As Abdellah Taïa stipulates: 'Il me semble que dire "je" dans ce pays est un acte politique. Nous sommes les enfants d'une période où l'oppression était omniprésente et le silence forcé. À un moment donné, il fallait que ça se libère'. (Orlando, 2009, p. 111)

(It seems to me that to use I in this country is a political act. We are the children of an omnipresent oppressive period, during which silence was forced. At a certain moment, it was necessary to liberate ourselves) [...] The confessional style of these works [...] more effectively encourages readers to consider the unsayable, the uncharted areas of the writer's imagined community.

Taïa refers in the embedded quotation to the controversial historical period of Hassan II's reign, which lasted from the 1960s to the 1990s, and whose social repression Taïa has captured in his award-winning fictional novel *Le jour du roi* (The King's day). For both Taïa and Orlando, the use of the 'I' in literature becomes a means of liberating oneself, in a manner which, I would add, micropolitically reclaims the individual self repressed by macropolitical Moroccan discourses. In embracing this first-person viewpoint, literature becomes a platform from which to utter the unsayable, chiefly the experiences of queer Muslim citizens at an angle from macropolitical ideologies. However, such a subversive act of self-expression cannot be safely undertaken in Morocco, where systemic homophobia continues to be rife. Taïa's diasporic plight lends his writing a melancholic tone, torn as he is between his longing for Morocco and his self-imposed exile, as between his fascination with Paris and his disenchantment with the French Republic's treatment of its ethnic minorities, particularly Muslims.[4] Alexandru Matei (2014) recognises a double cultural identity in Taïa: he lives in Paris, where he writes about Morocco from his current French cultural milieu, albeit, I would add, with a decidedly postcolonial consciousness.

Taïa's writing explores two interrelated strands of Islamicate homophobia: the systemic form that exists in Arab societies at a mundane level, and the state's official repression of homosexuality, best embodied by the character of Motjaba, the exiled gay Iranian in Taïa's *Un pays pour mourir* (A country to die in), which signals Taïa's consciousness about the precarious plights of queer citizens in the Middle East. Taïa's autofiction focuses most keenly on the former strand, as his autofictional characters face the hardships of growing up in Morocco. The opening of *An Arab Melancholia* narrates the near-rape of Abdellah, aged twelve, by a group of older Moroccan teenagers, led by the character dubbed Chouaïb. Here, Taïa's autofiction illustrates Jean-Paul Sartre's disquisition of active and passive homosexuals in Genet's work, whereby the active homosexual's subjugation of the lover 'moves to the inessential', since he 'derives his poignant beauty from the love that the girl queen bears him' (Sartre, 2012, pp. 336–7). In the episode's preliminaries, private and public perceptions surrounding sexual roles are also probed. Abdellah's neighbourhood friends routinely call him 'effeminate' and equate his effeminacy with being 'a *zamel*, a passive faggot' (Taïa, 2012a, p. 13); this correlation creates expectations in his assaulters, and before the encounter turns awry, Abdellah fantasises about having sex with Chouaïb, pondering '[w]e'd have sex, real sex. Serious sex. He'd always be in charge. *I'd let him think I was passive*' (2012a, p. 16, emphasis added). Taïa confirms here the almost automatic link made in Islamicate Arab societies between effeminacy, homosexuality, and the passive sexual role, illustrating static gender and sexual roles in collective Arab consciousness.

However, Taïa's narrator also queers the dynamic of these sexual roles. His autofictional self renders Chouaïb's imagined dominant role, to echo Sartre, 'inessential': he styles himself as passive, thus possessing Chouaïb's desire and making himself 'essential'. While undertaking this, Taïa forfeits personal vilification: the young Abdellah is surprisingly empathetic. Chouaïb is described as 'an adolescent who was tired of waiting and who wanted to become a man, fast – a big, strong, imposing man. [...] Chouaïb was in full metamorphosis. I could see it, feel it, understand it better than he did' (Taïa, 2012a, p. 19). The young boy can understand his aggressor's thirst for transformation because of his own struggle, as a homosexual, with becoming the man Moroccan society expects him to be; this makes him empathise with other young men who are going through parallel struggles with masculine performance and gender self-affirmation.

The tipping point in the episode, when Abdellah's strategic submissiveness is turned on its head, involves Chouaïb's persistent treatment of him as a girl, the 'girl queen' of Sartre's assessment of Genet. The narrator's young version of himself resists first inwardly and then outwardly this conflation of gender and sexual orientation:

> I wanted to tell him repeatedly that a boy is a boy and a girl is a girl. Just because I loved men and always would, didn't mean that I was going to let him think of me as the opposite sex, let him destroy my identity, my history like that. [...] I opened my eyes. I turned and shouted in his face, 'My name's not Leïla... I'm not Leïla... I'm Abdellah... Abdellah Taïa...' [...] We slugged it out, real punches, pretend punches. He called me all kinds of names: *zamel*, candy-ass, bitch, his little Leïla. I started biting him, biting him on the arms, the thighs. We were pushing and shoving. [...] This wasn't a game anymore. It was all about honor. Our honor as men. The honor we'd have to live with tomorrow. (Taïa, 2012a, pp. 21, 24).

Abdellah rebels both discursively, by invoking his own name, and materially against the erasure of his identity as a man and his substitution for the feminine construct of *Leïla*. Jean Zaganiaris argues that Chouaïb 'a besoin de voir Abdellah comme possédant des attributs de la femininité' (2013, p. 322) (needs to see Abdellah as possessing the attributes of femininity), since, I would add, this is the only way to ensure he remains properly male in his own eyes. Understood as a dialectic between masculinity – the active role – and femininity – the passive role – his sexual domination of Abdellah as Leïla would not detract from his perceived dominant heterosexuality.

Abdellah's prostration and near-rape is interrupted by the *muezzin*'s call to prayer. Chouaïb orders his friends to stop. The narrator observes: 'He was obviously a good Muslim. He feared God. [...] He could never worship sex and God at the same time. They each had their place', and hence he cannot yet tackle the 'boy about to be sacrificed' (Taïa, 2012a, p. 27). The *muezzin*'s chant is followed by Chouaïb's mother's call for 'Ali', Chouaïb's real name, which finally dispels the mood of sexual violence. Creeping up the stairs, the mother's voice renders all the adolescents children again, much like the scene of Izzi's murder in *My Brother the Devil*, and the group disbands. Apart from the violent means by which some Moroccans feel forced to become 'proper men', which recalls the toxic hypermasculinity explored in El Hosaini's film, I suggest Taïa's narrative critiques here the moral double standards of Moroccan society, where the rape of a man by another man can only be interrupted by the most superficial respect for religious duty.

Despite not having been penetrated by 'Chouaïb' or any of his peers, the young Abdellah's honour has been compromised; he is conscious of the encounter's consequences for his social status in his community, which plagues his psyche:

> From now on, people would only see me one way. I'd come with a warning label. A tag: effeminate guy. Sissy. [...] People would take advantage of me every day, abuse me more and more. In their own small way, people would kill me. Slay me alive. (Taïa, 2012a, p. 30)

Young Abdellah knows that his community's homophobia will fix his identity and obliterate his self. The sexual assault and Abdellah's internal struggle with its social implications create a trauma that drives him to touch a live power line. This moment of self-obliteration marks a before and after in the boy's life, resembling, yet again, Sartre's view of Genet's personal trajectory. As he intimates: 'Genet carries in his heart a bygone instant which has lost none of its virulence, and infinitesimal and sacred void which concludes a death and begins a horrible metamorphosis' (Sartre, 2012, p. 2). Like Genet, Abdellah is transformed by his own 'death' by electrocution, and what we witness is a crucial metamorphosis. The resurrected boy's first instinct is to part with his previous life by running, which incepts the theme of *l'errance*. He is no longer the 'effeminate boy':

> Now I was the boy who had been granted a miracle. For me, that marked a starting line. I'd break with the pack and start to run. [...] Run to save my hide? My soul? [...] I'd run towards the unknown me, the one that was found, the lost self. (Taïa, 2012a, pp. 33–4)

The renewed Abdellah is here molecularly enacting his own line of flight by running away from the heteronormative herd. Homosexuality and flight is also a theme that Taïa's work spectrally inherits from his autofiction writer forerunner, Genet; White surmises: 'Just as Genet later associated his first homosexual feelings with his first urges to steal, [...] the open declaration of his effeminacy is associated with running away [...]. Later, flight would always remain Genet's response to a crisis' (1994, p. 50). Orlando suggests that contemporary Moroccan authors 'question and explore sexual deviance and the social marginalization of those who refuse to kowtow to the norms of sociocultural traditionalism. Their narratives explore the desire to *break away* from the burden of family and tradition' (2009, p. 107, emphasis added). In Taïa's case, his young autofictional self's deathly experience triggers an urgent desire to flee from Moroccan society's strictures towards an unknown, deferred self that has been inexorably touched by his early experience of homophobia.

Such a wilful escape from the social pressures of 'the pack' also triggers religious doubt in Abdellah and a desperate – albeit diffident – embrace of matrilineal experiences and mystical manifestations of Islam at an angle from the homophobic and masculinist drive of majoritarian Sunni versions of the faith. This becomes blatant in the Cairo section of *An Arab Melancholia*, where, after a line of unhappy relationships with other Arab men, the narrator asserts:

> I wasn't myself any more. I had to rediscover who I was. That's why I left the apartment, to lose myself in the streets of Cairo. [...] A man without God. [...] I was losing it. The Arab world was losing it even faster than I was. [...] Nothing would ever be the same again. God no longer existed, that's what I really believed. I was going to hell. I was damned. Damned. I wandered around. What did I have left? A memory of an Algerian

named Slimane, [...] the ghost I found so miraculously soothing in Cairo. [...] What did I have left? Same as always, tombs, mausoleums, saints. (Taïa, 2012a, pp. 95–6)

In Egypt's capital city in the advent of the Arab Spring, Abdellah feels himself and his faith disintegrating alongside the rest of the Arab world; he feels judged and condemned for his 'sin' as a homosexual, and consigned to wandering the streets searching for himself, his only dim consolation being the memory of his past lover, the Algerian Slimane. This chimes with the spiritual search of Sufism, which gathers momentum in Taïa's novel. Amanullah De Sondy observes that '[t]he way of the Sufi has no set path; the other experiences that God grant the Sufi are added obstacles or tests that must be accepted in the hope that they will be overcomed [sic]' (2014, p. 154). Abdellah's spiritual practice of wandering is intermittently connected to this mystical dimension of Islam. The fragile recognisable features of the faith holding on to Abdellah are the tombs, mausoleums, and saints he has always revered, and which since *Mon Maroc* and *Le rouge du tarbouche* have been connected with women and with his mother, more specifically, honouring a matrilineal experience of Islam that serves as a form of identification and solidarity with Muslim women.

In *Le rouge du tarbouche*, the narrator recounts how he was initiated onto visiting saints' mausoleums by his mother, M'Barka, who took him to venerate Sidi Abdallah Ben Hassoun, Salé's patron saint, and Sidi Ben Acher, another saintly protector of the city. As the narrator observes: 'Je regardais à chaque fois cette communion de loin, peureux et en même temps complètement fasciné' (Taïa, 2012b, p. 13) (I watched every time this communion from afar, fearful and at the same time completely fascinated). Although, at first, Abdellah is both afraid and fascinated by his mother's religious homage to these saints, he will later in life embrace this popular aspect of religion and women's comforting spirituality. In a moment of wandering described in 'An Afternoon with Sidi Fatah', translated into English in *Another Morocco*, during which Abdellah experiences spiritual disorientation, he visits the mausoleum of the titular saint. The narrator recounts:

All around me, chatting, sat women, women whose spirituality I shared, with whom I was in communion. There were all kinds of women, old ladies in djellabas, young women in suits, women from the countryside who'd made the trip from very far away, rich women, poor ones. They mingled as they would never do anywhere but here. They didn't judge each other, they shared looks of such kindness. They were sisters. And amid all of them was me, the only man, the only boy. They inspired confidence in me. (Taïa, 2017a, p. 55)

In this episode of gender-inclusive religious consolation, the variegated group of Muslim women make Abdellah feel welcome and in spiritual communion with them at the saint's mausoleum, in a moment of gender integration that is linked to a female saintly benefactor rather than to a foreboding God who condemns him for his homosexuality. As the narrator surmises, the women 'didn't judge each other'. It is this non-judgemental feminine religiosity that clings on to Abdellah in the aforementioned moment of religious doubt in *An Arab Melancholia*. It connects affectively with the religiosity of women that he came to love as a child and young man in Morocco, and which remains with him despite his doubts about God. Taïa's work reorientates his understanding of Islam away from the patrilineal and towards the matrilineal, from patriarchal domination to maternal consolation, in a manner that temporarily disorganises heteropatriarchy.

Juxtaposed with Abdellah's episode of religious doubt is a moment of spiritual re-embodiment, where his confusion about his unrequited love for a Spaniard, Javier, intersects with memories of his sister Lattéfa:

I was caught up in the horror of my own state of confusion. [...] There were times when I could see my sister Lattéfa in myself, Lattéfa, the girl people said was possessed. [...] Lattéfa was possessed but I never understood how it had started for her. How was she to blame? I mean, what crime did she ever commit? [...] I was Lattéfa. And like her, I went to visit a saint, the nearest I could find. The saint was Sayyéda Zainab, the most important saint of Egypt. (Taïa, 2012a, pp. 97–8)

With Abdellah becoming his 'possessed' sister, Taïa undertakes an analogous critique of Islamic patriarchy and homophobia: both women and homosexuals are judged by normative Islamic ideologies, forced to kowtow to the image of the 'perfect Muslim' coined by his beloved Sufi poet Ibn Arabi (De Sondy, 2014). Yet, neither women nor homosexuals are, to echo Taïa's own words, 'to blame' for their difference; their resulting state of confusion when they fail to conform to society's strictures has much to do with their search for the beloved, a path to God through human love. Abdellah's spiritual disorientation leads him to the religiosity he was taught as a child, seeking the religious comfort of Sayyéda Zainab, a prominent saint of the Shia branch of Islam, and Prophet Muhammad's granddaughter. Although the narrator writes that he visited 'the nearest' saint 'he could find', it is important that this turns out to be a female descendant of Prophet Muhammad, and Shia, all of which signals a palpable ideological break from majoritarian Sunni Islam,[5] and a queer embrace of different forms of religiosity assembling Islam's often competing yet overlapping incarnations.

What Abdellah encounters at the saint's mausoleum remains most relevant to his spiritual reorientation. There, he runs into a Sufi crowd so heterogeneous that he feels instantly comforted, albeit still plagued by his lingering religious doubts about the nature of God:

Men, women, children, old people, women in veils, women in too much makeup, men with mustaches, men with beards, poor people, very rich people, Muslims, Copts, dwarfs, unhappy people, newlyweds, drug addicts, Blacks, whites, those who had a made a fortune in oil… A dense crowd, a single unit welded together across all social lines, a crowd joined as one in the unorthodox expression of their unique love. An overflowing crowd, one that cried out, louder and louder. Cried out in ecstasy. Cried out as the tenets of their sensuous, sexual religion demanded, cried out as Sufis. […] I jumped into the crowd. Enraptured. A dervish full of love and misfortune. A Moroccan child living in Paris in the middle of a major crisis. Someone without roots. With a very strident conscience. I sang along with them. I danced. I shouted. I didn't know whether I believed in anything anymore, but I did know that the crowd moving around the Lady of Cairo would do me good, maybe even save me. (Taïa, 2012a, pp. 98–9)

Unifying seemingly clashing models of gender, class, and social positioning, body types, and even religious identification – Copts being Christians – the colourful Sufi crowd that congregates in this time and place is constructed as inalienably *queer*, fluid, its assemblage of its multifarious identities into one single variegated whole helping Abdellah to assume his guilt-ridden difference. Abdellah embraces here a more sensual and less inhibited metaphysical manifestation of Islam, yet one which, despite its occasional subversion of gender roles and sexual normativity, as we will see now, remains partly steeped in patriarchal values. By becoming one with the Sufi crowd, however, Abdellah micropolitically assembles the different parts of his identity, in a manner that de-polemicises his seemingly conflicting sexual, cultural, national, and religious allegiances, thus placing a temporary hold on those societal pressures that force Moroccan Muslims to conform to the narrow moral standards of legalist and literalist versions of Islam.

De Sondy observes that Sufism 'has often detached itself from mainstream legalist movements in Islamic culture and society' (2014, p. 153), yet despite its 'basis of ungendered notions such as love, submission, and subservience, [...] these have often been gendered through an understanding that men are better suited to carry out such acts' (2014, p. 156). He notes that, for Sufis, Adam is created in God's image and Eve is only considered as being contained within Adam, hence femininity is still subservient to masculinity. De Sondy also argues that, despite its often subversive practice, aesthetics, and its sometimes open embrace of homoeroticism in so-called medieval and early modern Islamicate cultures, Sufism's basic theological tenets are still invested in masculine and feminine roles of dominance and subservience within heterosexual marriage, and in sexual abstinence. On the other hand, De Sondy also suggests that Sufis are often at loggerheads with the law, and that their conception of love often contradicts institutionalised state practices, arguing that 'Sufis [...] have long stated that same-sex relationships are a means to the beloved' (2014, p. 169), and that 'spiritual Sufis were led to a path to God which was often heterodox. In the path of submission to God, societal ideals can fall by the wayside' (2014, p. 171). Taïa's search for the beloved is often plagued by religious doubt because it fails to conform to a legalistic understanding of Islam as heteronormative. The Sufi crowd in *An Arab Melancholia* offers a temporary antidote for Abdellah's spiritual anguish: he feels there is a place for him in the 'heterodox' crowd that encompasses such a varied spectrum of humanity, and which does not automatically condemn his homoerotic path as intrinsically sinful.

Such powerful episodes of human intercommunion are short-lived in Taïa's work. As Zaganiaris surmises, 'L'amour est une *"possession"*. Sur un ton très proustien, où le narrateur passe d'un amour à un autre sous un register existentiel, le roman raconte les différentes relations d'Abdellah au Maroc et en France' (2013, p. 229, emphasis in original) (Love is a *'possession'*. In a very Proustian tone, the narrator moves from one love to another. Under an existential register, the novel recounts Abdellah's different relationships in Morocco and France.) Linked not so much to Proust as to Sufism and, as we shall see, pre-Islamic poetry, the existential theme of *l'errance* and the continuous search for the beloved are symptomatic of Taïa's melancholia[6] triggered by his precariousness as a gay diasporic Moroccan man. *L'errance* unites an urge to flee Moroccan homophobia, an affective mourning for his country of birth, and an endless spiritual search for the place of love and safety.

In the story 'Starobinski's Baraka', the autofictional narrator recounts his meeting with Jean Starobinski, the most prominent modern French thinker to examine the concept of melancholia. In Taïa's narrative, Abdellah, who at this point is studying in Geneva (Switzerland), becomes obsessed with touching Starobinski, so that his *baraka* – his 'blessing' – is passed on to him. In our interview, Taïa denied a direct influence of Starobinski's work on his writing and emphasised the personal way in which the French intellectual touched his life, explaining how, aesthetically, he 'attempted to do something Moroccan with him [...]: [he] wanted to touch his clothes' (Fernández Carbajal, 2017b, p. 498). Nonetheless, within the story, the narrator observes: 'We do not merely live with the people who surround us physically, we also live in the company of spirits – those we admire, those we adore, their sensibilities, their ways of looking at things. We evolve with them, thanks to them' (Taïa, 2017a, p. 65). Genon suggests, regarding this episode, that 'On peut aujourd'hui répondre que oui, la bénédiction, la réussite, la chance de l'auteur de *La relation critique* lui a bien été transmise' (2013, p. 94) (Today we can answer that yes, the blessing, the success, the luck of the author of *The Critical Relation* has been completely transmitted to him). Spiritually and phenomenologically, we could argue that the proximity of Starobinski to Abdellah, and the latter's wish to be granted the French thinker's 'blessing' in order to partake of his intellectual evolvement, both warrant a critical exploration of the way in which Starobinski's notion of melancholia can illuminate Taïa's queer mood as a sexually dissident diasporic Moroccan.

In his book *L'Encre de la Mélancolie* (The Ink of Melancholia), Starobinski explores the melancholic self, arguing that perceptions of movement have changed throughout history, as Western societies gradually became more detached from religious sensibilities:

> L'attente, l'errance, dans les versions premières de la légende, ont un terme lointain, et ce terme est défini selon l'eschatologie religieuse. À partir de l'époque des Lumières, la légende reste vivace, mais s'ordonne à une fin profondément modifiée. L'on assiste à un changement d'eschatologie, ou, plus radicalement, à la suppression de tout espoir en une parousie finale: l'errance, devenue agitation pure et mouvement sans but, détachée de toute finalité concevable, n'est plus qu'un emblème de l'absurde: un pas suit l'autre, mécaniquement, sans rejoindre ce qui jamais n'apparaîtra. (Starobinski, 2012, p. 532)
>
> (Waiting, wandering, in early versions of the legend, were a distant term, and that term is defined by religious eschatology. Since the Enlightenment, the legend is still alive, but it is put to a profoundly transformed end. We are witnessing a change of eschatology, or, more

radically, the elimination of any hope for a final parousia: wandering, now become agitation and aimless movement, detached from any conceivable purpose, is nothing but an emblem of the absurd: one step following another, mechanically, without rejoining that which will never appear.)

In view of Starobinski's work, Enlightenment secular conceptions of *l'errance* have taken away the spirituality embedded in the existential activity of wandering, rendering it a form of purposeless movement merely connected with psychic anxiety. I wish to argue here that Taïa's post-Enlightenment deployment of the theme of *l'errance* bypasses the secularist – and by extension colonial – legacy of the Enlightenment. His postcolonial melancholic wandering constitutes, instead, an assemblage of historical temporalities syncretising pre-Islamic and Islamicate Arab cultures, in a manner that situates his autofictional self in a diachronic line of lovelorn melancholia, whose thwarted longing for the beloved is not deviant or solipsistic, but culturally and spiritually linked to Arab history's long investment in conjoined erotic and spiritual searching.

The legacies in *An Arab Melancholia* of Sufi and pre-Islamic nomadic poetry allow for a queer transhistorical assemblage of various moments of errancy. In an episode following his visit to Sayyida Zeinab's mausoleum, Abdellah becomes lost again in Cairo:

> I needed to find someone, someone alive, in the flesh, someone real, someone visible, someone to save me. Someone to touch me. Someone who let me gaze upon him. Someone to carry me along. Someone who would make the decision for me about which path I ought to be following. Because I was now a *hayèm* [a man madly in love], a wanderer in the desert, as in Ibn Arabi's poetry. A vagrant. A man with no direction. A man with no God. [...] I wandered around for hours. [...] The cycle of blind death that I had already encountered as a child, as a young man, was starting again. I was lost in the desert. Lost and panicking. I was lost in the city, lost and panicking. Fear was all I felt, total panic as I felt the world slipping away. Slipping away inside me. (Taïa, 2012a, pp. 103–4)

With his repetitive, elegiac prosody, I argue Taïa writes himself into the tradition of the *qasida*, a poetic form hailing back to pre-Islamic Arabia, as Paul Smith testifies in his English translation of Ibn Arabi's poetry. According to Smith, this type of poem always starts 'with a nostalgic opening in which the poet reflects on what has passed, known as *nasib*. A common concept is the pursuit of the poet of the caravan of his love; by the time he reaches their campsite they have already moved on' (Arabi, 2012, p. 31). Ibn Arabi asks his friends in one of his *qasidas* to 'halt and beg for some words from / the remains of an abode that is ruined, since they left here / and let us mourn for the heart of this youth who was leaving it' (2012, p. 43). The poem contains a crucial element of longing for the departed beloved.

In *An Arab Melancholia*, Taïa self-confessedly becomes a comparable poetic vagrant, a *hayèm*, a wanderer in the desert searching for '[s]omeone to touch [him]', plagued by this unattainable love that constitutes, simultaneously, a grappling with his faith and his submission to God. The beloved pursued through the urban streets, here metaphorically transformed into a desert, often takes the shape of his past lovers in Europe and North Africa – i.e., Javier, Karim, Slimane – but in his crazed wandering through Cairo, this anguish is turned inwards, as Abdellah himself burns with longing for an abstract beloved who will steer him and who will send him, as a queer Arab, on the torturous path towards God. Crucially, this intersecting erotic and religious disorientation is not predicated at a remove from mainstream culture or in a different heuristic space, but is contiguous with well-established Islamic and pre-Islamic poetic traditions.

In our interview already cited, Taïa highlighted how a pre-Islamic poetic tradition, particularly the poems known as the *Mu'allaqat*, seven odes composed by pre-Islamic poets and deeply respected in Islam – they are said to have hung from the Kaaba in Mecca – awoke him to the cultural commensurability of his own situation:

> When I discovered this poetry, I felt such an emotional connection with it. For me, this is the true cosmopolitanism: the fact that being gay could be lived through an Arabic literary poetic tradition, like these poems that were written fourteen centuries before I was born, and which were already doing the same thing I am striving to do. (Fernández Carbajal, 2017b, p. 501)

In a manner emulated by his autofictional counterpart, the poets of the *Mu'allaqat* begin their poems by visiting the places where their beloved have camped, mourning the absence of these and other lovers. Imra'-ul-Qays intones:

> There, at that desolate place, I told my friends to halt their camels.../ [...]
> Ah no, the only cure for my grief is to allow my tears to flow.../ but what

remains here of her, that some solace to me is giving? / And even before I had met Unaizah I was grieving for two others. (*Seven Golden Odes of Arabia*, pp. 27–8)

The desert is the place where the poet searches for the traces of the beloved, where memories of previous lovers resurface, often tearfully, which recalls not just adult Abdellah's diasporic predicament but also his young self's crying as he wandered the streets of Salé. By assembling the legacies of the *Mu'allaqat* with those of Ibn Arabi's Sufi poetry, Taïa inscribes his homoerotic desire within a poetic tradition expressing both Islamic and pre-Islamic romantic melancholia. This transhistorical assemblage of cultural perspectives is purposefully *queer*, not just for its foregrounding of non-normative desires, but in its very anachronistic syncretisation of the theme of *l'errance*. Far from constituting a mere psychic reality, Taïa's exploration of errancy is spiritually connected to an Arab cultural tradition of unrequited love and spiritual wandering that places him in the continuum of Arab and Islamicate history.

For all of Taïa's queer assemblage of matrilineal and Sufi versions of Islam, and for his syncretic textual embodiment of the various literary histories of *l'errance*, his work is not altogether apolitical or unaware of the persisting power relations that constitute the legacy of European colonialism in postcolonial Morocco. The social hierarchies that allowed the colonisers to satisfy their sexual needs are now substituted by a not dissimilar form of neocolonial sexual tourism: foreign visitors entice Moroccans who are either desperate to flee Morocco's poverty or who want to partake in the West's alleged sexual freedom without the social stigma their fellow Moroccans attach to homosexuality. This topic is prominent in the novel and film versions of *Salvation Army*. The most central same-sex relationship in these narratives is between Abdellah, as a university student, and Jean, a French-speaking lecturer from the University of Geneva who intermittently visits Morocco. A homoerotic rapport is established between both men. The narrator relays: '[Jean] came three times to Morocco to see me. We visited three Moroccan cities together: Marrakech, Tangiers, Ouarzazate. I went to see him in Switzerland twice. We wrote each other at least five letters a week' (2009b, p. 78). Najib Redouane explains that 'Il n'est pas étonnant que le jeune narrateur-protagoniste considère sa relation avec Jean comme une opportunité tant attendue pour s'épanouir, se développer, et envisager même son élévation de son milieu modeste' (2007, p. 118) (It is not surprising that the young narrator-protagonist considers his relationship with Jean as a long-awaited opportunity to grow, to develop, and even to consider his elevation from his humble background.) For

Abdellah, brought up in a humble district of Salé, Jean offers attractive views of social mobility and a break from the apparent provincialism of his Moroccan life, in a way that also befits existing Islamicate relationships of mentorship. De Sondy states that '[o]ne may think of mysticism as a solitary path, but it's clear that Sufis venerate the master-discipline relationship, which is sometimes compared to the bond between husband and wife' (2014, p. 159). The relationship between Abdellah and Jean could be partly interpreted as that between a master and a disciple, yet contemporary Morocco holds a more traditionalist understanding of homosexuality.

During their visit to Marrakech, Abdellah is accosted by two policemen who suspect him of being Jean's prostitute. The policemen ask: 'What are you doing with this man? Why are you bothering him? [...] Where do you think you are, in America? [...] How much is he paying you?' (Taïa, 2009b, p. 91). Here, the toleration of homosexuality is predicated as a Western trait, alien to Moroccan society and by extension to Islam. Although they release Abdellah after checking his identification, as soon as they return to the car, the policemen shout: 'Make sure he pays you a lot ... and wash your ass good when he's done, dirty faggot' (2009b, pp. 91–2). Because the abuse is uttered in Arabic, Jean has not been privy to it, yet Abdellah is humiliated by the incident's homophobia. Despite the policemen's wilful misrepresentation of the relationship between Abdellah and Jean, it does not take Abdellah long to realise that there is not a great difference between Jean and other sexual tourists in Morocco.

The couple meet a character called Mohamed during their visit to Tangiers the following year. As the narrator candidly observes: 'Jean cruised him in the Delacroix Arcade. [...] And Mohamed followed him right away' (Taïa, 2009b, p. 99). The ease with which Jean procures Mohamed's charm unravels Abdellah's certainties about his lover's ulterior motives: 'Was this another reason Jean had come to Morocco, to get laid by cute, young Moroccans? Hadn't he come to Morocco to spend time with me, just me?' (2009b, pp. 99–100). In spite of the fact Jean indeed buys Mohamed's sexual services, Jean helps Abdellah secure a visa for a visit to Switzerland the following summer, thus establishing a more durable interpersonal link, yet one that cannot be extrapolated from a sense of neocolonial privilege on Jean's part. As Abdellah ponders: 'Maybe he and I shared the same love of books, but we *still* didn't have the same set of values nor the same set of doubts' (2009b, p. 100, emphasis added). The young man remains mildly hopeful that there will be an eventual ideological alignment between him and his lover, yet the narrative highlights the insurmountable structural inequality between the Swiss academic and his Moroccan lover.

Although Abdellah becomes Jean's guest in Europe for two months, the inequality of their relationship is further highlighted during his stay in Switzerland. The narrator tells us that living with Jean feels like being under a dictator. Moreover, while in a restaurant with Charles – Jean's friend and perhaps one-time lover – a man hands Abdellah a card reading 'I pay very well' (2009b, p. 114). This yet again brings home to Abdellah his subservience to Jean:

> For a lot of people, [...] I was nothing more than a prostitute, some kind of cheap hooker. Making the rounds with Jean, being part of this 'new' scene, meant a lot of people saw me as the object of his desire. What else could I be? After all, he was the one paying. And anybody could buy me, just like he did. [...] Deep inside me, this irreparable fracture opened. Several weeks later, the plane that brought me back to Morocco was full of Moroccan women trying to look chic. They were very expensive prostitutes. [...] Over there, just like back home, everything was for sale. (Taïa, 2009b, pp. 114–15)

It becomes plain that the sexual perpetuation of the colonial relationship is as prevalent in postcolonial Morocco as it is in contemporary Europe, and this creates a 'fracture' in Abdellah, who realises he will never be Jean's equal because of their socioeconomic differences and due to social perceptions of their relationship's transactionality. When Abdellah later secures a grant to study in Geneva, once he has broken up with Jean, Charles never shows up to collect him from the airport, prompting his desperate stay at the titular Salvation Army.

Here, the film provides a more explicit critique of social inequality. In the novel, when Abdellah runs into Jean, he has mixed feelings about his former lover: 'Seeing him that day, so near and yet so far, made me realize how much tenderness and attachment he aroused in me, and, despite my best efforts, always would' (Taïa, 2009b, p. 129). Abdellah cannot help feeling regret and avoids talking to Jean. Their prior emotional bond deters Abdellah from censuring the Swiss man in stern moral or political terms. By contrast, the film version of *Salvation Army* (2013) offers a fraught encounter that rings with important postcolonial tones. In their tense meeting in a university room, powerfully shot in profile and in chiaroscuro, Jean (Frédéric Landenberg) tries to soften the now wiser Abdellah (Karim Ait M'Hand) by complimenting him on his cropped hair before asking him what he is planning to do in Switzerland. Abdellah bluntly tells him that he wants nothing from him. Jean then changes tactic, accusing Abdellah of using him to make his way in Europe and calling him a whore. Abdellah appropriates the insult yet defiantly claims that he had to leave Jean because he needed to be free of Morocco and of him. This statement garners him a slap from Jean, followed by Abdellah's departure from the room. Taïa uses the film to expand on his novel's embedded postcolonial commentary: his younger autofictional self needed to flee Morocco in order to escape the persistent material inequalities and moral double standards of the postcolonial nation, but he had to simultaneously break free from the neocolonial liaison chaining him to Jean, whose financial sponsorship made him feel economically and emotionally imprisoned. The focus on a vocabulary of 'freedom' warrants a postcolonial critical approach that is attentive to the micropolitical impetus of Taïa's autofictional film, for, despite not being overtly political, it nonetheless provides an affective commentary on the complex nature of intercultural relationships in the wake of colonialism. Jean had offered the young Abdellah a means of partly escaping Moroccan homophobia, as well as broader cultural vistas, yet their socioeconomically uneven relationship cannot overstep the legacies of European colonialism.

Abdellah's only means of escaping the patriarchal strictures of Moroccan society, calcified conceptions of masculine dominance and feminine submission plaguing his relationships with other Arab men, as well as the neocolonial imbalances of his relationship with Jean, is the open embrace of a queer diasporic perspective that dissolves man-made borders. The most hopeful moment of queer diasporic communion in Taïa's work to date is his erotic encounter, retold in the novelistic version of *Salvation Army*, with Matthias and Rafaël, two gay men from Germany and Poland, respectively. The chapter depicts Abdellah on his way to see Jean in Geneva during a low point in their relationship, when he has already started seriously doubting the tenability of their liaison. On the boat from Tangiers to Algeciras, he chances upon this international couple, whose rocky relationship becomes a catalyst of Abdellah's queer diasporic desire.

The queer threesome between Matthias, Rafaël and Abdellah commences on a train from Algeciras to Madrid, and their diasporic connection is built up in Madrid's cosmopolitan spaces:

> Around midnight, just when we were supposed to get some sleep, the moment arrived, the single moment I think we all were waiting for, happened just like that, unplanned, no warning, and we took off our clothes and started to make love, all three of us naked together. We didn't sleep. The hot night kept us awake, ready for love and its pleasures. We were happy. Young and happy. The Spanish landscape hung like a frame around what surged within us and what we shared. Spain, the land of my

ancestors, the land I set foot in for the first time in my life. Spain, still Arab in certain places, despite the centuries and all the destruction. [...] I loved Madrid. I loved being part of Matthias' love. I loved being surrounded by two warm, naked bodies, by four hands caressing me. [...] I was them. I lived for them. And all three of us, by sharing this sensual and sexual love, became blood brothers, sperm brothers, far from our own borders. (Taïa, 2009b, pp. 138; 140)

It is significant that the queer connection between three men of different nationalities happens almost fortuitously, in the middle of the night, and while in transit, on a train linking the historically multicultural site of the former Arab and Berber Al-Andalus to contemporary Spain's cosmopolitan capital city. Abdellah abandons himself bodily and emotionally to the two men, at a moment when uprootedness does not signify cultural disorientation but queer diasporic reorientation. Sara Ahmed asserts '[b]odies may become orientated in this responsiveness to the world around them, given this capacity to be affected' (2006, p. 9). In Taïa's text, his body orients itself to Matthias and Rafaël's inviting bodies, in a simultaneous imaginative reappropriation of Spain's historically Islamicate spaces. According to Evan Beaumont Center, '[i]t was through this train experience – once again rooted in sexuality and bodies – that Taïa's power is restored from the colonial freedom in Jean that simultaneously acted as his greatest oppressor' (2012, p. 104). This moment of queer intercommunion allows Abdellah to disorganise geographical and personal borders, allowing him to revel in the eroticism of queer diasporic fraternity, at a remove from oppressive neocolonial sexual objectification and from nationalist social and religious ideologies.

Abdellah's arrival in Geneva clouds his mood of liberation and demonstrates the perniciousness of neocolonial power hierarchies. As he tells Jean about his experience of queer diasporic erotics with his two 'sperm brothers', his Swiss lover becomes furiously jealous. The narrator tells us: 'I was inside a prison, more and more inside a prison. Freedom in the West? What freedom?' (Taïa, 2009b, p. 141). Abdellah keeps pondering this freedom in the novel's closing, as he jointly considers diasporic disorientation and his personal grappling with Islam's legacies:

I thought going to live in Europe would mark the end of waiting and waging battles within myself. I was wrong. I would still live for quite some time in obscurity. I would have to make radical and immediate decisions very fast, take my stand, distance myself further and further from people I loved [...]. Learn how to love again. [...] Be happy on my own. Frequently vanish. Decide to drink or not to drink wine, to eat or not to eat pork. Little by little, reexamine my views about Arab culture, Moroccan tradition and Islam. Lose myself entirely, the better to find myself. (Taïa, 2009b, pp. 142–3)

This passage encapsulates the process of disorientation and reorientation involved in the queer Muslim experience of diaspora. Migration to Europe does not put a stop to Abdellah's internal wandering, and the theme of *l'errance* continues being of relevance, as he struggles to find a material and emotional footing in Europe. In addition, he also needs to establish distance from loved ones in order to extricate himself from the cultural and religious strictures of Moroccan homophobia. In distancing himself from the values inherited from his Moroccan upbringing, Abdellah's life in Europe involves a losing and finding of the self: Islamicate Moroccan culture is reassessed from a position of spatial and affective hindsight.

Despite the persistence of a melancholic form of wandering fuelled by social inequalities and by the precariousness of the queer diasporic citizen, Taïa's last words in *Salvation Army* sound a note of hope for the reconfiguration of the queer diasporic Muslim self. As his autofictions attest, he has learnt in the intimacy of his body about the required course of action: the need to rebel against neocolonial sexual oppression, to reassess the homophobia of inherited versions of Islam through the eclectic and unorthodox experience of various mystical and matrilineal practices of the faith, and to embrace the interpersonal pleasures of queer diasporas, whose challenges to personal and spatial boundaries micropolitically dissolve the discreteness of human categories. Taïa's process of losing and finding himself is an inexorable, endless journey towards self-definition, as he constantly looks for the place of safety in the often ethnically inhospitable spaces of contemporary Europe. Taïa's work becomes an embodiment of the jointly postcolonial and queer melancholia he so keenly feels, as he mourns the persistent social injustices of postcolonial Morocco and Europe, as well as the inability to find the elusive beloved in the ever-shifting urban desert. For Taïa's autofictional self, this search is still, in part, a quest towards spiritual self-affirmation, demonstrated in his queering of Sufi and pre-Islamic poetic traditions, whereby the poetic self mourns the absence of the beloved, and where a dualistic understanding of love is ultimately linked with the divine. The queer melancholia resulting from Taïa's errancy is thus jointly homoerotic and spiritual, disorganising both sexual and religious orthodoxies, yet inscribing his lovelorn queer melancholia onto the long continuum of Arab cultures historically pre- and post-dating the onset of Islam, hence also counteracting the contemporary Islamicate blindsiding and condemnation of homosexuality.

Notes

1. Rachid O. (b. 1970) is the author of several Francophone works of autobiographical fiction – or, as I shall propose, of autofictions – first published by Gallimard from the mid-1990s into the first two decades of this century, all yet unpublished in English: *L'enfant ébloui* (The amazed child), *Plusiers vies* (Many lives), *Chocolat chaud* (Hot chocolate), *Ce qui reste* (What is left) and *Analphabètes* (The illiterate). There has been contention around who is to be considered the first Moroccan writer to 'come out', with all its attendant fetishisation. I concur with Jean Zaganiaris (2013) in his assessment that, while Rachid O. may have been the first writer to relay his homosexuality autobiographically in his work, Taïa's public discussion of his homosexuality – including the disclosure of his full name in his 'coming out' piece in the progressive Moroccan magazine *TelQuel* in 2007 – single him out as the first Moroccan and Arab writer to assume his same-sex desire fully in the open, despite issues of family honour and potential risks to his safety.

2. In interviews, Taïa often describes himself as 'gay' – i.e., essentially and exclusively attracted to men – yet unlike his trajectory in the public eye, his literary and cinematic work does not make use of such identitarian labels, thus defying essentialist categorisation. It is reasonable to argue, then, that Taïa's narrative positioning in relation to power and his strategies are ostensibly *queer*: they aim at disorganising normative ideologies, both from heteronormative society and from the gay and lesbian civil rights movements in the West, preferring to disorientate his majority and minority readers with narratives that explore first-hand the identitarian contradictions experienced by queer diasporic Muslims.

3. There are so far two distinct strands in Taïa's literary work: one autofictional branch, in which Taïa writes about his own experiences as a gay man in Morocco, Europe, and Egypt, comprised to date by *Mon Maroc*, *Le rouge du tarbouche*, *Salvation Army*, and *An Arab Melancholia*; and a fictional branch, where Taïa creates imaginary characters and plots that are, according to our interview, still more or less indebted to his own experiences of Morocco and France, such as *Le jour du roi* (The King's day), *Infidels*, and *Un pays pour mourir* (A country to die in). In this latter fictional branch, Taïa still focuses, although to a lesser extent, on issues of sexual non-normativity and explores Moroccan and French societies from a more intersectional perspective, jointly exploring issues of gender, class, religion, ethnicity, and migration. I have chosen to focus on his autofictional works because they offer us the most direct views of the queer Muslim Moroccan self in time and place.

4. Taïa has written extensively, both online and in the press, about political topics, such as the 'Arab Spring' and queer issues in Morocco and the Middle East. In his article 'A Boy to be Sacrificed', published in *The New York Times*, he passionately asserts: 'Now, over a year after the Arab Spring began, we must again remember homosexuals. Arabs have finally become aware that they have to invent a new, free Arab individual, without the support of their megalomaniacal leaders. Arab homosexuals are also taking part in this revolution, whether they live in Egypt, Iraq or Morocco. They, too, are part of this desperately needed process of political and individual liberation. And the world must support and protect them' (Taïa, 2012c, p. 5). Taïa argues that the 'Arab Spring' should not forget its own homosexual rebels, whose efforts were often quelled, in the subsequent civil wars, by the Islamist parties

who coopted the revolutionary discourse. Taïa has also edited a collection of letters penned by prominent Moroccan literary figures – including himself, Tahar Ben Jelloun and Rachid O. – and addressed to contemporary Moroccan youth, entitled *Lettres à un jeune marocain* (Letters to a young Moroccan), in whose introduction Taïa states: 'Aujord'hui je sais que tout dans nos vies est politique' (2009c, p. 10) (Today I know that everything in our lives is political). Although Taïa does not ascribe to any parties' political agendas, he remains conscious of the necessary inclusion of homosexuals into the various forms of social revolution arisen in Islamicate societies; his own literary and cinematic work is a micropolitical articulation of such queer perspectives that vindicate and normalise them.

5 As Peter Mandaville (2007) observes, the Sunni branch of Islam composes roughly 90 per cent of the world's Muslim population. To offer a basic summary, the Sunni and Shia branches of Islam were founded straight after Prophet Muhammad's death, when succession was at stake. The Shiite sect decided to follow a religious leader, the *imam* Ali, the Prophet's son-in-law, who was allegedly appointed by Muhammad himself, and whose son and appointed successor, Hussein, would later be assassinated, thus giving Shia Islam its focus on martyrdom and sacrifice. On the other hand, the Sunni sect decided to appoint their leader, who turned out to be Abu Bakr, the Prophet's father-in-law, thus rejecting a generational hereditary line and choosing the Prophet's successor on the basis of his piety and moral fibre. According to Christopher M. Blanchard, 'Sunni Muslims do not bestow upon human beings the exalted status given only to Prophets in the Quran, in contrast to the Shiite veneration of imams' (2009, p. 14). Shiite Muslims remain a minority in most Islamicate societies, yet according to the demographic data cited by Blanchard, they are more numerous than Sunnis in several countries, most notably Iran and Iraq, but also in Azerbaijan, Lebanon, and Bahrain. Although Sunni Islam is the largest branch of Islam, their Shia counterparts hold much power in countries such as Iran and have had considerable influence since colonial times in Lebanon.

6 The notion of postcolonial melancholia used here is different from Paul Gilroy's iconic examination of postcolonial melancholia. For Gilroy, 'melancholic reactions are prompted by "the loss of a fantasy of omnipotence"' (2005). In other words, Gilroy's melancholia is hence symptomatic of the former colonisers' mourning for the lost empire. Conversely, my examination of Taïa's postcolonial melancholia is more concerned with the perspective of the formerly colonised, and with disaffection with the postcolonial state's persistent social inequalities, which is intimately linked with the repression of queerness.

8

The druzification of history: queering time, place, and faith in the diasporic novels of Rabih Alameddine

THIS CHAPTER shifts our focus from the construction of the autofictional self in Abdellah Taïa's work, as well as his struggle with issues of masculinity, sexual orientation, and faith within the continuum of Arab history, to how the narratives by queer diasporic Muslims become in themselves a queer relaying of time and place. The work of Lebanese-American painter and novelist Rabih Alameddine crucially interweaves themes that are highly autobiographical – the Lebanese Civil War (1975–90), the Lebanese diaspora in America, and the American AIDS crisis of the 1980s and 1990s – yet he does so in such a way that history and myth, as well as time and place, are routinely queered. As I will show here, Alameddine's literary work deftly explores the temporal and spatial sutures and raptures that are endemic to queer diasporic experience. As a preliminary example of his particular positioning, Alameddine's first novel, *KOOLAIDS: The Art of War*, published in 1998 and depicting the interwoven human tragedies of the Lebanese Civil War and the American AIDS crisis, contains the most quoted two lines of its author's fiction: 'In America, I fit, but I do not belong. / In Lebanon, I belong, but I do not fit' (Alameddine, 1999a, p. 40). At first glance, this statement appears perfectly to encapsulate the personal conundrum of living in the Lebanese diaspora, with conflicting issues of ethnic alienation in America and sexual ostracism in Lebanon. However, Alameddine's highly postmodern fiction complicates such clear-cut mapping, demonstrating that the diasporic subject is, in his narrator's words, more of an '[a]malgam' (1999a, p. 14), or, to use our conceptual vocabulary, an *assemblage* of seemingly competing affiliations.

Alameddine has written, so far, six books of fiction: his aforementioned debut novel, *KOOLAIDS*, an experimental novel of juxtaposed narrative voices and perspectives; the rare and sought-after short-story collection *The Perv*, published in 1999; *I, the Divine*, published in 2001, a novel about the arduous textual construction of the Lebanese female diasporic self; the masterful and ambitious assemblage of Lebanese and Islamicate myth and history, *The Hakawati*, published in 2008; *An Unnecessary Woman*, released in 2014, a realist novel about an unpublished Lebanese translator; and a novel set in one single day exploring the life of a queer Yemeni man living with AIDS, *The Angel of History*, published in 2016. In his latest novel, Alameddine returns to many of the themes of *KOOLAIDS*, which evinces his ongoing commitment to memorialising the victims of the AIDS epidemic. Here, I retrospectively explore Alameddine's fiction specifically dealing with the Lebanese diaspora in America – *The Hakawati*, *I, the Divine*, and *KOOLAIDS* – in an attempt to retrace his footsteps to the root of his diasporic sensibility. My critical intervention begins by considering *The Hakawati*'s reinscription of homosexuality in Islamicate (hi)stories and its problematic silencing in contemporary Muslim communities. I subsequently explore Alameddine's critique of homonormativity, his favouring of queerness, and his critique of Druze patriarchy in *I, the Divine*. Finally, I analyse the queering of time and place (Halberstam, 2005) in *KOOLAIDS*, a narrative that assembles the past, the present, and various human geographies, through the mouthpiece of a queer Muslim prophetic narrator living with AIDS. In this combined critical examination of Alameddine's fiction, I demonstrate that Alameddine's general disorganisation of heteropatriarchal mores is rendered possible through his 'druzification' of history from a diasporic perspective, as he interweaves and adapts Lebanese, Arab, and Western cultures and tropes, ultimately asking his majority- and minority-ethnic readers to question societies' and families' alleged discursive and identitarian hermeticism.

The phrase 'the druzification of history' is a self-consciously playful refashioning of Salman Rushdie's oft-quoted 'chutnification of history'. Rushdie's narrator in *Midnight's Children*, Saleem Sinai, famously proclaims: 'Every picklejar [...] contains, therefore, the most exalted of possibilities: the feasibility of the chutnification of history; the grand hope of the pickling of time!' (Rushdie, 1982, p. 459). This 'chutnification' can be understood both as a preservation of history for posterity and as a purposeful blending of history's multifarious ingredients. Rushdie is arguably Alameddine's most prominent literary forerunner, with his comparable investment in Muslim family sagas, father-and-son relationships, and playfully hybrid textualities. Nonetheless, while admitting to being 'not a religious person at all' (Shannahan, 2011, p. 131), Alameddine remains, in terms of his ethnic filiation, a *queer* sort of Muslim: he is a Druze, member of a Middle

Eastern religious minority initially spread out across Israel, Palestine, Syria, and Lebanon, whose faith is an esoteric offshoot of Ismaili Shia Islam (Halabi Abbas, 2015). The Druze are, traditionally at least, a secretive religious sect keen on avoiding sectarian violence and discrimination through the process of *al-taqiyya*, defined by Intisar J. Azzam as 'safeguarding the faith by simulating the ways and rituals of other communities' (2007, p. 3). Although *al-taqiyya* is no longer a feature of contemporary Druze experience, the ability of the Druze to assimilate into various ethno-religious communities is still felt in Alameddine's routine-like enmeshing of cultural traditions. Coupled with the fact that religious initiation into the Druze faith is not compulsory, and that Druze religious scriptures are traditionally only made available to those formally incepted into the community of believers, it is little wonder that, as Halabi Abbas suggests, contemporary Druze, especially those in the diaspora, often adopt secularist or Westernised cosmologies. This seems to be certainly the case with Alameddine, who has relinquished faith and embraced instead a postmodern canon of 'world literature' including the literary experiments of Jorge Luis Borges, Roland Barthes, Fernando Pessoa, and Javier Marías, while invariably drawing from the cultural themes developed by his Islamicate Lebanese upbringing. Islam therefore still plays an important role in Alameddine's work, despite his personal distance from the faith, and its cultural influence clearly pervades his work.

I demonstrate here that Alameddine cannot completely extrapolate himself from his Druze ethno-religious heritage. In etymologically tracing the naming of the Druze, Robert Brenton Betts concurs with

> the most common assertion that the Druze take their name from the heretic *al-Darazi*, whose name in Arabic means the tailor, from the verb *daraza*, to sew, stitch. The plural of the word *darz* (seam, hem, suture) is *duruz*, which is the identical spelling in Arabic of the Druze. (Betts, 1988, p. 28)

This etymology is curiously in keeping with the eclectic and syncretic nature of Druzism: the Druze stitch together religious elements from various cults and philosophies, such as Greek neoplatonism and Sufism; due to their peculiar history of social persecution and protective cultural and religious assimilation, they also suture themselves with other ethnic communities, adopting their cultural habits and religious rituals. As a diasporic writer and artist of Druze heritage, Alameddine is adept at interweaving different cultural traditions in such a way that new, unconventional connections are forged. In the face of various national and diasporic parochialisms, Alameddine's narratives defy what Salaita (2011) calls 'ethnonationalism' – i.e., the organisation of nationalist belonging around particular ethnic groups.

Alameddine's work strives to reveal the arbitrary and imagined nature of sturdily constructed roots, in narratives whose variegated cultural tapestries are invested in queering the demands of bloodlines, as well as of ethno-religious orthodoxies. Judith/Jack Halberstam advocates, via Michel Foucault, 'queer friendships, queer networks, and the existence of these relations in space and in relation to the use of time' (2005, p. 1). Alameddine's diasporic sensibility questions the temporal and spatial logics of Western thought, especially when confronted with the traumatic histories of war-induced displacement and the human tragedies effected by the AIDS epidemic. In Alameddine's work, these forms of queer dissidence are interwoven with instances of diasporic ethnic resistance. We have already established, as Gopinath suggests, that '*[s]uturing* "queer" to "diaspora" [...] recuperates those desires, practices, and subjectivities that are rendered impossible and unimaginable within conventional diasporic and nationalist imaginaries' (2005, p. 11, emphasis added). The focus on the act of 'suturing' makes Gopinath's point even more semiotically prescient: Alameddine's work makes sexual orientation inalienable from the experiences of diaspora and sutures both personal conundrums in a way that makes them intelligible to his readership.

To begin our examination of Alameddine's work, his third novel, *The Hakawati*, is a revisionist tale that stitches together different temporalities and forms of (hi)story-telling. Zuzana Tabačková (2015) describes it as a postmodern version of the *Thousand and One Nights*, a series of stories within stories dealing with characters who have a penchant for storytelling. This is the case with the *emir* and his wife, the fictional figures that feature in the novel's opening. In Alameddine's text, stories are collectively shared, and they are channelled through the novel's main narrator, the diasporic character Osama al-Kharrat, a member of a mixed-heritage Lebanese family of *hakawatis* – storytellers – turned car dealers. Osama moved to America to study during the Lebanese Civil War. His family name, which means 'the fibster' (Alameddine, 2009, p. 37), was bestowed upon them by Osama's grandfather's benefactor, a *bey* from Beirut. As Osama explains,

> [a] hakawati is a teller of tales, myths, and fables (hekayât). A storyteller, an entertainer. [...] Like the word 'hekayeh' (story, fable, news), 'hakawati' is derived from the Lebanese word 'haki,' which means 'talk' or 'conversation.' This suggests that in Lebanese the mere act of talking is storytelling. (Alameddine, 2009, p. 36)

As Salaita (2011) helpfully summarises, the al-Kharrat clan is multiethnic: Osama's heritage is English, Armenian, and Lebanese. While he is Druze, his sister Lina is a Maronite Christian, and his uncle Hovik is Armenian. The siblings Mariella and Fatima are of Iraqi Christian and Italian Jewish heritage. This complex intermixing presents a human mapping of Lebanon not familiarly organised around ethnically 'pure' sectarian groupings, as is the wont of the country's accepted historiographies, but as a richly interwoven loom of faiths, cultures, and nationalities.

In Osama's transcribed oral narratives, which are passed down to him by his grandfather and his uncle Jihad, as well as by various other *hakawatis*, the distant Islamic mythical and historical pasts, the recent past of the Six Day War of 1967 and of the Lebanese Civil War, and the postwar present, are all seamlessly druzified: history and myth become tightly interwoven; fictional and historical characters happily coexist in narratives that constitute an irreverent reminder about the mythologising undertaken during the task of assembling human (hi) stories. Alameddine acknowledges his indebtedness to unexpurgated texts in his novel's postscript, where he cites the 'uncensored' versions of the *Thousand and One Nights* and of *Kalila wa Dimna*, the Arabic translation of the Sanskrit *Panchatantra*, alongside the Old Testament, the Qur'an, Italo Calvino's fiction, and Ibn Hazm's *The Ring of the Dove*. The explicit reference to the uncensored version of the text popularly known as the *Arabian Nights* demonstrates Alameddine's choice to reinstate in his own narrative those elements deemed controversial or deviant by later editors and translators, such as the blunt exploration of Islamicate same-sex desire.

Alameddine's work recovers a censored Islamicate tradition in which homosexuality had a visible, if not altogether uncontroversial, role. To recapitulate, Khaled El-Rouayheb charts the textual history of the *Thousand and One Nights*, explaining how Richard F. Burton's highly eroticised version of the work published in 1885, which is testament to Orientalism's exaggerated fascination with Arab sexuality, was subsequently expurgated in the 1930 edition published in Cairo. This postcolonial Egyptian version of the text elided all the homoerotic stories, including those featuring the famous Baghdadi poet Abu Nuwas. El-Rouayheb suggests that the reason behind this censorship was the postcolonial elite's distaste for homosexuality, which partly emulated the homophobia of the former British colonisers, and which resulted in their disavowal of any homoeroticism in the Islamicate past. It is the legacies of this homoerotic element in Arab culture that Alameddine excavates and sutures in *The Hakawati*, in which one of the main stories' subplots deals with the sentimental relationship between two Muslim men. In the section of the novel set in the mythical Islamicate past, the slave Fatima is sent on a mission to secure the *emir*'s wife an elixir that will make her conceive a long-expected son. On her way, Fatima and her six attendants, including the stable boy Jawad, are accosted by a group of Bedouin thieves, who attempt to rape them. Using her wit, she turns the men against each other, with Fatima killing the last man standing, with the exception of the thief Khayal, who does not desire Fatima and repeatedly states: 'I still want the boy. I just want the boy' (Alameddine, 2009, p. 13).

Much of the remaining first chapter is devoted to Khayal's desperate seduction of Jawad. Fatima sets the terms thus: '[Jawad] is neither captured nor a slave [...]. Since he has free will, you must convince him, charm him into your tent. We have seven nights before we reach my home city, Alexandria. You have seven nights to seduce him. You may begin tomorrow' (Alameddine, 2009, p. 14). Fatima's words corroborate the tacit toleration of homosexuality in the Islamicate past, even if homosexual acts were, at worst, publicly punished and, at best, mourned as socially untenable. Like a lowly version of King Sharyar of the *Arabian Nights*, Jawad must be entertained by Khayal's wit in order to grant him his romantic wish. After a failed initial attempt at quoting the Prophet Muhammad's *hadith*, Khayal makes recourse to the Arab homoerotic archive. Two of his attempts involve the poetry of Abu Nuwas, which Fatima finds charming but which Jawad resists. Khayal recites: '*A woman once berated me / Because of the love I feel / For a boy who huffs and struts / Like an untamed young bull* [...]. */ Know you not that the Holy Book / Speaks the definitive truth: / Before your daughters / Your sons shall be preferred?*' (Alameddine, 2009, p. 20, emphasis in original). Fatima is stricken by the desert-dweller's knowledge of Abu Nuwas' work, cleverly interposing that the preference for boys is '[i]n matters of inheritance, my boy, but the poet took some liberties' (2009, p. 20), ostensibly to justify his penchant for young men. Fatima asks for more recitation of Abu Nuwas, yet Jawad is unmoved. As he asserts, 'his poetry speaks nothing other than his preference for a certain kind of love. That he likes boys does not make him more desirable to me. It simply means he has good taste' (2009, p. 21). Alameddine is here giving expression to popular perceptions of Arab and Islamicate age-structured romance, involving the tacitly accepted admiration of older men towards younger men, which, although not synonymous with our contemporary and Westernised understanding of homosexuality, is portrayed as being an indelible part of collective Arab consciousness.

Khayal eventually resorts to the work of Andalusian writer and jurist Ibn Hazm. As we have seen, Scott Kugle (2010) cites Ibn Hazm as one of the classical Islamic jurists who advised against applying the death penalty to Muslims engaged in homosexual acts. Moreover, his revisionist exegesis of the story of Sodom also interpreted Lot's people's rejection of his prophethood as the main reason for their divine punishment, not their homosexuality, as traditionalist Islamic interpretation insists nowadays. The tragic story from Ibn Hazm's *The Ring of the Dove* that Khayal retells involves a poet from Córdoba called Ahmad ben Kulaib al-Nahawi and his unreciprocated love for his student, Aslam. Once the poet's affections become known to him, Aslam stops his classes and chides his former teacher for his 'improper' feelings towards him. The lovelorn poet dies, after which Khayal narrates, via Ibn Hazm, how 'years later, on a horribly rainy day, [...] the cemetery warden recognized Aslam, who by then had become a grand poet himself, sitting on the grave of Ahmad ben Kulaib al-Nahawi, paying his respects [...]. Rain streaked his face like tears' (Alameddine, 2009, pp. 31–2). The story makes Fatima weep and Jawad is self-confessedly touched, but he is not seduced. By this point, Khayal's attempts at wooing Jawad have included *ahadith*, the poetry of Abu Nuwas and al-Mutanabbi, and the stories of Ibn Hazm. Some of these works are among the most prominent in the Islamicate homoerotic archive, yet Jawad, like a contrary version of King Sharyar, remains unconvinced.

Alameddine's Druze-like suturing of religious traditions is what ultimately works on Jawad's sensibility. At his wit's end outside Alexandria's gates, Khayal pleads:

> 'I have nothing to offer, nothing but myself. If you want me to leave you, I will depart before the dawn, but if you take my hand, I will make you the same covenant that Ruth made with Naomi: Where you go I will go, and where you stay I will stay. Your people will be my people and your God my God. Where you die, I will die and there I will be buried.' Jawad took Khayal's hand. (Alameddine, 2009, p. 33)

The pledge that finally wins over Jawad does not involve the Arab penchant for bawdiness, sentimentality, or the tragic lack of fulfilment of one man's love for a younger man, but a covenant of companionship that is drawn from the Bible, not the Qur'an or its attendant traditions. Alameddine's novel performs two feats here: as Waïl S. Hassan argues, the effect of Alameddine's narrative is 'to project an image of an Arab cultural tradition that is much more tolerant of homosexuality' (2011, p. 213), which counteracts contemporary traditionalist Islamism and its erasure of homosexuality; he also sutures Islamic, Judaic, and Christian traditions by drawing two queer Muslims towards each other

The druzification of history

through the Bible's invocation. This druzifying gesture of ethno-religious syncretism disorganises dominant contemporary Islamist views on homosexuals as sexually perverted or morally deviant, as Fatima's tacit toleration of same-sex desired evinces. However, it is telling that we do not witness much of Khayal and Jawad's burgeoning relationship. At one point, Fatima catches Jawad coming out of Khayal's tent: 'Embarrassed to be discovered, he blushed, tried to speak, but ended up stuttering' (Alameddine, 2009, p. 66), which suggests a lingering sense of social and/or moral impropriety in his relations with Khayal. Nevertheless, Fatima expresses admiration for Khayal.

As a follow-up, the section of Alameddine's novel set in our contemporary moment suggests that Arab attitudes towards homosexuality have been mixed throughout history, and in the al-Kharrat contemporary family saga, secrecy and shame surround the expression of queer desires, to the point of censorship. Both Osama, the novel's main narrator, and his uncle Jihad, his *hakawati* mentor, have homosexual tendencies. Although their same-sex desire is not discussed explicitly in the text, uncle Jihad's queerness is gradually revealed through unsubtle hints. For instance, when Osama walks into his late uncle's 'den', his 'movie wall was still up' (Alameddine, 2009, p. 365). The long list of male and female film stars and posters ends with a triple invocation of 'Judy Garland, Judy Garland, Judy Garland', a reference to a gay icon that seems to echo Dorothy's homeward-bound three clicks of her ruby slippers' heels in the 1939 film *The Wizard of Oz*. The most revealing picture is now conspicuously absent from Jihad's collage: as Osama narrates,

> one image was scraped away, with the wall's plaster showing through. I didn't have to be told who scraped it off or what picture it was. After Uncle Jihad's death, my father wouldn't have wanted anyone to see the image of Alan Bates and Oliver Reed kissing fiercely. (Alameddine, 2009, p. 366)

This intriguing apocryphal image is linked to the 1969 adaptation of D. H. Lawrence's *Women in Love*, in which Bates and Reed come close to kissing during a torrid naked wrestling scene charged with homoeroticism. The behaviour of Osama's father Farid demonstrates, as Hassan observes, that 'Jihad's close family members must hide his shame' (2011, p. 214). In addition, in *Queer Beirut*, Sofian Merabet argues that '[t]urning from politics to affect, homophobia grows ultimately into a shared trauma fostered by social exclusion' (2014, p. 232). By scraping off the prominent queer image, Farid is ostensibly excluding his brother's alleged 'deviance' from the family record, revealing both the clandestine workings of Lebanese queerness and the traumatising workings of collective Islamicate homophobia.

Salaita describes Jihad as 'a witty and intelligent character who serves as something of a confidant and father figure to Osama', arguing that he 'functions as a catalyst in other ways. It is to Jihad, not to Farid, that Osama's mother, Layla, was initially attracted. Jihad is gay, however, a fact that Alameddine suggests but never states explicitly' (2011, p. 56). When Osama asks his mother to tell him the story of Jihad's seduction of her, she playfully denies her attraction to him:

> I recognised – oh, what shall we call it? – [Jihad's] special ability to be best friends with women, the instant I saw his impish grin from across the room. My God, how could I not, given the way he crossed his legs or what he did with his hands? No one would talk about it, but that didn't mean anyone was fooled. (Alameddine, 2009, p. 418)

Layla is here skirting around the topic of Jihad's unspoken but implied homosexuality, unable to give it its proper name, and only going as far as describing his camp demeanour and to presuppose everyone's knowledge of his alleged 'condition', which is never openly debated. Hassan comments on Kaelen Wilson-Goldie's review of *The Hakawati*, in which she describes Jihad as 'a fabulous gay man whose homosexuality is apparent to and relished by all but never discussed and altogether not so much of an issue' (Hassan, 2011, p. 213). Hassan retorts that

> homosexuality is 'not so much of an issue' precisely because it is never discussed. It can be tolerated, even relished, only when it is *not* openly acknowledged (don't ask, don't tell, don't show), or when it is clothed in poetic or belle-lettristic forms and enshrined among the literary classics. (Hassan, 2011, p. 213, emphasis in original)

In other words, homosexuality is clandestinely tolerated and sometimes granted its place in the Arab and Islamicate collective imaginary, but it is not considered socially proper. I would argue that the Druze family's internalised homophobia, which forces them to disavow Jihad's queerness through omission, is intimately linked to the Druze practice of *al-taqiyya*: in the face of sexual difference, they choose dissimulation, adopting the general homophobic stance of much of contemporary Arab culture, with its joint emphasis on socio-religious orthopraxy and heteronormativity.

In the absence of sexual self-validation in Osama's and Jihad's life stories, both *hakawatis* use their storytelling medium as a means of disorganising the heteronormative status quo, through the subversive retelling of stories and the queering of religious traditions. For example, the story of the slave Fatima constitutes a druzification of different religious stories that are queerly retold: she is named after Prophet Muhammad's daughter, and her miraculous amulet, bestowed upon her by her demon lover, is Fatima's Hand, a popular symbol in Phoenician, Berber, Jewish, and Arabic cultures. Fatima is seduced by Afreet-Jehanam, a Satanic figure who severs and magically restores her real hand; Fatima expresses surprise at this turn of events, stating she did not expect hell to be like this. The *afreet* is vexed by this simple association: 'Ah, humans. Your ideas of hell are nothing more than the lees and dregs of unimaginative minds long since dead. Listen. Let me tell you a story' (Alameddine, 2009, p. 81). It is clear from the demon's invocation that the stories in *The Hakawati* are an imaginative reworking of religious scriptures, unravelling longstanding associations and weaving new ones that give irreverent expression to queer desires.

Through Fatima's story of surrogacy, Osama's narrative reworks the seminal story of Abraham, the patriarch of the three Abrahamic religions — Judaism, Christianity, and Islam — seen through a queer Orientalist lens. The *emir* and his wife are the equivalents of Abraham and Sarah, and Fatima becomes the slave maternal surrogate, Hagar. Fatima secures an elixir of fertility from an Alexandrian healer, but the phial breaks before reaching the palace; she eventually solves the situation through a double impregnation from Afreet-Jehanam, who helps her conceive cherubically white Shams and dark and ugly Layl — whose names mean 'sun' and 'moon' in Arabic — a dualistic refashioning of the fathers of Judaism and Islam, Isaac and Ishmael. Fatima carries Shams and the *emir*'s wife carries Layl, who are swapped at birth, with Fatima bringing up the black child and the emir and his wife the white one. The twins, whose magical powers render them celebrated prophets, develop queer incestuous desires towards each other, starting with a passionate kiss on their seventh birthday: 'Not a friendly kiss, not a brotherly kiss, but a full mouth-to-mouth, indecently lasting kiss' (Alameddine, 2009, p. 320). The emir and his wife, who are censuring of their son's friendship with a slave's child — despite the fact he is the child the emir's wife carried in her womb — find their patriarchal and hierarchical attitudes checked by a queer case that disorganises their traditionalist Islamicate values.

The sexual activity between the twins escalates as they get older. The prepubescent pair are later caught having sex by the *emir*'s wife:

> Her twelve-year-old son lying on his stomach without a stitch of clothing, his white behind saluting the sky, his head nestled between his dark twin's spread thighs. The dark one, naked and hairless, lying on his back, his head cradled in one hand and his other hand curled into the prophet's golden strands as Sham licked his testicles, an effortless indulgence. The boys formed a calm, sinewy interlacing of alabaster and onyx. When Layl opened his eyes and noticed the emir's wife aghast, a devilish grin appeared on his face. (Alameddine, 2009, p. 380)

Sham and Layl's sexual indulgence allows them to blend light with darkness through bodily performance, syncretising their dualistic nature in a manner that seems to point to the binaries inherent in human storytelling. However, their incestuous queer desire is mirthfully intended to shock the *emir*'s wife, who stands for traditionalist morality and patriarchal hierarchies. She ultimately blames Layl and Fatima for Sham's perversion and orders Layl – the son she carried in her womb – castrated and killed. The connections between motherhood, duality, child sexuality, castration, parricide, and the emphasis on the underworld – the traditional symbolic recipient of man's instinctual nature – all suggest an assembled psycho-sexual rendering of the original Abrahamic religious story. I argue that Alameddine is here queering religious scripture through a reworking of Orientalist storytelling that brings to the forefront the deep psychic undercurrents and queer desires repressed in the contemporary part of his novel. This subversive tale of same-sex fraternal incest could be interpreted as Jihad's – and by extension Osama's – storytelling 'revenge' for the lifelong personal and familial concealment of their desire towards the same sex. As a druzified tapestry of tales interwoven by a queer narrator, *The Hakawati* ultimately suggests that human stories must necessarily exceed the narrow strictures of religious orthodoxy and patriarchal morality, as well as the selective retelling of history. Alameddine's text remains patently conscious of the limitations assailing those queer subjects, like Jihad and Osama, who are positioned at an angle from social normativity, and whose identities and experiences are ostensibly muted by contemporary Islamist homophobia. Alameddine's diasporic imagination creates an irreverent narrative medium through which to explore the complexities of human desire, exorcising through overtly sexualised queer stories the repressed ghosts of the Islamicate past and present.

In turn, *I, the Divine*, whose subtitle is *A Novel in First Chapters*, constitutes a critique of Lebanese Druze patriarchy that also takes to task normative forms of homosexuality in the West. The novel charts fictional character Sarah Nour el-Din's subsequent attempts at creating a narrative about her experiences as a Lebanese woman of mixed Lebanese and American heritage. As she confesses in one of her later exercises:

> I have been blessed with many curses in my life, not the least of which was being born half Lebanese and half American. Throughout my life, these contradictory parts battled endlessly, clashed, never coming to a satisfactory conclusion. I shuffled ad nauseam between the need to assert my individuality and the need to belong to my clan. (Alameddine, 2003, p. 229)

In this confession, Sarah becomes the perfect embodiment of identitarian assemblage: she is constantly torn by her clashing need to embrace American individualism and Lebanese clannishness. Her frustrated narrative attempts paint a fragmentary but overall cogent picture of her family life in Lebanon and America; they are mostly written in English, but some of them are relayed in French, a reminder of Lebanon's colonial history and its ongoing legacies in the fraught postcolonial present (Hirst, 2010; O'Ballance, 1998; Fisk, 2001). Sarah's father, Mustapha, is a Lebanese Druze who divorced Sarah's late mother, Janet, because of 'her' inability to conceive a son. Janet never overcomes her ostracism and eventually commits suicide. Quoting from Maya Jaggi's review, Tabačková observes that Sarah's

> continual attempts to tell her story prove to be a chain of constant failures. Since her identity is broken in multiple ways, her narrative is also ruptured, chaotic, irregular and, therefore, it could be equaled with an irritable 'quest for a fictional form to reflect trauma and self-invention'. (Tabačková, 2015, p. 120)

Sarah's narrative fragments are ultimately metonymic of her identitarian fracture, as she struggles to make sense of her own self between nation and diaspora, the Lebanese past and the American present.

Sarah's long-awaited little brother, Ramzi, turns out, ironically, to be gay, hence proving yet another challenge to their family's heteropatriarchal values. Nevertheless, in her perception, his life in America with his boyfriend Peter is disappointingly normative:

> No one would be able to guess Ramzi and I are related. My apartment looks like a hurricane went through it, his is ready for a photo spread in *House*

and Garden. They cooked salmon soufflés that never, ever, collapsed for Princess, their white Persian cat. They made a perfect couple – too perfect, for they were carbon copies, exact replicas, never challenging, never arguing, never having to allow the other within the boundaries of their erected walls, a relationship based on mutual convenience, complementary neuroses, and loneliness. (Alameddine, 2003, p. 124)

In Sarah's ruthless description of Ramzi and Peter's relationship, the emphasis is on sameness, sanitisation, and emotional disconnection: they make the perfect couple because of their affectively detached affluence and the picture-perfect superficiality of their life together. In Alameddine's parodic depiction of Ramzi, the Lebanese gay man embodies the conservative strand of diasporic selfhood. A namesake of Alameddine's protagonist, Sara Ahmed, reflects: 'Bodies that experience disorientation can be defensive […]. So, too, the form of politics that proceed from disorientation can be conservative, depending on the "aims" of their gestures, depending on how they seek to (re)ground themselves' (Ahmed, 2006, p. 158). Ramzi's diasporic disorientation results in becoming the 'carbon copy' of his American boyfriend Peter's stylised but emotionally detached version of the homosexual. To his half-sister Sarah, he is not queer, but homonormative, failing to challenge American sexual taxonomies.

After Ramzi explains to Sarah about Peter's condescension towards her being a symptom of his problem with his family, Peter flatly denies queerness with blunt biphobia, telling Sarah about her former lover David's relationship with a man:

David is gay. Or bisexual or whatever they call themselves these days. We met him and his lover of ten years. They're an openly gay couple. David cheats on him with women. […] I told his lover […] I'd never want to be seen with a closet heterosexual. (Alameddine, 2003, p. 249)

Alameddine renders Peter a mouthpiece of American homonationalism. Jasbir K. Puar argues:

National recognition and inclusion, here signaled as the annexation of homosexual jargon, is contingent upon the segregation and disqualification of racial and sexual others from the national imaginary […]. At work in this dynamic is a form of sexual exceptionalism – the emergence of national homosexuality, what I term 'homonationalism'. (Puar, 2007, p. 2)

Peter disqualifies David's implied bisexuality and enforces a narrative of the closet that can only envisage the binary of homosexual vs. heterosexual. Peter's defensiveness around Ramzi's family also belies his American homonationalist fear of citizens of 'Other' countries, such as Lebanon, whose cultures are considered by Western 'homosexual jargon' to be inherently and uniformly homophobic. Alameddine's text is therefore highly conscious of the problematic normative dimensions of Western gay identities, which, in his view, favour assimilation rather than ethnic resistance. The various cultural histories that make up the American national narrative are thus conflated into the present of homogenous sexual exceptionalism.

Of all the characters in Alameddine's second novel, Sarah is arguably the most queer in terms of her intermittent challenges to societal gender and sexual expectations. As she narrates in the first chapter entitled 'The Divine Sarah': 'I grew up infatuated with Sarah Bernhardt, having been named after her by my grandfather. [...] I did not realise when I was younger how much anguish my being a tomboy caused my family' (Alameddine, 2003, p. 59). Young Sarah likes playing football and is obsessed with the cross-dressing classical actress, to the point of dying her head red to emulate her. She is 'initiat[ed] into total femininity' – by which she means using makeup liberally – by her school friend Dina when she is fifteen years old. Dina will remain Sarah's best friend into adulthood. In this narrative attempt, Sarah tells us Dina 'did not care for boys at all' (Alameddine, 2003, p. 60). In a later first chapter entitled 'The People in My Life' that tells of Sarah's and Dina's diasporic lives in New York and Boston, respectively, Dina is explicitly described as 'a lesbian' (2003, p. 83).

It is to Dina that Sarah turns for emotional support after being raped by three Lebanese men, when she is too frightened by her family's perception of the implications to the family honour of her forced deflowering. However, after this episode of aggressive masculinity and sexual trauma, Alameddine refuses to couple Sarah and Dina sentimentally; he does not force Sarah to turn to the female gender in repudiation of male sexuality. As I have already noted in my examination of Rolla Selbak's film *Three Veils*, Samar Habib's critique of the work of Kuwaiti scholar Ålia Shuåib finds problematic 'its inability to fathom homosexuality outside the framework of religious prohibitions and inadequate heterosexual relations' (Habib, 2007, p. 11). Alameddine's work resists this misguided Arab instinct to link homosexuality with heterosexual inadequacy, and to regard all same-sex practices in Islamicate societies as a result of religious or ideological strictures impeding heterosexual relations. So, while Alameddine resists the homogeneity predicated by Western gay identities, he also rejects the commonplace logic of Arab homosexualities.

What is more visibly triggered by Sarah's traumatic experience is her move away from Lebanon to America. In this respect at least, trauma and diaspora are intimately connected; yet Alameddine's series of fractured narratives render Sarah a queer character who disorganises gender and sexual expectations, refusing to become a lesbian despite her early tomboyish inception and her dramatic experience of violent male sexuality. In addition, at one point, her brother Ramzi's boyfriend Peter arrogantly states: 'Simply thinking of you as a mother is disconcerting' (Alameddine, 2003, p. 246), for she does not have an emotionally dependent relationship with her son Kamal, and it is his father, Omar, who primarily brings him up after their return to Lebanon while Sarah stays on in America. In a manner similar to her irresolutely mixed Lebanese and American identities, Sarah's gender performance, best embodied during adulthood in her unconventional motherhood, as well as her responses to external expectations about her relationships and her sexuality, all refuse to exist along binary axes or to kowtow to hetero- or homonormative patriarchal ideologies.

The gradual dawning on Sarah's consciousness of the patriarchal dominance at work in her family brings on the novel's climax in the latter part of the novel's first chapters. As she grows up, Sarah begins to realise that her grandfather, Hammoud Nour el-Din, is telling her apocryphal stories about her namesake Sarah Bernhardt: her later knowledge of his male chauvinistic treatment of her mother, Janet, as well as of the omitted story of Druze Sarah, reveal the insidious workings of patriarchy. In her study of Druze women, Intisar J. Azzam observes that 'despite the fact that the *Tawhīd* Scriptures establish and confirm fundamental principles of equality between men and women', she perceives 'a serious gap between these egalitarian principles and the actual experience of the Druze woman' (2007, pp. 42–3). Sarah's mother quotes to her daughter Hammoud's hurtful words after giving birth to her: 'You know, Janet, I love this girl so much. Do you know why? [...] [B]ecause she's the reason I am going to be able to return you to your fucking country' (Alameddine, 2003, p. 295). Hammoud's obsession with having a male grandchild and his harsh treatment of his daughter-in-law corroborate the gender bias of the Druze community. Azzam confirms the Druze 'preference for male children', and that 'it is women who are held responsible for the sex of their offspring. Although such attitudes have been changing with increases in levels of education, many women continue to feel insecure when they do not have sons, while others are divorced for giving birth solely to daughters' (Azzam, 2007, p. 175), which perfectly fits Janet's predicament in *I, the Divine*.

Despite being an eager *hakawati*, Hammoud refuses to tell Sarah about her Druze namesake. It is her sister Amal that tells her the story of the woman sent to save the Druze community from violent sectarianism. As she recounts, in the light of the faith's belief in the equality of men and women in God's eyes, the Druze leader Al-Muqtana sent Sarah to lead the negotiations and to reconfirm the vows of the faithful. According to Amal, 'Sarah was the reason we are here. [...] Don't you find it strange that [our grandfather] would not mention her? He preferred to fill your head with stories of the Divine Sarah, but not the Druze Sarah' (Alameddine, 2003, p. 289). Azzam observes that the decision to send Sitt Sarah was 'a decision in keeping with the teachings of the *al-Tawḥīd*, which gave women the self-assurance and self-reliance needed to participate in the community's political life and to be entrusted with leading roles as emissaries in vital endeavours' (2007, p. 30). Hammoud's decision to omit the story of Sitt Sarah reveals his refusal to acknowledge the 'self-assurance and self-reliance' of women, a patriarchal attitude that Alameddine's novel is keen to challenge through his portrayal of mixed-heritage diasporic Sarah, and which reveals her dismay about the patriarchal values of the Lebanese Druze community. Alameddine's novel thus reinscribes the wilfully forgotten stories of the Lebanese past, which reveal the central role of women to the Druze community. While Hammoud represents the contemporary sway of Islamist patriarchy in the present, Sarah's inquisitiveness purposefully queers the received narratives of the Islamicate Druze past.

In spite of her belated realisation about her grandfather's patriarchal bias, Sarah is ultimately unable to extrapolate herself completely from patriarchal ideologies because of her personal trauma. In the novel's last first chapter, Sarah is shocked by a nature documentary depicting a male lion's killing of his rival's cubs; she then dwells on the importance of collectivity: 'If I wanted to know about *lion*, I had to look at the entire pride. [...] All of them together, not all of them individually summed up' (Alameddine, 2003, p. 308, emphasis in original). Hassan argues that 'in allegorizing the behavior of lions, *I, the Divine* naturalizes patriarchal violence, an ironic and surely unintended consequence of a rape victim [...]. This solution is philosophically and ethically problematic, through psychologically understandable as a trauma victim's repression of painful experience' (2011, p. 211). Despite Sarah's celebration the notion of the clan, which she self-consciously perceives as part of her Lebanese identity, this gesture confirms the resilient power of Druze patriarchy. In Alameddine's text, Sarah's self-imposed exile and her mixed heritage do not provide an easy ideological escape from masculinist oppression. Withstanding this caveat, she remains productively queer in terms of her irresolute strangeness: she constitutes Alameddine's assemblage of conflicting discourses of nationality, gender, and sexuality, as she becomes the diffident embodiment of the Lebanese diaspora in America, a cipher of the ravages of the past and the unsettlements of the present.

Alameddine's debut novel, *KOOLAIDS: The Art of War*, arguably contains the seeds of his later fiction, such as the diasporic critique of homonationalism and Druze patriarchy of *I, the Divine* and the interwoven multiple narrations of *The Hakawati*, yet in its queer suturing of the American AIDS crisis and the Lebanese Civil War, it remains Alameddine's most formally ambitious work to date. Salaita describes it as 'a pastiche that mixes not only story lines and temporal sequences, but also styles and genres' (2011, p. 43). *KOOLAIDS* contains numerous narrators whose identities are often merely implied, which requires the reader to disentangle its textual mesh of subjectivities. As Hout observes, '[w]ith the exception of Samir's mother, whose dispersed diary entries [...] appear in a non-chronological fashion, and his sister, Joumana Bashar, who supplies one letter, most other narrators are gay Lebanese and American men' (2012, p. 25), the majority of them living with AIDS, and some of whom are located in the diaspora. The novel's most prominent narrators are Lebanese-born Mohammad, a Muslim painter, and Samir, a Druze, both living in America. Although Alameddine's novels are purportedly not autobiographical, Mohammad's occupation reveals some resemblance to his creator. In the last part of this chapter, I examine Alameddine's use of AIDS dementia for the queering of time and place, in a manner that illustrates the plight of the Lebanese diasporic subject. I also propose that, given his significant name and his constant reference to religious texts, Mohammad becomes a queer form of prophet, whose druzification of scriptures and manifold religious traditions reveals the influence of Alameddine's Druze sensibility.

In *AIDS in America*, Susan Hunter charts the syndrome's effect on humanity, stating that 'AIDS kills three times more people *each day* than died in the World Trade Centre attack on September 11, 2001, and if we count those infected *each day*, it is five times more lethal' (2006, p. 199, emphasis in original). Hunter's statistics bring home the enormity of the global AIDS epidemic, which significantly puts into perspective 9/11 and Islamic terrorism. The American AIDS crisis of the 1980s and 1990s and the Lebanese Civil War were taking place at the same time in different parts of the world, yet, as Alameddine's novel illustrates, for some citizens, these events were happening simultaneously in the same affective plain. Therí Pickens argues that '*Koolaids* is not possible without the interaction between the displacement caused by the Lebanese Civil War and the experiences of embodiment germane to the early days of the HIV/AIDS epidemic. The very structure of the novel *sutures* these two stories together as uneasy analogies' (2013, p. 85, emphasis added).

This queer suturing of time and place establishes uneasy analogies because, as Alameddine knows as a postcolonial and diasporic subject, contextually bound human histories can never become fully synonymous. Indeed, his novel summarily debunks the perspective of an American Muslim man who attempts to compare the Lebanese and American Civil Wars and who sanctimoniously proposes the American South as an epitome of postwar healing and national assimilation (Alameddine, 1999a, p. 72). Nonetheless, despite Alameddine's awareness of perils of historical conflation, Lebanon featured so prominently in global media at the time of the AIDS crisis that the conflict became a symbolic touchstone of human embattlement. For example, in an essay on American AIDS literature, John M. Clum links Lebanon with AIDS when discussing the writer and activist Paul Monette: 'Monette, HIV positive himself, waits for the time bomb to turn his body into another Beirut' (1990, p. 648). Given that Clum is not directly dealing with Lebanon, it is all the more significant that he compares the body living with HIV with the bellicose ravaging of Lebanon's capital: this simile reveals the assemblage of human tragedies in the American collective consciousness.

This is the context in which Alameddine wrote *KOOLAIDS*, wherein collective human tragedies became interrelated, even assembled, in a queering of time and place that remains keenly diasporic. Judith/Jack Halberstam argues that

> queer time, even as it emerges from the AIDS crisis, is not only about compression and annihilation; it is also about the potentiality of a life unscripted by the conventions of family, inheritance, and child rearing. […] Queer subcultures produce alternative temporalities by allowing their participants to believe that their futures can be imagined according to logics that lie outside of those paradigmatic markers of life experience – namely, birth, marriage, reproduction, and death. (Halberstam, 2005, p. 2)

In light of Halberstam's work, I argue Alameddine's first novel undertakes one such 'compression and annihilation' of queer time during the AIDS crisis, whereby temporalities become queerly assembled and affectively interconnected. I also suggest that Alameddine's queer communities challenge the 'markers of life experience' established by heteronormative patriarchy. Yet, Alameddine's focus on Lebanese diasporic and American men living with AIDS does not seem as concerned with futurity – although death and the afterlife are a central concern in the book – as with the subjective overlapping of the war-ridden and AIDS-infected present. To Alameddine's diasporic text, such traumatic human temporalities must learn to live in unsettling emotional contiguity.

Mohammad's narrative possesses a dream-like quality, connected to AIDS dementia, that allows for the subjective assemblage of genders and sexual categories, time and place. Let us consider a vignette containing one of the text's prominent queerings of spaces and temporalities:

> Amalgam.
> I am back at the Berkeley campus. I am passing by the Arts building. Bullets fly overhead. A soldier shouts at me to get out of the sniper fire. He leads me into a warehouse. We enter an office together. I find the soldier extremely masculine. I am terrified of him. I am in awe of his sexuality. I ask him if I can suck his cock. He shrugs. I kneel in front of him as he leans back on the desk. I unbutton his fly. I take out his cock. I am surprised at its size and rigidity. I start sucking. As I do, the soldier beings to transform. He develops breasts. His hair grows longer and fairer. I am still sucking his cock as she becomes a gorgeous woman. I still find her exciting. I do not want to ever stop sucking her cock. I can feel her getting bored. She takes her cock from my mouth, stuffs it back into her panties, and straightens her dress. She exists the building as I run after her, offering her money to let me suck her cock. She walks on the arms of a handsome man. She looks back at me and smiles. She keeps walking away. We are back in Beirut. (Alameddine, 1999a, pp. 14–15)

In Mohammad's AIDS-influenced reverie, the alliterative cities of Berkeley and Beirut become assembled in queer time: the Lebanese city where he spent his childhood and the American city of his university education are amalgamated, with the Lebanese Civil War's violence queerly erupting in America. As an antidote to AIDS-related sexual guilt and celibacy, Mohammad's trance queers his desire: the soldier partly transitions in mid-scene, yet Mohammad's attraction remains unabated, dissolving sexual binaries. By the end of the episode, the opening statement is mirrored – 'I am back at the Berkeley campus. [...] We are back in Beirut' – indicating a fusing of both spaces and of Mohammad's life's temporalities. In Alameddine's text, AIDS dementia is not posited as a stigmatising condition, but as a form of diasporic visionary queerness, subverting dominant temporal and spatial logic by suturing global human histories demanding our collective attention.

I would also suggest that Alameddine's utilisation of AIDS dementia subverts, as well, religious orthodoxies in a way that challenges their aggressive heteronormativity, and which druzifies their meaning. Mohammad specifically queers the Qur'anic and biblical story of Lot, the main episode that has historically informed the contemporary categorical Islamic condemnation of homosexuality. To recapitulate, in this controversial story, the Prophet Lot offers to the men of Sodom and Gomorrah his unmarried daughters, one of whom is reported to have slept with him while drunk in order to continue the family line; he sacrifices them in order to preserve intact the dignity of the visiting angels, whom the men of his community want to rape. Mohammad ironically summarises the lesson ultimately learnt:

> God destroys the faggots with fire and brimstone. He turns a disobedient wife into salt. But he asks us to idolize drunks who sleep with their daughters or offer them to a horny, unruly mob. This is the lesson of Sodom and Gomorrah: Homosexuals are bad. (Alameddine, 1999a, p. 64)

Dervla Shannahan argues that '[s]uch overt critique of Prophetic behaviour in Sodom reveals the patriarchal politics of heteronormative genealogies conflated in the Abrahamic traditions, and undresses the positioning of a God who politically aligns with such injustices as absurd' (2011, pp. 135–6). She also remarked earlier that '[w]hen I asked Alameddine if he was trying to reinterpret Sodom in *Koolaids*, he answered "I'm not sure it was an alternative interpretation as much as a rejection of superficial ones"' (Shannahan, 2011, p. 134).

Alameddine's queer prophet Mohammad highlights the heteronormativity of dominant scriptural interpretation, which discerns the patriarchal bias in Lot's behaviour. In doing so, however, he is suturing sacred texts: while the story of Lot is told in both the Bible and the Qur'an, the story of his daughter's sexual history with him is present only in the Bible, which demonstrates, yet again, Alameddine's druzification of religious traditions by suturing them together and thus undertaking a joint critique of Judaic, Christian, and Muslim hegemonies. However, Alameddine's character is not drawn towards queer-friendly commentary. As I have already suggested, Kugle (2010) interprets God's punishment of the men of Sodom as being based on their rejection of Lot's prophethood and on their betrayal of their wives through their intended rape of the visiting angels. Partly influenced by Ibn Hazm's classical exegesis, Kugle regards rape and apostasy, not homosexuality, as being of centrality to this episode. By contrast, Mohammad does not rehearse a queer interpretive reclamation and simply rejects interpretive literalism, in keeping with the esoteric tendency of the Druze, as inspired by Ismaili Shia Islam. Halabi Abbas suggests that Ismailism 'developed the idea that the true knowledge of the divine realities is contained in their hidden or esoteric meaning', adding that 'this is the point of distinction between the Sunnis, who adhere to the literal meaning of the text and are called the people of the Shar'ia, and the Shi'is, who adhere to interpretation, and are called the people of the Way' (Abbas, 2015, n.p.) What Alameddine resists through his rejection of 'superficial' religious interpretation is the literalism of Sunni Islam, opting instead for a more esoteric approach to scripture that does not fix religious meanings and which renders them a matter of subjective mysticism, even going as far as suturing the Bible and the Qur'an, thus signalling more generally the heteropatriarchal biases of the three Abrahamic religions.

Alameddine further druzifies religious scriptures by stitching them together, thus revealing their parochialism and the conservative advancement of particular religious texts, in detriment of others, in American culture. One of the most recurring episodes in Mohammad's narrative is that of the Four Horsemen of Apocalypse, from the Bible, which signals Mohammad's obsession with death and Judgement Day. At one point, the white rider starts at the mention of Paradise in the horsemen's collective chant, exclaiming:

> What the hell is this? [...] Those are not my words. I never said that. You guys are reading from the wrong fucking book, you idiots. That's the Qur'an. You're not allowed to read from that when you're with me. The Bible is my book. [...] We're in America now. (Alameddine, 1999a, p. 99)

Mohammad's AIDS-induced rant highlights the Jewish and Christian bias of American religiosity and its blindsiding of Islam: the Qur'an is considered the 'wrong fucking book', which assumes that the Bible is America's foundational religious text. Shannahan (2011) argues that Mohammad's fourth rewriting of Apocalypse reveals an 'exclusivist Judeo-Christian vision' that nonetheless takes place in the same eschatological plain, since Judaism, Christianity and Islam ultimately believe in the same God. In subversively critiquing the 'Othering' of Islam in narratives of American religiosity, *KOOLAIDS* constitutes a Druze response to prominent queer versions of the Judaeo-Christian alliance, such as Tony Kushner's popular plays *Angels in America*. Claudia Barnett argues that Kushner's prophet, Prior Walter, while being of Yankee WASP – i.e., White Anglo Saxon Protestant – stock, is also 'the pilgrim whose journey recalls the beginnings and diasporas of both Mormons and Jews. While his ancestors appear comically and formidably onstage, his more nuanced heritage explicitly recalls the different scriptures and positions him as prophet' (Barnett, 2010, p. 473). Kushner's two plays, *Millennium Approaches* and *Perestroika*, syncretise Judaism and Christianity, and Prior's diasporic heritage allows him to stand for members of both religions.

In turn, Alameddine reinscribes Islam within the diasporic mythos of the American nation, offering his own Muslim diasporic prophet who remains willing to amalgamate religious traditions. The reiterations at work in Alameddine's text evidence a Druze sensibility keen on a cyclical conception of both life and textuality. According to Betts (1988), the Druze do not believe in Paradise or in Judgement Day as conceived by the Abrahamic faiths, but in reincarnation and the perfection of the human soul, which helps explain Alameddine's fixation with textual repetition and revision. As Mohammad states, 'I wanted to write an endless book of time. It would have no beginning and no end. [...] I was not able to do it. Besides, I would have been copying the master. Borges did it before me' (Alameddine, 1999a, p. 118). If Mohammad failed to succeed because of his own unavoidable death from AIDS complications, Alameddine himself did eventually achieve an endless book of time with *The Hakawati*. As Tabačková perceptively observes, '[t]he last words of the novel, in a Finnegans-like-way bring the reader back to the beginning of the story' (2015, p. 115). Whereas Alameddine's atheistic diasporic perspective drives him towards postmodern poetics, via experimental writers such as Borges, the resulting assembled textualities can be regarded as a unique diasporic overlapping of Western postmodern poetics and Alameddine's Lebanese Druze heritage, with its emphasis on suturing cultural traditions and on religious syncretism.

The queer community living with AIDS in Alameddine's novel also resists a conception of family organised around the concept of the ethnic or religious clan, hence exceeding the logic of bloodlines. In his work on transcultural adoption, John McLeod asserts that '[t]he prizing of blood-lines, birthrights and national and cultural "roots" has become the modern norm, regardless of how arbitrary it may be firmly to establish these things extra-discursively' (2015, p. 15). AIDS also brings with it a crisis in traditional conceptions of family in *KOOLAIDS*:

> In 1982, [James] decided not to go back home for Thanksgiving. A group of friends formed the We Are Family group. There were seven of them that year. They came over for a Thanksgiving dinner at his house. When dinner was over, they played Sister Sledge's disco hit full blast. They played that song at every Thanksgiving since. Through the years the

group got bigger with lovers joining in. Through the years the group got smaller with friends dying. (Alameddine, 1999a, p. 40)

The 'We Are Family' group is united around ideas of sexual dissidence and in rejection of conservative ideologies shunning homosexuality. Together, these queer men create a shrinking yet stoic model of family living with the harrowing realities of AIDS, in defiance of the shame emanating from their heteronormative families hailing from America and elsewhere. As Mohammad told us a few lines earlier, his Lebanese family disowned him after he was 'outed' by an art magazine: 'I was alone. A piece of my heart was forcibly taken out. Eradicated. Expurgated. Obliterated. Emasculated'; deeply hurt by familial rejection, he invites his friend Scott to live with him, after which he recalls '[w]e became one word, Mohammad and Scott, Scott and Mohammad. One person. One life. One love' (Alameddine, 1999a, p. 40). The affective assemblages and the networks of desire forged in Alameddine's novel push against the boundaries of sexual propriety and ethno-religious exclusivism, reaching beyond the impositions of bloodlines and ultimately revealing the necessity to challenge monolithic constructions of identity. In suturing subjectivities from different cultural, religious, and national backgrounds, Alameddine is contributing to the druzification of his vision of America and diversifying its foundational diasporic narrative.

Alameddine's fiction, which translates into English his complex assemblage of East and West, past and present, is a repository of networks of affect woven in the face of collective embattlement. Given Alameddine's diasporic sensibility, which is equally at loggerheads with American ethno-nationalism and with Lebanese religious sectarianism, his fiction becomes a space for dissidence with normative discourses which seek to homogenise communities and to scapegoat 'Others' because of their different ethnicities or their seemingly 'deviant' sexualities. Alameddine's oeuvre queers the units that we have created to explain the world's temporal and spatial workings: as Salaita observes, via Saree Makdisi, Alameddine's debut novel illustrates 'how the political upheaval entailed in the civil war eliminated both temporal and ontological certainties' (Salaita, 2006, p. 77), leading to the queering of time and place, and, meanwhile, to the questioning of the heteronormative bias of religious interpretation. In the face of imposed religious certainties from the three Abrahamic religions, Alameddine's work opts, instead, for esoterism, druzifying the Islamicate mythical and historical past while disorganising religious orthodoxies in the literalist Islamist present. Alameddine's texts ultimately posit an assemblage of textual perspectives that corroborates the syncretic nature of queer diasporic subjectivity, as well as the impossibility of holding on to any one single, holistic narrative. As past and present coexist in both spatial and temporal assemblage, the narratives that are woven to alienate queer subjects are revealed to be invariably heterosexist and patriarchal; as their discreteness unravels, out of their enmeshed discursive strands, queer citizens find ways of stitching new forms of becoming and belonging against the certainty of bloodlines, heteropatriarchal social expectations, and the sidestepping of the queer person living with AIDS.

9

Written on the body: a queer and cartographic exploration of the Palestinian diaspora in Randa Jarrar's *A Map of Home* (2008) and *Him, Me, Muhammad Ali* (2016)

A RAB-AMERICAN WRITER Randa Jarrar conjures in her long and short fiction a mode of mapping the diasporic self which is irreverent, culturally and linguistically idiosyncratic, and inexorably queer. In a *Beirut39* interview excerpted in her website, she candidly asserts: 'That's actually what I love about literature – how the submerged of the world can finally get their say. I love to write about the disenfranchised, the fatties, the cast-offs, the queers, the dirty kids, the ones history doesn't love' (Jarrar, n.d.). In her own words, Jarrar's literature brings to the surface and reclaims those human subjects who are persecuted, misunderstood, or maligned, including, crucially, queer people. Like Abdellah Taïa's work, Jarrar's fiction draws significantly on her own life experiences; yet, unlike Taïa's autofictions, Jarrar's narratives are only semi-autobiographical: her narrators are fictional, which allows both for poetic licence and comedic distance. In fact, in terms of her fiction's overall tone, Jarrar's writing is more akin to Rabih Alameddine's than to Taïa's: whereas Taïa's narratives are suffused with pathos, borne out, as I have suggested, of his postcolonial queer melancholia, Jarrar's work brims instead with bathos, one of the author's main tools of insurgence against Arab and Islamic heteropatriarchy. Jarrar's creative imagination imbues serious themes such as gender violence and patriarchal oppression with humour, while interrogating the impact of Arab heteropatriarchy on queer bodies. The last chapter of this book examines Jarrar's debut novel, *A Map of Home*, published in 2008, and her recent short story collection, *Him, Me, Muhammad Ali*, and their queer and cartographic mapping of the queer female body in the diaspora.

In her recent book *Living a Feminist Life*, Sara Ahmed self-confessedly embodies the figure of the 'feminist killjoy'. Ahmed recalls how American black feminists and feminists of colour 'taught [her] to think about the figure of the angry black woman, the angry woman of color, as well as the angry indigenous woman, as another kind of feminist killjoy: a feminist killjoy who kills feminist killjoy' (2017, p. 177). Although Jarrar's female characters sometimes find themselves responding angrily to parental – and, indeed, chiefly paternal – control, it is humour, rather than anger, that constitutes Jarrar's main tool as a feminist writer, an irreverent vantage point which she partly inherits from her Arab ethnic background, which she applies to her diasporic characters' shifting surroundings. Nancy El Gendy suggests, via Kimberly Christen, that Jarrar's 'trickster humour has Arab origins', to be traced back, most notably, to the figure of Juha, a fool from Arab folk tales '[k]nown for his drunkenness, homosexuality, eroticism, satire' (El Gendy, 2016, p. 4). According to El Gendy, trickster figures refuse to view tragedies as sacrosanct or as solely victimising the individual. She proposes that '[t]rickster humour in [Jarrar's] novel [*A Map of Home*] liberates readers, as well as characters, from long-standing tragic ideologies about the diasporic Muslim female body' (El Gendy, 2016, p. 5). Through semi-autobiographical mouthpieces and other narrators, I argue Jarrar recasts Ahmed's figure of the 'feminist killjoy' into a 'feminist trickster', deploying humour in order to illustrate the ideological biases and inconsistencies of national and diasporic Arab Muslim communities and the complex predicament of living out queer, Arab, and Palestinian identities in America.

Jarrar's fiction often mobilises first-person narrators with more or less autobiographical intent, hence exploiting the interstices between fiction and memoir and assembling genres. Dwelling on the role of Palestinian memoir in dialogue with Norbert Bugeja's work, Lindsey Moore observes that '[t]he self is historicized through his/her reconfiguration of meaning out of "the vast, evanescent bodies of national, communal or social memory" [...]: personal experience, while not necessarily representative, has a wider collective resonance' (2017, p. 168). Moore recognises the importance for Palestinian writers of personal experiences of dispossession and how their own narratives resonate with collective histories of exile. In addition, Anna Bernard suggests that

> any Palestinian or Israeli literary text, fictional or not, that is structurally reliant on the "recourse to biographical form" for its project of

sense-making will produce its own demographic imaginary – its own mediated infinity – and so its own criteria for national citizenship and national belonging. (Bernard, 2013, p. 40)

In light of Moore's and Bernard's perspectives on Palestinian memoirs, I suggest that Jarrar forges an assemblage out of the most productive aspects of both fiction and memoir. Jarrar makes recourse to her biographical experiences as a diasporic subject of mixed Palestinian heritage who has lived in Kuwait, Egypt, and the USA. Her peripatetic history helps her complicate in her fiction issues of national identity and ethnic and religious affiliations. However, Jarrar draws from her own experiences in a highly fictionalised manner, which allows her to experiment freely with received commonplaces about both Arab and American cultures, which also frees her from the strictures of mimesis. Nonetheless, this does not altogether exonerate her from the burden of collective representation, since Jarrar's narratives are meant to play into the Palestinian collective imagination. However, the double orientation in Jarrar's work ultimately complicates its effect. As she intimates: 'One of my hopes as I was writing [*A Map of Home*] was for its audience to be both Arab and non-Arab; for it to work with both camps' (Albakry and Siler, 2012, p. 119). Jarrar's writing is simultaneously meant to ring familiar to Arab readers, to disorientate both Arab and non-Arab readers unfamiliar with issues of sexual dissidence, and to generate readerly empathy for the queer Muslim diasporic subject of Palestinian heritage.

It needs to be noted that Jarrar's various feminist tricksters tread a fine line between comedy and caricature, as well as between realism and hyperbole, often perilously tipping into the latter. Nonetheless, as Jarrar seems about to confirm Western readers' internalised stereotypes about Arabs, and Arab commonplaces about 'Western culture', these are often unceremoniously turned on their head with unabashed irony. In this regard, Jarrar's writing is visibly keen on disorganising her implied readerships' ideological preconceptions, as she blurs the boundaries of hyphenated identities with the disruptive thrust of queer diasporic bodies. Similarly to Taïa's fiction, Jarrar's writing is highly conscious of issues of linguistic[1] and literary embodiment, and of the role of these textual bodies in disrupting Arab, Islamicate, and Palestinian societal and familial mores.

For Jarrar, the human body constitutes a cultural and countercultural archive. In the British postmodern queer novel *Written on the Body*, Jeanette Winterson's genderqueer narrator declares: 'Let me penetrate you. I am the archaeologist of tombs. I would devote my life to marking your passageways, the entrances and exits of that impressive mausoleum, your body' (1993, p. 119). *A Map of*

Home takes up Winterson's exordium and becomes invested in the examination and opening up of bodies; yet, if exploration of old mausoleums and penetrating imagery resemble the stuff of colonial fantasy, Jarrar's perspective remains postcolonial, for it deals with Palestinians' national dispossession and their constant search for a home in an exilic world precariously negotiated between Israeli colonialism and Palestinian postcolonial resistance. As I will show, in the physical absence of a collective homeland, Jarrar's diasporic fiction maps home onto the diasporic subjects' bodies, rendering the diasporic self the personal repository of Palestinian exile. Jarrar's characters' bodies also tackle the inheritance of Arab and Islamicate gender and sexual cartographies delimiting and constraining the queer and female body, while drawing attention, in a manner bordering into the metafictional, to the importance of writing and storytelling for the expression of the displaced Palestinian citizen's memory.

While at odds with her Islamic heritage due to its mainstream condemnation of homosexuality, Islam looms large in Jarrar's diasporic imaginary. To start at the end, *A Map of Home* finishes with reference to a chapter from the Qur'an which she relates to her central family's history. As her narrator, Nidali, writes:

> The pen is a *sura* in the Qur'an that starts: '*Nun*. By the pen, and that they write, you are not mad: thanks to the favour of your Lord. [...]" One afternoon, shortly after we'd moved to America, I found Mama and Baba fighting about a pen a woman had given him [...]. [I]t became clear after a few minutes that [Mama] believed this pen to be a spy pen. [...] "Our lives have been recorded," she said. "Someone out there knows everything that's gone on inside our house." [...] Mama reached over and threw the pen out of the window. I catch the pen now and listen to all our stories.' (Jarrar, 2009, pp. 289–90)

The Qur'an's pen *sura* starts with God's assurance to Prophet Muhammad that no matter what defamers write with their pens about his alleged madness, his revelations are real, which chimes with the narrator's efforts to record her family's lives. Obsessed with privacy and family honour in a manner that resonates with contemporary concerns in the Arab world, as well as, via Jasbir K. Puar (2007), with the Western obsession with the statist surveillance of Muslims, the narrator's mother is worried that a pen gifted to her husband contains a concealed microphone which has recorded their every word. This episode constitutes almost a metafictional disclaimer, since Jarrar's narrative has indeed offered us the family's intimate histories of uprooting and diaspora. Here, Jarrar transposes the Qur'an's concern with scripture and defamation to our modern concern with technology and surveillance, while reminding us of the necessity of recording histories in order to give textual embodiment to the dispossessed and the displaced, in this case the Palestinian diaspora.

Self-conscious textuality and embodiment are intimately linked in Jarrar's endeavours, which is in agreement with queer theory. In the introduction to *Bodies that Matter*, Judith Butler asks herself and her readers a series of probing questions:

> How, then, can one think through the matter of bodies as a kind of materialization governed by regulatory norms in order to ascertain the workings of heterosexual hegemony in the formation of what qualifies as a viable body? How does the materialization of the norm in bodily formation produce a domain of abjected bodies, a field of deformation, which, in failing to qualify as the fully human, fortifies those regulatory norms? What challenge does that excluded and abjected realm produce to a symbolic hegemony that might force a radical rearticulation as what qualifies as bodies that matter, ways of living that count as 'life,' lives worth protecting, lives worth saving, lives worth grieving? (Butler, 1993, p. 16)

Poignantly writing at the height of the AIDS crisis, Butler begs which bodies matter and are worth recounting and how they are constructed against the normative. She also asks us to consider in what ways difference itself can strengthen the norm and how such norm is to be subverted. In response to these questions posed by queerness, Jarrar's writing forges queer bodies torn between gender binaries and between attraction to both genders. As I demonstrate in the forthcoming pages, Jarrar's fiction grapples with the idea of what constitutes a 'viable body' in heteronormative societies. Her writing creates queer bodies challenging gender binaries and torn between attraction to both genders, thus disorganising received Arab and Islamicate ideas and values. This chapter interrogates issues of home mapping and war-induced deterritorialisation, while examining the articulation of bodies as maps and as the physical and textual repositories of colonial and patriarchal violence. Here, bodies are also explored as cyphers disorientating national and diasporic Arab and Islamicate gender and sexual expectations. *A Map of Home*'s first-person viewpoint conveys a sense of urgency about the self-validation of queer bodies in both literal and symbolic ways.

In order to understand the multiple connections between Jarrar's diasporic experiences and her fiction, it is necessary to have a basic knowledge of her life trajectory. Born in Chicago in 1978 to a Palestinian father and an Egyptian mother of Greek heritage, Jarrar was brought up in Kuwait, until the outbreak of the Gulf War (1990–91). In 1991, her family moved initially to Cairo, in her maternal native country of Egypt, and then, eventually, to the East Coast of the USA (Espinoza, 2017; Ali, 2017). Educated as a creative writer and occasionally working as a translator of Arabic, Jarrar currently teaches creative writing at Fresno State University, in California. Palestine is given due prominence in Jarrar's imaginary, although having grown up in the diaspora, she also has a complicated history of political reclamation of the lost homeland and a desire for a more durable home at a remove from the demands of Palestinian nationalism. Jarrar observes in a short memoir entitled 'Imagining Myself in Palestine': 'Growing up, my Palestinian identity was mostly tied to my father. He was the Palestinian in the family, and when we went back to the West Bank it was to see his brothers and sisters and parents' (2012, n.p.). Jarrar's last successful trip to Palestine was in 1993.

Jarrar's Palestinian memoir recounts how she has since been denied entry into Palestine to visit her sister, the only member of her immediate family from which she has not been estranged following the publication of *A Map of Home*, and who has since moved to California. Jarrar tells us about the familial fallout after the publication of her debut novel:

> My father and I hadn't spoken since he read my first novel, nearly four years ago. He had sent me an angry email, and told me that we would no longer be seeing one another, or speaking. [...] My father had said in his email that, by writing about sex in my novel so shamelessly, I had disregarded the legacy of my Palestinian family, which, he claimed, had defeated Napoleon. (Jarrar, 2012, n.p.)

Jarrar's memoir mirrors the humorous contradictions examined in her fiction, with her father's almost comical reclamation of his family's seemingly anti-colonial history, while refusing to acknowledge his daughter's unflinching denouncement of Arab patriarchal oppression. Here, her father justifies his repudiation of her on account of her frank depiction of sex, which is deems un-Palestinian, and by extension un-Islamic, since religious identity is intimately interwoven with his Palestinian identity. Jarrar's memoir highlights how conservative sexual morality often impedes the honest acknowledgement of lingering patriarchal violence in Arab and Muslim communities; in the face of these problematic realities, it is easier to resort to familial self-mythologising. Jarrar's candour in dealing with sexuality and her flouting of inherited morality position her at loggerheads with her cultural and religious heritage. In addition to being self-confessedly queer, and having had premarital sex, Jarrar has also had a son out of wedlock, which is also anathema to her Arab heritage and which has further estranged her from her family.

A Map of Home is the fictional autobiography of Nidali Ammar, a young Arab woman who closely resembles Jarrar's own persona: Nidali is the daughter of a Palestinian father, Waheed, who left Palestine during the 1967 Arab–Israeli war, and a Greek-Egyptian mother, Fairuza, whose ancestors originally migrated to Egypt from Crete. Written in the tradition of the *bildungsroman*, Nidali's narrative begins with the particulars of her birth in America and of her naming, which is an initial source of friction between her parents, and which preliminarily demonstrates the preponderance of patriarchal values. According to the narrator:

> While filling out my certificate, Baba realized that he didn't know my sex for sure but that didn't matter; he'd always known I was a boy, [...] and as he approached the box that contained the question, NAME OF CHILD, he wrote [...] Nidal (strife; struggle). (Jarrar, 2009, p. 3)

Instead of following the tradition of naming the child after his own father, Waheed chooses a name that speaks meaningfully to his experience as an exiled Palestinian; but in wrongly presuming that his offspring is male, he gives away his deep desire for a son, which foreshadows his ambivalent treatment of Nidali and her own future gender-bending attitude. Nidali is eventually joined by a brother, Gamal, whose submissiveness fails to fulfil his father's high expectations of his masculinity. The theme of affective investment in male children and traditional masculinity belongs in a lineage of Arab writing critiquing Arab and Islamicate patriarchy, such as Tahar Ben Jelloun's *The Sand Child* and *The Sacred Night*, as well as Rabih Alameddine's *I, the Divine*, which we examined in the previous chapter.

Here, Nidali is claimed as the property of her father and brought up to fulfil his desire for a son. Following the discovery of his daughter's femaleness, Nidali recounts how Waheed 'grabbed a pen and added at the end of my name a heavy, reflexive, feminizing, possessive, cursive, cursing "I" ' (Jarrar, 2009, p. 5). Nidali becomes 'my struggle' and is thus labelled his father's inalienable possession, a feat he spends the rest of the novel reasserting both verbally and physically throughout the family's various migrations, first to Kuwait City, where the family spends much of Nidali's formative years; then, after Saddam Hussein's invasion of Kuwait, to Alexandria, where they precariously survive in their holiday apartment; and finally, when Waheed gets offered a job in America, to Texas, where the whole family lives huddled up in a trailer. Their lack of a conventional house is attributed to Waheed's criminal record, gained after being reported to the US police for beating up Nidali, which means he cannot secure a mortgage. It is significant that Waheed's most notorious acts of parental control, chiefly his violent beatings of Nidali, are also the crimes that deter him from fulfilling his duty as the traditional 'breadwinner' in America.

Because of these multiple migrations and pervasive parental surveillance, Nidali only manages to develop fleeting emotional and sexual relationships with various men and women, which constitute her own line of flight from her cultural and familial heritage, but which, in the case of same-sex liaisons, also involves guilt and shame due to the internalised Islamic condemnation of homosexuality. In *A Map of Home*, the themes of the mapping of home in the Palestinian diaspora and the self's exploration of gender and sexuality are intimately assembled. Ahmed suggests that

> [i]f we think of the second-wave feminism motto 'the personal is political,' we can think of feminism as happening in the very places that have historically been bracketed as not political: in domestic arrangements, at home, every room of the house can become a feminist room. (Ahmed, 2017, pp. 3–4)

Jarrar's novel advances the idea that the mundane coming together of queer bodies in everyday spaces acts as a micropolitical revulsive against Arab and Islamicate heteronormativity, but rather than enacting a purely individualist – and hence Americanised – quest for self-expression, the queer self transversally grapples with gender and sexuality at the same time as it struggles with the displacement of the Palestinian people. In other words, I argue that Nidali's gender and sexual fluidity cannot be extrapolated from her homelessness and uprootedness.

One of the main conundrums assailing Nidali in the novel is her disidentification with constraining models of femininity and masculinity, while being limited by her father's Arab and Islamicate patriarchal values. Her gender ambivalence is foreshadowed by Waheed's desire for a son. However, Waheed's ideological position regarding gender roles remains inconsistent: he wants Nidali to be free from traditional Arab conflations of femininity and domesticity, yet he also polices her body and her behaviour in order to uphold the Islamicate concept of family honour. At one point in the novel, Waheed collects Nidali from a party she has attended with her then-boyfriend Fakhr al Din without asking for his permission. Music and paternal violence blend together during the drive home and the ensuing beating:

> I wanted to sing 'You Are My Life' and pretend that I was Umm Kulthum, who began singing when she was little. I'd heard stories about how her baba didn't want her to stop but he was scared that his little girl would be taken advantage of or not be taken seriously because of her sex, so he put her in boys' clothes and pretended to others, and soon to himself, that she was a boy, and in this costume she was safe to be herself and to be happy. [...] Baba had been pretending all my life that I was a boy, from the moment of my birth, even before. Tonight was possibly the first time he actually realized that I was on my way to becoming a woman. [...] Slap. My cheek burned. [...] He grabbed my hands and held them both with his one big hand. With his free hand he slapped me again. I hated it when he held both my hands; it made me feel so powerless. [...] I wondered if Umm Kulthum's dad hit her. [...] I put an Umm Kulthum tape in and brought the small stereo into bed with me. I listened to her mournful voice and pretended she was singing only to me, that she was in bed with me, her black sunglasses and beehive and white handkerchief and fat body, all with me. [...] I didn't ever want to be like Mama; I wanted to be free and forever unmarried like Umm Kulthum was, and someday have my own money and my own house so I wouldn't have to answer to anyone. (Jarrar, 2009, pp. 121–3)

Nidali is here inspired by the model of the Egyptian singer Umm Kulthum, a prominent artistic figure in the Arab collective imagination, and who also happens to embody the contradictions of Islamicate conceptions of gender. After Waheed beats Nidali up for daring to socialise with boys and for her slightly worsening school results, Nidali's queer imagination blends Umm Kulthum's unconventional and abjected body and her own in her bed, while imagining her potential financial freedom from her father in a yet unforeseen future. This episode of *A Map of Home* is in keeping with Alameddine's depiction of Sarah Nour el-Din in *I, the Divine*, whereby the grandfather figure connects his granddaughter's name with that of the cross-dressing classical actress Sarah Bernhardt. Genderbending artists such as Umm Kulthum and Bernhardt thus become inspirational symbols of unconventional femininity that is simultaneously oriented towards heteronormative male fantasy and queer subversion. The strategic appropriation of Umm Kulthum allows Nidali to locate herself in the continuum of Arab culture: at once a part of mainstream Arab culture, yet also in defiance of Arab patriarchal values with her embrace of queerness.

The troubled yet complex relationship between Waheed and Nidali is central to *A Map of Home*. As a diasporic Palestinian man committed to anti-colonialism and political secularism, Waheed remains sympathetic to his sisters' submission to traditional gender roles back home in Palestine: ' "All my sisters," Baba said, "got married before they were fifteen. No, I'm lying; Kameela was seventeen. They got married against the whitewashed wall outside... like prisoners awaiting execution." Baba stopped and exhaled wearily' (Jarrar, 2009, p. 105). Waheed then reflects on how, as a man, going to university in Egypt liberated him, and he regrets his sisters' lack of access to education and their submission to Palestinian and Arab gender roles. As he tells Nidali, 'I want more than anything in the world for you to have that opportunity' (2009, p. 105). As a Nasser sympathiser, he also forbids Nidali from donning the *hijab*, even when her Kuwaiti classmates do so. However, Waheed's dreams of Nidali earning a PhD and becoming an academic remain an extension of his own thwarted personal ambitions and therefore a sign of his lingering patriarchal control over his daughter's destiny.

Despite such paternal determinism, Jarrar's narrative also conveys Nidali's empathy towards her father:

> Poor Baba. He used to be a good poet. Now he was a dad and a husband, and he couldn't write any more. He had an idea in his head, but that, unfortunately, was all he had. [...] Because he wanted it to come out of his head perfectly, fully formed, like Athena out of Zeus (like, on some days, he believed I had come out of him), he could never let it go. When I saw that Baba was afraid, I felt sorry for him. (Jarrar, 2009, p. 109)

Jarrar adeptly captures the patriarchal expectations that constrain Waheed himself: his literary potential is thwarted by family obligations that constitute his duties as an Arab man. In addition, his stubborn literary sterility is here channelled through Nidali's maternal imagery, inherited matrilineally from her mother's Greek-Egyptian heritage. Waheed is rendered in Nidali's hyphenated Palestinian-Egyptian sensibility a Zeus-like figure, a godlike masculine archetype who regards his daughter as an Athena-inspired extension of his own ego. I would suggest that, given Jarrar's overall depiction, Waheed is constructed as both subject and perpetrator of Arab patriarchy. Yet, Nidali remains sympathetic towards him in his inability to convey his Palestinian identity because of the pressures exerted on his Arab masculinity.

Nidali's narrative and, metonymically, Jarrar's novel become the belated fulfilment of Waheed's literary ambitions. Nonetheless, no amount of filial sympathy can erase the reality of his continued violence towards Nidali, which springs from his internalised patriarchal values. Waheed's depiction has divided reviewers and critics. Dina Jadallah argues that 'Nidali has a slightly racist and Western-influenced perception of Arabs, perhaps a reflection of her divided self, being American, Palestinian, and Egyptian' (2010, p. 112). While it is reasonable to assert that sometimes Jarrar's representation of Arab masculinity seems to border on caricature, other critics have perceived complexity in Jarrar's work. According to Steven Salaita, 'Waheed is not the stereotypical Arab male of American lore, though he does exhibit a need for too much control over Nidali's decisions. Nevertheless, he is too multifaceted to be read as a simple representation of one or a few things' (2011, p. 132). Indeed, Waheed's wish for his daughter to be free from Arab and Islamicate patriarchy through gaining an education and his resistance to seeing her married intersect with his fixation with Nidali earning a doctorate, his prohibition of socialising, and his corporal punishment. I would suggest Waheed constitutes the 'multifaceted' embodiment of the contradictions assailing modern Arab men: he becomes the embodiment of their struggle overturning Islamicate patriarchy, which they punctually oppose, for instance in regard to female education, while helping to perpetuate it in others, such as gender violence and the enforcement of traditionalist family honour.

As regards the inheritance and subversion of inherited values, Jarrar's fiction explores how this inheritance also involves an internalisation of Arab homophobia, steeped as it is in Islamicate dogma, which makes her characters conflicted about their queerness. Although Nidali's most lasting sentimental relationship is with the aforementioned boy Fakhr, she has intermittent relationships with girls that, she gradually realises, disorganise her inherited values about sexual orientation. Her first same-sex encounter is with her friend Rama, just before Nidali leaves war-torn Kuwait with her family. While Rama cross-questions Nidali about her relationship with Fakhr, a fortuitous homoerotic episode develops:

She reached over and pinched my boob.
  "Ow! You pinched my boob!"
  "I know."
So I pinched hers.

> Soon we were tickling each other and she stuck her knee right in between my legs. A moan escaped from my mouth; it felt good, her knee there, and she moved it over me in a circle. I grabbed her thigh and guided the circle until I felt the way I felt whenever I sat over the bidet for too long. I turned away from Rama and jumped off the bed. I had no idea what had just happened and Rama seemed just as confused as I was. [...] When we got in the car and I turned and saw Rama's dark hand shutting her heavy front door, I knew I'd never see her again. In a few days, my family would pile into our cars and leave Kuwait through Iraq. I cried quietly on the way home, at my bewilderment and at all the injustice that had been decreed unto me, unto us. I felt as though I no longer understood the world. (Jarrar, 2009, p. 142)

Nidali and Rama instinctively follow the movements of female self-gratification in a moment of fortuitous homoerotic connection, whose source or implications neither girl seems fully to grasp, but which Jarrar's narrative interweaves with issues of war and migration. When Jarrar writes about Nidali's 'injustice that had been decreed unto *me*, unto *us*' (emphasis added), it is difficult to establish whether this unfairness applies to Nidali's Palestinian-Egyptian diasporic family or to the homoerotic duo of Nidali and Rama, which is torn by Nidali's need to flee Kuwait. As regards Nidali's sense that she no longer understands the world, this can be comparably related to her short-lived homoerotic relationship with Rama as to her notion of home. Nidali is seemingly disorientated on both counts: her unexpected homosexual experience with Rama and her imminent uprooting from her family home in Kuwait are both sources of emotional upset that Jarrar assembles in Nidali's consciousness. This is one useful example of the assemblage of Palestinian uprootedness and queerness in Jarrar's depiction of the queer diasporic Muslim self.

Nidali gradually comes to realise that she has feelings for both boys and girls. Her next homoerotic experience takes place in Alexandria, where the Amaar family takes refuge during the Gulf War. In this case, Nidali feels jealousy towards her schoolmate Jiji's boyfriend:

> I wanted to tell Jiji that I'd give her her first kiss. I hadn't thought of it before but just then, when I saw that slimy frog, I thought, *I* should give her her first kiss. I'll go to hell, I thought. I liked boys, I assured myself, because I did. I wanted to kiss them. But I wanted to be the first one Jiji kissed instead of some slimy toad of a guy. (Jarrar, 2009, p. 170; original italics)

Nidali's narrative reveals here that she is conflicted about her queer orientation: she needs to remind herself that she likes boys while being irresistibly attracted to Jiji. Nidali is unequivocal about the moral implications of her desire: 'I'll go to hell.' Subsequently, Nidali tries to avoid Jiji in order not to confront her feelings for her. As she confesses, 'I wished Mama and Baba had saved the money they'd spent on this stupid school so I would have never met Jiji and never felt *guilt*' (Jarrar, 2009, p. 171, emphasis added). When her brother Gamal becomes the object of her father's violence due to his poor performance at school, Nidali does not intervene: 'I thought, I'm already going to hell for having lesbian thoughts and I might as well bide my time here on earth' (2009, p. 171). She focuses, instead, on her homework, doing the washing up, and her masturbation at the bathroom bidet, where she self-confessedly has 'shuddering orgasms' (2009, p. 171). So far, Nidali's narrative does not contain any mention to any religious scripture, and she consigns herself to hell for the mere thought of kissing another woman, without having wilfully acted on her homosexual desires.

I would suggest that, given the lack of any explicit reference to Islam, Nidali has internalised Arab and Islamicate cultural 'guilt' about homosexuality. In the face of this self-imposed ethno-religious repression, Nidali opts for sexual self-gratification. The water imagery surrounding Nidali's choice for autoeroticism also connects symbolically with her queer sexual fluidity and the rejection of sturdy sexual binaries. El Gendy argues that Jarrar's novel 'contributes to third-wave Arab American women writers' ongoing battle against normative productions of the Muslim female body by questioning a web of interwoven institutions, ideologies and mythologies that fabricate the body and sexuality' (2016, p. 14). Indeed, Jarrar's fictional autobiography takes to task assembled Arab cultural habits and Islamicate values; in the face of the powerful institutions whose ideologies Nidali has visibly internalised, she still claims ownership over her own body, her self-stimulation constituting an ongoing form of defiance against imposed ideas about Arab and Islamicate femininity.

The theme of homosexuality and religious guilt is further explored in the story 'Building Girls' collected in *Him, Me, Muhammad Ali*. The first-person narrator, Aisha, is an Egyptian concierge who takes care of a four-storey building in a small town between Alexandria and Abu Qir. Divorced, with a little girl called Shadia, and living with her parents, Aisha finds herself erotically entangled with a woman called Perihan, one of the clients in her building. The narration of their homoerotic encounter offers a combination of internalised homophobia, exegetical unconventionality, and queer consolation:

'Sometimes,' I divulged, 'I see men beautiful enough to invite here. But I don't, I just come here by myself and imagine them touching me.'

'You come here to masturbate?'

My face flushed and I looked away.

'Don't, Aisha. Don't be embarrassed,' she said, and took my face in her hands. [...] She kissed my cheek. 'Don't be embarrassed,' she said and stroked my face. 'Don't be embarrassed,' she said and kissed my eyelids. 'Don't be embarrassed,' she whispered and pecked my lips. 'Don't be embarrassed,' she said, her tongue sliding into my mouth. I hadn't kissed anyone in a long time. I knew what we were doing was wrong, but I didn't know why. I imagined my mother finding us, spitting on me, her mouth grimacing in disgust, and I pulled away. Perihan put her hands on my waist and said again, 'Don't be embarrassed,' and slowly wedged her knee between my legs. [...] She slid her hands over me, then kissed my neck, my shoulders, my breasts, my stomach, my hips, all the while whispering for me not to be embarrassed. I couldn't help it. [...]

'Have you done this to many women?'

'No. But I was scared at first that there was something wrong with me. I went to many imams and they all said the same thing: what I felt was haram and I should control it. Then I found an imam who told me that nothing in the Koran says a woman can't love a woman. There's one verse that says if two women are found together they should be locked up in the house. Then the imam told me that two women locked up in a house could only lead to one thing.' We both laughed. I smelled myself on her breath and hugged her close.

In the following days, I averted my eyes when Mother looked at me. I was ashamed and confused, but then I would hear Peri chanting, 'Don't be embarrassed,' her voice like a phantom-like sheet, and I would feel better. (Jarrar, 2016, pp. 30–1)

Perihan coaches Aisha in the act of sexual liberation: in her view, neither masturbation, nor same-sex eroticism, ought to warrant the embarrassment that Aisha feels. Aisha has visibly internalised negative views on female homosexuality. As she confesses, 'I knew what we were doing was wrong, but I didn't know why', which suggests she cannot trace the formal source of Arab or Islamicate homophobia. Perihan explains how she herself struggled with her attraction towards women, and when approaching *imams*, she was given mostly conventional but also one unconventional exegetical position regarding the Qur'an's *sura* on women.

Scott Siraj al-Haqq Kugle comments on the Qur'anic verses that mention an ambiguous immorality committed by women:

> As for those of your women who commit the immorality [al-fahisha], have four from amongst yourselves bear witness against them. If they do witness, then confine them [the women] to their rooms until death causes them to perish or until God makes them a way [of release]' (Kugle, 2010, p. 64, emphasis in original)

Although, as already noted, according to Kugle, the tenth-century *tafsir* scholar al-Isfahani was the first religious commentator to hazard that such nebulous 'immorality' refers specifically to female homosexuality, Scott's grammatical analysis reveals the pronoun used in the verses denotes a group of women rather than just a couple. This point notwithstanding, the *imam* advising Perihan irreverently suggests the prescribed course of action – i.e., domestic confinement – would only lead towards more same-sex practices. This is a comedic pronouncement because it references the Arab commonplace highlighted by Samar Habib, which assumes that 'the homosexualities of the Middle East are brought on by the segregation of the sexes' (2009, p. 34). In this case, both women have internalised negative messages about female homosexuality, despite the fact that the Qur'an is purposefully ambiguous and that it is only through heteropatriarchal exegesis and cultural encoding that lesbianism has ever been found to be at the root of Qur'anic female immorality. Aisha feels 'ashamed and confused' after having sex with Perihan, yet her lover's repeated motto offers her queer consolation in the face of familial and societal censure. Jarrar's short story playfully subverts several tropes in Arab and Islamicate cultures: it offers an unorthodox perspective on the Qur'an's alleged condemnation of female homosexuality, and it satirises the gender segregation at the heart of traditional Arab culture and its usual construction as a further instigator of same-sex erotic practices. I suggest Jarrar's creative intervention is undertaken through the entangling of queer bodies and the humorous disorganisation of cultural and religious values. Jarrar's feminist trickster once again highlights the biases at the heart of Arab cultures.

As regards the role of maps in the tracing of home and the individual's identity, *A Map of Home*, as its very title indicates, is both literally and symbolically invested in maps. In this text, maps constitute not just the repositories of national ideologies and aspirations, but also highly personal cartographies that are, to borrow Winterson's phrase, written on the body. In the first instance, Jarrar's maps signify the unresolved deterritorialisation of Palestine's first-generation diaspora; in the second, they denote the related but distinct homelessness of the second-generation queer diasporic Muslim subject. From the start of the novel, Nidali shows sympathy towards the plight of Palestinians, while recognising the enormity of their nationalist task. She narrates how her father teaches her that

> moving was part of being Palestinian. 'Our people carry their homeland in their souls,' he would tell me at night as he tucked me in. [...] 'You can go wherever you want, but you'll always have it in your heart.' I'd think to myself: 'That's such a heavy thing to carry.' (Jarrar, 2009, p. 9)

Indeed, a large part of the novel's dealings with Nidali's 'imagined community' involves the burden of carrying on Palestinian nationhood and identity as a diasporic subject. She develops an urgency to relay her family's perishable experiences in a way that preserves them; this reportage entails a conscious mapping of her family's migrations.

In taking up the role of family raconteur, Nidali creates a textual collage of her family's memories, desperately attempting to capture Palestine during her brief childhood sojourns there and thenceforth also *in absentia*:

> I asked Mama for some paper and a pen and she fished them out of her bag. I wanted to draw everything I saw [...]. I realized I couldn't draw all these things but I wanted terribly to record them, to make order of my surroundings, so I made a list of them. [...] When I was done I gave Mama the sheet of paper and she folded it in half without looking at it. Now I wished the wind would whisk the list I made and placed it in Baba's lap; then, he'd open it up and read it and he'd feel better. [...] We then looked for a taxi to take us to Baba's village, Jenin, and found a van pull of people who were going there too. [...] I watched the ponies, the olive trees, the almond trees; I noticed how neat the rows of trees were, the small sprinklers that shot water at them, the green army jeeps that zoomed past us, Baba's face, which resembled the sliced rocks and mountains on our left. (Jarrar, 2009, pp. 96; 101)

Nidali's powerful urge to capture her impressions of Palestine is thorough, albeit unsystematic: all she can do is randomly list everything she sees as the family heads towards her father's native town. Her cartography refuses to be taxonomic, yet despite her childish perception, her initial account of Palestine manages to capture both the beauty and the peril implicit in the landscape: nature and warfare become assembled in a way that reminds us of the precariousness of Palestine's political status, since even the guiltless trees are 'shot' with water. Bodies and landscape also become superimposed in the girl's imaginary, with her father's face being mirrored in the Palestinian mountains, a physical and geographical comparison that is suffused with nationalism, since it moulds her father's figure after the Palestinian land itself. Although not fully assimilatory or syncretic, this episode purposefully compares the land and its citizens, mapping and firmly aligning the self with the Palestinian landscape, and thus making a semiotic case for Palestinian nationalism.

Somewhat unexpectedly, it is not her Palestinian family, but her Egyptian grandfather, Geddo, who awakens Nidali to the importance of map-making and to its reliance on perspective:

> Do you know that a large-scale map creates a better relationship between people and their land? I know they didn't teach you that in the English school in Kuwait because they knew that power is the knowledge and command of the land, and they wanted that knowledge and power for themselves! So here I am standing on the land, and you should learn that when it comes to maps, accuracy is always a question of where you stand. (Jarrar, 2009, pp. 188–9)

Through Nidali's grandfather, Jarrar articulates here a postcolonial critique of map-making: maps are rendered not infallible but subjective documents tied to perspective and power, and they are also impregnated with affect. Yair Wallach states that maps are 'privileged symbol[s] of the nation', and that they have 'a role in discourses of cultural memory, history and identity' (2011, p. 361). He argues that ideas of the homeland are not strictly territorial but discursive. As he suggests, '[m]aps are not simply rational statements to be interpreted through a logical calculus, but rather are material objects invested with emotions, love and pain' (2011, p. 361). Instead of fixed official documents, maps are thus part of the discursive construction of the nation, and it is in keeping with this conceptualisation that Jarrar deploys maps in her fiction. I suggest Jarrar's narrative relies not on the impossible demarcation of the ever-changing and inexorably more encroached Palestinian territories, but on the affective and discursive charting of the Palestinian homeland.

As Christine Leuenberger and Izhak Schnell observe, 'maps do not reveal, but produce reality; they do not represent, but become inscribed in the landscape; they are not fixed, but are continuously made and re-made' (2010, p. 805). In other words, maps do not demarcate an external landscape but ideologically create such landscape, in ways that are clearly political. Writing on a task set for Palestinian and Israeli students to draw maps of Palestine, Efrat Ben-Ze'ev reflects on the difficulty of arriving at an incontrovertible charting of the Palestinian nation:

> border lines were more difficult to demarcate. Nevertheless, a geo-body emerged from the maps [...]. More often than not, this geo-body was detached from its surroundings, forming the image of an island-like country. [...] Perhaps the geo-body, in essence, is more of an idea or a message rather than a projection of a reality. (Ben-Ze'ev, 2015, p. 250)

The map of Palestine drawn by both Palestinian and Israeli students is, more often than not, amorphous, floating, with undecided borders, which reveals the shifting nature of the Israeli and Palestinian nations and the ongoing shifting of the various Palestinian borders. What transpires here is that mental maps produce disparate versions of the nation, demonstrating its ideological and emotive construction and, in the case of Palestine, its precarious and unequal negotiation.

Similarly to the young subjects of Ben-Ze'ev's study, Nidali desperately attempts at one point to draw a map of Palestine which she creates from memory. The difficulties in doing so and the pain it causes her father makes her want to be free from the map's and the nation's affective demands:

> One afternoon, I sat at the dining table and drew a map of Palestine from memory. Baba walked by, coffee cup in hand, and said, 'You still remember that?' I nodded and looked at the map nervously, hesitant about whether I'd drawn it right. I pointed at the western border and asked, 'Is that right?' 'Who knows,' he said, waving his hand dismissively. [...] I approached him timidly. I wanted to know more.
>
> 'What do you mean, Baba, when you say "who knows"?'
>
> 'Oh, *habibti*. That map is from a certain year. The maps that came earlier looked different. And the ones that come after, even more different.'
>
> 'What do you mean?'
>
> 'I mean... there's no telling. There's no telling where home starts and where it ends.'
>
> I sat with him on the cold balcony for a while. When I got up to go back inside, I noticed that Baba's eyes were filled with tears.
>
> I took the map I drew to my room, flipped my pencil and brought the eraser's tip to the page. I erased the western border, the northern border.

I erased the southern and eastern border. I surveyed what remained: a blank page, save from the Galilee. I stared at the whiteness of the page's edges for a long, long time. The whiteness of the page blended with the whiteness of my sheets. 'You are here,' I thought as I looked at the page and all around me. And oddly, I felt free. (Jarrar, 2009, pp. 192–3)

In the light of this episode, there is no 'right' map of Palestine. Nidali's nervousness reveals the difficulty in drawing an accurate map of the 'homeland', and Waheed's pain at the ongoing and ever more flagrant dispossession of the Palestinian people does not elude his young daughter. Her response is to erase the map's borders in such a way that only the primal landmark of Galilee is left. And here, a forfeiture of national aspirations is enacted: the blank page blends with Nidali's bedsheets, and the only feasible map is the one marking her current location. Nidali's, and metonymically Jarrar's, freedom from the demands of the Palestinian nation may be fragile, yet it usefully illustrates the affective pull of map-making and the diasporic struggle with mapping the Palestinian homeland. In view of these complications, nationhood starts to give way to personhood, veering from an impossible objective demarcation of the nation-state to a subjective articulation of the person's location. Such is the distinct, yet perhaps politically unsatisfying, predicament of the diasporic subject. Daniel Rabinowitz is conscious of the suspicion vested on the Palestinian diaspora, when he writes that '[n]arrators of the nation are weary of diasporas. They have a vested interest in blocking diasporic subjectivities from entering mainstream discourse. Such entry, after all, might encourage deterritorialization and god forbid, denationalization of the national project' (2000, p. 771). Jarrar does not shirk the important themes of home and nation, yet she also remains suspicious of totalising narratives that curtail the complexity of the subject who is queer, diasporic, and of mixed heritage. Her writing does not betray a lack of commitment to the lost homeland; rather, it articulates frustration with the nation's constant demands on diasporic subjects.

Due to the deterritorialisation of the Palestinian people, the means to freedom become removed from the nation-state, and new homes must be found in the diaspora. As Nidali narrates, ' "I lost my home," Baba said, [...] "and I gained an education... which later became my home. That can also happen for you. [...] War is terrible. Terrible! But good things come out of it too" ' (Jarrar, 2009, p. 106). Waheed is referring here to Six Day War (1967) which banished him from Palestine and propelled him towards his university education in Egypt. Nidali already told us earlier in the novel that 'I knew from the beginning that home meant fighting, arguing, and embellishing, and that's why I loved school. School was where my parents were not' (2009, p. 10). If, for Waheed, an education was the consolation prize for losing his homeland, then, for Nidali, it is an escape from family vicissitudes, a tool of familial disidentification. School can become both a home and an escape for Palestinian people who bear the burdens of direct dispossession, in the case of the first generation, and the task of honouring the stolen homeland, in the case of the second generation. Jadallah suggests that 'Jarrar maps home, but does not *define* it. The distinction is significant because the latter implies limits, while the former is forever boundless as well as relative' (2009, p. 111, emphasis in original). Jarrar's lack of clear definition agrees with the idea that maps are subjective, contingent, and ultimately linked to the individual and their struggle with collective notions of the nation.

In the end, the difficulties of mapping home objectively devolve onto the individual and their body. Jarrar's novel renders bodies the ultimate maps bearing the political weight of Palestinian dispossession. Both Nidali and her brother are the usual victims of their father's violence, and their bodies become metaphorically linked with Palestine:

> Gamal and I compared our bruises like bomb sites on two different maps. "This is where Baba's foot landed; this is where his palm exploded; here is the site of the house slipper mine; please note the series of detonations along this arm's terrain, the craters in this butt's field, see how this cheek encampment was burned down to the ground." We giggled. [...] I tickled him until he said mercy and we passed out, our bodies folded-up maps under the thin sky of our worn blue blanket. (Jarrar, 2009, pp. 177–8)

Nidali maps her and her brother's bodies as metaphorical maps, with each part of their bodies becoming a feature of the war-torn landscape, yet their childish game has more serious political implications: we are privy here to how the diasporic Palestinian body becomes a site of Arab patriarchal aggression that reproduces the violence done onto the Palestinian nation and its people. This supports my argument that, while Waheed may be the victim of the Israeli occupation, he also perpetuates Arab and Islamicate patriarchal habits, whose comparable oppression he is unable to recognise and check despite his more progressive political values regarding women and their social opportunities in Arab societies. Jarrar's discursively multilayered deployment of maps, bodies, and cultural inheritance ensures that Palestinians are not solely victimised, but that they are also shown as involved in an arduous war with queer and feminist subjects, in an assemblage of different national and personal wars: the macropolitical battle for the Palestinian homeland and its diasporic memorialisation, as well as the micropolitical battle within the diasporic family, and against Arab and Islamicate patriarchy, for gender and sexual equality.

The queer diasporic body, as I have shown, becomes the simultaneous repository of Palestinian national dispossession and of ethno-religious sexual repression in Jarrar's work, and national maps are forfeited in favour of the mapping of queer subjectivities. In the face of these intersecting dilemmas of self, home, and belonging, Jarrar shows us how the queer body can claim ownership over itself. The mapping of bodies helps us to consider what it means to be queer, Arab, of Palestinian and Muslim heritage, simultaneously; it is instrumental to begin questioning the influence exerted by heteropatriarchal societies on what are considered acceptable or normative bodies. If Taïa's autofictional works narrate the self within the continuum of pre- and Islamic Arab history and occasionally opts for esoteric manifestations of Islam, such as Sufism, while Alameddine's work queers religious texts by amalgamating them and offering irreverent queer exegesis revealing the heteropatriarchal bias of religious interpretation, then Jarrar's texts offer the queer female body as the repository of both Palestinian dispossession and heteropatriarchal violence and shame. These texts reveal that how the queer self is located in space and time remains politically relevant to the configuration of Muslim identities and the inheritance of Arab and Islamicate cultures: through queer melancholic autofictionality, the druzification of history, and the mapping of queer bodies, these writers demonstrate that the queer Muslim diasporic self is productively located at an angle from the inherited logic of Western and Arab and Islamicate hegemonies, struggling for a more stable and self-affirming definition of the queer self and searching for a durable place of safety at a remove from Islamicate heteropatriarchal expectations.

Note

1 Mohammed Albakry and Jonathan Siler have written persuasively on the use of the English language in Jarrar's first novel, commenting on Nidali's fluency in American English and her parents' struggle with it. However, what is arguably more interesting is what they perceive as 'numerous instances of Arabic and English code mixing related to the domain of cursing or obscenities' (2012, p. 115). Jarrar chooses to use more or less direct translations

of Arabic cursing, as well as of other expressions, in order to preserve some of the flavour of Arabic in her English text. As Albakry and Siler argue, 'in using English, these Arabic-English bilinguals create a new variety that deploys, bends, and mixes languages to suit their communicative purposes, aware of the limitations inherent in using any one language and the risk involved in using a hybrid one' (2012, p. 119). Jarrar's choice to use a hybrid form of English arguably pays off: a large part of the novel's originality and humour rely on its characters' Arabic-infused English, which conveys more powerfully the predicament of the Palestinian and Arab diasporas in America.

Conclusion: Thinking across

A RETROSPECTIVE GLANCE at all the writers and filmmakers whose work I have examined in this book should illustrate, at a most primal level, the sheer variety of Muslim identities and the multiplicity of directions that queer diasporas take across national borders: we have two secular British Muslims of South Asian heritage, one of them via South Africa; a Canadian Ismaili Muslim of East African and South Asian heritage living in Britain; a Turkish man of Islamicate heritage living in Italy; a British Muslim of mixed Egyptian and Welsh heritage; an American Muslim and a former Muslim of Palestinian and mixed Palestinian heritage; a Moroccan Muslim settled in France; and a secular Lebanese Muslim of Druze heritage living in America. The wide range of cultural reference, the plethora of ethnic configurations of Islam, and a number of unusual minorities within Islam – such as Ismailism and Druzism – all help us reflect on how the lived experiences of Muslims and their assembled identities easily outgrow the narrow dictates set by modern iterations of Islam, such as Salafism or Wahhabism. According to these relatively recent minority tendencies within contemporary Islam, the number of people around the world who qualify as Muslim would be very small indeed. The material realities creatively explored by queer artists of Muslim heritage demonstrate otherwise: there are many ways of being Muslim, and many mundane struggles that need to be met in defining one's identity against the sway of heteropatriarchal hegemonies.

The three sections of *Queer Muslim Diasporas in Contemporary Literature and Film* have systematically examined the distinct struggles queer Muslims undertake when dealing with the cultural and ideological negotiations of interethnic queer desire, the legacies of normative constructions of Islamic gender, and having to position themselves in time and place in the light of calcified Islamicate histories and knowledges. Queer Muslims routinely disorganise, as we have seen in the work of Hanif Kureishi, the social hierarchies inherited from colonialism against the contemporary clout of neoliberal ideologies, while purposefully resisting the

Conclusion: Thinking across

thrust of diasporic heteronormativity and ethnic exclusivism, while also being subject to the lure of dominant white culture. Muslim and non-Muslims must also, as per Ian Iqbal Rashid's work, become attuned to each other's wavelengths; that is, to the various demands placed on them by their different histories, located as they are at the interstices between colonial and postcolonial modernities and diasporic postmodernity. Queer Muslims also excavate, from their diasporic vantage points, the homoerotic cultural archives buried by modern homophobia, as we saw in the work of Ferzan Özpetek.

In turn, disquisitions of Islamic gender saw the work of queer Muslim women qualify Western stereotypes of the submissive and oppressed Muslim woman while fighting racism, as we saw in the literature and films of Shamim Sarif. Although occasionally subscribing to homonationalist ideologies that construct the West as the site of sexual exceptionalism, I argued Sarif's work offers countermemories of female same-sex desire against queer Muslim women's discursive erasure. We then examined the exploration of Islamic masculinities in the work of Sally El Hosaini, who posits Islam as a relational ethno-religious identity enabling the creation of new forms of queer masculinity at a remove from familial first-generation diasporic heteronormativity and second-generation diasporic gang hypermasculinity. The work of Rolla Selbak unites some of the strands of Sarif and El Hosaini's work: her depiction of Muslim American women explores the challenges they face in conforming to received ideas of Islamic and Arab femininity, while denouncing the homophobia assailing diasporic Muslim communities, positing, meanwhile, a vision of Islam which, while resiliently heterosexist, is also tuning itself to the diverse plights of women.

Finally, interrogating the position of the Muslim self in queer time and place allowed us to investigate Abdellah Taïa's postcolonial queer melancholia, triggered by social injustice in the postcolonial nation and by systemic homophobia, while offering Sufism, women's religiosity, and queer diasporic fraternity as places of safety against the strictures of racism and Islamicate heteronormativity. We then examined how Rabih Alameddine's Druze sensibility sutures religious traditions and undertakes irreverent queer exegeses debunking ossified heteronormative interpretation of religious scripture, offering the person living with AIDS as a pseudo-prophetic figure amalgamating places and histories against the dominance of Western logic. Finally, the work of Randa Jarrar drew our attention to the persistent heteropatriarchal biases of diasporic Muslim communities, even when male figures attempt to distance themselves from Arab patriarchal values. Jarrar's work undertakes a reclamation of the queer female body in its own terms, liberated from the constraints of received ideas of nationality, gender presentation, and sexuality.

It is useful to remember that none of these artists hold the self-same relationship with Islam, and, despite their Muslim heritage, they are placed along a continuum of adherence to, and distance from, the precepts of their faith, often on account of their assembled diasporic sensibilities, which are at odds with orthopraxy, or because of their personal rejection as members of sexual minorities. We also ought to remember that Islam is not organised in the fashion of other religious institutions such as the Catholic Church and that, while figures and pockets of religious authority do exist, Islam's structures are not routinely built in a hierarchical manner, and thus, with some exceptions, no single person has the moral authority to establish who is or is not to be considered a Muslim. Hence, while queer Muslims may be often castigated as sinners or apostates by those subscribing to mainstream heteropatriarchal Islamicate values, their level of identification, or disidentification, with their faith is a matter that concerns their own relationship with God. However, the artists whose work I have explored here establish different relationships with Islam without cancelling the importance of their Islamicate heritage, with its tight interweaving of faith and culture. In addition, as I have illustrated throughout this book, sexual orientation does not remain a mere issue of private morality. Queer Muslims do not live out their multifarious identities strictly in private; they do not inhabit their own reified semiotic spaces, physically and ideologically removed from the world's heteronormative majority. On the contrary, queer Muslims' continuous lines of flight from normativity demonstrate that their micropolitical trajectories are publicly relevant, as they redefine the contours of macropolitical societal segments attempting to categorise humanity according to neat identitarian parameters. As I have evinced, one can be queer *and* Muslim: these identities coexist in tension, in harmony, or in an assemblage of jagged edges, depending on how and to what extent individual Muslims have managed to wrest themselves from the strictures of hetero- and homonormativity.

Exploring queer Muslim's *jihad* in coming to terms with their assembled identities is also an issue of visibility, of readership and audience. The authors and filmmakers whose work has been selected for this book do not belong in a single, well-defined lineage of queer Muslim art; they are not members of any individual queer Muslim *community*, in the singular; rather, they forge their own communities – when they do or can – both in the physical immediacy of their own diasporic surroundings and in the active imagination of their uprooted sensibilities, often disorganising the demands of bloodlines and ethno-nationalism. However, their visibility remains a contentious issue. Some of these writers, such as Kureishi, Taïa, and occasionally Alameddine and Jarrar, are published by prominent Western presses, but Shamim Sarif, for instance, publishes her work through her own imprint co-owned by her partner; in addition, all the films explored in this book are eminently independent, often transnational coproductions attempting to gather enough funds to tell their unconventional tales. Queer diasporic Muslims' arduous attempts at getting their stories heard should draw our attention to the relatively recent public attention their plights have received and to the limited audiences they ultimately reach. The belated public interest in queer Muslims can be linked to the infamous 'War on Terror': misery stories of oppressed Muslim women and repressed Muslim homosexuals are central to the interventionist ideologies of Western imperialist powers, but the writers and filmmakers invoked in this study try not to play into the hands of Western interventionists: their depictions of the mundane existence of queer Muslims in the diaspora evinces the common humanity of their experiences, and while Islamicate homophobia and patriarchal values are certainly large stumbling blocks to be reckoned with, they routinely qualify Western stereotypes of the violent patriarchal Muslim male, of repressed and submissive Muslim women. The stories of queer Muslims illustrate a patent wish for survival and for cross-cultural commensurability.

Due to time, spatial, and linguistic constrains, my coverage of queer Muslim perspectives has been unavoidably partial. I have only been able to explore queerness as far as it concerns sexual orientation, although with some reference to the queering of gender conventions, such as those of Alameddine's protagonist in *I, the Divine* and Jarrar's narrator in *A Map of Home*. Trans Muslim art still needs to be broached, and great places to start would be the work of Canadian poet Trish Salah and Jordanian playwright Amahl Khouri, which I aim to examine in my ongoing research. In addition, I have consciously chosen to focus on diasporas where the West is the so-called destination, chiefly Britain, France, Italy, the USA, and Canada. 'Clash of civilizations' rhetoric often constructs Muslims as the 'enemy within', so I have chosen to explore identitarian tensions in the work of queer Muslims located in the West in order to gauge their challenges to sturdy ideologies of both the nation and the diaspora. Other European national perspectives and, indeed, genres remain to be explored, such as Beldan Sezen's *Snapshots of a Girl*, a semi-autobiographical graphic novel depicting Turkish same-sex desire in Turkey, Germany, the Netherlands, and the USA. Another Germanic example is Kutluğ Ataman's *Lola and Billy the Kid*, released in 1999, a film about Turkish queerness and transvestism in contemporary Germany. Although the distinctiveness of Turkish Islamism has been explored in Özpetek's work, the negotiation of Turkish queerness in other European locales would continue qualifying Kemalist and Islamist homophobia.

If my critical attention in this book has been devoted to, chiefly, queer Muslim artists located in the Anglophone West, with the exceptions of France and Italy, the North/South axis ought to be the next 'frontier' tackled in future studies. The study of Islam from a *decolonial* perspective reveals the prominence of liberation theology in South America and the belated critical acknowledgement of Islam's position in the global South. The recent collective work of decolonial thinkers and theologians working on Islam – and Judaism – in the South (Esack, 1997; Grosfoguel, 2013; Maldonado-Torres, 2016, 2018; Sayyid, 2015; Slabodsky, 2014, 2017) questions the centrality of northern and Western European empires in postcolonial enquiry; it envisages 1492 as the key date of the 'metaphysical catastrophe' (Maldonado-Torres, 2016): this is the momentous year of the fall of Granada, the last Islamic kingdom in what would become modern Spain, and also of the so-called 'discovery' of the Americas, with the simultaneous birth of modern imperialism. Decoloniality seeks to reach beyond the alleged Eurocentric discursive constraints of postcolonialism, although it has some blatant conceptual overlaps with well-established postcolonial discourses, such as those of Edward Said and Frantz Fanon. One of its key aims is to bring liberation to oppressed peoples through the decolonisation of the mind, which, in the light of Islam, ought to involve a liberation from Eurocentric paradigms, be they linguistic, cultural, philosophical, or educational. The inception of decoloniality involves, then, not simply a material liberation from colonialism, but a metaphysical liberation from *coloniality* – i.e., the colonial imposition of ontological states of being – which entails wrestling free from the troubling legacies of European colonialism in the global South. This is an ambitious and sobering enterprise that ought to receive attention in future discussions of global Islam.

Such a decolonial liberation, I must add, should entail decolonisation from Eurocentric networks of desire as much as from hegemonies within Islam itself. Although I do not believe queer Muslims' liberation will take place chiefly in the theological plain – and, indeed, theology might remain, to the end, one of the last standing bastions informing Muslim heteronormativity – the emancipation of sexually anti-normative Muslims needs to be undergirded by a spiritualism that is capacious and enabling. Some of the writers in *Queer Muslim Diasporas*, such as Alameddine and Taïa, break away from both the literalism and traditionalism of mainstream Sunni Islam, opting instead for esoteric approaches: in the case of Alameddine, this becomes manifest in a highly subjective, culturally syncretic, and complicated interpretation of religious scripture; in Taïa, it involves a colourful and unorthodox Sufi crowd that liberates him from sturdy heteropatriarchal notions of Islamic masculinity. As the mystical dimension of Islam, Sufism may well hold the key to Muslim metaphysical decolonisation, including queer emancipation, and significant progress has been made to this regard in world regions such as Central and South America. Writing on the history of Islam in Mexico, Zidane Zeraoui especially mentions the *Sheikha* and *murshida* Amina Teslima, a Puerto Rican Sufi leader settled in Mexico. As Zeraoui notes, 'Amina Teslima has broken the traditional stereotypes of Islam. Female, Muslim, inter-religious leader, pacifist and head of the Sufi Order in Mexico, she has made several pilgrimages to Mecca as well as to Medina, Jerusalem, and India' (2011, p. 76). Teslima's trailblazing work, which pushes for the emancipation of women, while conjoined with a pacifist and inclusive agenda, suggests that there are alternative ways of 'doing' Islam against the sway of traditionalist Muslim practices and at an angle from problematic Western views on Islam as the 'religion of the sword'. Islam's diasporic trajectory in South America, coupled with a decolonial perspective, offers glimpses of hope for a more diverse and less masculinist understanding of Islam which can aid the emancipation of women and queers from the heterosexist bias of majoritarian versions of the faith. While Sufism may be regarded by some Muslims and their allies as too apolitical and Westernised, or too strategically invested in private and emotional religiosity, it is worth arguing that decoloniality starts with one's own metaphysical being, and from there it expands, tuber-like, as a rhizome, to the rest of the world.

There are ethnic partialities to be recognised in global discussions of Muslims, which usually remain focused on the Arab and Middle Eastern inception of Islam and its ongoing developments in the region and its diasporas. Benjamin F. Soares points out how 'in an effort to keep West Africans beyond the influence of other Muslims, the French [...] promot[ed] what they called *Islam noir* that was localised and distinct from *Islam blanc* (White Islam), as practised elsewhere' (2000, p. 279, emphasis in original) In the light of Soares' work, it would seem that the racial segmentalisation of Islam dates as far back as colonial times, and that 'white Islam' – i.e., connected with Semitic peoples – was purposefully kept separate from the seemingly more animist Islam of the black peoples of Africa. The Islam of black people in America, Europe, and elsewhere, ought to be more routinely examined. The character of Aisha in El Hosaini's film *My Brother the Devil*, a black Muslim girl from Ethiopia living in London, acts a compelling reminder of the need to include black Islam in any present or future discussions of its position in the West, following the lead of guiding revolutionary figures such as Malcolm X and the Black Panthers in America, whose Islam proved a powerful tool of epistemic and ideological liberation from white supremacy in the 1960s and 1970s.

I would argue, in conclusion, that de-essentialising Islam may be the most important task to be undertaken in order to break free from both Islamophobic and literalist Islamic conceptions of Muslim identities in the West and elsewhere; and coupled, potentially, with mystical manifestations of the faith, such as Sufism, which are respectful of both pluralism and individualism and celebratory of human diversity. The focus of critical discourses surrounding queer Muslims in the diaspora, whether in the humanities, arts, social sciences, or other fields of enquiry, should also be on intersectionality – i.e., on critiquing the structural intersection of racism, sexism, Islamophobia, homophobia, classism, and other forms of social discrimination. But, without forfeiting intersectionality, it should also be self-consciously transversal. Scholar of transgender studies Patricia Elliot (2016) develops the notion of transversality previously tackled by Michel Foucault and Félix Guattari. In her view, bodies that meet are at once confronted with their similarities and their differences and must learn to respect them. Indeed, for a truly emancipatory form of political Islam to arise, Muslims and their allies ought to consider vindicating the plights of those who similarly struggle with received normativities but who may also be, in some fundamental ways, *unlike themselves*. This transversality must be, crucially, a two-way street of political affiliation; it would require cisgender, heterosexual, and queer Muslims, Muslims with varying degrees of (dis)identification with 'religion', and, indeed, non-Muslims, to consider the perspectives of those who are *different* from themselves.

In other words, for a successful liberating manifestation of Islam to arise in our contemporary times, Muslims should be ready to take up the causes of those people on the other side of racial, sexual, gender, class, and theological borders, by championing their challenges to Euro-American and Islamicate hegemonies alongside their own. While this position may be deemed too idealistic in its inclusivity, too Westernised or even potentially imperialist in its hopes of universality, it nonetheless follows the postcolonial critique of the 'divide and rule' logic of colonialism: communities that are kept separate, convinced about their hermetic and discrete natures, are easier to dominate; those who challenge the contours of societal categorisation, who refuse to fit the neat boxes predicated by macropolitical discourses, are insidious agents of change that threaten to disturb the highly partisan fabric of contemporary societies. In short, *queer* needs to join with *straight*, *Muslim* needs to join with *non-Muslim*, *us* needs to join with *them*. We especially need to dissolve the *us* against *them* dichotomy in order to start debunking 'clash of civilisations' rhetoric productively. As Hwa Yol Jung suggests, '[t]ransversality means to overcome and go beyond ("trans") the clash of ethnocentrisms both "Orientalist" and "Occidentalist" as a result of "essentializing" (to use Edward W. Said's phrase) the Orient or the Occident' (2011, p. xii). Indeed, without a critique that disorganises the segments and binaries of both Orientalist and Occidentalist thought, we remain in the prison-house of rampant identity politics and their isolationist hermeneutics. For Muslims and non-Muslims of all kinds – traditionalist, revolutionary, queer, or non-queer – it is time to think transversally – it is time to think *across*.

Bibliography

Abbas, H. 2015. *The Druze: A New Cultural and Historical Appreciation*. Reading: Ithaca Press.
Abbas, S. 2014. *At Freedom's Limit: Islam and the Postcolonial Predicament*. New York: Fordham University Press.
Abboud, S., L. Jemmott, and M. Sommers. 2015. "'We are Arabs': The Embodiment of Virginity Through Arab and Arab American Women's Lived Experiences." *Sexuality & Culture* 19.4: 715–36.
Abdel Haleem, M. A. S. 2005. *The Qur'an*. Oxford and New York: Oxford University Press.
Abu Hassan, R. M. 2005. "Jordan." In: S. Nazir and L. Tomppert, eds., *Women's Rights in the Middle East and North Africa*. Lanham, MD: Rowman and Littlefield, pp. 105–23.
Ahmad, A. 1992. *In Theory: Classes, Nations, Literatures*. London: Verso.
Ahmad, W. I. U. and Z. Sardar. 2012. *Muslims in Britain: Making Social and Political Space*. London and New York: Routledge.
Ahmed, L. 2011. *Quiet Revolution: The Veil's Resurgence, from the Middle East to America*. New Haven and London: Yale University Press.
Ahmed, R. 2015. *Writing British Muslims: Religion, Class and Multiculturalism*. Manchester: Manchester University Press.
Ahmed, S. 2006. *Queer Phenomenology: Orientation, Objects, Others*. Durham and London: Duke University Press.
——— 2017. *Living a Feminist Life*. Durham and London: Duke University Press.
Alameddine, R. 1999a. *KOOLAIDS: The Art of War*. New York: Picador.
——— 1999b. *The Perv: Stories*. New York: Saint Martin's Press.
——— 2003. *I, the Divine: A Novel in First Chapters*. London: Phoenix.
——— 2009. *The Hakawati: A Story*. New York: Anchor.
——— 2015. *An Unnecessary Woman*. London: Corsair.
——— 2016. *The Angel of History*. London: Corsair.
Albakry, M. and J. Siler. 2012. "Into the Arab-American Borderland: Bilingual Creativity in Randa Jarrar's *A Map of Home*." *Arab Studies Quarterly* 34.2: 109–21.
Ali, K. 2006. *Sexual Ethics and Islam: Feminist Reflections on Qur'an, Hadith, and Jurisprudence*. Oxford: Oneworld.
Ali, L. 2017. "Irreverent Stories of Arab-American Women Fill Randa Jarrar's 'Him, Me, Muhammad Ali'." *LA Times*. 13 January. Available at: www.latimes.com/books/jacketcopy/la-ca-jc-randa-jarrar-20170113-story.html.

Bibliography

Al-Solaylee, K. 2004. "A Touch Too Pink?" *Saturday's Globe and Mail*. 24 July. Available at: www.theglobeandmail.com/arts/a-touch-too-pink/article18268745/.

Anderlini-D'Onofrio, S. 2007. "Bisexual Games and Emotional Sustainability in Ferzan Ozpetek's Queer Films." *Journal of Bisexuality* 6.4: 121–34.

Ansari, H. 2004. *"The Infidel Within": Muslims in Britain since 1800*. Hurst & Company: London.

Arabi, I. 2012. *Selected Poems*. Translated by P. Smith. Victoria, Australia: Book Heaven.

Asad, T. 1993. *Genealogies of Religion*. Baltimore: Johns Hopkins University Press.

Azzam, I. J. 2007. *Gender and Religion: Druze Women*. London: Druze Heritage Foundation.

Badin, A. 2016. "Between Men: Homosocial Desire and the Dynamics of Masculinity in the Novels of Rachid O. and Abdellah Taïa." *Contemporary French and Francophone Studies* 20.1: 111–20.

Barnett, C. 2010. "AIDS = Purgatory: Prior Walter's Prophecy and Angels in America." *Modern Drama* 53.4: 471–94.

Beaumont Center, E. 2012. "The Pleasures of *Salvation Army*: Exploring Agency and the Body in Queer Moroccan Spaces." In: D. Talbott, M. Janzen and C. E. Forth, eds., *Bodies and Culture: Discourses, Communities, Representations, Performances*. Newcastle: Cambridge Scholars, pp. 95–108.

Ben Jelloun, T. 2000a. *The Sacred Night*. Translated by A. Sheridan. Baltimore and London: Johns Hopkins University Press.

——— 2000b. *The Sand Child*. Translated by A. Sheridan. Baltimore and London: Johns Hopkins University Press.

Ben-Ze'ev, E. 2015. "Blurring the Geo-Body: Mental Maps of Israel/Palestine." *The Middle East Journal* 69.2: 237–S30.

Bereket, T. and B. Adam. 2008. "Navigating Islam and Same-Sex Liaisons Among Men in Turkey." *Journal of Homosexuality* 55.2: 204–22.

Berghnd, D. and C. Sternberg, eds. 2010. *European Cinema in Motion: Migrant and Diasporic Film in Contemporary Europe*. Basingstoke and New York: Palgrave Macmillan.

Bernard, A. 2013. *Rhetorics of Belonging: Nation, Narration, and Israel/Palestine*. Liverpool: Liverpool University Press.

Bery, A. 2001. "The Redbeck Anthology of British South Asian Poetry." *Wasafiri* 16.33: 75–6.

Betts, R. B. 1988. *The Druze*. New Haven and London: Yale University Press.

Blanchard, C. M. 2009. *Islam: Sunnis and Shiites*. Congressional Research Service. Available at: https://fas.org/irp/crs/RS21745.pdf.

Bocock, R. J. 1971. "The Ismailis in Tanzania: A Weberian Analysis." *The British Journal of Sociology* 22.4: 365–80.

Boone, J. A. 2015. *The Homoerotics of Orientalism*. New York and Chichester, West Sussex: Columbia University Press.

Boschi, E. 2015. "Loose Cannons Unloaded. Popular Music, Space, and Queer Identities in the Films of Ferzan Özpetek." *Studies in European Cinema* 12.3: 246–60.

Brah, A. 1996. *Cartographies of Diaspora: Contesting Identities*. London and New York: Routledge.

Brown, J. 2007. *The Canonization of al-Bukhārī and Muslim: The Formation and Function of the Sunnī Ḥadīth Canon*. Leiden: Brill.

Buchanan, B. 2007. *Hanif Kureishi*. Basingstoke and New York: Palgrave Macmillan.

Bullock, K., ed. 2005. *Muslim Women Activists in North America: Speaking for Ourselves*. Austin: University of Texas Press.

Burton, R. F. 2006. *The Book of the Thousand Nights and a Night: A Plain and Literal Translation of the Arabian Nights Entertainments*. Available at: https://ebooks.adelaide.edu.au/b/burton/richard/b97b/.

Butler, J. 1993. *Bodies that Matter: On the Discursive Limits of "Sex"*. New York and London: Routledge.

Caramel. Directed by N. Labaki. 2007. France and Lebanon: Les Films des Tournelles and Les Films de Beyrouth. Momentum Pictures, 2008. DVD.

Cestaro, G. P., ed. 2004. *Queer Italia: Same-Sex Desire in Italian Literature and Film*. Basingstoke and New York: Palgrave Macmillan.

Chandran, R. 1987. "The Asian Stars." *India Today*, July 31. Available at: http://indiatoday.intoday.in/story/new-crop-of-asian-actors-in-britain-confront-the-problems-frontally-and-make-its-way/1/337335.html.

Chatterjee, D. 2000. *The Redbeck Anthology of British South Asian Poetry*. Bradford: Redbeck.

Cherry, P. 2017. "'I'd Rather My Brother was a Bomber than a Homo': British Muslim Masculinities and Homonationalism in Sally El Hosaini's *My Brother the Devil*." *The Journal of Commonwealth Literature*. Available at: https://doi.org/10.1177/0021989416683761.

Cichocki, N. 2005. "Continuity and Change in Turkish Bathing Culture in Istanbul: The Life Story of the Çemberlitaş Hamam." *Turkish Studies* 6.1: 93–112.

Clarke, P. B. 1976. "The Ismailis: A Study of Community." *The British Journal of Sociology* 27.4: 484–94.

Clum, J. M. 1990. "'The Time before the War': AIDS, Memory, and Desire." *American Literature* 62.4: 648–67.

Le Cuore Sacro. Directed by F. Özpetek. 2005. R&C Produzioni. CG Home Video, n.d. DVD.

Daftary, F. ed. 2010. *Modern History of the Ismailis, A Continuity and Change in a Muslim Community*. London and New York: I. B. Tauris.

Dalacoura, K. 2014. "Homosexuality as Cultural Battleground in the Middle East: Culture and Postcolonial International Theory." *Third World Quarterly* 35.7: 1290–306.

Dave, P. 2006. *Visions of England: Class and Culture in Contemporary Cinema*. New York and London: Berg.

Dawson, N. 2013. "Five Questions with *My Brother the Devil* Writer/Director Sally El Hosaini." *Filmmaker Magazine*. 22 March. Available at: https://filmmakermagazine.com/67337-five-questions-with-my-brother-the-devilwriterdirector-sally-el-hosaini/#.Vwu3PWNc7lJ.

A Day with a Muslim: Trump Supporters. Web Documentary. 2016. Rolla Selbak Pix. Available at: https://vimeo.com/164076565.

Deleuze, G. and F. Guattari. 1996. *A Thousand Plateaus: Capitalism and Schizophrenia*. London: Athlone Press.

De Sondy, A. 2014. *The Crisis of Islamic Masculinities*. London and New York: Bloomsbury.

Despite the Falling Snow. Directed by S. Sarif. 2015. UK: Enlightenment Productions.

Don't Call Me Urban! The Time of Grime. 2010. Available at: www.dontcallmeurban.com.

East is East. Directed by D. O'Donnell. 1999. UK: FilmFour.

Bibliography

Elliot, P. 2016. *Debates in Transgender, Queer, and Feminist Theory*. Abingdon and New York: Routledge.

el-Gallal, H. S. 2014. *Islam and the West: The Limits of Freedom of Religion*. Bern: Peter Lang.

El Gendy. N. 2016. "Trickster Humour in Randa Jarrar's *A Map of Home*: Negotiating Arab American Muslim Female Sexuality." *Women: A Cultural Review* 27.1: 1–19.

El-Rouayheb, K. 2005. *Before Homosexuality in the Arab-Islamic World, 1500–1800*. Chicago and London: University of Chicago Press.

El Tayeb, F. 2011. *European Others: Queering Ethnicity in Postnational Europe*. Minneapolis and London: University of Minnesota Press.

Esack, F. 1997. *Qur'an, Liberation and Pluralism: An Islamic Perspective of Interreligious Solidarity against Oppression*. Oxford: Oneworld.

Espinoza, A. 2017. "Taking Down the House: An Interview with Randa Jarrar." *LA Review of Books*. 5 January. Available at: https://lareviewofbooks.org/article/taking-down-the-house-an-interview-with-randa-jarrar/.

Esposito, J. L. 2002. "Preface." In: Y. Y. Haddad, ed., *Muslims in the West: From Sojourners to Citizens*. New York: Oxford University Press, pp. vii–viii.

Le Fate Ignoranti. Directed by F. Özpetek. 2001. R&C Produzioni, Films Balenciaga. Parasol Pecadillo Releasing, 2003. DVD.

Fernández Carbajal, A. 2014. *Compromise and Resistance in Postcolonial Writing: E. M. Forster's Legacy*. Basingstoke and New York: Palgrave Macmillan.

——— 2017a. "The Postcolonial Queer and the Legacies of Colonial Homoeroticism: Of Queer Lenses and Phenomenology in E. M. Forster, David Lean and Hanif Kureishi." In: E. Cavalié and L. Mellet, eds., *Only Connect: E. M. Forster's Legacies in British Fiction*. Bern: Peter Lang.

——— 2017b. "The Wanderings of a Gay Moroccan: An Interview with Abdellah Taïa." *The Journal of Postcolonial Writing* 53.4: 496–506.

Fisk, R. 2001. *Pity the Nation: Lebanon at War*. Oxford: Oxford University Press.

Fitzgerald, T. 2007. *Discourse of Civility and Barbarity: A Critical History of Religion and Related Categories*. Oxford and New York: Oxford University Press.

Flagg, F. 2000. *Fried Green Tomatoes at the Whistle Stop Cafe*. New York: Ballantine Books.

Fried Green Tomatoes. Directed by J. Avnet. 1991. USA: Universal Pictures.

Gairola, R. K. 2009. "Capitalist Houses, Queer Homes: National Belonging and Transgressive Erotics in *My Beautiful Laundrette*." *South Asian Popular Culture* 7.1: 37–54.

Galt, R. 2005. "Back Projection: Visualizing Past and Present Europe in *Zentropa*." *Cinema Journal* 45.1: 3–21.

Galt, R. 2013. "The Prettiness of Italian Cinema." In: L. Bayman and S. Rigoletto, eds., *Popular Italian Cinema*. New York: Palgrave Macmillan, pp. 52–68.

Galt, R. and K. Schoonover. 2016. "Hypotheses on the Queer Middlebrow." In: S. Faulkner, ed., *Middlebrow Cinema*. Abingdon and New York: Routledge, pp. 200–15.

Genon, A. 2013. *Autofiction: Pratiques et Théories*. Paris: Mon Petit Éditeur.

Gerhards, J. 2010. "Non-Discrimination towards Homosexuality." *International Sociology* 25.1: 5–28.

Gibson, M. and D. T. Meem. 2002. *Femme/Butch: New Considerations of the Way We Want To Go*. New York: Harrington Park Press.

Bibliography

Gilroy, P. 1987. *"There Ain't No Black in the Union Jack": The Cultural Politics of Race and Nation*. London: Routledge.

——— 2005. *Postcolonial Melancholia*. New York and Chichester, West Sussex: Columbia University Press.

Girelli, E. 2007. "Transnational Orientalism: Ferzan Özpetek's Turkish Dream in *Hamam* (1997)." *New Cinemas: Journal of Contemporary Film* 5.1: 23–38.

The Good, the Bad and the Ugly. Directed by Sergio Leone. 1966. Produzioni Europee Associate.

Gopinath, G. 2005. *Impossible Desires: Queer Diasporas and South Asian Public Cultures*. Durham and London: Duke University Press.

Grosfoguel, R. 2013. "The Structure of Knowledge in Westernized Universities: Epistemic Racism/Sexism and the Four Genocides/Epistemicides of the Long 16th Century." *Human Architecture: Journal of the Sociology of Self-Knowledge* 11.1: 73–90.

Grrl's Guide To Filmmaking. Reality TV series. 2014. Rolla Selbak Pix. Available at: https://vimeo.com/103069340.

Gunning, D. 2010. *Race and Antiracism in Black British and British Asian Literature*. Liverpool: Liverpool University Press.

——— 2015. "The First-Person Plural in Hanif Kureishi's Essays." *The Journal of Commonwealth Literature* 50.2: 133–49.

Habib, S. 2007. *Female Homosexuality in the Middle East: Histories and Representations*. New York and London: Routledge.

——— 2009. *Arabo-Islamic Texts on Female Homosexuality: 850–1780 AD*. Youngstown, NY: Teneo Press.

——— 2010. *Islam and Homosexuality*. 2 vols. Santa Barbara, CA: Praeger.

Haddad, Y. Y., J. I. Smith, and K. M. Moore. 2006. *Muslim Women in America: The Challenge of Islamic Identity Today*. New York: Oxford University Press.

Halberstam, J. 2005. *In a Queer Time and Place: Transgender Bodies, Subcultural Lives*. New York and London: New York University Press.

Hall, S. 1990. "Cultural Identity and Diaspora." In: J. Rutherford, ed., *Identity: Community, Culture, Difference*. London: Lawrence and Wishart, pp. 222–37.

Hamam: The Turkish Bath. Directed by F. Özpetek. 1997. Sorpasso Film, Promete Film, Asbrell Productions. Parasol Pecadillo Releasing, 2004. DVD.

Harem Suare. Directed by F. Özpetek. 1999. R&C Produzioni, Films Balenciaga, AFS Film. CG Home Video, n.d. DVD.

Hassan, W. S. 2011. *Immigrant Narratives: Orientalism and Cultural Translation in Arab American and Arab British Literature*. New York: Oxford University Press.

Hawley, J. C., ed. 2001. *Post-Colonial, Queer: Theoretical Intersections*. Albany: State University of New York Press.

Hazm, I. 1994. *The Ring of the Dove: A Treatise on the Art and Practice of Arab Love*. Translated by A. J. Arberry. London: Luzac.

Heeney, A. 2015. "SFFS Artist-in-Residence Sally El Hosaini on Writing and Directing 'My Brother the Devil'." *Seventh Row*. 15 February. Available at: www.seventh-row.com/2015/02/15/sffs-artist-in-residence-sally- el-hosaini-on-writing-and-directing-my-brother-the-devil/.

Henna Night. Directed by S. El Hosaini. 2009. UK: Yalla Film Company. Available at: https://vimeo.com/26166968.

Hennessy-Fiske, M., J. Jarvie, and D. Q. Wilber. 2016. "Orlando Gunman had Used Gay Dating App and Visited LGBT Nightclub on Other Occasions, Witnesses Say." *Los Angeles Times*. June 14.

Heyndels, R. 2009. "Entremêlements Narratifs sur la Tombe de Jean Genet, Abdellah Taïa et Rachid O." *Travaux de Littérature* 22: 473–81.

Hill, J. 1999. *British Cinema in the 1980s: Issues and Themes*. Oxford: Oxford University Press.

Hipkins, D. 2014. "Hamam – the Turkish Bath". In: L. Bayman, ed., *Directory of World Cinema: Italy*. Chicago and Bristol: Intellect, pp. 94–5.

Hirst, D. 2010. *Beware of Small States: Lebanon, Battleground of the Middle East*. New York: Nation Books.

Hodgson, M. G. S. 1974. *The Venture of Islam: Conscience and History in a World Civilization*, vol. 1. Chicago and London: University of Chicago Press.

Hoggard, L. 2013. "Sally El Hosaini: 'I'm Interested in People on the Margins of Society'." *The Observer*. 27 January. Available at: www.theguardian.com/film/2013/jan/27/sally-el-hosaini-film-interview.

The Holy Bible: King James Version. n.d. Collins Bible.

Hope, W. 2005. *Italian Cinema*. Bern: Peter Lang.

Hout, S. 2012. *Post-War Anglophone Lebanese Fiction: Home Matters in the Diaspora*. Edinburgh: Edinburgh University Press.

Hunter, S. 2006. *AIDS in America*. New York and Basingstoke: Palgrave Macmillan.

Huntington, S. P. 2002. *The Clash of Civilizations and the Remaking of World Order*. London: Free Press.

Hussain, A. 2004. "Muslims in Canada: Opportunities and Challenges." *Studies in Religion/Sciences Religieuses* 33.3/4: 359–79.

I Can't Think Straight. Directed by S. Sarif. 2008. UK: Enlightenment Productions. Enlightenment Films, 2010. DVD.

IndieWire. 2007. "Ian Iqbal Rashid: 'My Main Influences Were the Dance Films I Grew Up With'." 17 January. Available at: www.indiewire.com/2007/01/park-city-07-interview-ian-iqbal-rashid-my-main-influences-were-the-dance-films-i-grew-up-with-75383/.

——— 2012. "Meet the 2012 Sundance Filmmakers #29: Sally El Hosaini, 'My Brother the Devil'." 11 January. Available at: www.indiewire.com/article/meet-the-2012-sundance-filmmakers-29-sally-el-hosaini-my-brother-the-devil.

Jadallah, D. 2010. "Randa Jarrar: A Map of Home." *Arab Studies Quarterly* 32.2: 109–13.

Jahangir, J. B. 2010. "Implied Cases for Muslim Same-Sex Unions". In: S. Habib, ed., *Islam and Homosexuality*, vol. 2. Santa Barbara, CA: Praeger, pp. 297–326.

Jaikumar. P. 2012. "Sabu's Skins." *Wasafiri* 27.2: 60–7.

Jarrar, R. n.d. "Interview with Beirut39." Available at: https://randajarrar.com/interviews/.

——— 2009. *A Map of Home*. New York: Penguin.

——— 2012. "Imagining Myself in Palestine." *Guernica*. 14 May. Available at: www.guernicamag.com/randa-jarrar-imagining-myself-in-palestine/.

——— 2016. *Him, Me, Muhammad Ali*. Louisville: Sarabande.

Jung, H. Y. 2011. *Transversal Rationality and Intercultural Texts: Essays in Phenomenology and Comparative Philosophy*. Athens, OH: Ohio University Press.
Kalila wa Dimna. 2012. Available at: https://dl.wdl.org/8933/service/8933.pdf.
Kamboureli, S., ed. 1996. *Making a Difference: Canadian Multicultural Literature*. Toronto and New York: Oxford University Press.
Karim, K. H. 2010. "Crescent Dawn in the Great White North: Muslim Participation in the Canadian Public Sphere." In: Y. Y. Haddad, ed., *Muslims in the West: From Sojourners to Citizens*. New York: Oxford University Press.
Kelly, C. G. "Is There a 'Gay-Friendly' Islam? Synthesizing Tradition and Modernity in the Question of Homosexuality in Islam." In: S. Habib, ed., *Islam and Homosexuality*, vol. 2. Santa Barbara, CA: Praeger, pp. 247–68.
Kempley, R. 1986. "'Laundrette': Soap and Sympathy." *The Washington Post*, March 28.
Keown, M., D. Murphy, and J. Procter, eds. 2009. *Comparing Postcolonial Diasporas*. Basingstoke and New York: Palgrave Macmillan.
Khan, A. 2017. "LGBTQ Muslims Have Always Existed, and We Deserve to Tell Our Own Stories." *Think Progress*. 12 June. Available at: https://thinkprogress.org/in-the-days-following-the-tragic-shooting-at-a-gay-nightclub-in-orlando-on-june-12-2016-we-3c66d9d6a172/.
Khan, M. M. 1997. *Sahîh Al-Bukhâri*. 9 vols. Darussalam, Saudi Arabia: Riyadh.
Kılıçbay, B. 2008. "Queer as Turk: A Journey to Three Queer Melodramas." In: R. Griffiths, ed., *Queer Cinema in Europe*. Chicago and Bristol: Intellect, pp. 117–28.
Kirby, J. 2016. "Orlando Gunman Omar Mateen Name-drops Obscure ISIS Terrorist in 911 Transcripts." *New York Magazine*. 26 September. Available at: http://nymag.com/daily/intelligencer/2016/09/orlando-gunman-omar-mateens-911-transcripts-released.html.
Kiss Her I'm Famous. Web Series. 2013–14. Rolla Selbak Pix. Available at: https://vimeo.com/62584712.
Koller. V. 2008. "'Not Just a Colour': Pink as a Gender and Sexuality Marker in Visual Communication." *Visual Communication* 7.4: 395–423.
Kramer, G. M. 2013. "Arab Gangs of London." *Gay City News*. 13 March. Available at: http://gaycitynews.nyc/arab-gangs-of-london/.
Kramer, M. 2010. "Sexual Orientation: The Ideological Underpinnings of the Gay Advance in Muslim-Majority Societies as Witnessed in Online Chat Rooms." In: S. Habib, ed., *Islam and Homosexuality*, vol. 1. Santa Barbara, CA: Praeger, pp. 133–62.
Kugle, S. S. a-H. 2010. *Homosexuality in Islam: Critical Reflections on Gay, Lesbian, and Transgender Muslims*. Oxford: Oneworld.
Kureishi, H. 1996. *The Black Album*. London: Faber and Faber.
——— 1999. *The Buddha of Suburbia*. London: Faber and Faber.
——— 2000. *My Beautiful Laundrette*. London: Faber and Faber.
——— 2002a. *Dreaming and Scheming: Reflections on Writing and Politics*. London: Faber and Faber.
——— 2002b. *Gabriel's Gift*. London: Faber and Faber.
——— 2005. *The Word and the Bomb*. London: Faber and Faber.
——— 2008. *Something To Tell You*. London: Faber and Faber.
——— 2010. *Collected Stories*. London: Faber and Faber.
Kushner, T. 2007. *Angels in America, Parts One and Two*. London: Nick Hern Books.

Bibliography

Lang, A. 1898. *The Arabian Nights Entertainments*. London: Longmans.

Lawrence. B. 2014. "Islam: Unbound and Global". In: J. T. Kenney and E. Moosa, eds., *Islam in the Modern World*. London and New York: Routledge, pp. 209–30.

Leaman, O. 2014. *Controversies in Contemporary Islam*. London and New York: Routledge.

Leuenberger, C. and I. Schnell. 2010. "The Politics of Maps: Constructing National Territories in Israel." *Social Studies of Science* 40.6: 803–42.

Lola and Billy the Kid. Directed by Kutluğ Ataman. 1999. Germany: Boje Buck Produktion, Westdeutscher Rundfunk, Zero Film GmbH.

The L Word. Television series. 2004–9. USA and Canada: Showtime.

MacDonald, M. 2014. "SUR/VEIL: The Veil as Blank(et) Signifier." In: L. K. Taylor and J. Zine, eds., *Muslim Women, Transnational Feminism and the Ethics of Pedagogy: Contested Imaginaries in Post-9/11 Cultural Practice*. New York and Abingdon: Routledge, pp. 25–58.

Mahadeen, E. 2018. "Hymen Reconstruction Surgery in Jordan: Sexual Politics and The Economy of Virginity." In: G. Griffin and M. Jordal, eds., *Body, Migration, Re/constructive Surgeries: Making the Gendered Body in a Globalized World*. Abingdon and New York: Routledge, pp. 159–72.

Mahmood, S. 2005. *Politics of Piety: The Islamic Revival and the Feminist Subject*. Princeton and Oxford: Princeton University Press.

Makdisi, U. 2002. "Ottoman Orientalism." *The American Historical Review* 107.3, 768–96.

Making Maya. Directed by R. Selbak. 2003. USA: Zahra Pictures. Available at: www.youtube.com/watch?v=XWKkIuT8ZEI.

Maldonado-Torres, N. 2016. "Outline of Ten Theses on Coloniality and Decoloniality." *Frantz Fanon Foundation*. Available at: http://frantzfanonfoundation-fondationfrantzfanon.com/article2360.html.

—— 2018. "The Decolonial Turn." Translated by R. Cavooris. In: J. Poblete, eds., *New Approaches to Latin American Studies: Culture and Power*. New York and London: Routledge, pp. 111–27.

Malik, K. 2010. *From Fatwa to Jihad: The Rushdie Affair and its Legacy*. London: Atlantic.

Mandaville, P. 2007. *Global Political Islam*. London and New York: Routledge.

Marler, R. 2008. "Mogul in the Making." *The Advocate*. 4 November, p. 57.

Marshall, S. E. and J. G. Read. 2003. "Identity Politics Among Arab-American Women." *Social Science Quarterly* 84.4: 875–91.

Massad, J. A. 2007. *Desiring Arabs*. Chicago and London: Chicago University Press.

Matei, A. 2014. "L'Autre du Corps et l'Autre de l'Esprit. Abdellah Taia, *L'Armée du Salut*." *Journal of Research in Gender Studies* 4.1: 859–74.

Maxey, R. 2006. "'Life in the Diaspora is Often Held in a Strange Suspension': First-Generation Self-Fashioning in Hanif Kureishi's Narratives of Home and Return." *The Journal of Commonwealth Literature* 41.3: 5–25.

McCrum, K. 2013. "Welsh-Egyptian Director Sally El Hosaini on her Inspiration." *Wales Online*. 1 April. Available at: www.walesonline.co.uk/news/local-news/welsh-egyptian-director-sally-el-hosaini-2494271.

McLeod, J. 2015. *Life Lines: Writing Transcultural Adoption*. London: Bloomsbury.

Bibliography

Meer, N. 2010. *Citizenship, Identity and the Politics of Multiculturalism*. Basingstoke and New York: Palgrave Macmillan.

Meghani. S. A. 2014. "Queer South Asian Muslims: The Ethnic Closet and its Secular Limits." In: C. Chambers and C. Herbert, eds., *Imagining Muslims in South Asia and the Diaspora: Secularism, Religion, Representations*. London and New York: Routledge, pp. 172–84.

Meherali, Z. 2004. "Pride and Prejudice." *Samar Magazine*. 11 March. Available at: www.samarmagazine.org/archive/articles/174.

Merabet, S. 2014. *Queer Beirut*. Austin: University of Texas Press.

Mishra, V. 2007. *The Literature of the Indian Diaspora*. London and New York: Routledge.

Modood, T. 2010. *Still Not Easy Being British: Struggles for a Multicultural Citizenship*. Stoke and Sterling, USA: Trentham Books.

Moore, L. 2017. *Narrating Postcolonial Arab Nations: Egypt, Algeria, Lebanon, Palestine*. New York and London: Routledge.

Moore-Gilbert, B. 2001. *Hanif Kureishi*. Manchester and New York: Manchester University Press.

Morey, P. and A. Yaqin. 2011. *Framing Muslims: Stereotyping and Representation after 9/11*. Cambridge, MA and London: Harvard University Press.

Morrison, J. 2003. *Contemporary Fiction*. London and New York: Routledge.

Murray, S. O. 2007. "Homosexuality in the Ottoman Empire." *Historical Reflections/Réflexions Historiques* 33.1: 101–16.

Murray, S. O. and W. Roscoe. 1997. *Islamic Homosexualities: Culture, History, and Literature*. New York and London: New York University Press.

My Beautiful Laundrette. Directed by S. Frears. 1985. UK: FilmFour. Channel 4, 2008. DVD.

My Brother the Devil. Directed by S. El Hosaini. 2012. UK: Wild Horses Film Company and Rooks Nest Entertainment. Blood Brothers Films Limited, 2013. DVD.

Naber, N. 2012. *Arab America: Gender, Cultural Politics, and Activism*. New York and London: New York University Press.

Naguib, S. 2010. "Horizons and Limitations of Feminist Muslim Hermeneutics: Reflections on the Menstruation Verse". In: P. Anderson, ed., *New Topics in Feminist Philosophy of Religion: Contestations and Transcendence Incarnate*. Dordrecht: Springer Press, pp. 33–49.

Navratilova, M. and G. Vecsey. 1985. *Being Myself*. London: Collins.

Ncube, G. 2014. "Writing Queer Desire in the Language of the 'Other': Abdellah Taïa and Rachid O." *Rupkatha Journal of Interdisciplinary Studies in Humanities* 6.1: pp. 87–96.

Needham, J. 2013. "After the Arab Spring: A New Opportunity for LGBT Human Rights Advocacy?". *Duke Journal of Gender Law and Policy* 20: 287–323.

A New Day in Old Sana'a. Directed by B. Ben Hirsi. 2005. UK and Yemen: Felix Films Entertainment and Yemen Media Centre.

Nguyen, V. 2017. "Queer Intimacy and the Impasse: Reconsidering *My Beautiful Laundrette*." *ARIEL: A Review of International English Literature* 48.2: 155–66.

Noor, A. M. 2010. "Rape: A Problem of Crime Classification in Islamic Law." *Arab Law Quarterly* 24: 417–38.

Nuwas, A. 2013. *Selected Poems*. Translated by P. Smith. Victoria, Australia: Book Heaven.

O., R. 1995. *L'enfant ébloui*. Paris: Gallimard.

———— 1996. *Plusieurs vies*. Paris: Gallimard.

——— 1998. *Chocolat chaud*. Paris: Gallimard.
——— 2003. *Ce qui reste*. Paris: Gallimard.
——— 2013. *Analphabètes*. Paris: Gallimard.
O'Ballance, E. 1998. *Civil War in Lebanon, 1975–92*. Basingstoke and New York: Palgrave Macmillan.
Onaran, Y. 1997. "Gay Turkish Movie Loses Oscar Bid." *Associated Press*. 3 November. Available at: www.apnewsarchive.com/1997/Gay-Turkish-Movie-Loses-Oscar-Bid/id-39de4798ce959fa37e1044bd585c37c7.
Orlando, V. K. 2009. *Francophone Voices of the "New" Morocco in Film and Print: (Re)presenting a Society in Transition*. Basingstoke and New York: Palgrave Macmillan.
Oumano, E. 2010. *Cinema Today: A Conversation with Thirty-Nine Filmmakers from Around the World*. New Brunswick, New Jersey and London: Rutgers University Press.
Özbay, C. 2010. "Nocturnal Queers: Rent Boys' Masculinity in Istanbul." *Sexualities* 13.5: 645–63.
Öztürkmen, A. 2005. "Turkish Tourism at the Door of Europe: Perceptions of Image in Historical and Contemporary Perspectives." *Middle Eastern Studies* 41.4: 605–21.
Özyurt, B. E. and V. Duyan. 2017. "The Comparison of Grandparents', Parents', and Young People's Attitudes Toward Lesbians and Gay Men in Turkey." *Journal of GLBT Family Studies* 13.1: 40–55.
Patton, C. and B. Sánchez-Eppler, eds. 2000. *Queer Diasporas*. Durham and London: Duke University Press.
Perez, E, S. Prokupecz, C. E. Shoichet, and T. Hume. 2016. "Omar Mateen: Angry, Violent 'Bigot' who Pledged Allegiance to ISIS." *CNN*. 14 June. Available at: https://edition.cnn.com/2016/06/13/us/orlando-shooter-omar-mateen/index.html.
Pickens, T. 2013. "Feeling Embodied and Being Displaced: A Phenomenological Exploration of Hospital Scenes in Raboh Alameddine's Fiction." *Multi-Ethnic Literature of the United States* 38.3: 67–85.
Pilkington, E. and J. Elgot. 2016. "Orlando Gunman Omar Mateen 'Was a Regular at Pulse Nightclub'." *The Guardian*. 14 June. Available at: www.theguardian.com/us-news/2016/jun/14/orlando-shooter-omar-mateen-was-a-regular-at-nightclub.
Procter, J. 2003. *Dwelling Places: Postwar Black British Writing*. Manchester and New York: Manchester University Press.
Puar, J. K. 2007. *Terrorist Assemblages: Homonationalism in Queer Times*. Durham and London: Duke University Press.
Quinn, B. 2011. "David Starkey Claims 'The Whites Have Become Black'." *The Guardian*. 13 August. Available at: www.theguardian.com/uk/2011/aug/13/david-starkey-claims-whites-black.
Rabinowitz, D. 2000. "Postnational Palestine/Israel? Globalization, Diaspora, Transnationalism, and the Israeli-Palestinian Conflict." *Critical Inquiry* 26.4: 757–72.
Rahman, M. 2014. *Homosexualities, Muslim Cultures and Modernity*. Basingstoke and New York: Palgrave Macmillan.
Rahman, M. and A. Hussain. 2014. "Muslims and Sexual Diversity in North America." In: D. Rayside and C. Wilcox, eds., *Faith, Politics, and Sexual Diversity in Canada and the United States*. Vancouver and Toronto: University of British Columbia Press, pp. 255–74.

Ramji, R. 2016. "Examining the Critical Role American Popular Film Continues to Play in Maintaining the Muslim Terrorist Image, Post 9/11." *Journal of Religion and Film* 20.1: 1–19.

Ranasinha, R. 2002. *Hanif Kureishi*. Tavistock: Northcote.

Rashid, I. I. 1991. *Black Markets White Boyfriends and Other Acts of Elision*. Toronto: Tsar.

——— 1993. *Song of Sabu*. Calgary: disOrientation.

——— 1995. *The Heat Yesterday*. Toronto: Coach House Press.

——— 2007. "Memory of Fingertips." *Wasafiri* 22.1: 50–1.

Robins, K. and A. Aksoy. 2000. "Deep Nation: The National Question and Turkish Cinema Culture." In: H. S. M. Mette, ed., *Cinema And Nation*. London and New York: Routledge, pp. 191–208.

Roy, O. 2004. *Globalized Islam: The Search for a New Ummah*. New York: Columbia University Press.

Rushdie, S. 1982. *Midnight's Children*. London: Picador.

——— 1992. *Imaginary Homelands: Essay and Criticism 1981–1991*. New York: Penguin.

——— 1998. *The Satanic Verses*. London: Vintage.

Ryan, L. 2012. "Young Muslims in London: Gendered Negotiations of Local, National and Transnational Places." In: W. I. U. Ahmad and Z. Sardar, eds., *Muslims in Britain: Making Social and Political Space*. London and New York: Routledge, pp. 101–19.

Sa Ğlam, B. G. 2014. "Rocking London: Youth Culture as Commodity in *The Buddha of Suburbia*." *Journal of Popular Culture* 47.3: 554–70.

Said, E. W. 1983. *The World, the Text, and the Critic*. Cambridge, MA: Harvard University Press.

——— 1997. *Covering Islam: How the Media and the Experts Determine How We See the Rest of the World*. London: Vintage.

——— 2003. *Orientalism*. London: Penguin.

Saikal, A. and A. Acharya, eds. 2014. *Democracy and Reform in the Middle East and Asia: Social Protest and Authoritarian Rule after the Arab Spring*. London: I.B. Tauris.

Salah, T. 2002. *Wanting in Arabic*. Toronto: TSAR.

Salaita, S. 2006. *American Literature Readings in the Twenty-First Century: Arab American Literary Fictions, Cultures, and Politics*. New York: Palgrave Macmillan.

——— 2011. *Modern Arab Fiction: A Reader's Guide*. Syracuse, NY: Syracuse University Press.

Salvation Army. Directed by Abdellah Taïa. 2013. Morocco, France and Switzerland: Les Films de Pierre, Les Films Pelléas, Rita Productions, Ali n' Films, Radio Télévision Suisse, SRG SSR Idée Suisse.

Sammy and Rosie Get Laid. Directed by S. Frears. 1987. London, UK.

Sarif, S. 2008. *I Can't Think Straight*. London: Enlightenment Press.

——— 2011a. *Despite the Falling Snow*. London: Enlightenment Press.

——— 2011b. *The World Unseen*. London: Enlightenment Press.

Sartre, J. P. 2012. *Saint Genet: Actor and Martyr*. Translated by B. Frechtman. Minneapolis: University of Minnesota Press.

Sayyid, S. 2015. *A Fundamental Fear: Eurocentrism and the Emergence of Islamism*. London and New York: Zed Books.

Scheib, R. 2008. "I Can't Think Straight." *Variety*, 24 November, p. 37.

Seedat, F. 2013. "Islam, Feminism, and Islamic Feminism: Between Inadequacy and Inevitability". *Journal of Feminist Studies in Religion*, 29.2: 25–45.

Selbak, R. 2014. "Coming Out in a Muslim Family." *The Huffington Post*. 14 October. Available at: www.huffingtonpost.com/rolla-selbak/coming-out-to-a-muslim-fa_b_4086152.html?guccounter=1.

Sen, A. 2006. *Identity and Violence: The Illusion of Destiny*. London: Penguin.

Seven Golden Odes of Arabia: The Mu'allaqat. 2014. Translated by P. Smith. Victoria: Australia. Book Heaven.

Sezen, B. 2015. *Snapshots of a Girl*. Vancouver: Arsenal Pulp Press.

Shaheen, J.G. 2001. *Reel Bad Arabs: How Hollywood Vilifies a People*. New York: Olive Branch Press.

Shakespeare, W. 2008. *Romeo and Juliet*. Oxford: Oxford University Press.

Shannahan, D. 2011. "Reading Queer A/theology into Rabih Alameddine's *Koolaids*." *Feminist Theology* 19.2: 129–42.

Sharlet, J. 2010. "Public Displays of Affection: Male Homoerotic Desire and Sociability in Medieval Arabic Literature". In: S. Habib, ed., *Islam and Homosexuality*, vol. 1. Santa Barbara, CA: Praeger, pp. 37–55.

Shatto, R. 2013. "Three Veils." *Curve* 23.1: 30.

Sher Vancouver Out and Proud Project. n.d. "Five Questions with Ian Iqbal Rashid – a Critically Acclaimed Poet, Script-writer, and Filmmaker of Such Films 'Touch of Pink' and 'How She Move'." Available at: https://shervancouver.wordpress.com/category/ian-iqbal-rashid-poet-script-writer-filmmaker/.

Shryock, A. ed. 2010. *Islamophobia/Islamophilia: Beyond the Politics of Enemy and Friend*. Bloomington and Indianapolis: Indiana University Press.

Siddiqi, M. Z. 1993. *Ḥadīth Literature: Its Origin, Development and Special Features*. Cambridge: Islamic Texts Society.

Sjo, S. 2013. "Go with Peace Jamil – Affirmation and Challenge of the Image of the Muslim Man." *Journal of Religion and Film* 17.2: 1–31.

Slabodsky, S. 2014. *Decolonial Judaism: Triumphant Failures of Barbaric Thinking*. New York: Palgrave Macmillan.

——— 2017. "Eternal Enmities: A Jewish Decolonial Re-Evaluation of Western Altruism." *Contending Modernities*. Available at: http://contendingmodernities.nd.edu/theorizing-modernities/eternal-enmities/.

Soares, B. F. 2000. "Notes on the Anthropological Study of Islam and Muslim Societies in Africa." *Culture and Religion* 1.2: 277–85.

Spivak, G. C. 1993. *Outside in the Teaching Machine*. London and New York: Routledge.

Spurlin, W. J. 2001. "Broadening Postcolonial Studies/Decolonizing Queer Studies: Emerging 'Queer' Identities and Cultures in Southern Africa." In: J. C. Hawley, ed., *Postcolonial, Queer: Theoretical Intersections*. Albany: State University of New York Press, pp. 185–205.

Stag. Directed by Ian Iqbal Rashid. 2002. Garsington, Oxfordshire: Martin Pope Productions. Available at: www.youtube.com/watch?v=po7BUFZXGaI.

Starobinski, J. 2012. *L'Encre de la Mélancolie*. Paris: Seuil.

Sternberg, C. 2010. "Migration, Diaspora and Metacinematic Reflection." In: D. Berghnd and C. Sternberg, eds., *European Cinema in Motion: Migrant and Diasporic Film in Contemporary Europe*. New York: Palgrave Macmillan, pp. 256–74.

Stobie, C. 2003. "Somewhere in the Double Rainbow: Queering the Nation in Recent South African Fiction." *Current Writing: Text and Reception in Southern Africa* 15.2: 117–37.

Surviving Sabu. Directed by Ian Iqbal Rashid. 1997. London: Hindi Pictures. Available at: www.youtube.com/watch?v=_umTkBgkJcM.

Tabačková, Z. 2015. "The Thousand and One Tries: Storytelling as an Art of Failure in Rabih Alameddine's Fiction." *Journal of Language and Cultural Education* 3.3: 112–24.

Taïa, A. 2009a. *Mon Maroc*. Biarritz: Séguier.

——— 2009b. *Salvation Army*. Translated by F. Stock. Los Angeles: Semiotext(e).

——— 2009c. *Lettres à un jeune marocain*. Paris: Seuil.

——— 2010. *Le jour du roi*. Paris: Seuil.

——— 2012a. *An Arab Melancholia*. Translated by F. Stock. Los Angeles: Semiotext(e).

——— 2012b. *Le rouge du tarbouche*. Paris: Points.

——— 2012c. "A Boy To Be Sacrificed." *New York Times*. Available at: www.nytimes.com/2012/03/25/opinion/sunday/a-boy-to-be-sacrificed.html.

——— 2015. *Un pays pour mourir*. Paris: Seuil.

——— 2016. *Infidels*. Translated by A. Strayer. New York: Seven Stories.

——— 2017a. *Another Morocco: Selected Stories*. Translated by R. Small. South Pasadena, CA: Semiotext(e).

——— 2017b. *Celui qui est digne d'être aimé*. Paris: Seuil.

Taylor, L. K. and J. Zine. 2014. *Transnational Feminism and the Ethics of Pedagogy: Contested Imaginaries in Post-9/11 Cultural Practice*. New York and Abingdon: Routledge.

Thiara, N. W. 2009. *Salman Rushdie and Indian Historiography: Writing the Nation into Being*. Basingstoke and New York: Palgrave Macmillan.

Thomas, S. 2007. "Something to Ask You: A Conversation with Hanif Kureishi." *Changing English: Studies in Culture and Education* 14.1: 3–16.

Three Veils. Directed by R. Selbak. 2011. USA: Three Veils Production Company and Zahra Pictures. Peccadillo Pictures, 2012. DVD.

Touch of Pink. Directed by Ian Iqbal Rashid. 2004. Canada and United Kingdom: Martin Pope Productions.

Toye, W. and E. Benson, eds. 1997. *The Oxford Companion to Canadian Literature*. Toronto and Oxford: Oxford University Press.

Tumini, A. 2009. "A Landscape of Their Own: Space and Identity in Ozpetek's *Hamam: The Turkish Bath* and Julio Medem's *Cows*." *Film International* 7.5: 50–6.

V Tape. n.d. "Ian Rashid." Available at: www.vtape.org/artist?ai=694.

Wadud, A. 1999. *Qur'an and Woman: Rereading the Sacred Text from a Woman's Perspective*. New York and Oxford: Oxford University Press.

Wallach, Y. 2011. "Trapped in Mirror-Images: The Rhetoric of Maps in Israel/Palestine." *Political Geography* 30: 358–69.

Waters, S. 2002. *Fingersmith*. London: Penguin.

Bibliography

Waugh, T. 2006. *Romance of Transgression in Canada: Queering Sexualities, Nations, Cinemas.* Montreal and Kingston, London, Ithaca: McGill-Queen's University Press.

Weber, D. 1997. "'No Secrets Were Safe from Me': Situating Hanif Kureishi." *The Massachusetts Review* 38.1: 119–35.

Wheatley, S. 2010. *Don't Call Me Urban! The Time of Grime.* Newcastle Upon Tyne: Northumbria University Press.

White, E. 1994. *Genet.* London and Basingstoke: Picador.

Williams, J. S. 2010. "Queering the Diaspora." In: D. Berghnd and C. Sternberg, eds., *European Cinema in Motion: Migrant and Diasporic Film in Contemporary Europe.* Basingstoke and New York: Palgrave Macmillan, pp. 196–214.

Winterson, J., ed. 1986. *Passion Fruit: Romantic Fiction with a Twist.* London: Pandora.

——— 1993. *Written on the Body.* London: Vintage.

Women in Love. Directed by K. Russell. 1969. UK: Brandywine Productions.

Woolf, V. 1943. *A Haunted House and Other Short Stories.* London: Hogarth Press.

The World Unseen. Directed by S. Sarif. 2008. South Africa and UK: Enlightenment Productions. Enlightenment Films, 2009. DVD.

Yates, K. 2015. "Simon Wheatley: 'Not All Grime had to be about Confrontation. It was a Celebration of Being Here'." *The Guardian.* 28 July. Available at: www.theguardian.com/music/2015/jul/28/simon-wheatley-not-all-grime-had-to-be-about-confrontation-it-was-a-celebration-of-being-here.

Young, R. J. C. 2007. *Postcolonialism: An Historical Introduction.* Oxford: Blackwell.

Zabus, C. 2013. *Out in Africa: Same-Sex Desire in Sub-Saharan Literatures and Cultures.* Woodbridge, Suffolk: James Currey.

Zaganiaris, J. 2013. *Queer Maroc: Sexualités, Genres et (Trans)identités dans la Littérature Marocaine.* Editions Des Ailes Sur Un Tracteur.

Zahedi, A. 2011. "Muslim American Women in the Post-11 September Era: Challenges and Opportunities." *International Feminist Journal of Politics* 13.2: 183–203.

Zanghellini, A. 2010. "Neither Homophobic nor (Hetero) Sexually Pure: Contextualizing Islam's Objections to Same-Sex Sexuality". In: S. Habib, ed., *Islam and Homosexuality,* vol. 2. Santa Barbara, CA: Praeger, pp. 269–95.

Zeraoui, Z. 2011. "Arabs and Muslims in Mexico: Paradiplomacy or Informal Lobby?" In: M. E. Cruset, eds., *Migration and New International Actors: An Old Phenomenon Seen With New Eyes.* Newcastle Upon Tyne: Cambridge Scholars, pp. 51–90.

Zine, J. 2004. "Creating a Critical Faith-Centered Space for Antiracist Feminism: Reflections of a Muslim Scholar-Activist." *Journal of Feminist Studies in Religion* 20.2: 167–87.

Zollner, B. 2010. "Mithliyyun or Lutiyyun? Neo-Orthodoxy and the Debate on the Unlawfulness of Same-Sex Relations in Islams." In: S. Habib, ed., *Islam and Homosexuality,* vol. 1. Santa Barbara, CA: Praeger, pp. 193–221.

Index

9/11 x, 23, 34, 42, 57, 109, 120, 128, 156–8, 220

Abbas, Sadia 24, 33–4, 45, 148
Abraham 213
Aga Khan 80–1
Aga Khan University 86n.3
Ahmad, Aijaz xiii
Ahmed, Leila 26n.3, 158
Ahmed, Rehana 57, 129n.5
Ahmed, Sara xv, 152, 174, 176, 200, 216, 229, 235
   queer phenomenology 21, 38, 40, 47, 100–1, 117, 125
Ahmadinejad, Mahmoud 3
AIDS xvii, 60n.3, 63, 204–5, 207, 220–7, 232, 251
al-'Alwani, Taha Jaber 11–12
Al-Bukhari, *Sahîh* 144, 154n.3
Al-Ghazali, Zaynab 177n.3
al-Isfahani 11, 242
Alameddine, Rabih 204–27, 228, 234, 236, 251, 253, 254
   Angel of History, The 205
   Hakawati, The 205, 207–14, 220
   I, the Divine 205, 214–20, 234, 236, 253
   KOOLAIDS: The Art of War 204–5, 220
   Perv, The 205
   Unnecessary Woman, An 206
Ali, Kecia 27n.4, 165, 170–1
Anderlini-D'Onofrio, Serena 98, 100, 104–5
Ansari, Humayun 137, 138, 139
Arab Americans 156–7
'Arab Spring' 138, 153–4n.2, 166, 189, 202–3n.4
Arabi, Ibn 142, 190, 194–6
Arabian Nights, The 8, 25–6n.1, 129n.5, 207, 208, 209
Asad, Talal 23

assemblage 20, 25, 37, 40, 42, 48, 51, 59, 70, 84, 89, 93, 97, 100, 109, 119–20, 126–7, 142–3, 183–4, 191, 194, 196, 204, 215, 219, 221–2, 226–7, 230, 239, 248, 252
Ataman, Kutluğ
   Lola and Billy the kid 253
Attenborough, Sir Richard
   Gandhi 35

Bedouin 26–7n.4, 209
Ben Jelloun, Tahar 183, 203n.4, 234
Bernard, Anna 229–30
Bernhardt, Sarah 217, 218, 219, 236
Bible, the 9, 10, 210–11, 223–4
Boone, Joseph Allen 91, 95
Borges, Jorge Luis 206, 225
Bowie, David 53
Bowles, Paul 6
Brah, Avtar
   diaspora space 140
British Arabs as minority within British Muslim minority 136
British imperialism and sexual dominance 67–8, 68–9
Buchanan, Bradley 37–8, 42, 46, 60n.4
Burton, Sir Richard 8, 25–6n.2, 208
butch and *femme* lesbian gender presentations 122, 129–30n.6
Butler, Judith 129n.6, 232

Ceccatty, René de 184

Daftary, Farhad 80, 85n.1
De Sondy, Amanullah 125, 136, 142–3, 189, 190, 192
decoloniality 254–5

Index

Deleuze, Gilles and Félix Guattari 2
   micropolitics 19–20, 28n.9
   plateau 20
Druze 205–6, 208, 210, 212, 214, 218–19, 224–5, 250

Egyptian Revolution (1952) 138
El Gendy, Nancy 229, 240
El Hosaini, Sally 131–53, 155, 181, 187, 251, 255
   Henna Night 133–4
   My Brother the Devil 131–2, 134–54, 187, 255
Elliot, Patricia 276
El-Rouayheb, Khaled 4, 5, 8, 67, 208
El-Tayeb, Fatima 146–7

Fanon, Frantz 254
fiqh 9, 12, 145, 164, 166
Fitzgerald, Timothy 2
   secularism and religion 22–3
Flagg, Fannie
   Fried Green Tomatoes (at the Whistle Stop Café) (novel and film) 111, 121–2
Forster, E. M.
   Passage to India, A 60n.2
Foucault, Michel 4, 207, 256
Frears, Stephen 33, 35, 38, 42, 95

Gairola, Rahul K. 44, 61n.6, 61n.7
Gandhi see Attenborough, Sir Richard
Garland, Judy 211
Genet, Jean 6, 181–3, 185–6, 187–8
Genon, Arnaud 183, 193
Gilroy, Paul 48–9, 203n.6
Girelli, Elisabetta 87, 91, 94, 95–6, 103
globalisation 7, 15, 89, 167, 176
Gopinath, Gayatri 2, 17, 33–4, 41, 45, 46, 67, 72, 73, 104, 112, 118, 120, 126, 207
Grant, Cary 74, 76–8, 82–4
Greek (Hellenistic) homoeroticism, and Roman Islamic indebtedness to it 5, 67
grime 136, 140, 153n.1
Guattari, Félix 256
   see also Deleuze, Gilles and Félix Guattari
Gulf War 59n.1, 156, 233, 239

Habib, Samar 1, 7, 9, 11, 12, 26n.3, 124–6, 166, 175, 217, 242
hadith (sing.) *ahadith* (pl.) 9, 11, 12, 27n.7, 85n.1, 144–5, 166

Halberstam, Judith/Jack 207, 221
Hall, Stuart 134
Hawley, John C. 14
Hazm, Ibn 10, 208, 209–10, 223
heteronormativity xii, xvi, 14, 17–18, 20, 37, 42–4, 49, 55–8, 61n.6, 63, 66, 74, 79–83, 85–6n.2, 93, 96, 98, 101, 105, 118, 122, 129n.3, 130n.6, 134, 142–3, 147, 151–2, 167, 171, 188, 192, 202n.2, 212–13, 221, 223, 226, 232, 235–6, 251–2, 254
hijab 148–9, 154n.2, 158–9, 167, 171, 173, 177n.1, 237
hijra 18
Hill, John 35, 37, 60n.4
hip-hop 136, 139, 141, 146, 153n.1
Hollywood romantic comedy 63, 74, 76–8, 82–4, 85, 85–6n.2
homonationalism 15, 124, 129n.3, 135, 151–2, 155, 176
   see also Puar, Jasbir K.
homonormativity xvi, 16, 20, 68, 112, 125, 151–2, 215–16, 218, 252
homophobia xi–ii, xvi, xvii–iii, 1–3, 7–9, 12–13, 18, 54–5, 71–2, 81–2, 87–8, 93–4, 97–8, 100, 102, 110–12, 119–21, 127, 131, 142–3, 146, 150–2, 167, 171, 185–8, 190, 192, 197, 199, 201, 208, 211–12, 214, 240–1, 251–4, 256
homosociality 44–5, 66, 89, 91, 95–6, 98, 105, 142, 169
Huntington, Samuel T.
   clash of civilizations 28–9n.10
Hussain, Amir 65–6, 75–6
hypermasculinity and machismo 140, 141–2, 146, 148, 151, 152, 187, 251

ijtihad 9
intersectionality xii, 2, 18–19, 20, 25, 34, 36, 40, 48, 58, 63, 94, 110, 114–15, 121, 127, 146, 202n.3, 256
Iranian Revolution (1979) 156
Islamic traditionalism and conservatism xvi, 18, 53–6, 66, 73–4, 76, 79–82, 109, 126–7, 131, 155, 159, 167, 176–7, 188–9
Islamophilia *see* Shryock, Andrew
Islamophobia xiii–xiv, 2, 16, 18, 28n.8
Ismailism 63, 64–5, 74–5, 76, 78, 80, 82, 85n.1, 86n.3, 206, 224, 250

Index

Jagose, Annamarie 14, 46
Jaikumar, Priya 71, 72–3
Jarrar, Randa 228–49, 251, 253
   Him, Me, Muhammad Ali 229, 240–2
   Map of Home, A 228, 229, 231–40, 242–8, 248–9n.1, 253
Jewel in the Crown, The (TV series) 60n.2, 68–9
   see also Scott, Paul
Jung, Hwa Yol 256–7
Jungle Book, The (film, 1942) 72

Karim, Karim H. 66, 83
Kemalism 88, 94, 96, 99, 101
Khan, Aamina xi
Khouri, Amahl 253
Kılıçbay, B. 97–8
Kugle, Scott Siraj al-Haqq 9–11, 12, 27n.5, 27n.7, 209, 223, 241
Kulthum, Umm 236–7
Kureishi, Hanif 33–61, 62, 95, 103, 131–2, 183, 250
   Black Album, The 59n.1
   'Bradford' 59n.1
   Buddha of Suburbia, The 34, 49–59, 62
   Gabriel's Gift 56–7, 59
   My Beautiful Laundrette 33–49, 58–9, 62, 73, 87, 95, 104, 136, 147, 150
      critical perspectives 35
   'My Son the Fanatic' (short story and film) 59n.1
   Sammy and Rosie Get Laid 35, 58
   Something to Tell You 57
   Word and the Bomb, The 59n.1
Kushner, Tony 224–5
Kutchi 76, 79

Lawrence, Bruce 3, 23–4
Lawrence, D. H. 211
Leaman, Oliver 3
Lean, David 60n.2
Lebanese Civil War 204, 207, 208, 220–6
London riots (2011) 135, 138, 141

Mahmood, Saba 158, 177n.1, 177n.3
Maldonado-Torres, Nelson 254
Mandaville, Peter 18, 29n.11, 145
marriage xi, xvi, 6, 36, 55–8, 95, 97, 106n.1, 110, 112–16, 121, 133, 157, 158, 160–2, 167–8, 174, 192, 221

Martin, Robert K. 64, 69
Massad, Joseph 2, 6, 7, 15, 124
Mateen, Omar x–xi
McLeod, John 225
Meer, Nasar 136–7
Meghani, Shamira 78, 82, 83
Merchant Ivory
   Room with a View, A 60n.2
Mernissi, Fatima 26n.3, 177n.1
modernity xvi, 9, 15–16, 53, 55, 65–6, 68, 70, 73, 74, 76, 78–85, 88, 91, 94, 99, 101–3, 167
Modood, Tariq 117
Moore, Lindsey 229–30
Moore-Gilbert, Bart 35, 37, 40, 55–6, 60n.2, 60n.3
Morey, Peter and Amina Yaqin 16, 23, 34, 147
Mu'allaqat 195–6
Muhammad (Prophet) 9, 11–12, 18, 28n.10, 142, 144, 166, 190–1, 203n.5, 209, 213, 231
multiculturalism 34, 37, 38, 39, 41, 48, 59, 116, 125, 132, 134, 135, 137, 139, 157
Murray, Stephen O. 96, 99
Murray, Stephen O. and Will Roscoe 1, 2
Muslim Brotherhood 166, 177n.3
Muslim diversity in Britain 136–7
Muslim patriarch, image of the 113–14, 119–20, 162–3, 174, 237–8, 253

Naber, Nadine 160, 168, 171
neoliberalism xv, 48, 50, 59, 66, 81, 89, 176
Nuwas, Abu 4, 8, 208, 209

O., Rachid 183, 202n.1, 203n.4
Orientalism xiii–iv, xvi, 87–8, 93–6, 99, 103, 106n.2, 124, 156, 159, 160, 176, 208, 257
   see also Said, Edward W.
Orlando, Valérie K. 184–5
Ottoman homoeroticism 88–9, 95, 97, 99, 102
Ottoman multiculturalism 96, 98
Ottoman Orientalism 96
Ovid 100
   Metamorphoses 99–100
Özpetek, Ferzan 87–106, 183, 251
   cuore sacro, Le 90
   Hamam, The Turkish Bath 87–106
   Harem Suare 89–90, 105, 106n.1
   His Secret Life 90

Index

Passage to India, A see Forster, E. M. (novel); Lean, David (film)
Patton, Cindy and Benigno Sánchez-Eppler 16–17
pink 39–40, 84, 85–6n.2
postmodernity 34, 37, 66, 73–4, 83–4, 129n.6, 204, 206–7, 225, 230, 251
Powell, Enoch 48–9
Procter, James 16, 139
Puar, Jasbir K. 15, 20, 42, 124, 216, 231
Pulse nightclub x–xi
punk 51–3

queer micropolitical disorientation xv, 2, 21–2, 25, 36, 38, 58, 105, 131, 132, 134–5, 142, 146, 152–3, 201, 238–9
queer phenomenology 41
  see also Ahmed, Sara
Qur'an, the 9, 13, 22, 144–5, 165, 166, 167, 169, 172, 208, 223–4, 231, 241–2
  Lot's people 9–12, 26n.2, 26–7n.4, 210, 223
  maktoob 144
  pen *sura* 231
  on women 11, 26n.3, 27n.5, 241–2

race 16, 19, 33–5, 41, 48–9, 58, 82, 99, 111, 117, 121, 140–1
  mixed-race 39, 42, 47, 60n.5
racism xiii, 18, 39, 41, 47, 66, 67, 71, 73, 78–9, 114–15, 172, 251, 256
Rahman, Momin xii, 18, 75–6
Raj Revival *see* Rushdie, Salman
Ramji, Rubina 156
Ranasinha, Ruvani 35, 40, 45
rape 163–5
Rashid, Ian Iqbal 62–86, 87, 103–4, 183, 251
  Black Markets White Boyfriends and Other Acts of Elision 63–4, 68–70
  Heat Yesterday, The 63–4, 79–80
  Song of Sabu 63, 70
  Stag 64, 66–8, 73
  Surviving Sabu 64, 66, 70–3, 104
  Touch of Pink 62–4, 66, 73–86, 87, 104
Roach, Joseph 112, 126
Roy, Olivier 8, 120, 145, 148, 149
Rushdie, Salman 29n.11, 33, 36, 120, 129n.5, 205
  Imaginary Homelands 60n.2
  Midnight's Children 129n.5, 205

Raj Revival 35, 60n.2
Satanic Verses, The 33, 58, 59n.1, 129n.5

Sa Ğlam, Berkem Gürenci 53
Sabu 70–1
  see also Rashid, Ian Iqbal
Said, Edward W. xiii–xiv, 3, 6, 254, 257
  Covering Islam 24–5
  Orientalism xiii–iv
  The World, the Text and the Critic 52, 53
Salafism 145, 165, 250
Salah, Trish 253
Salaita, Steven 206, 208, 212, 226, 238
Sammy and Rosie Get Laid see Kureishi, Hanif
Sarif, Shamim 109–30, 134, 136, 155, 163, 169, 174, 181, 251
  Athena Protocol, The 129n.1
  House of Tomorrow, The 128n.1
  I Can't Think Straight (film and novel) 105, 110, 111, 115–28, 136, 155, 163, 169, 174
  World Unseen, The (novel and film) 110–15, 121–2, 128
Sartre, Jean-Paul 185–6, 187–8
Scott, Paul 60n.2, 69
  Raj Quartet, The 60n.2, 69
Selbak, Rolla 105–76, 181, 217, 251
  Day with a Muslim, A: Trump Supporters 157
  Grrl's Guide to Filmmaking 157
  Kiss Her I'm Famous 157
  Three Veils 105–77, 217
Sen, Amartya 39
Sezen, Beldan 253
Shaheen, Jack G. 156
Shakespeare, William
  Romeo and Juliet 133
Shia Islam 65, 190–1, 203n.5, 224
Shryock, Andrew
  Islamophilia xiv
Siddiqi, Muzammil 8–9, 10
Six Day War or Arab-Israeli War 208, 234, 246
Soares, Benjamin F. 255
Spivak, Gayatri 48
Spurlin, William J. 2, 15
Starkey, David 141
Starobinski, Jean 192–4
Stobie, Cheryl 113, 121

submissive Muslim woman, pervasive image of the 45, 112, 115, 132, 135, 148–9, 156–7, 162–3, 251, 253
Sufism xvii, 4, 183, 189, 190–2, 196, 201, 206, 248, 255–6
Sunni Islam 65, 85n.1, 191, 203n.5, 224, 254

tafsir (sing.), *tafasir* (pl.) 9, 10, 11, 26n.3, 85n.1, 145, 164, 165, 166, 242
Taïa, Abdellah 181–203, 204, 228, 230, 248, 251, 254
  Another Morocco 183
  Arab Melancholia, An 183, 185–95
  jour du roi, Le 185
  Mon Maroc 183, 189
  rouge du tarbouche, Le 181–3, 189–90
  Salvation Army (film) 183, 196, 198–9
  Salvation Army (novel) 183, 196–201
terrorist, stereotype of the Muslim 135, 147–8, 152–3
Teslima, Amina 255

Thatcherism 33, 37, 39, 40, 43, 48, 50, 132
  Section 28 60n.3
Thousand Nights and a Night, A see *Arabian Nights, The*
transversality 256–7

virginity 160–3

Wadud, Amina 26n.3, 172–3
'War on Terror' 24, 157–8, 177n.1, 253
Western sexual exceptionalism 20, 66, 82, 123–4, 155, 217, 251
White, Edmund 183, 188
white supremacy xiii
Winterson, Jeanette 123, 230–1, 242
Wizard of Oz, The 211

X, Malcolm 255

Zabus, Chantal 110, 113
Zanghellini, Aleardo 26–7n.4
Zine, Jasmin 109

EU authorised representative for GPSR:
Easy Access System Europe, Mustamäe tee 50,
10621 Tallinn, Estonia
gpsr.requests@easproject.com

www.ingramcontent.com/pod-product-compliance
Lightning Source LLC
Chambersburg PA
CBHW070235240426
43673CB00044B/1800